AS CRUEL AS ANYONE ELSE

THE ITALIAN LIST

T0405714

ANGELO DEL BOCA

As Cruel as Anyone Else

Italians, Colonies and Empire

Translated with an Introduction by
Richard Braude

Seagull
BOOKS

LONDON NEW YORK CALCUTTA

This book has been translated thanks to a translation grant awarded by the Italian Ministry of Foreign Affairs and International Cooperation.

Questo libro è stato tradotto grazie a un contributo alla traduzione assegnato dal Ministero degli Affari Esteri e della Cooperazione Internazionale italiano.

Seagull Books, 2024

First published in Italian as *Italiani, brava gente?*
© Neri Pozza Editore, Vicenza, 2005

First published in English translation by Seagull Books, 2024
Introduction and English translation © Richard Braude, 2024

Paperback ISBN 978 1 80309 372 7

Hardcover ISBN 978 1 80309 348 2

British Library Cataloguing-in-Publication Data
A catalogue record for this book is available from the British Library

Typeset by Seagull Books, Calcutta, India
Printed and bound by WordsWorth India, New Delhi, India

This book is dedicated to the volunteers,
especially the younger ones, who, three times now,
have carried me in emergencies to hospital
in their ambulances.
They represent the best of Italy,
so far from everything of which these pages tell.
My deepest thanks.

CONTENTS

In the house of the hangman one should not mention the noose;
one might be suspected of harbouring resentment.

—Theodor W. Adorno[1]

Resistance to Italian colonialism contributed to the foundation of at least four modern states and one world religion: the Somali Dervish movement led by Mohammed Abdullah Hassan (heinously remembered as the 'Mad Mullah'); the revolutionary coup of General Gaddafi in Libya, who was inspired by the anti-Italian resistance leader Omar Al-Mukhtar (rather than King Idris); the armies of the Ras Tafari (*Ras* meaning 'Lord'), later Emperor Haile Selassie of Ethiopia, whose legend has been crystalized and deified by the Rastafarians; as for Eritrea, the nation's very name was dreamed up by Italian colonizers, who—in the words of the historian Ruth Iyob—left the artificial country as an 'unfinished script to an uncompleted play, and a stage on which the ill-prepared Eritrean actors were left to devise their own lines and action.'[2] The history and founding ideologies of these states are as tied to the defeat of Italy's Fascist empire as are those of the modern Republic of Italy—as, indeed,

---

1 Theodor W. Adorno, 'The Meaning of Working Through the Past' (1959) in *Critical Models: Interventions and Catchwords* (Henry Pickford trans.) (New York: Columbia University Press, 2005), p. 89. My thanks are due to Danny Hayward, Francesca Di Pasquale and Alberto Toscano for their careful comments on this preface. Any errors remain my own.

2 Ruth Iyob, *The Eritrean Struggle for Independence* (Cambridge: Cambridge University Press, 1995), p. 4.

is the history of the world, given that it was from this small country that Fascism was born, an ideology which, in name at least, led to one World War and has inspired violent, White supremacist movements across the globe for over a hundred years.

Despite the global repercussions of Italy's colonial past, its beginnings, development and end are not widely known—neither globally, nor, indeed, within Italy itself. The Italian title of this book, *Italiani brava gente*—'Italians, good people'—is an ironic reprisal of a colloquial phrase used to invoke the supposedly benevolent nature of Italian interventions in other countries. The words, rendered in a mock-Italian, lend it the tone of a warm, avuncular racist joke hovering over a very dangerous misconception: that Italians' 'hearts weren't really in it', in which *it* stands for settler colonialism, concentration camps and genocide. This book's intervention is that the positive recollection of the Italian colonial experience represents a myth that 'has no right to citizenship'. The late Angelo Del Boca demonstrates this by tracing the story of Italian violence perpetrated not only in its formal colonies (Eritrea, Ethiopia, Libya and Somalia) and other theatres targeted by its armies (whether in Eastern Europe or East Asia), but also against Italians themselves during the internal conflicts following national unification in the nineteenth century and over the two World Wars of the twentieth.

Translating this work from Italian to English has the potential result of restoring the facts to a very different audience; whereas Del Boca wrote with the aim of making Italians conscious of their own history as oppressors, and of the violence that formed them as a people, in English this work's meaning is transformed, becoming a guide for *non*-Italians. English is, of course, a global language due to the legacies of the British Empire and American cultural imperialism, leading to the ironic reflection that today's inhabitants of Italy's former colonies are more likely to read that history in English than Italian; the very fact that Italy's empire was defeated and dismantled by an Anglophone alliance determines the importance of translating this work from one imperial idiom to another.

To fully appreciate Del Boca's intervention, it is useful for the reader to have a general outline of this colonial and imperial trajectory, which, if little known to a contemporary Italian audience, is likely to be shrouded in mystery for an Anglophone one. This introduction thus attempts to trace the Italian Empire's contours, drawing largely on Del Boca's many works as well as other important recent publications—nearly all of which cite Del Boca's writings as fundamental to confronting both the tactical amnesia and imperial nostalgia which, over the past two decades since this book's original publication, is slowly but thankfully being reversed.[3] I then provide a summary of Del Boca's biography, as an account of his intellectual formation will help the reader understand still better his historiographic intervention. A third and final section provides a brief account of the postwar decline of the Italian Empire and some aspects of its afterlives, drawing again on Del Boca's works and reflections, and indicating some ways in which these help us to understand Italy's place in the world today.

CONTOURS OF THE ITALIAN EMPIRE

Throughout ancient and medieval history, the position of the Italian peninsula in the middle of the Mediterranean Sea—'the only large inland sea on the circumference of the earth [to offer] marine speed of transport with terrestrial shelter from the highest wind or wave, for a major geographical zone'[4]—had determined the fortunes of Italy's many cities, kingdoms and communes. But in the modern era, its inhabitants yearned for

---

3 See Alessandro Triulzi, 'Displacing the Colonial Event', *Interventions* 8(3): 430–43; see also Mia Fuller, 'Italy: Beyond the Clichés that Obscure Unacceptable Histories', *Journal of Genocide Research* 24(2) (2021): 298–307.

4 Perry Anderson, *Passages from Antiquity to Feudalism* (London: New Left Books, 1974), p. 21.

the Atlantic on the one side, and for the oil fields of West Asia on the other. Benito Mussolini railed against Italy's ambitions being thwarted by the grip the French and British Empires held over the confines of the sea:

> Italy has no free communication with the oceans and is thus a prisoner in the Mediterranean [. . .]. The bars of this prison are Corsica, Tunisia, Malta and Cyprus; the prison guards are Gibraltar and the Suez Canal.[5]

In the age of global capital, Italy's apparent geographical centrality had turned from blessing to curse. Indeed, the Suez Canal—in construction from the end of the 1850s—had immediately confronted the newly unified country as a central geopolitical fact, 'forcing its destiny', driving the expansion of its ports to become destinations for the new European maritime traffic.[6] In this new Mediterranean, the centres of capital in Europe remained elsewhere, and those powers that did reap the benefit of the new trade with the East also owned majority shares in the Canal—first France, and then Britain.[7]

Even before the opening of the Canal, however, Italians had looked beyond the Mediterranean—especially through the busy activities of Savoyard administrators who had inherited the global connections of Genovese merchants, connections that stretched across both the Atlantic and the Pacific (which included a significant interest in the trade in enslaved persons).[8] The Savoyard consul to Peru even bought an island

---

5 Renato De Felice, *Mussolini il duce. Lo Stato totalitario 1936–1940* (Turin: Einaudi, 1996), pp. 321–22.

6 Quoted in Del Boca, *Gli italiani in africa orientale*, VOL. 1 (Rome and Bari: Laterza, 1976), p. 33.

7 See Barbara Curli (ed.), *Italy and the Suez Canal from the Mid-Nineteenth Century to the Cold War* (London: Palgrave Macmillan, 2022).

8 Giulia Bonazza, *Abolitionism and the Persistence of Slavery in the Italian States, 1750–1850* (London: Palgrave Macmillan, 2019); Guido Abbattista (ed.), *Global Perspectives om Modern Italian Culture: Knowledge and Representation of the World*

in the Galapagos before the royal government in Turin rejected his proposal to acquire the whole archipelago.[9] Similarly, various proposals were made to establish colonies in Southeast Asia—Pulau Weh, Borneo, Maluku—including as penal colonies to hold prisoners taken in the nineteenth-century war against Southern 'bandits'.[10]

Such proposals were invariably denied by the new Italian nation-state on account of both potential conflict with other European powers and exorbitant costs. Indeed, the governor of Zhejiang, reporting to Emperor Dezong of Qing, the Guangxu Emperor, at the end of 1899, described the Italian global predicament well enough:

> The Italians are not worthy of concern for five reasons. First, it is a small and a poor country, and has difficulty in raising the costs for war. Second, every soldier needs two hundred silver *taels*, and it will be difficult for the public in Italy to be persuaded to support this. Third, the sea route from Naples to China is 7,000 miles, along which Italy lacks its own coaling and supply stations. Fourth, every soldier must be transported from the motherland itself—unlike the British who could send troops from India, or the French from Annam. Fifth, even if Italy were to acquire land in China, it would not have the forces necessary

in Italy from the Sixteenth to the Early Nineteenth Century (London and New York: Routledge, 2021). Also see the project Atlantic Italies: Economic and Cultural Entanglements (15th–19th Centuries): www.atlanticitalies.net.

9 Lucy Riall, 'Hidden Spaces of Empire. Italian Colonists in Nineteenth-Century Peru', *Past and Present* 245 (February 2022): 209.

10 Alessandro Di Meo, 'Italian Explorations in Southeast Asia' in Edoardo Tortarolo (ed.), *Cosmopolitan Italy in the Age of Nations* (London and New York: Routledge, 2023), pp. 161–74; Olindo De Napoli, 'Colonialism through Penal Deportation in the Italian Political and Legal Debate: from the Unification to the Beginning of the Colonial Enterprise', *Quaderni fiorentini per la storia del pensiero giuridico moderno* 49 (2020): 185–220.

to garrison it, and hardly enough financial resources to promote Italy's commercial interests.[11]

He was entirely right: when the Italians attempted to occupy the Sanmen Bay that year with two battleships, they were soon forced to back down. The ensuing invasion of Beijing, and the impotence of the eventual Italian concession at Tianjin, arguably only confirmed the accuracy of the governor's assessment (see Chapter Four).

More successful transatlantic colonial activities, such as in Peru, constituted what the historian Lucy Riall has recently called an 'informal empire', in which Italian pioneers were actively involved in extracting petroleum, establishing plantations and importing indentured Chinese labourers—as well as other Italian would-be landowners—all enacted within a racist framework of a 'civilizing' mission, settler colonialism and Catholic proselytizing.[12] Garibaldi's well-known adventures with Italian-born republicans in South America—and his donning of their distinctive poncho—testifies to this global reach.[13]

In terms of constructing a formal empire for the new nation-state, however, the situation was far more restricted. The coast of North Africa facing Italy at the birth of the new nation in 1861—and the brutal wars of Unification that ensued (described in Chapter Two below)—was domi-nated by other colonial powers as well as other deadly, on-going conflicts. The Hispano-Moroccan War had established the permanence of the Spanish colonies in Ceuta and Melilla; Algeria had been yoked under French occupation for over three decades; the Ottoman Empire had regained total control over Tripolitania and the Cyrenaica (modern Libya).

---

11 Yanwei Wang, *Diplomatic Documents of the Qing Dynasty* (Taipei: Wen Hai Press, 1973), cited in Lamxin Xiang, *The Origins of the Boxer War: A Multinational Study* (London and New York: Routledge, 2003), p. 101. Translation modified.

12 Lucy Rial, 'Hidden Spaces'.

13 Alfredo Sciorocco, *Garibaldi: A Citizen of the World* (Allan Cameron trans.) (Princeton, NJ: Princeton University Press, 2007).

Egypt and Tunisia were both independent states, but economic modernization and militarization was effectively propelling both countries into becoming debt colonies. In 1881, to the dismay of the Italian community living there, France invaded Tunisia and forced the constitutional monarchy to submit as its 'protectorate'; the following year, Britain invaded Egypt to 'protect' the viceroy from a nationalist insurrection.

As Del Boca succinctly noted, politicians of the new Italy with a mind for expansion thus had three routes into those parts of Africa that lay beyond British and French rule: down the Nile Valley, through the ports of the Red Sea or approaching from the north coast of the Horn of Africa. Thanks to Catholic missionaries, geographic societies and mercenary Egyptologists, an Italian vanguard with good knowledge of the area already existed.[14] Already in the late 1850s—when similar consuls were plotting in South America and Borneo—the Foreign Minister of the Savoyard Kingdom of Sardinia had pushed for a colony to be established in Ethiopia, a plan rejected by Cavour (including in his later guise as Prime Minister of Italy) as being too diplomatically complex.

Indeed, entrance into East Africa during the 'ideological preparatory years' of the 1870s brought the new Kingdom of Italy into consistent vying and diplomatic negotiation with the British state.[15] While the British looked to northern Somalia as a key location to support its Indian trade, they strategically supported Italian claims to the coast of Eritrea in the late nineteenth century—including the eventual invasion at Massawa (see Chapter Three)—as a useful counterbalance to potential French claims. In 1870, the port of Assab was bought outright by the Florio shipping company, finally realizing Italian dreams of an

---

14 Del Boca, *Gli italiani in africa orientale*, VOL. 1, p. 4. See also Cristina Lombardi-Diop, 'Gifts, Sex, and Guns: Nineteenth-Century Italian Explorers in Africa' in Patrizia Palumbo (ed.), *A Place in the Sun* (Berkeley, CA: University of California Press, 2003), pp. 119–36.

15 Del Boca, *Gli italiani in africa orientale*, VOL. 1, p. 51.

overseas naval base—and what would eventually become the Colony of Eritrea.

Through diplomatic relations with Emperor Menelik II, the Italians then used their position on the north coast to pass through Ethiopia and to the southern regions of Somalia.[16] Menelik's appeasement of these invaders did not pass without criticism, as evidenced by a poetic, scathing letter sent to him by one of his former advisors—after escaping from the Italian concentration camp on the Eritrean island of Nokra (described by Del Boca below in Chapter 3):

> Moving slowly like a turtle, encouraged by the concessions that were made to them, the Europeans broke the treaty and occupied the cradle lands of Ethiopia, including the lands of its monasteries. The Italians reached the point of claiming that your majesty— a pagan King!—had no power whatsoever, that you were merely our Italian protectorate. Your feeding hand got bitten.[17]

The 'turtle-like' Italians eventually felt confident enough to claim the strip of Banaadir facing the Indian Ocean, leased by the Sultan of Zanzibar to a company founded by a former consul.[18] Italian 'explorers' made their way up the coastline, with the Italian state providing financial and military backing. Through a series of treaties with different Somali sultanates, in 1888, Italian Somaliland was born in all but name, managed by state-licenced companies (whose practices of enslavement are covered in Chapter Seven). The colonizing push at the end of the nineteenth century in East Africa, which relied on the participation

---

16 Ioan Myrddin Lewis, *A Modern History of Somalia* (London and Boulder: Westview Press, 1965), pp. 40–41.

17 Tekeste Negash, *No Medicine for the Bite of a White Snake: Notes on Nationalism and Resistance in Eritrea, 1890–1940* (Uppsala: Nordiska Afrikainstituet, 1986), p. 11. Blatta Gebre Egziabeher Gila Mariam escaped from Nokra despite Del Boca's claims that this was impossible.

18 Lewis, *Modern History of Somalia*, pp. 42–52.

of Menelik II, was foreclosed by the reckless invasion of Ethiopia in 1893 and the Italians' resounding, historic defeat at the Battle of Adwa three years later (see Chapter Ten). Del Boca noted that this defeat also coincided with the violent end of two of Italy's most celebrated colonizing explorers: 'with the deaths of [Antonio] Cecchi and [Vittorio] Bottego, an epoch came to an end, that of an adventurous, inconclusive, beggar's imperialism. Italy remained in Africa, but she did so in silence, on the defensive.'[19]

But one chapter closed and another began. By the time of the Great War, the Italian Empire was decidedly less limited. Gone were the adventurers; in their place came demographic colonization—even while millions of starving Italians emigrated across the world of their own accord. As Mark Choate has pointedly described in *Emigrant Nation*, the defeat at Adwa heralded new state-backed attempts to unify the informal empire: 'the government collapsed the analytical concept of emigrant, exile, expatriate and unredeemed into the single theoretical concept of "Italians Abroad".'[20] It is in this context of mass emigration that the new phase of Italian imperialism is now widely understood. Over the first decade of the twentieth century, different Italian governments took steps to formalize and consolidate *Somalia italiana*, and Italian families were encouraged to immigrate both there and to Eritrea. After stymied experiments at introducing Italian economic interests into Ottoman Libya, Italy decided to expand its *Lebensraum* definitively in 1911, invading Tripoli (see Chapter Five) and employing air warfare for the first time in the process.[21]

---

19 Del Boca, *Gli italiani in africa orientale*, VOL. 1, p. 749.

20 Mark Choate, *Emigrant Nation* (Cambridge, MA: Harvard University Press, 2008), p. 5. For the 'unredeemed', see below in this volume, p. *xix*.

21 Charles Stephenson, *A Box of Sand: The Italo-Ottoman War 1911–1912* (Ticehurst: Tattered Flag, 2014), pp. 105–110; Thomas Hippler, Prologue to *Governing from the Skies: A Global History of Aerial Bombing* (David Fernbach trans.) (London and New York: Verso, 2017).

Libya was not, at the time, of great strategic concern to the Ottoman Empire—paling in comparison to the centrality of the contemporaneous war in the Balkans—but it was *ideologically* important, especially in the light of the 'Young Turks' reformist movement that had only just taken control. İsmail Enver, one of the movement's leaders and later Minister of War, smuggled himself through Greece and across to Egypt to repel the Italian invasion. He wrote in his diary on his way to the war:

> We will prove to civilized Europe that we are not lawless bar-
> barians. We will show that we are worthy of respect. Let the
> great powers leave our fate to us. Poor Tripoli is now lost. Who
> knows, maybe forever! Why am I going to Tripoli? I am going
> to perform a moral duty. The whole Islamic world expects this
> from us.[22]

Enver did not complete his 'moral duty'; he was soon called back to the Balkans, where the same fervour contributed to the Armenian genocide. The occupation of Libya was consolidated through the Treaty of Lausanne a year later, after Italian naval ships had bombarded Beirut and occupied several Ottoman island naval bases in the Eastern Mediterranean.[23]

By unsettling a delicate geopolitical balance, the Italian invasion of Ottoman Libya arguably contributed to the outbreak of war in 1914,[24] a conflict in which Italy initially remained neutral, even—as Del Boca noted—while the new Ministry for Colonies saw an opportunity to

---

22 M. Şükrü Hanioglu, *Kendi Mektuplarında Enver Paşa* (Istanbul: Derin Yayınları, 1989), p. 79; partly cited in Jonathan McCollum, 'Reimagining Mediterranean Spaces: Libya and the Italo-Turkish War, 1911–1912', *Diacronie* 23(3) (2015). See also *Diario della guerra libica* (Salvatore Bono ed.) (Bologna: Cappelli, 1986). My thanks to Ceylan Begüm Yıldız for help with the reference.

23 Ryan Gingeras, *The Fall of the Sultanate* (Oxford: Oxford University Press, 2016), pp. 98–99.

24 Christopher Clark, *The Sleepwalkers: How Europe Went to War in 1914* (London: Penguin, 2012), p. 242.

overturn relations with France and Britain and expand its influence over East Africa.[25] But when they joined the Great War in 1915, Italy's main territorial ambitions were not in Africa, but were concerned instead with the expansion of the borders of the nation out into those areas of former kingdoms and republics of the peninsula that had remained under the control of other European powers following the wars of unification in the 1860s, above all Croatia and Dalmatia—historical regions of the Republic of Venice that had remained under Austro-Hungarian rule, generating claims that have resurfaced periodically through Italy's modern history (see Chapter 11).[26]

Del Boca passionately describes how the violence wreaked upon the Italian working classes by aristocratic generals along these fronts during 1915–18 laid the grounds for the composition of the future Fascist Party (see Chapter Six). Commenting on the earliest of Mussolini's speeches, he claims that 'in the confused and still undefined Fascist ideology, the only stable point was this imperialist desire, feeding off myths of Imperial Rome and rancour over the "mutilated victory".[27] Italian Fascists and socialists alike lamented the continuing 'beggars' imperialism' of their nation, defending Italy's attempts to create an empire in order to catch up with other European powers.[28] But—as Lenin had noted years earlier, when Italy was busy bombing the Ottomans—the only real way in which Italy's imperialism belonged to 'beggars' was through the more than five million members of Italy's working classes who now constituted an enormous global diaspora.[29] (Indeed, following Lenin's

---

25 Del Boca, *Gli italiani in africa orientale*, VOL. 1, p. 843.

26 Other areas to which some Italians laid claim culturally and historically included Corsica, Malta and the Savoy lands extending to the county of Nice. Indeed, in the postwar treaties, it was for these territories that Italy pushed most fervently, rather than other claims in East Africa, the Adriatic, and the Middle East (with the exception of the concession of Jubaland).

27 Del Boca, *Gli italiani in africa orientale*, VOL. 1, chap. 13.

28 Especially Labriola: see Del Boca, *Gli italiani in africa orientale*, VOL. 1, p. 363.

lead, Italian communists were often more forward-thinking in their relation to the colonies, as Neelam Srivastava has recently demonstrated.)[30]

Del Boca broke the historiographical mould by arguing that pre-Fascist liberal colonial methods were no less violent, predatory and criminal than Fascist ones. Indeed, his argument linking Italy's potentially *greater* use of violence to its role as a 'late-comer' within European imperialism echoes similar arguments about the violence employed by both Germany and Japan.[31] Yet while this was a fundamental, corrective intervention—Italy's colonial history can certainly no longer be reduced only to its Fascist past—in the accounts below, the Fascist invasions of Libya and Ethiopia do seem to signal a new, qualitative change. These differences also related to the tactical approaches to colonization employed in each territory, as Nicola Labanca has argued.[32] Somalia was effectively ruled through delegation to private companies (and their thugs); in Eritrea, the approach was fundamentally military, from invasion through to martial law. In Libya, the Italian state attempted overarching demographic control, especially through the concentration of one third of the population of Cyrenaica into camps. Fascist Ethiopia, on the other hand, witnessed the forging of a civil administration that attempted to found an imperial outpost along Italian lines of governance, in what Haile Larebo has called a 'virtually permanent war economy'.[33]

---

29 For a detailed tracing of the term 'beggar's imperialism', see Carlo Carbone, *Italiani in Congo* (Milan: FrancoAngeli, 2019), pp. 68–70. My thanks to Enrico Gullo for this reference.

30 Neelam Srivastava, *Italian Colonialism and Resistances to Empire: 1930–1970* (London: Palgrave Macmillan, 2019), pp. 34–48.

31 See Enzo Traverso, *The Origins of Nazi Violence* (New York: The New Press, 2003); Nikolaus Mavrapoulos, 'The Latecomers' Early Colonial Experiment—The Uniqueness of the German Case', *Athens Journal of History* 6(2) (April 2020): 157–74.

32 Nicola Labanca, *In marcia verso Adua* (Turin: Einaudi, 1993), p. *xiii*.

33 Haile Larebo, 'Empire Building and Its Limitations: Ethiopia (1935–1941)' in

It was arguably this attempt to fully subject and mould the population and economy of Ethiopia that led to the peaks of Italian colonial violence, through both the use of gas warfare and genocidal commands from Mussolini himself.

Fascist leaders arrived in Eritrea and Somalia in 1923 with an eye to retaking control of colonies from liberal governors they suspected of having a soft touch. Others in the dictatorship looked initially towards the Ottoman Empire and the Balkans with a taste for invasion, but the years of national economic crisis (1926–28) discouraged any military expansion. Ironically, it was in 1929—when the world economy crashed— that Fascism began its real offensive, above all as a demographic solution. As a regime propaganda paper claimed, 'the entire Fascist system stands beneath the slogan "expand or explode".'[34]

From Mussolini's standpoint, the Quadripartite Agreement of 1933 (between Italy, France, Britain and Germany) and the Franco-Italian Agreement of 1935 were meant to guarantee a decade of peace in which the Fascists could pursue dominance in East Africa, especially Ethiopia.[35] The eventual invasion is described in detail in Chapter Nine. Haile Selassie's faith in the League of Nations was revealed as naive, and his hopes that other foreign powers would come to his aid—including Japan, Saudi Arabia and the 'Little Entente'—came to nought.

Aid did come, however, from individuals and non-state actors across the globe, 'a wave of sympathy and solidarity which perhaps only Vietnam enjoyed in the postwar period, overcoming racial, religious and political

---

Ruth Ben-Ghiat and Mia Fuller (eds), *Italian Colonialism* (New York: Springer Link, 2005), p. 85.

34 Del Boca, *Gli italiani in africa orientale*, VOL. 2, chap. 1. The reference is *Fame coloniale*, 'Echi e commenti', 25 June 1931.

35 For the historiographical debate around the motivations behind the invasion, see G. Bruce Strang (ed.), *Collision of Empires: Italy's Invasion of Ethiopia and its International Impact* (New York and London: Routledge, 2016).

barriers,' as Del Boca noted.[36] This was true from Peru to the Dodecanese, from London to New York: 'Ethiopia is the country of our forefathers, an' I feel somehow that if we can help them now, that some day they'll help us,' a young activist in Harlem told a reporter in 1935.[37] Or, as a Guyanese-born activist later recalled:

> It's very important to put the response of the black world to the Ethiopian War into perspective, especially since it is easy to get the impression that pan-Africanism was just some type of petty protest activity [. . .]. But the real dimensions can only be gathered by estimating the kind of vast support that Ethiopia enjoyed among blacks everywhere. [. . .] When the Italians entered Addis Ababa, it was reported that school children wept in the Gold Coast.[38]

International outcry and activist support was not enough to defeat the Italian armies, however, and Selassie fled Ethiopia. In Italy, the conquest represented the foundation of the Empire: 'The occupation of Addis Ababa,' Del Boca writes, 'provoked an unprecedented and very genuine enthusiasm. According to the data gathered by the Interior Ministry, at least thirty million Italians poured into the streets, responding to the

---

36 Del Boca, *Gli italiani in africa orientale*, VOL. 2, chap. 5.

37 William R. Scott, *The Sons of Sheba: African-Americans and the Italo-Ethiopian War 1935–1941* (Bloomington: Indiana University Press, 2006), p. 137. See also Arlena Buelli, 'The Hands Off Ethiopia campaign, racial solidarities and intercolonial antifascism in South Asia (1935–36)', *Journal of Global History* 18(1) (2023): 47–67; and Cedric Robinson, 'Fascism and the Intersections of Capitalism, Racialism, and Historical Consciousness', in *On Racial Capitalism, Black Internationalism, and Cultures of Resistance* (H. L. T. Quan ed.) (London: Pluto Press, 2019).

38 T. Ras Makonnen, *Pan-Africanism from Within: As Recorded and Edited by Kenneth King* (Nairobi and London: Oxford University Press, 1973), cited in Priyamvada Gopal, *Insurgent Empire: Anticolonial Resistance and British Dissent* (London and New York: Verso, 2019), p. 324. Makonnen was born George Thomas Griffiths; he took an Ethiopian name in 1935 in direct reaction to the Fascist invasion.

cry of the sirens.'[39] But the colony was, ultimately, both a demographic and then a military failure. Despite the vast African territory now under direct Italian rule, Italians continued to emigrate to other continents: in 1939, 'the Italian population of New York was still ten times more than that of the entire Italian empire.'[40] It was six full years later, at the Battle of Gondar, that a combined army of almost 20,000 Ethiopian and British soldiers—including many from Britain's African and Asian colonies—finally forced the Italians to surrender.[41]

ANGELO DEL BOCA: A PARTISAN LIFE

Piedmont

Having plotted the coordinates of Italy's colonial and imperial trajectories down to the closing of the war, it is possible to zone in on the author's own course through this moment and beyond. Angelo Del Boca lived a long and varied life, and in some respects the current book represents an auto-biographical journey, composed as it was over a few months in 2005, when its author was 80 years old. Sometimes this autobiographical thread is entirely explicit, such as when he turns to the stories his father told him about General Cadorna, or the episode of General Miani's family presenting him with their infamous relative's archive (both in Chapter 6), or indeed when he recalls his decades-long diatribe with the journalist and former Fascist Indro Montanelli. At other times, one needs to know the facts of Del Boca's life to glimpse the traces of his different professional and political careers, especially during his account of Fascism and the Civil War.

Del Boca came from a middle-class family in Piedmont, in the Ossola Valley, very near to the Swiss border. His grandfather had bought

---

39 Del Boca, *Gli italiani in africa orientale*, VOL. 2, chap. 13.

40 Larebo, 'Empire Building and Its Limitations', p. 90.

41 Del Boca, *Gli italiani in africa orientale*, VOL. 3, chap. 4.

the land around the natural thermal springs in the small mountain village of Crodo and, over the first decades of the twentieth century, attempted to transform these into an attractive site for naturalists and tourists. His attempts failed, and the family fell on harder times, especially following the global economic depression of 1929. The springs were bought by another aspiring capitalist, who bottled and sold its water under the label *Crodino*, a fizzy drink still popular throughout Italy. What may seem a minor detail regarding the highs and lows of commodified beverages contributes to understanding some of Del Boca's class attitudes: haunted by the circumstances that had propelled his own family one rung down the ladder of social class, throughout his work he considers honourable generals, accomplished professionals and dignified aristocrats with an esteem that perhaps covers a mild envy. No revolutionary, he rarely questions the capitalist resolution to the Civil War, feeling instead a limited affinity for the bourgeoisie from which he had been excluded by birth and which should have led Italy with greater honour.[42]

He faced his roots in Piedmont—the dominant region of the old Savoyard state—with a slightly different sentiment, however. Not having any doubts as to his place in Italian society on a geographical level, Del Boca revels in underscoring the frequency with which his wealthy region gave rise to some of the very worst figures in Italy, such as Pietro Badoglio and Cesare Maria De Vecchi (see Chapters Seven and Twelve). More telling still is Del Boca's inclusion of the war on banditry in the volume, which he describes as a violent invasion of the Italian South by the Piedmontese armies. Such an attitude is not to be taken for granted in today's Italy any more than it was 20 years ago when Del Boca wrote the chapter. Anglophone readers may recall Eric Hobsbawm's well-known essay on the topic as well as Antonio Gramsci's own approach to the

---

42 An exception is his admiration for the utopian republic of Domodossola; see Angelo Del Boca, *Il mio novecento* (Vicenza: Neri Pozza, 2008), pp. 106–10.

Southern Question.[43] But both Gramsci and Hobsbawm's accounts tend to interpret the repression of the South as a necessary evil for the unification and progress of the nation.[44] Del Boca, on the other hand, was well aware of his privileged position as a Northerner and has no truck with such triumphalist renderings of the nation's birth. Having painfully felt the ideological scales falling from his eyes, he approaches the Southern question with an iconoclastic rebellion learnt from decades of studying both Fascism and colonialism.[45]

The fundamental turning point in Del Boca's life, which provides a key to the book, was this relationship with Fascismo. In Chapter Nine, he turns to describing Fascism on an ideological level, making use of the autobiographies and diaries of prominent one-time Fascists—Indro Montanelli, Bruno Mussolini (the dictator's son)—taking their words at face value, presenting them as in a court of law. Boasting, bragging even, about their acts of duty and valour, these writer-soldiers' words are transformed by Del Boca into confessions of war crimes. But this usurpation of their texts has another aspect, when read through Del Boca's own biography: these are also the words of his childhood heroes.

---

43 Eric Hobsbawm, *Bandits* (London: Weidenfeld and Nicolson, 1969).

44 See Nicola Labanca and Carlo Spagnolo (eds), *Guerra ai briganti, guerra dei briganti (1860–1870). Storiografia e narrazioni* (Bari: Unicopli, 2021).

45 This approach took on a different tone some years after Del Boca's book, in 2011 and the 150th anniversary of Unification, when a Southern malcontent was expressed in part through a historical revisionism, claiming that genocide had been committed in the South and proto-Nazi concentration camps set up in the North. The historian Alessandro Barbero has argued against this Southern-populist interpretation in *I prigionieri dei Savoia* (Bari and Rome: Laterza, 2012). Also see the important recent critique of this position 'from the South' by Carmine Conelli, *Il rovescio della Nazione. La costruzione coloniale dell'idea di Mezzogiorno* (Naples: Tamu, 2022).

The Choice

Until 1943, Del Boca's world was a purely Fascist one. In his memoirs, he describes with a rare honesty the cultural smothering performed by the insular, domineering ideological apparatus of the dictatorship. All he knew was Fascism and, to a large extent, it was all that he could have known. 'I had seen my mother spitting on the portrait of Mussolini that we kept in the kitchen, but she was no anti-Fascist of any kind: just a mother who was sick and tired of scraping the cash together for her children's costly uniforms.'[46] The fighter pilots sweeping over Ethiopia's mountain plateaus are thus the images of his adolescence, the propaganda pasted across school exercise books and magazine pullouts, the stuff of adventure stories and playground games. Undermining the universe of his childhood can be understood not only as the motor of his criticism of those 20 years of Fascist rule, but also, more fundamentally, as driving the overarching thesis of the book. Del Boca demonstrates in minute detail how the myth of the 'good Italian' is unmerited, asking how it is possible that this myth could be maintained despite all the evidence to the contrary. He does not, in the end, provide a real response to this question—the text is too focused on demonstrating the fallibility of the myth to truly delve into its functioning. But he does provide a response, instead, to a different and related question, that of how it was possible for Italians to act with such violence and cruelty. His answer is an anthropological and pedagogical one: the creation of Italian man, *homo italicus*, as a reaction to centuries of Italy's identity as a second-rate European nation, and especially in the wake of the mid-nineteenth-century liberal project of unifying the peninsula as a single nation-state. Over the book's sprawling first chapter—doubtless for him the most original chapter with respect to his life's work—Del Boca traces the modernist, Fascist project of creating new Italians back to the broader bourgeois, Enlightenment mission of educating the Italian people. In so doing, he

---

46 Angelo Del Boca, Introduction to *La Scelta* (Vicenza: Neri Pozza, 2006).

not only lays at the door of liberalism—rather than just Fascism—the blame for the violence and horror wreaked by Italians across the world, but also finds meaning in his own teenage attendance of the Saturday schools, the Fascist choirs and, ultimately, his months in Mussolini's army.

The burdensome choice that Italians were called upon to make in September 1943 is a central moment in the chapter on the Civil War (Chapter Twelve), in which Del Boca recalls how his own friends and acquaintances took different paths, whether that of non-decision, of disappearing into the mountains to join the Resistance units or to enrol in the army of the Italian Social Republic, i.e. the residue of the Fascist forces that now fought alongside the German troops. This was the path taken, at least initially, by Del Boca himself. In his autobiography, he describes how in September 1943, at the mere age of eighteen, faced with this momentous decision, he turned to someone he respected and admired, who might counsel him—his favourite schoolteacher. She opened the door to him and, instead of the hoped-for discussion of ethics and principles, of the potential to finally criticize the regime, she simply asked him why he was not in the uniform of the Fascist youth, with a note of anger. So much for the trusted schoolteacher.

The ensuing experience was to mark his life. After a short-lived attempt to tarry in Modena, the political police threatened to arrest his father unless Del Boca junior enrolled in the Fascist army. He enlisted and was sent for training in the German town of Münsingen; he recalls seeing Mussolini in July 1944 at the Gänsewag training grounds.[47] Del Boca's division, the Monterosa, left for the Ligurian coast shortly afterwards, under the command of Rodolfo Graziani.[48] Over the following

---

47 Del Boca, *Il mio novecento*, p. 69.

48 Carlo Gentile and Francesco Corniani, 'Zur Geschichte der italienisch-faschistischen Division Monterosa im deutsch besetzten Italien 1944–1945', *Quellen und Forschungen aus italienischen Archiven und Bibliotheken* 102(1) (2022): 432.

summer months, a large number of soldiers deserted, either to return home or to join the Resistance fighters. Del Boca claims that, of the 13,000 troops in the Monterosa division, half fled, and by November the count included himself, enrolled in the 7th Alpine Brigade (a division of Giustizia e Libertà), fighting under Italo Londei against the 162nd Turkestan Division of the German Army and for the liberation of the town of Bobbio[49]—'the most difficult and memorabile months of my existence.'[50] Aspects of those 20 months—first with the Fascists, then with the anti-Fascist resistance—surface throughout his writings as fragments, not least in Chapter Twelve below, when he mentions the massacre perpetrated by the Monterosa division against the resistance fighters in Bobbio, likely the 240 rebels killed in the report provided by the Lombardy Generalkommando for the final week of August 1944.[51] He does not clarify which side he was on at this stage. It is as if, of all the stories he had to tell, these traumatic facts could not be expressed without mediation. Indeed, following the war, it was to fiction that Del Boca turned in order to communicate what he had experienced, a form of expression utilized by many other survivors of the conflict.

From Italian Neo-realist To Global Journalist

Nearly all of Del Boca's works of fiction are set in the Second World War, collected in the volumes *Dentro mi è nato l'uomo* (A man was born within me) of 1947, *L'anno del giubileo* (The jubilee year) a year later and *Viaggio nella luna* (Journey to the moon) in 1955. In these works, we find the voice of a young writer who was immersed in that same psychological and literary process undergone by other former partisans,

---

49 Del Boca, *Il mio novecento*, pp. 70, 236.

50 Del Boca, *La scelta*.

51 Gentile and Corniani, 'Zur Geschichte der italienisch-faschistischen Division Monterosa': 435.

including Italo Calvino, Beppe Fenoglio and Elio Vittorini.[52] It also produced writers who experienced the Civil War under other guises, such as Carlo Levi, Cesare Pavese, Leonardo Sciascia and, last but not least, Primo Levi. Of these central figures of postwar Italian literature, Del Boca knew personally—and corresponded with—Pavese and Vittorini. Calvino recalled that Del Boca was, at one time, the rising star:

> The young writer who was typical of that time, the one that Vittorini banked on as the real discovery by *Il Politecnico*, was Angelo Del Boca, from Vercelli. Del Boca was lyrical and effusive; I tried to write stories like that but Vittorini just threw them in the waste basket.[53]

But it was in 1963 that Del Boca finally confronted his contradictory experience of the Civil War head-on, in the autobiographical (yet semi-fictionalized) work, *La scelta* (The choice). The title was apt for several reasons. First, because of its ambiguity regarding which choice, which decision, was truly central to Del Boca's experience of the war: that of joining the Republic of Salò, or that of deserting and joining the Resistance, and all the trauma, pain and indeed courage that this entailed. Yet the title is also apt as marking the moment when Del Boca made another significant decision, that of definitively abandoning literature as his mode of expression.

From 1948 till 1967, Del Boca wrote for *La Gazzetta del Popolo*.[54] Writing in a period which saw the influx of Southern Italians to the North, including Turin's FIAT car factories, Del Boca was frequently

---

52 See Lucia Re, *Calvino and the Age of Neorealism: Fables of Estrangement* (Stanford, CA: Stanford University Press, 1990); see also Srivastava, *Italian Colonialism and Resistances to Empire*, pp. 215–18.

53 Italo Calvino, *Letters: 1941–1985* (Martin McLaughlin trans.) (Princeton, NJ: Princeton University Press, 2014), p. 400. See also Francesco Mereta, 'Quando Italo Calvino ammirava Angelo Del Boca', *Studi piemontesi* 35(1) (2006): 83–87.

54 Del Boca, *Il mio novecento*, p. 96.

sent to report on the conditions of Sicily and Calabria at the beginning of the decade—another motivation for the Southernist sympathies expressed in Chapter Two.[55] The *Gazzetta* was the key rival to *La Stampa*, the Turin-based newspaper controlled by the director of FIAT; and when working as head of local news in 1956, he often found himself in opposition to the city's modernization.[56]

Turin was, however, more often than not Del Boca's point of departure over this period. The number of countries—indeed, continents—from which Del Boca began to send reports is astonishing. His new role as special correspondent led to his first journeys to North Africa in the mid-50s, then to India, Iran and Israel–Palestine, and in 1959 an important tour of ten countries across West Africa. In 1961, he extensively toured both North Africa and the Middle East, and the following year visited East Asia.[57] When the material favoured it, he would transform a series of articles into a book: on the tenth anniversary of the creation of Israel, on West Africa on the eve of postcolonial independence, on anti-Francoist Spain, South Africa after the Sharpeville massacre, Japan, Yugoslavia, as well as hundreds of articles covering everywhere from Algeria to Vietnam.[58]

---

55 Del Boca, *Il mio novecento*, pp. 123–39, 158.

56 See the diary extracts in Del Boca, *Il mio novecento*, pp. 160–74 (Del Boca erroneously dates the diary to 1958; from p. 126 onwards, one deduces that these relate instead to 1956).

57 Del Boca, *Il mio novecento*, pp. 125, 175–86.

58 *Israele anno dieci* (Turin: Lattes, 1958); *L'Africa aspetta il 1960* (Milan: Bompriani, 1959); *L'altra Spagna* (Milan: Bompriani, 1961); *Apartheid. Affanno e dolore* (Milan: Bompriani, 1962); *Occhio giapponese* (Novara: De Agostino, 1963); *Rapporto dalla Jugoslavia* (Genoa: Valnoci, 1968). Also see Angelo Del Boca, 'Vietnam' in *Lotte di liberazione e rivoluzioni* (Turin: Giappichelli, 1968). His account of an episode from the Algerian War of Independence in 1954 was picked up by Jean-Paul Sartre for *Temps modernes*.

Del Boca was also politically involved over this period. He had joined the Italian Socialist Party on its formation at the end of the war, and his international correspondence often overlapped with his political projects. In the early 1960s, he was part of the *Circolo della Resistenza* in Turin, a group of intellectuals, historians and writers who were particularly concerned with new Fascist forces accumulating in Italian politics.[59] This local concern also flowed into another rich and detailed book which Del Boca collaborated on, reporting on neo-Fascist movements (interpreted very broadly) around the world, translated into English shortly after.[60] His reports on the anti-Francoist front of the early 1960s had led him to supporting aspects of the armed struggle in Spain, but this was an exception—he had no connections with the revolutionary movements of Italy's long '68. He was, instead, a figure of committees and petitions, whether in defence of journalism or of opposition movements in the countries he had visited, such as the Committee of Friendship and Aid with the Algerian People[61] or the Movement of Democratic Journalists.[62] He also produced a journalistic inquiry into the situation of Italy's psychiatric hospitals—anticipating Franco Basaglia's paradigm-changing intervention by two years.[63]

---

59 See the account provided in Claudio Dellavalle, 'Il politico e l'organizzatore di cultura' in Luciano Boccalatte (ed.), *Guido Quazzi. L'archivio e la biblioteca come autobiografia* (Milan: FrancoAngeli, 2008), pp. 33–60.

60 Angelo Del Boca and Mario Giovana, *Fascism Today: A World Survey* (R. H. Boothroyd) (London: William Heinemann, 1970).

61 See Caterina Roggero, 'The Italian Left and Ben Bella's Authoritarianism in Algeria, between Unconditional Support and Faint Criticism (1962–1965)', *Journal of Asian and African Studies* 58(6) (2022): 16.

62 See Enzo Forcella, 'Grandezza e miseria del *movimento dei giornalisti democratici*' in *Il potere delle parole: come si diventa giornalista* (Rome: La Città del Sole, 1983).

63 Angelo Del Boca, *Manicomi come lager* (Turin: Edizioni dell'Albero, 1966).

Historian

Fundamental among these journalistic works for the current volume—
and indeed for signalling another important 'choice' in his life—was
that which brought him to East Africa, and the publication in 1965 of
his book on the Ethiopian war, a work based on archives and diaries as
well as copious interviews with high-ranking Ethiopian figures, including
Haile Selassie himself.[64] 'The idea was to reconstruct the Abyssinian
campaign, but—for the first time—by also listening to the voices of the
conquered.'[65] It was in the articles for this volume that Del Boca first
proposed that chemical weapons had been utilized by the Italians in the
invasion of Ethiopia.

In 1967 Del Boca left *La Gazzetta* to concentrate on a year-long
inquiry into the economic and cultural crisis faced by the newspapers
themselves, financed by the Agnelli Foundation.[66] Returning from this
'sabbatical', from 1968 to 1980 Del Boca worked as the vice-director for
Il Giorno in Milan. Having been tempted by un unfulfilled promise that
he might become director, he described this as 'the worst decision of my
life',[67] trapped in a failing paper run by an unpleasant editor with a politically ambiguous orientation.[68] He overcame his frustration by dedicating
himself to his historical work, continuing the mission already begun
with *The Ethiopian War* and producing the volumes that were to establish

---

64 Angelo Del Boca, *La guerra d'Abissinia 1935–1941* (Milan: Feltrinelli, 1965);
translated as Angelo Del Boca, *The Ethiopian War 1935–1941* (Phyllis Deborah
Cummins trans.) (Chicago, IL: University of Chicago Press, 1965).

65 Del Boca, *Il mio novecento*, p. 183.

66 Angelo Del Boca, *Giornali in crisi: Indagine sulla stampa quotidiani in Italia e nel
mondo* (Turin: Aeda, 1968).

67 Del Boca, *Il mio novecento*, p. 249.

68 See Del Boca's account in Ada Gigli Marchetti (ed.), *'Il Giorno'. Cinquant'anni di
un quotidiano anticonformista* (Milan: FrancoAngeli, 2007), pp. 193–98; also
Giampaolo Pansa, *Comprati e venduti. I giornali e il potere negli anni '70* (Milan:
Bompiani, 1977).

his legacy: multi-volume historical works on *Gli italiani in africa orientale* (The Italians in East Africa) and *Gli italiani in libia* (The Italians in Libya), totalling six weighty books published over the decade 1976 to 1986.[69] As has been noted, the first volumes rely heavily on secondary sources, but as Del Boca continued his investigations, he increasingly delved into the archives, making constant discoveries and undergoing a professional transformation from journalist to historian.[70] At the end of the 1970s, several factors induced him to return to Turin and definitively change careers: the need to dedicate himself more fully to archival work, the transformation of the Italian Socialist Party under the leadership of Bettino Craxi and the death of his first wife, Maria Teresa: 'without her, I could not bear to live in that horrifically empty house' in Milan.[71]

Thus, while Italy was passing through a fiery period of convulsions and transformations, Del Boca was shoulder-deep in papers. His approach was that of an idiosyncratic collector, maintaining and expanding an archive of military records that complemented those he could access in governmental collections—indeed, throughout the text below, especially in the chapters on the invasion of Ethiopia, Del Boca references these items from his personal store. This approach reaches a climax with the account of General Miani in Chapter Six, based almost entirely on records brought to him by Miani's descendants,[72] but is equally present in Chapter Eight, where he demonstrates the use of gas in Ethiopia through reference to the telegrams held in his own archive.[73] These

---

69 *Gli italiani in Africa orientale*, 4 vols (Bari: Laterza, 1976–84); *Gli italiani in Libia*, 2 vols (Bari: Laterza 1986).

70 Nicola Labanca, *In marcia verso Adua*, p. xiii.

71 Del Boca, *Il mio novecento*, pp. 258–59.

72 Del Boca more fully analysed the events emerging from Miani's archive in *La disfatta di Gasr Bu Hàdi. 1915: Il colonnello Miani e il più grande disastro dell'Italia coloniale* (Milan: Mondadori, 2004).

73 Del Boca brought together other interventions (including by Giorgio Rochat) in *I gas di Mussolini* (Rome: Editori Riuniti, 1996). Further evidence has since been

documents were tracked down and produced by Del Boca repeatedly in his decades-long diatribe with Indro Montanelli (see p. 211 below), an exchange that helps us understand much about Del Boca's character: theirs was a battle of words in which ideas of honour and honesty played a greater role than those of justice and punishment. For Del Boca, his disagreement with Montanelli had to be removed from the realm of political ideologies—a socialist campaigning journalist engaged in a predictable attack on a hyper-conservative editor-in-chief—and instead waged on the field of a shared ideology, that of the honourable soldier.

Del Boca's transformation into a professional historian was accompanied by a continuous and successful attempt to encourage students and colleagues, from both Italy and the former colonies, to delve into scientific research. In 1985, Del Boca took up the presidency of the Institute for the History of the Resistance at Piacenza, the location of his own war-time activities, establishing an office, archive and academic journal, with articles concentrating on the local history of Piacenza on the one hand and of Italian colonialism on the other. In addition to a range of interventions relating to Italy's relations with Somalia and other former colonies over the 1990s, in the last decades of his life Del Boca dedicated himself to autobiographical works as well as specific studies into different aspects of his life's research,[74] often relying on personal archives. The present volume, published in 2005, may have been written over a period of six months,[75] but by now it should be clear to the reader

---

provided through the important oral histories recovered in Irma Taddei, *Autobiografie Africane* (Milan: FrancoAngeli, 1996) and Matteo Dominioni, *Lo sfascio dell'impero* (Rome and Bari: Laterza, 2008) among other studies.

74 *Un testimone scomodo* (Domodossola: Grossi, 2000), *Il mio novecento* (Vicenza: Neri Pozza, 2008), *Nella notta ci guidano le stelle: La mia storia partigiana* (Milan: Mondadori, 2015). We can also mention here the collection of his interviews, *Da Mussolini a Gheddafi: Quaranta incontri* (Vicenza: Neri Pozza, 2012).

75 Del Boca, *Il mio novecento*, p. 445.

that it represents, in truth, the product of six decades of research and engagement.

The fate of Italy's empire in Africa—defeated in a global war by other imperial forces—meant that there was little continued connection between the formerly colonized and the population of the new Italian Republic.[76] 'Italy's Empire ended not in a groundswell of nationalist revolts by colonized peoples [. . .] but by military defeat and diplomatic fiat.'[77] Of course, even if not on the same scale as in Britain or France, there were many former colonial subjects who moved to Italy and with whom the new Republic had to reckon with.[78] And indeed, over half a million Italian refugees had to be integrated from the former possessions in Africa, Eastern Europe and China.[79] Yet this influx of new citizens did not translate into a mass consciousness regarding the crimes of the colonies, and Italian progressives were more engaged in confronting two decades of Fascist rule at home than the longer, and equally (or more) brutal, history of violence abroad.

In part, the myth of the 'good-natured Italians' was born in this moment, when Italian governments attempted to convince both their electorate and their international allies that they could be trusted to return to their former colonies and govern them amicably. Eritrea was occupied by British forces in 1941, who remained there for over a decade. Italy had hoped then to regain the colony and campaigned

---

76 Srivastava, *Italian Colonialism and Resistances to Empire*, pp. 204–5.

77 Ruth Ben-Ghiat and Mia Fuller (eds), Introduction to *Italian Colonialism*, p. 2.

78 See Valeria Deplano, 'Within and Outside the Nation: Former Colonial Subjects in Post-War Italy', *Modern Italy* 23(4) (2018): 395–410.

79 Pamela Ballinger, *The World Refugees Made: Decolonization and the Foundation of Postwar Italy* (Ithaca and London: Cornell University Press, 2020). See also her argument on the *unexceptional* nature of Italian decolonialization, pp. 17–20.

diplomatically to this end—even under agreement to accompany the country into independence—but in 1952 the UN supported annexation by the Ethiopian empire, a military expansionism that continued for decades, even after Haile Selassie was overthrown by the Derg. As Ruth Iyob has written, 'while Ethiopia's revolutionary transition from an anachronistic feudal empire to a Marxist–Leninist republic altered the terms of ideological reference, the same goals remained regarding the Eritrean problem.'[80] In his own assessment, Del Boca criticized Italy for losing all interest in Eritrea after 1952, even during the decades of open warfare with Ethiopia, a conflict in which he believed Italy could have had a key diplomatic role for peace. The end of the war—and Eritrean independence—saw no greater engagement from Italy, despite Del Boca's hopes. Nor did the Eritrean askari receive any pension from Italy, despite having effectively built their empire. Italy abandoned her African veterans much as it had abandoned its Italian ones—a situation with which Del Boca no doubt felt a certain affinity (see p. 307 below).

In Ethiopia, there was, of course, no question of a return. The Treaty of 1947 made assurances for the return of all Ethiopian works stolen by Italy during the occupation, and in 1956, war reparations were agreed upon after lengthy negotiations.[81] Tens of thousands of Italians left during the 40s and 50s, leaving a small and broken Italian community in the capital.[82] And whereas in Eritrea, Italian schools remained and the Italian

---

80 Iyob, *Eritrean Struggle for Independence*, p. 58. See also her account of the 1940s anti-Italian resistance movement and the postwar negotiations between the Axis powers regarding Eritrea's future: pp. 61–81.

81 Artworks in state collections were eventually returned, but not from private ones. Other works include the Weber Tsehai airplane, only very recently returned by the Meloni government. See Angelo Del Boca, 'Il colonialismo italiano tra miti, rimozioni, negazioni e inadempienze', *Italia contemporanea* 212 (September 1998): 590–603. The fourth-century obelisk of Axum, stolen in 1937, was returned in 2004.

82 Alessandro Pes, 'Senza l'impero: le comunità italiane in Africa orientale tra mito

past maintained a certain traction among the ruling elites, this was not so in Ethiopia. And whereas in Eritrea the askari were viewed as a founding element of the country, in Ethiopia they were regarded as a shameful secret of the past:[83] the history of collaboration with Italian authorities was suppressed, and the resistance movement celebrated. Selassie returned and was hailed as the harbinger of modernity to the region.

In Somalia, Italy had greater diplomatic success: although occupied by the British during the Second World War, Italy effectively returned to the colony from 1950 to 1960, mandated by the UN with overseeing the transition to independence. The occupation continued the same exploitative prewar approach, treating the country as an agricultural colony, with capital in the hands of Italian companies. Not only did General Nasi (whose crimes in Ethiopia are described in Chapter Seven) return as Commissioner, but Italy also deployed 6,000 troops.[84] Continued interference in Somalian politics arguably sowed the seeds for a political conflict that was to undermine the future of the Somali state: the democratic government established after independence lasted less than a decade, when Siad Barre's army overthrew it.[85] In an interview from 1970, Barre's views on Italian colonialism were clear enough: 'Italian colonialism never saw anything beyond the bananas, and aside from the bananas developed practically nothing [. . .] Then there was independence, and things did not change much, because the old rulers were nothing other than remote controlled puppets of the old colonial

imperiale e fine del colonialismo', *Rivista dell'Istituto di Storia dell'Europa Mediterranea* 10 (June 2022): 45–62.

83 Triulzi, 'Displacing the Colonial Event': 31.

84 Antonio Maria Morone, 'How Italy Returned to Africa' in Paolo Bertella Farnetti and Cecilia Dau Novelli (eds), *Colonialism and National Identity* (Newcastle: Cambridge Scholars Publishing, 2015), pp. 130–36.

85 See Abdi Ismail Samatar, *Africa's First Democrats* (Bloomington and Indianapolis: Indiana University Press, 2016).

interests.'[86] The bloody invasion of Ethiopia in 1977 saw Barre's army defeated by Soviet and Cuban forces sent to support the Derg, leaving Somalia devastated, a country of refugees. Here, Del Boca was critical of successive Italian interventions: first, of the mysterious, shameful diplomatic support offered to Barre in the mid-80s by Bettino Craxi (Del Boca's old nemesis in the Italian Socialist Party); then, of Giulio Andreotti's abandonment of Somalia following Barre's overthrow; and finally, of how Italy was drawn into the American invasion—'Operation Restore Hope'—in 1992.[87] The myth of the 'good Italians' that had accompanied the Italian troops' mission in Somalia was scandalously dismantled some years later when evidence of their utilization of torture came to light.[88] In the final pages of the present volume, Del Boca downplays this episode, choosing instead to focus on the 'honourable' behaviour of Italian troops in other engagements—over-optimistically.

As for Libya, at the end of the war, Italy argued that no war damages were due because, in 1938, Libya had already been a colony; and reparations for damages during colonization were out of discussion, as no European power had agreed to this. A sum was finally decided upon with King Idris—again in 1956—merely as a contribution to postwar reconstruction. When Gaddafi seized power in 1969, the new military government renewed the demands for reparations. As Muhammed Jerary, Director of the Libyan Studies Center, has commented, Libyans 'felt thrice betrayed: by Italian colonization, by the devastation of a World War whose mines continued to kill them, and by being denied compensation that had been paid even to the aggressor powers.'[89] When Italy

---

86 Cited in Angelo Del Boca, *Una sconfitta dell'intelligenza. Italia e Somalia*, Laterza (Rome: Laterza, 1993), p. 15.

87 Del Boca, *Una sconfitta dell'intelliigenza*, pp. *vii–xi*.

88 Del Boca, 'L'operazione Ibis in Somalia: Luci ed ombre in una missione di *peace-keeping*', *I sentieri della ricerca* 3 (June 2006): 247–51.

89 Muhammed T. Jerary, 'Damages Caused by the Italian Fascist Colonization of Libya' in Ben-Ghiat and Fuller (eds), *Italian Colonialism*, p. 204. A hospital promised

refused, Gaddafi confiscated all the property belonging to the 20,000 Italians still in Libya and carried out their expulsion. The Italian president, and former communist, Massimo D'Alema visited Libya in 1999 and finally apologized for the crimes of Italian colonialism, as well as returning the statue of Venus that had been looted from Leptis Magna (and gifted by Mussolini to Goering); Del Boca himself was enthusiastic at the time about the new diplomatic relations, Libya's improved economy and the trans-Mediterranean pipelines.[90] Good relations also included a renewed engagement to recover information regarding the Libyans who had been deported to and imprisoned in Italy during the resistance movement, as well as—especially from 2008—Libya's important role in blocking maritime immigration to Italy's southern shores and islands.[91]

These relations were obviously entirely interrupted by the NATO aerial assault of 2011, the assassination of Gaddafi and the ensuing decade of civil war. Throughout this period, Libya has become an increasingly central partner in Italy's role as Europe's gatekeeper, its governments (and militias) identified as privileged interlocutors of border control.[92] This interlocution has created a new and horrifying partnership from 2017 onwards, in which Italy directly finances the construction of concentration camps for the tens of thousands of people from across Africa and the Indian subcontinent attempting to depart from Libya as a means to circumvent Europe's apartheid-style visa regime. As some have provocatively noted, today's camps for would-be immigrants disturbingly mirror those constructed by the Italian army in the Cyrenaica a hundred

---

in 1956, and again in the 1980s, was finally built—in 2016, as a military operation.

90 Del Boca, 'Obligations of Italy Toward Libya' in Ben-Ghiat and Fuller (eds), *Italian Colonialism*. See also Natalino Ronzitti, *The Treaty of Friendship* (Rome: Istituto Affari internazionali, 2009).

91 See Luciano Monzali and Poalo Soave, *Italy and Libya: From Colonialism to Special Relationship (1911–2021)* (London and New York: Routledge, 2023).

92 See Sally Hayden, *My Fourth Time, We Drowned* (London and Brooklyn: Melville House, 2022); Nancy Porsia, *Mal di Libia* (Milan: Bompiani, 2023).

years' earlier.[93] The anthropologist Stefania Malia Hom has called this the 'mobius strip' of empire, in which the tools of empire's past constantly return in an imperialist present, modified and transformed but nevertheless—or rather, necessarily—violent and racialized.[94] In one of his last interventions in 2019, Del Boca was crystal clear in placing the current agreement with Libya in the lineage of Italian 'colonial and neo-colonial wrongdoings'.[95]

Del Boca's approach to the 'myth' behind the apparently good character of Italian colonialism takes a leap of faith beyond the boundaries of imperial history and returns to a more general question of character and violence; the success of the volume perhaps lies precisely in a global view of history that nevertheless returns over and over again to the Italian mainland, to understand how the Italian people have not only been formed by external events, but even actively moulded by internal actors. The long opening chapter on the constant denigration to which Italians were subjected by both foreign travellers and, indeed, other Italians (for the most part aristocrats) prior to unification forms a masterful, tense overture that leads us from the comic peculiarities of sarcasm and mockery to the violent formation of working masses to be disciplined by their new national government. Knowing the pains to which Del Boca went throughout his life to broaden our attention from the horrors of Fascism to those of liberalism, we can stress the implied thesis: that it was liberalism that was responsible for inculcating into Italians the ideals of obedience, unity and national pride—virtues valorized in reaction to decades of perceived humiliation and structural poverty—which

---

93 Eric Salerno, *Genocidio in libia* (Rome: manifestolibri, 2019).

94 Stefania Malia Hom, *Empire's Moebius Strip: Historical Echoes in Italy's Crisis of Migration and Detention* (Ithaca, NY: Cornell University Press, 2019).

95 Tommaso Di Francesco, interview with Del Boca, *il manifesto* (1 November 2019). Del Boca died in 2021, at the age of 96.

ultimately found the very worst expression in Mussolini's Fascism. This for him is the motivation behind the cruelty displayed by Italians, a cruelty which has led them to perform all manner of violent acts across the world, to no lesser extent than other peoples.

Del Boca says little about the functioning of 'myth' as such: he is, we might say, fully Crocean—the secret to understanding a people's character is to be found by understanding their history.[96] Ever the journalist, for him *myth* is no more than a lie, superficial propaganda that belies the scandalous truth.[97] Again and again he asks the question of how Italians could have brought themselves to act in this manner, in a way that only partially opens the reader's mind to questions of psychology. More frequently, we can feel him standing shocked, open mouthed, at a double scandal: of the violence itself, and of the historical disavowal that seems to have subsequently been enacted. He implicitly rejects Bollati's posing of the question (in *L'Italiano*, 1983, which he cites in Chapter Two) as one of national character, opting instead to make distinctions: not all Italians are to blame, but instead a powerful minority that manipulated the masses, transforming them into warriors.

Del Boca maintains throughout a juridical or forensic orientation, investigating the records for the numbers and circumstances that would allow not only for the violence of Italy's generals to be evaluated as (war) crimes, but even the extent of such indictments. As Nicola Labanca argued at the time, there is a danger in reducing matters to these terms, as this potentially blocks an assessment of the whole system or structure of colonialism and racism in which these acts occurred.[98] It is only in

---

96 Benedetto Croce, *Teoria e storia della storiografia* (Bari: Laterza, 1966).

97 The opposite, of course, would be the case for Furio Jesi, for whom myths can be used or abused, but in their authentic form are bearers of validity. See Furio Jesi, *Secret Germany* (Richard Braude trans.) (London: Seagull Books, 2021) and Alberto Toscano, *Late Fascism* (London: Verso Books, 2023), pp. 114–31.

98 Nicola Labanca, 'Colonial rule, colonial repression and war crimes in the Italian colonies', *Journal of Modern Italian Studies* 9(3) (2004): 300–313.

the final pages on the construction of the national character in the 'second republic' of Silvio Berlusconi that Del Boca returns to a more strictly psychological reasoning. In Berlusconi's political project, Del Boca sees a new version of 'making Italians', this time not the obedient soldier of the *homo italicus*, but the dutiful consumer who nevertheless follows orders and curtails their own powers of criticism. The burden of the violent formation of an Italian nation is not, therefore, posed in a dialectical relation to the projection of a marginalized Other—as David Forgacs has argued, for example[99]—but instead weighs upon the conscience of a struggle that remains *internal* to Italy. This (faintly Marcusian) appeal in the final pages for a united front against *homo economicus*, although written 20 years ago in a very different country, now seems to foreshadow the project of Trumpism—and one facet of its opposition.

Yet, there is perhaps another way to understand Del Boca's proposal in light of more recent events. The oscillations of Italian political life—in which it is rare now for a government to last a full term—have, at the time of writing, brought the Brothers of Italy party to power, under the leadership of Giorgia Meloni. Meloni rose through the ranks of the Italian Social Movement (MSI), indirect heirs to the Fascist Party, and her current party continues to brush off accusations of neo-Fascism while rarely confronting them.[100] Yet, even when she is criticized for drawing on Fascist support, the horrors of the Empire are not part of this legacy; Fascism means Mussolini and Italianness, but the silence that still reigns so successfully over Italy's bloody colonial past—despite decades of research and campaigning—means that her ideology does not threaten her claim to an international presence. Relations between Italy and Libya are better than they have been for a long time, with

---

99 David Forgacs, *Italy's Margins: Social Exclusion and Nation Formation Since 1861* (Cambridge: Cambridge University Press, 2014).

100 See David Broder, *Mussolini's Grandchildren: Fascism in Contemporary Italy* (London: Pluto Press, 2023), pp. 147–52.

direct flights between Rome and Tripoli having recently recommenced, and elaborate proposals for Italy's geopolitical, energy-focused position in the Mediterranean are being made under the rubric of the 'Mattei Plan', even while repressing the intertwined histories of postcolonial and state violence that led to the assassination of Enrico Mattei himself (and others).[101] Italy's old unique geographical centrality returns, now as a hub for gas and oil lines, along with its apparently ambiguous relation to countries once colonized by European powers—Italian or otherwise. Fortunately, over recent years, activists, writers and scholars have returned to the histories of Italian colonialism from a contemporary perspective, whether through the lens of the 'Black Mediterranean'[102] or through practices of radical 'street-naming' as a mode for remembering and reclaiming struggles against Italian colonialism.[103] Understanding the histories of the entirely *unambiguous* past relations with peoples across the world detailed in the pages below may indeed help the international community—from above or below—to better conceive the legacy underpinning much of the war-mongering ideology and racist border policies promulgated by Italy's leading politicians today.

---

101 See Giuseppe Lo Bianco, *Profondo Nero: Mattei, De Mauro, Pasolini* (Milan: Garzanti, 2009).

102 See Alessandra Di Maio, 'Il mediterraneo nero. Rotte dei migranti nel millennio globale' in Giulia de Spuches (ed.), *La Città Cosmopolita* (Palermo: Palumbo Editore, 2012), pp. 143–63; The Black Mediterranean Collective (ed.), *The Black Mediterranean: Bodies, Borders and Citizenship* (London: Palgrave Macmillan, 2021); Camilla Hawthorne, 'Black Mediterranean Geographies: Translation and the Mattering of Black Life in Italy', *Gender, Place and Culture: A Journal of Feminist Geography* 30(3) (2023): 484–507.

103 See Tenley Bick, 'Ghosts for the Present: Countercultural Aesthetics and Postcoloniality for Contemporary Italy: The Work of Wu Ming 2 and Fare Ala' in Martin Munro et al. (eds), *Global Revolutionary Aesthetics and Politics After Paris '68* (London: Lexington, 2020), pp. 45–78.

PREMISE

In February 1937, following an attempt on the life of Marshall Rodolfo Graziani—then viceroy of Ethiopia—several thousand Italians, civilians and soldiers alike came out of their houses and barracks and let loose the most violent and bloodthirsty mass lynching that Africa had ever seen.

Armed with clubs, cudgels and iron bars, they took aim at anyone—men, women, children, the elderly—they met in the forest-city of Addis Ababa. And because it had already been decreed that the massacre was to last for three days, and because the use of clubs turned out to be too tiring, by the second day they had decided to make use of more efficient and effective methods. The most practical was to drench a hut in petrol and set fire to it, with all its occupants still inside, and then lug a hand grenade at it.

No one has ever drawn up a precise account of the Ethiopians murdered between 19 and 21 February 1937. The estimates range from a minimum of 1,400 to a maximum of 30,000, depending on the source one consults.

The thousands of Italians who participated in the massacre of so many innocent people—people who had nothing to do with the assassination attempt—never paid for their crimes. They were never investigated. They never spent even one day in prison. After the extended bloodbath, they went back to their homes and barracks as if nothing had happened. Those who had families in the city resumed their lives without any problems, without feelings of guilt, managing their own affairs, hugging their children, making love, as if their intense murderous activities over those three blood-soaked days had been the most natural and admirable thing in the world.

The episode of Addis Ababa, for all its severity, is but one of many episodes in which Italians have proved themselves to be capable of unspeakable cruelty. As a rule, these massacres have been carried out by 'ordinary people'—people neither exceptionally fanatical, nor trained in mass liquidation. They acted in the spirit of discipline, by emulation, or because they were convinced of being in the right by eliminating 'barbarians' or 'subhumans'. It is not uncommon to find, among the officers, those who even boasted of their ferocious actions, providing extended accounts full of macabre details. For example, one provided an account about how to transform a partisan captured in Slovenia into a human torch. All that was necessary, they assure us, were a pole and a tree to which to tie the prisoner, a flask of petrol and a match.

This book spans the history of Italy from the war against brigandry through to the Second World War, stopping to examine some of the most striking episodes that have taken place in Italy, in some of the European countries occupied by Axis forces during the war, and of course in the Italian overseas colonies; and attempts to illustrate the dynamics of these moments in their specific historical contexts. We can, however, already anticipate that the protagonists of these episodes will find no extenuating circumstances, because their evident culpability is all too obvious and unmistakable. The myth of Italians as 'good folk'—*italiani brava gente*—which has covered over so many horrors, including those that we present to the reader here, is in realty, under the cold light of the facts, no more than a hypocritical and fragile artifice. It has no right to exist; it simply has no historical basis. It is a myth that has been arbitrarily and cunningly utilized for more than a century, and has its followers even today—but the simple truth is that Italians, given the circumstances, have behaved as cruelly as any other people in analogous situations. They have no right to claim any particularly clemency, and certainly no self-absolution.

Before examining the episodes of violence which we have selected from the years between 1861 and 1946, a first chapter is dedicated to the history of Italians in their difficult journey to national unification. During this journey, Italians were often judged extremely harshly by foreign observers, often cruelly so, frequently without any motivation—a treatment they often received from many Italian politicians and writers as well.

We will see the difficulties faced by the first Italian governments, not only during the process of unification itself but also in the delicate and complex task of 'making Italians', to use Massimo d'Azeglio's phrase.[1] This meant tearing them away from their localisms in order to provide them with a national consciousness and a precise identity. It was no easy task. And yet, from the governments of the Right to those of the Left—and from Giovanni Giolitti to Benito Mussolini—everyone, even if to differing degrees, was engaged in the attempt to build a different model of Italian. Only Mussolini, over the course of 20 years, took this process of radical transformation of the individual to its extreme conclusions—the results of which we are all well aware.

The objective of 'making Italians' in a country that had known the greatest kinds of social fragmentation for centuries, and the almost continuous influence of other peoples—always in the form of invaders—was no doubt a legitimate one, perhaps even an unavoidable one. But the means employed to do so were not always appropriate. In some periods, these means have even been poisonous, and instead of producing virtuous citizens and disciplined soldiers, ended up producing the most terrifying instruments of death, as we shall see.

---

1 Massimo d'Azeglio (1798–1866): Italian liberal politician; Prime Minister of Sardinia; and later, member of the Italian Senate.

ONE

MAKING ITALIANS

Italians, taken as a whole, have never enjoyed a particularly good reputation over the last three centuries. No foreign traveller who journeyed across the peninsula, whether for business or pleasure, failed to express, in their diaries or letters, opinions about the Italians that were far from complimentary. But even our own internal observers, those of the educated classes, have been no less prone to uncover the vices and defects of their countryfolk. These range from making witty comments to passing down harsh sentences, from ironic observations to pseudo-scientific conjecture. And then, of course, there are the instances of self-flagellation.

To provide a few examples: the Italians have been described as lazy indifferent slackers; as ignorant, gullible, sycophantic Papists; and as untrustworthy, stupid, servile turncoats. And furthermore, as unfeeling towards all admonishment, all insults, even beatings. I could go on.

How is it possible that a people who had conquered the world with its armies, laws and culture, could have fallen so far as to become, as Otto von Bismarck maintained, 'the fifth wheel on the cart' in the great array of European nations—and to remain, for centuries, a passive object in the hands of foreign diplomacy? And yet this is simply fact. The decline has been slow but unstoppable. The wondrous decades of Rome were followed by centuries of darkness, interrupted by the miracle of the Renaissance. And then, again, night fell upon a divided Italy, bringing it to the peaks of its fragmentation and impotence, with governments whose courts spoke in French, German and Spanish but not in Italian.

We had to wait until the Peace of Aquisagrana (1748) and the end of Spanish domination before Italy, even while continuing as a mosaic of separate states, began to exit its long isolation and, after so many wars that had laid waste to its territory, to know the benefits of neutrality and peace. But the idea of forming a federation of Italian states remained nonetheless utopian. Indeed, the opinion of Francesco Guicciardini was the dominant one, who not only praised Italy's political division but also attributed its 'blossoming' to precisely this fact.

Over the century of the Enlightenment, Italy still seemed, in terms of reform, a world away from other European nations. We certainly had our progressive intellectuals, who augured radical change for the peninsula, above all in matters concerning social inequality, feudal hangovers, rural poverty and widespread illiteracy. From his chair in political economy in Naples, Antonio Genovesi emphasized the importance of launching practical and technical education as soon as possible. Among the reformers in Lombardy, on the other hand, first and foremost we find Pietro Verri and Cesare Beccaria, while in Naples it was Gaetano Filangieri who pushed for freedom of the press and of speech, and expounded his hope for a judiciary free of corruption.[1] But the relationship between princes and reformers was never an easy one. The reformers always took second place, and if they were given a hearing in Lombardy and Tuscany, and tolerated in Naples on condition that they tone down their requests, in Piedmont they were openly persecuted and forced into exile. In Venice, Genova and the Papal states they simply had no voice at all.

---

1 Antonio Genovesi (1713–69) and Pietro Verri (1728–97) were fundamental political economists, while Cesare Beccaria (1738–94) and Gaetano Filangieri (1753–88) were the founders of liberal Italian juridical thought. [Trans].

From the start, the French Revolution thus inflamed enthusiasm and hope for the majority of Italian intellectuals. The arrival of the French army in Italy, led by Napoleon Bonaparte, and the creation of his 'Cisalpine Republic', along with other 'sister' republics in Europe, raised great expectations, above all among Jacobins who saw the day of Italian independence nearing and the creation of an entirely new society. But these expectations soon gave way to disappointment and finally revolt. For Napoleon, Italy was in reality merely a pawn in his great game. Betraying the dreams of Francesco Melzi d'Eril, who had invoked a truly free Italy that would no longer be subordinate to France, in 1805 Napoleon crowned himself as sovereign ruler over the Kingdom of Italy, and distributed his family members across the peninsula's various regions.[2]

Nevertheless, the outcome of the years of French domination was not entirely negative. Italy witnessed noteworthy changes. For even if the form of independence conceded by Napoleon presented very precise, stultifying limitations, it nevertheless allowed a few leading groups to experiment with their own political and administrative skills, concretizing some reforms and reaping the benefits of the Napoleonic Code, which constituted an extraordinary and beneficial novelty. It was also significant that tens of thousands of soldiers donned a uniform and learnt to fight—even if in the name of causes that had nothing at all to do with Italy's own interests and independence. In the end, even while the country was still clearly divided, there was a certain encouragement to be found in the fact that whether in Milan or Naples, Turin or Florence, you could now find people who cultivated ideas of unity and were ready to fight to realize them.

Following the Congress of Vienna, which gave a new arrangement to a Europe that had been turned upside-down by the Napoleonic wars,

---

2 Melzi d'Eril (1753–1816) was the vice-president of the short-lived Italian Republic between 1802 and 1805; Napoleon was the president. [Trans].

Austria took control of all of Italy save for Piedmont—without any consultation of Italy herself. Between failed insurrectionist movements and increasingly severe repression, and notwithstanding unbridgeable divisions between democrats and moderates, Italy (defined with malice by Duke Metternich as nothing other than a 'geographic expression')[3] nevertheless took the final and difficult steps towards unification, despite all the seemingly insurmountable obstacles, including the presence of a foreign emperor in the North East and a reactionary pontiff in the country's heartland.[4]

There were very few who translated such aspirations into plans, and such plans into decisive action. As Stuart J. Woolf has rightly pointed out:

> The total number of individuals actively engaged in transforming Italy's conditions and attempting to gain independence did not count more than a minimal percentage of the country's 20 million inhabitants. Nevertheless, they existed as a growing proportion of the educated classes, even if still a minority, and were increasingly concerned with conquering the trust of the 'multitudes'—even if in often rhetorical and generalizing terms.[5]

At the end of a perilous journey marked by extraordinary episodes (such as the insurrectionary Five Days of Milan, and clamorous failures (such as the defeat of Carlo Alberto at Novara), out of the different versions of Italy (Mazzini's republican Italy, Gioberti's neo-Guelfian one, Cattaneo's federalist version, Ferrari and Pisacane's socialist one) it was Cavour's 'strong', Savoyist Italy that won out.[6] It was eventually imposed through

---

3 The phrase was coined by Klemens von Metternich, Chancellor of the Austrian Empire, in a note to the Lord Chancellor of Hungary in 1847. See *Mèmoires, documents et écrits* (Paris, 1883), VOL. 7, p. 415. [Trans].

4 Ferdinand I of Austria and Pope Pius IX, respectively. [Trans].

5 Stuart Josef Woolf, 'La storia politica e sociale' in *Storia d'Italia Einaudi* (Ruggiero Romano and Corrado Vivanti eds), VOL. 3 (Turin: Einaudi, 1973), p. 241.

6 For Pisacane, see pp. 22–23 below.

violence and rigged plebiscites by a kingdom that, in terms of its legal codes and administrative systems, was one of the most backward in the whole peninsula. It certainly was not the Italy that many had dreamt of and fought for. But what counted, what prevailed over everything else, cancelling out the disappointment and anger, was that Italy had been made, and no force existed that would be able to tear asunder this new reality. And now—as Massimo d'Azeglio had suggested—making Italy meant making Italians; and this was true, above all for those multitudes who had been sitting in the wings, had never lifted a rifle, had never known the trials of prison or the bitterness of exile. The task ahead was clearly among the most challenging, and it could have no certain time-scale. But one fact was certain: it would require an investment of energy, of innovation, of courage, of imagination and money superior to all that had been necessary to unify the country, a fact that had been produced more through diplomacy than through the shedding of Italian blood. To put it in another way: there were more deaths at Adwa, in the first Italian-Abyssinian war of 1895/96, than in all the wars and uprisings of Unification.[7]

But just who were they, these Italians, subjects of a seemingly unstoppable decline? Did they truly deserve being so heavily criticized? Let us first take a look at what foreign travellers—well known and otherwise—had written about them. Benedictine abbot Jean Mabillon, who had come to Italy at the end of the seventeenth century to finish his research into primitive and medieval Christianity, was particularly shocked by the extreme poverty he encountered from Tuscany down to Campania, by the abandoned or under-cultivated fields, the sparse villages, the famished farmers and the prematurely ageing women. The rich and educated people he met in the cities also seemed to him completely deaf to the progress taking place in Europe; they seemed to be characterized by a

---

7 For Adwa, see pp. 83–84 below.

passivity and general sluggishness. Their only drive was to 'try and get by.'[8]

Italy through the eyes of Scottish theologian Gilbert Burnet, Bishop of Salisbury, was not so different in 1865. It was dominated by ignorance, oppressed by Papal intolerance and undoubtedly one of the poorest and most unfortunate regions of Europe. Burnet was even convinced that the Italians were entirely aware of their inferior situation and political and moral passivity. Not even the glorious and ancient republics of Venice and Lucca were saved from this process of regression.[9] For his own part, Joseph Addison, who visited Italy in the early years of the eighteenth century, proposed a comparison between the glory and glamour of Italy's past and its present poverty and desolation, maintaining that Italy—by now isolated and stagnant—no long exercised any influence at all on the rest of Europe. He was especially critical of Roman Catholicism: 'Here they are so concerned with people's souls that they entirely overlook the health of their bodies.'[10]

Writer, philosopher and scholar of both science and law, Charles-Louis de Secondat, baron of La Brède and Montesquieu, came to Italy at the end of summer in 1728, and remained for a year. His fame preceded him for having penned the wonderfully satirical *Persian Letters*, and he was welcomed everywhere with great kindness, enjoying the privilege of speaking freely with sovereigns, princes, high prelates and scholars. Gifted with a boundless curiosity and an unusual proficiency in every field of study, there was no one better to provide an exhaustive account of the Italian situation. Reading through his *Voyage en Italie*, his conclusion

---

8 Jean Mabillon, *Correspondance inèdite de Mobillon et de Monfaucon avec l'Italiei* (Antoine-Claude Pasquin Valery ed.) (Paris: J. Labitte, 1847).

9 Gilbert Burnet, *Some Letters Containing an Account of What Seemed Most Remarkable in Travelling Through Switzerland, Italy, Some Parts of Germany, etc., in the Years 1685 and 1686* (Rotterdam: Abraham Acher, 1686).

10 Joseph Addison, *Remarks on Several Parts of Italy* (London, 1705), p. 184.

seems, on the whole, negative. For example, he writes that: 'The Italian republics are little more than poor aristocracies, that only continue through the pity one has for them; and whose nobles—without any sense of greatness or glory—aim merely to conserve their idleness and privileges.'[11]

When providing details, Montesquieu openly criticized Venice's decline, a place when laws go unobserved and where the thousands of prostitutes performed a function unknown elsewhere. He recalled with great irritation how he was besieged by beggars in Verona; and he also noted the backward laws of Savoy, writing that 'one cannot leave the country without permission, on pain of confiscation and arbitrary punishment.' As for the Genovese, he noted their extreme stinginess: 'There is no falsity like their buildings: the exterior is that of a wonderful house, but inside there is only an old spinster.' Fortunately, however, there was Rome: 'where my stay was extremely pleasant: you enjoy everything. The stones themselves seem to speak. One never lacks things to see.' And yet it was a shame that the Eternal City was governed by Pope Benedict XIII, 'a man most hated by the Roman people, and even his devotion is despised, given that he leaves them to die of hunger.'[12] Montesquieu pulled no punches on the same theme:

> Today a simonious public reigns in Rome. Never in the government of the Church has crime been seen to rule so openly. Vile men are installed in every position. And the papacy, for its own part, gives little attention to what is going on. As things

---

11 Charles Louis de Secondat, Baron de Montesquieu, 'Voyage d'Italie' in *Oeuvres complètes de Montesquieu*, VOL. 10: *Mes voyages* (Paris: Classiques Garnier, 2012), p. 296.

12 Montesquieu, 'Voyage d'Italie', p. 105, pp. 183–84, p. 200, p. 277 and p. 245, respectively.

stand, it is impossible that a worthy man be elected pope: they do not want one.[13]

The great scholar who, a few years later, was to publish the fundamental *Spirit of the Laws*, and who formulated the three-fold division of state powers, one of the pillars of democratic thought, could not but note the infinite number of Italy's contradictions. 'A meeting of nobility and abjection', to use Giovanni Macchia's pithy summary, 'of decorum, of the utmost heights and poverty'.[14]

Exactly ten years following Montesquieu's travels, Charles de Brosses—president of the Parliament of Burgundy, then governed by the princes of Condé—was to visit the peninsula. Though an important scholar of the history of navigation in Oceania, he did not possess Montesquieu's encyclopaedic knowledge and often indulged in picturesque descriptions when he did not descend into outright gossip. From the pages of his *Lettres familières sur l'Italie* emerges a sad, wretched, depressed and divided Italy, a country with neither ideas nor program, a land continually crossed and devastated by foreign armies. In a famous summary, de Brosses wrote: 'Imagine a land where a quarter of the people are priests, a quarter statues, a quarter work very little, and a quarter do nothing whatsoever.'[15]

Italy was not visited only by tourists searching for the sun or historians tracking down documents—or literati besieged by strong feelings. There were also jurists like Joseph Michel Antoine Servan and Charles Dupaty, economists such as Jean-Marie de la Platière, scientists like Joseph-Jérome de Lalands, agriculturalists such as John Symonds and Arthur Young. These latter two provided a complete overview of Italian

---

13 Montesquieu, 'Voyage d'Italie', p. 247.

14 Giorgio Macchia 'Introduzione' to Montesquieu, *Viaggio in Italia* (Rome and Bari: Laterza, 1995), p. *xviii*.

15 Charles de Brosses, *Lettres familières sur l'Italie*, VOL. 2 (Paris: Firmin-Didot, 1931), p. 6.

agriculture, with particular attention to Piedmont and Lombardy. The image they provide is far from an exhilarating panorama, above all due to the total lack of political freedom and an abnormal limitation on civil liberties. Unlike many other travellers who poured out descriptions of monuments, churches, sculpture and paintings, Symonds and Young provided the first precise information on Italy's oddly backward economic systems and techniques of production. Thus stripped bare, Italy could no longer coincide with that vision dreamt of and idealized by Northern European countries. Similarly, for the German Johann Wilhelm Archenholz, Italy was no paradise but a land ruled by a politics of falsity, poverty and ignorance. 'Despite their palaces'—he wrote in *England und Italien*—'their churches, painting galleries and other works of art, the Italians remain among the most unhappy inhabitants of our hemisphere.'[16]

Even Johann Wolfgang Goethe, who had wanted to travel to Italy his whole life—and who would go on to write to his friend Eckermann that 'Yes, I can truly say that only in Rome have I felt what it means to be a man'—did not hold back on heavily criticizing the character and behaviour of the Italians, even while attempting to mitigate his judgement with tolerance and understanding. Deploring the terrible state of the means of transport, for example, he observed that: 'This Italy, so greatly favoured by Nature, has lagged far behind all other countries in mechanical and technical matters, which are, after all, the basis of a comfortable, agreeable life.' The sight of rubbish heaps that accumulated in every angle of the streets disturbed him, especially during his stays in Verona and Venice. But with great generosity he attributed 'the squalor and lack of comfort of their houses, which shock us so much' to the fact that, thanks to the warmer climate, 'they are always out of doors and too carefree to think about anything.' Once he reached Rome, he was attracted to and fascinated by the wonderful monuments; yet he did not fail to

---

16 Johann Wilhelm von Archenholz, *England und Italien*, VOL. 2 (Michael Maurer ed.) (Heidelberg: Winter, 1993), p. 2.

observe that 'one comes upon both traces of magnificence and of devastation, which stagger the imagination. What the barbarians left, the builders of Modern Rome have destroyed.' Struck by the sheer frequency of murders in the city, he wrote that 'they are children of nature, who, for all the pomp and circumstance of their religion and art, are not a whit different from what they would be if they were still living in forests and caves.'[17]

After the grand tour in Italy—a ritual which over the eighteenth century had become almost obligatory for an upper stratum of English society, reaching mythic status—over the first two decades of the nineteenth century a second, mass arrival of Englishmen in the peninsula was so significant that people spoke of an Italo-mania. The most celebrated visitor was certainly Lord Byron, whose *Childe Harold's Pilgrimage* represented an extraordinary journey in verse across the sites and monuments of the obligatory itinerary. He certainly noted the ruins both old and new, but for him this ruinous Italy—stagnant and dead— was fascinating. In his words, the crumbling of its glorious past held an 'immaculate charm'.[18] The poet Percy Bysshe Shelley was less tolerant and benevolent, however, when he travelled through Italy in the same years. Even while indicating some positive aspects of Italy, in his *Letters from Italy*, he found the Italians to be a 'miserable people, without sensibility or imagination', even comparing them to a 'tribe of stupid and shrivelled slaves'.[19]

The opinion of poet and politician Alphonse Marie-Louis de Lamartine recalled Shelley's, save for perhaps being more negative still.

---

17 Johann Wolfgang von Goethe, *Werkausgabe, Volume 7: Italienische Reise* (Bettina Hessa ed.) (Cologne: Könemann, 1998), p. 128; *Italian Journey* (W. H. Auden and Elizabeth Mayer trans) (New York: Schocken Books, 1968), p. 110, p. 45, p. 120 and p. 155, respectively.

18 George Gordon Byron, *Childe Harold's Pilgrimage*, IV: 26.

19 Percy Bysshe Shelley, *The Prose Works*, VOL. 2 (Richard Herne Shepherd ed.) (London: Chatto and Windus, 1888), pp. 226 and 232.

He denied the Italian people any chance of redemption and unification because they had lost the ancient virtue of the warrior, they sat back while other peoples advanced and were born already old. Incapable of ridding themselves of Austrian absolutism, they looked to France not as an emancipating country but as a more tolerant master. And he added: 'For a part of these unfortunate peoples, freedom is nothing more than an alternative to servitude.'[20]

While sharing Lamartine's opinion on Italy's impossibility of become a nation like France, due to a whole series of obstacles (beginning with the fact that it had no capital city), Jules Michelet—author of the celebrated *History of France*—did not demonstrate any particular contempt for the Italians themselves, instead indulging in pity and commiseration. And this was understandable because—as he himself confessed—'I was born from Virgil and Vico.'[21] Stendhal's position was similar, of these writers the one who probably knew Italy best, having experienced an extended stay. While Stendhal enjoyed Italy's endless attractions, he also criticized its religious debasement, its bigotry and superstition. Yet he always looked for attenuating circumstances within the continued and overwhelming catastrophes that had struck the country. 'I am afraid for the future of Italy,' he wrote in *Rome, Naples and Florence*. 'This nation will continue to bring forth philosophers like Beccaria, poets like Alfieri, soldiers like Santa-Rosa; but the trouble is that these industrious individuals are too isolated from the masses of the people.'[22]

Sent to Rome by Napoleon in 1803 as secretary to the ambassador, Chateaubriand stayed in Italy for seven months, from which remains

20 Alphonse de Lamartine, *Correspondence*, VOL. 3, 1825.

21 Verdun-Louis Saulnier, *La littérature francaise du siècle romantique* (Paris: Presse universitaires, 1961), p. 55. The remark is reported by Gabriel Monod in his *Jules Michelet* (Paris, 1875). [Trans.]

22 Stendhal, *Rome, Naples et Florence* (Paris: Delaunry, 1826), p. 151; *Rome, Naples and Florence* (Richard N. Coe trans.) (London: John Calder, 1959), p. 238.

his *Voyage en Italie*—certainly not among his best works and a far cry from *René*, the work that inspired all the Romantics. He was completely fascinated by the monuments of ancient Rome, which he visited systematically, filling his pockets with fragments of porphyry, alabaster and painted plaster; he rarely took note of the people who actually inhabited the country, who for him represented little more than a worthless frame around the overall picture. The few sketches he provides of the people he met nevertheless display a squalid, miserable, hopeless world. Describing his ascent of Vesuvius, he wrote: 'Not a living creature do I find in this region of desolation except a poor, thin, sallow, half-naked girl, bending under a load of wood, she has cut on the mountain.'[23] An uneducated man he met in the Roman countryside, in an abandoned farmhouse, also belonged to a seemingly subhuman race:

> A sort of savage, half-naked, pale and emaciated by fever, guards these melancholy dwellings, like those spectres in our Gothic legends that defend the entrances to abandoned castles. One might say that no nation has dared to succeed those masters of the world in their native land, and that these plains are as they were left by Cincinnatus's plough, or the last Roman ploughshare.[24]

The Italy described by German poet and writer Heinrich Heine, Enlightenment scholar and follower of Hegel, in his *Reisebilder* was again composed of poverty, ignorance, superstition, oppression and extraordinary theft. But it was also worthy of pity: 'The whole Italian race is internally sick, and sick people are invariably more refined than the robust, for only the sick man is really a man, his limbs have a history of suffering, they are spiritualized.' Attempting to distance himself from

---

23 Francois de Chateaubriand, *Oeuvre complètes*, VOL. 7 (Paris: Honoré Champion, 2008); *Voyage en Italie* (A. S. Kline trans.) (London: Poetry in Translation, 2010); here, *Voyage en Italie*, p. 90.

24 Chateaubriand, *Voyage en Italie*, p. 112.

his forerunners who had waxed lyrical with monotonous descriptions of arcadia and tourism, Heine went straight to the point: 'There is nothing so stupid on the face of the earth, as to read a book of Travels in Italy—unless it be to write one—and the only way in which its author can make it in any degree tolerable is to say as little in it as possible of Italy.'[25]

Among the Protestant clergymen who visited Italy, some—such as Reverend Drummond—revealed a marked intolerance in relation to the Catholic population and their religious practices. Crossing the Val d'Ossola and the 'glittering snows of Monte Rossa', Drummond happened to come across a throng of the faithful pouring into a small church. Denying that this could be 'truly the house of the Lord and the gate of heaven', Drummond added that 'this was no watch-tower of Zion—it was a citadel of the enemy—there, souls were deceived not warned—there, a lie never ceased upon its stone altar, and truth never entered—and there, wolves in sheep's clothing enriched themselves at the expense of the flock.'[26] Even if Drummond's opinion was particularly factional, the Roman Catholic church's part in the Italian decline was undeniable. Jean-Charles-Léonard Simonde de Sismondi, writing in the early years of the nineteenth century, wrote that Italy was 'the land of the dead', adding that: 'One might say that religion in modern Italy, instead of serving as a moral support, has instead perverted its principles.'[27]

At the end of that same century, 40 years after Italian Unification, René Bazin—one of the sharpest observers of habits and events in our country—came up against nearly all the ills denounced by travellers who preceded him: from the extreme poverty of some regions through

25 Heinrich Heine, *Gesammelte Werke, Volume 3: Reisebilder* (Berlin: Grote'sche Verlag, 1887), p. 238; *Pictures of Travel* (Charles Godfrey Leland trans.) (Philadelphia: Schaefer and Koradi, 1879), p. 286 and p. 291, respectively.

26 David Thomas Kent Drummond, *Scenes and Impressions in Switzerland and the North of Italy* (Edinburgh: W. P. Kennedy, 1854), pp. 181–83.

27 Jean Charles Léonard Simonde de Sismondi, *Histoire des républiques italiennes du moyenâge*, VOL. 8 (Brussels: Société typographique belge, 1839), pp. 461 and 511.

to the scourge of pellagra, from an excess of taxes to the torment of usury, from a Calabria dominated by a handful of idle, greedy barons through to the countryside where the same tools described by Virgil were still in use.[28] Visiting one of the worst neighbourhoods of Naples, near the port, Bazin was struck by both pity and rage:

> Alas! What miserable meeting of poverty and human suffering. What a sight for those who come to Italy with the allusion of a Naples mad with joy, happy to live under the sun! [. . .] The news of our presence had already run through the whole neighbourhood and the crowds rushed around us. [. . .] We climbed up to a mezzanine, where five children sleep in the same bed while their mother combs her hair. I can see neither table nor any trace of furniture, save for a stool, a pot and a ladle.[29]

This ghastly spectacle of desolation contrasted, as Bazin observed, with the country's efforts to maintain an army of hundreds of thousands of soldiers and to reinforce a navy that was said to be the third greatest in the world.

We have seen how foreign travellers in Italy, from the seventeenth to the nineteenth centuries, did not hold back on their criticism of Italians even when—from the second half of the eighteenth century onward—Italy's reawakening was quite clear, at least in the cultural sphere. One thinks, for example, of the appearance of works such as Cesare Beccaria's *Dei delitti e delle pene*, and Pietro Verri's *Meditazioni sull'economia politica*, works that were well known beyond the Alps. Nevertheless, when criticisms by foreigners were particularly severe, above all in terms of denouncing the backwardness and passivity of the Italians, they

---

28 *Pellagra* ('sour-skin'): a disease caused by Vitamin-B deficiency that can result in symptoms similar to leprosy. See Daphne Roe, *A Plague of Corn* (Ithaca: Cornell University Press, 1973). [Trans.]

29 René Bazin, *Les Italiens d'aujourd'hui* (Paris: Calmann-Lévy, 1894), pp. 244–47.

revealed a certain detachment natural to those who essentially had not been forced to partake in the trials and tribulations of a foreign country.

The opinions expressed by Italian exponents of culture and politics took on a quite different tone. The discussion was more direct, without euphemisms and circumlocution. Here one finds passion and bitterness, pity and contempt, the cry of the prisoner and the curse of the exiled. In general, these took the form of exhortations and admonishments aimed by the educated minority at the distracted masses—or, put more simply, at those who were concentrated exclusively on finding what they needed from day to day to survive. One should not forget that, right up to the nineteenth century, the population of Lombardy—today among the country's richest—was still struck by pellagra, i.e. a lack of vitamin B3, because they ate corn almost exclusively.

Among the harshest and immovable flagellates of Italian customs was the poet of Recanati, Giacomo Leopardi, whose volume '*Zibaldone* of Thoughts' was not only full of sharp and precious observations about Italy and its inhabitants, but who also dedicated an entire book to the topic, his 'Discourse on the Present State of the Customs of the Italians'. For Leopardi, the Italians of his own time were cruel, unfeeling and indifferent, incapable of having true customs. 'Italy's upper classes' he clarified, 'are more cynical than any of their peers in other nations. And the Italian commoners are the most cynical of all commoners.' Furthermore, 'in terms of philosophical science and a developed, deep awareness of man and the world', Italy was 'incomparably inferior to France, England and Germany.' But there was worse still: Italian life was 'without prospect of a better future, without any occupation or goal, it is limited to the present.'[30] Italy, in the end, did not know any other version of collective life beyond the stroll, Mass and holidays (religious or otherwise).

---

30 Giacomo Leopardi, *Discorso sopra lo stato presente dei costumi degli italiani* (Milan: Rissoli, 1998), pp. 65–66, p. 57 and p. 59, respectively.

Ugo Foscolo was more pessimistic still, one-time a Napoleonic soldier and successively the Emperor's adversary when—with the Peace of Campoformio—Bonaparte had ceded Venice to Austria. His celebrated protagonist, Jacopo Ortis, constantly on the run before committing suicide, served as a warning to Italians to not entrust themselves to foreign armies: 'So many of us think freedom can be purchased with money; they think foreign nations are coming here out of a love for justice to slaughter each other on our battlefields just to free Italy!'[31] Referring to the total lack of agreement among Italians themselves, that undermined every struggle for independence, Jacopo Ortis exclaims: 'Every day we wretches recall the liberty and glory of our ancestors because those qualities are all the more splendid when contrasted with our present-day slavery. While we invoke the names of the great men of the past, our enemies are trampling on their tombs.'[32]

While for Pietro Giannone all of Italy's ills could be traced back to a loss of military discipline—meaning that there was no choice for recovering this discipline and honour than to entrust oneself to the princes of Savoy (who eventually repaid the compliment by letting him rot in a cell in the castle of Ceva)—for Melchiorre Gioia, the path to be taken ought instead to have been that of an 'undividable republic': 'Once we take a closer look at our national character and our material position, we are increasingly persuaded that an indivisible republic can be the only tool to recover our freedom. [. . .] A republic that will silence jealousies, mute dissent and in which there will be no echo save for that of public happiness.'[33]

---

31 Ugo Foscolo, *Ultime lettere di Jacopo Ortis* (Cles: I libri dell'Unità, 1993), p. 34; *Ugo Foscolo's* Ultime Lettere di Jacopo Ortis: *A Translation* (Douglas Radcliff-Umstead trans.) (Chapel Hill: University of North Carolina Press, 1970), p. 56.

32 Foscolo, *Jacopo Ortis*, p. 117; *A Translation*, p. 134.

33 Melchiorre Gioia, 'Dissertazione sul problema 'Quale dei governi liberi meglio convenga alla felicità d'Italia', in *Letture del Risorgimento. 1749–1870* (Giosuè Carducci ed.) (Bologna: Zanichelli, 1920), pp. 68–71.

Yet first of all, Giuseppe Parini claimed, it was necessary to remove the education of the people from the clergy, because 'the friars are not teaching people good manners, nor have they ever; indeed, they do not teach anything at all, because they do not themselves have any idea of how to do so.'[34] Giuseppe Baretti went further still, who could not bear the idea that in Tuscany alone there were 5,600 friars, 12,000 priests and 8,000 monks—all at the expense of the community. Above all, he could not tolerate 'the shocking ignorance of the friars, who were charged by their holy authorities to impart learning through words and writings as well as by good example.' He suggested the establishment of an extremely severe state exam in order to weed out 'those so many baboons of friars.'[35]

For the Neapolitan Gaetano Filangieri, the monster to be beaten back and destroyed was, instead, the land owners, the great lords of the earth—in his opinion, they were the cause of the great poverty that afflicted Southern Italy. In his unfortunately unfinished masterwork, *La scienza della legislazione*, he maintained in no uncertain terms that: 'No, it is not within their hands that farming will be perfected; it is not these happy few, surrounded by an immense mass of paupery, that make up a national happiness; it is not the great land owners who constitute the wealth of a nation.'[36] We do well to note that these were not the words of someone of Masaniello's ilk, but of Filangieri, knight of the realm, son of the prince of Arianello. A figure in the court of King Ferdinand IV of Naples, Filangieri was convinced that agriculture was the primary source of wealth and should thus be developed by forcing land owners to cultivate their fields, nurturing the smaller landowner and abolishing primogeniture and *fideicommissium*.

---

34 Giuseppe Parini, 'Cagioni del presente decadimento delle belle lettere e delle belle arti in Italia', in Carducci, *Letture*, p. 20.

35 Giuseppe Baretti, 'Degli ordini monastici e dei frati in Italia a mezzo il secolo XVIII' in Carducci, *Letture*, pp. 20–29.

36 Gaetano Filangeri, 'Molti gran proprietarii, pochi proprietarii piccoli, ostacolo alla popolazione' in Carducci, *Letture*, p. 30.

In nearly the same years in Milan, another aristocrat, Marquis Cesare Beccaria Bonesana, expressed his concern for the world of Italy's poor, who enjoyed no attention at all. In his celebrated book *Dei delitti e delle pene*, he suggested this defence for an unfortunate man who had fallen into crime:

> What are these laws that I must respect, that leave such a great distance between myself and the rich man? [. . .] Who made these laws? Rich and powerful men who have never deigned to visit the squalid hovels of the poor, who have never broken a mouldy crust of bread among the innocents cries of their famished children and the tears of wives.[37]

What hope was there that Italy might awake from its long, interminable lethargy? For how long would Italians still be objected to these ferocious criticisms, malevolent considerations, malicious analyses and insults? Even if they were perhaps in part responsible for their own misfortune, did they really merit this constant punishment? In 1832, while plotting plans for an improbable series of insurrections in Naples and Tuscany, Giuseppe Mazzini's opinion on Italy was particularly severe: 'Broken, divided, untrusting, uneducated, uncertain—caught between the threats of tyrants and the perfidious flattering of all those who, while lauding its ancient greatness, put her to sleep so that she will not attempt a new greatness; all the strength of her elements counterbalanced and annulled by the lack of any unity and faith.'[38]

Not even the cries and curses arriving from within the prisons managed to interrupt the lethargy of the masses—and even less the calls to act, to rebel, to struggle. Carlo Pisacane's appeal went unheard, who addressed his old comrades in battle in October 1855: 'Raise the cry of

---

37 Cesare Beccaria, *Dei delitti e delle pene* (Turin: Einaudi, 1994), p. 66; *On Crimes and Punishments* (David Young trans.) (Indianapolis: Hackett, 1986), pp. 50–51.

38 Giuseppe Mazzini, 'Della giovine Italia' (1832), *Opere*, VOL. 1 (Milan: Daelli, 1861), p. 150.

freedom, wave on high the three-hued banner, rid yourselves of the absurd formulas of sects, the heraldic symbols of towns and dynasties, which construct the greater meaning: cry out Italy! Italy! And the people, from the Alps to Lilibeo, will respond with a raging joy.'[39]

Two years later he would make his way, with a very small group of comrades—badly armed and poorly advised—to meet his fate at Sapri.[40]

Working on his masterpiece from his Parisian exile, *Dal primato civile e morale degli italiani*, Abbot Vincenzo Gioberti also employed sarcasm and mockery in his attempt to shake up the Italian people:

> Is there a modern nation that, in terms of the result of its works and the energy of its spirit, does not beat Italy? Dear God! [...] Is there anything great and beautiful that we Italians do? What are the feats of our labours and hearts? Where are our fleets and colonies? Of what glory, wealth and power can I speak? Can Italy claim to be of this world?[41]

The barbs launched by Gioberti—who a few years later returned to Turin and spent three months as the head of the Council of Ministers—held a particular sting. Yet there was comfort to be found in the fact that at this point Italy was clearly on the threshold of unification. Even if the majority of Italians continued to hold little interest in the nation's destiny, the Savoyards and a small fighting minority of patriots were about to reach the coveted goal. Unification and independence opened up new frontiers, the most challenging of which would be the making of Italy as a nation, that is, 'making Italians', as d'Azeglio had put it.

---

39 Giuseppe Amoroso (ed.), *Lettere di patrioti italiani del Risorgimento* (Bologna: Cappelli, 1971), p. 151.

40 In July 1857, Carlo Pisacane and his troops were massacred in a failed revolutionary expedition to Sapri, a port in south-west Italy. [Trans.]

41 Vincenzo Goberti, *Del primato morale e civile degli italiani*, VOL. 1 (Capolago: Tipografia Elvetica, 1846), p. 433.

To borrow the words of Martin Clark, 'this was a formidable task. "Italy" in 1871 consisted of a number of very different regional societies, with different economies and ways of life, different cultures, different histories and different religious practices.'[42] The greatest obstacle to the building of a nation was the fact that the majority of Italians did not know how to read and write, and nearly all of them expressed themselves in regional dialects. Italian, to all effects, was a dead language, just like Latin, used almost exclusively by the educated classes. According to the estimates provided by Tullio De Mauro, out of a population of 27 million Italians, those who utilized the national language counted no more than 620,000.[43] The necessity of erecting schools in every corner of the country was thus pressing, as well as utilizing the three years of military conscription to impart a minimum of education upon the drafted soldiers. But this operation took time—elementary-school education only became obligatory in 1877; furthermore, at this time, the pupils in the secondary schools—public and religious combined—numbered 60,000, while the universities were populated by only a fraction of that number.

The first draft of a scholastic regulation bore Carlo Pisacane's signature, and it is a great shame that it was not introduced, because it is characterized by a surprising modernity. According to the hero of Sapri, the state should take care of the citizens from the youngest age and maintain them through schooling until they turn 18—an extremely ambitious goal that Italy has not reached even in the twenty-first century. Pisacane wrote in his essay *La rivoluzione*:

> Maternal care is essential for children up till the age of seven, and is prescribed by Nature herself; once this age of physical development has been fully attained, the education of a child ought to be entrusted to the state. Every town ought to have its

---

42 Martin Clarke, *Modern Italy: 1871 to the Present* (London and New York: Routledge, 2014), p. 37.

43 Tullio De Mauro, *Storia linguistica dell'Italia unita* (Bari: Laterza, 1963), p. 43.

own school that houses all the instruments necessary for the complete development of both the physical and moral faculties [. . .]. People should be educated in these schools up to 15 years of age, in which timespan every pupil would learn a skill to its conclusion. Between the age of 15 and 16, everyone would be obliged to attend a course on civic philosophy and on the origin of religions, whereby each pupil would learn the rights of citizens and how to protect themselves from superstition. [. . .] The state would then attribute two years of education to each person in a specialty of its choosing, at technical colleges located in the principle Italian cities. At 18 years of age, the state's care would come to an end.[44]

It was instead the 'Casati Law' that came into effect from 15 November 1859, first in the Kingdom of Sardinia and then across the Kingdom of Italy. Despite being widely criticized for its rigidly centralizing plan, it remained active—with a few 'adjustments'—for decades, until the Gentile Law of 1923. These 'adjustments' included the Coppino Law of 15 July 1887, which established obligatory scholastic attendance from the age of 9, and a fine for parents found lacking; and the Daneo-Credaro Law of 1911, which absorbed elementary schools into the state, thus resolving a problem common to many towns of not being able to cover the costs of basic education.

The unification of the country's schooling systems provided an important push to the development of publishing. While 600 presses were present in 1859, this number rose to 911 by 1873—and by 1871, teachers could draw on 2,000 textbooks. The leaders in the production of syllabi, textbooks, anthologies, auxiliaries, history books and geography manuals, as well as texts for classical, technical and normal education,

---

44 Carlo Pisacane, *La rivoluzione* (Turin: Einaudi, 1970), p. 210. [Original translation, but also see *Revolution* (Richard Roberts trans.) (Leicester: Troubador, 2010), p. 180.]

were editors such as Paravia, Bemporad, Sandron, Vallardi, Sansoni and Zanichelli.[45] The need to support the national-education project benefited the valorization of a range of disciplines, including history, geography and the Italian language. As Paolo Bianchini has noted:

> the role attributed to the formation of a national sentiment represents the roots of the decision to insert into the reading collections songs, stories and poems aimed at celebrating love for one's country through exulting the Italian genius in sciences, literature and the arts [...]. Just as significant was the recollection of episodes of national history through deeds of exponents of the House of Savoy, as well as of men and women from more humble backgrounds, and of entire cities that had been engaged in struggle against foreign rule.[46]

In the ideological and pedagogical framework of these anthologies, it was values inspired by God, Patria and the Family that predominated— but not without space being given over to civic, secular and military values as well. A good example is Giovanni Pascoli's *Flower of Flowers: Prose and Poetry Chosen for the Italian School*, an anthology that reached its eighth edition in 1929. Compiled for the improvement of young men, to instil in them a love of their country and make them into aware and proud Italians, the volume could not but begin with a eulogy to Dante, 'the upmost' of human genius, 'the first and greatest author of our language'.[47] Nor could it ignore the letter written from the prison of Santo Stefano by the Neapolitan patriot Luigi Settembrini, addressed to his son:

---

45 The main liberal publishing houses of nineteenth-century Northern Italy. [Trans.]
46 Paolo Bianchini, 'I testi di lingua italiani prima e dopo l'unità' in Giorgio Chiosso (ed.), *Teseo. Tipografia e editori scolastico-educativi dell'Ottocento* (Milan: Editrice bibliografica, 2003), p. *lii*.
47 Giovanni Pascoli, *Fior da fiore. Prose e poesie scelte per la scuola italiana* (Palermo: Sandron, 1929), p. *vi*.

Never forget to be Italian. Know that this is a sacred name, the name of a people who have been unlucky and slandered through no demerit of their own. Maintain the honour of your fatherland through the health of life, purity of habit, knowledge of the word, sweetness of approach, strength of ambition [. . .]. Make it so that anyone, upon seeing your actions, remarks: This is true Latin blood. Love this land, love it with a fierce love.[48]

Of course, Pascoli's anthology had to include a sketch of Garibaldi, provided by his friend, biographer and fervent admirer, Giuseppe Guerzoni. And of course this *Flower of Flowers*, read by generations of Italians, had to close with the words of Pasquali Villari: 'There once was a day— indeed, an entire century—when we were the most cultured country in the world. Europe hung ecstatic upon the lips of our professors.'[49]

Yet it was above all in the field of national history, abundantly present among the anthologies of Italian literature, that post-Unification governments—and with them, authors and editors—aimed to provide the new generations with sublime examples and values. As Lorenzo Cantatore has observed:

History was consulted and ransacked like an immense repertoire of ideas, a catalogue of images to be reused as supporting documents for the new collective myths. It was thus that the country, sifting through the 'storeroom of tradition', furnished its anthological museum by which to educate new generations in a cult of behavioural, aesthetic, linguistic, ethical, religious and moral examples, authorized and prescribed by a past that was persistently present.[50]

---

48 Pascoli, *Fior da fiore*, p. 110.

49 Pascoli, *Fior da fiore*, p. 513.

50 Lorenzo Cantatore, 'La letteratura italiana sui banchi di scuola. Valori, modelli e antimodelli nelle antologie dell'età iberale', in Chiosso, *Teseo*, p. *lxviii*.

The same effort was engaged in the editing of history books. Simply citing some of the titles provides a clear idea of the content: *The History of Italy through her Pains and Glories, Recounted for the Use of the People and Schools*;[51] *For the Love of One's Country: Dialogues for Young Men, For the Use of Schools and Families*;[52] *The Moral and Civic Duties: Teaching the Youth through Precept and Example*.[53] And still more: *Italy's Redeemers: The Contemporary History of the Patria as Narrated through Short Extracts for Young People*.[54]

Adults also needed to be educated, through expansive works such as Giuseppe Mazzini's *Duties of Man*, Francesco De Sanctis' *History of Literature* and Carlo Cattaneo's *The City Considered as the Principle Ideal of Italian Histories*. But there were also smaller, more accessible works, such as *Examples of Italian Virtue*,[55] a collection of 150 historical episodes ranging from Berengario's pardoning of Lamberto to the death of Pasquale Paoli: a thousand years of Italian glory proffered for the reader's rumination. For his own part, Michele Lessona took inspiration from *Self-Help*, the well-known volume by Scottish writer Samuel Smiles, and produced his own book entitled *Will Is Power*, in which he indicated for his Italian public a rich gallery of their fellow citizens who had been born poor but achieved great fame simply by being educated with a 'tenacious will'. The cast of protagonists included Gioacchino Rossini, Pietro Thouar, Giovanni Dupré, Giulio Richard, Niccolò Paganini,

---

51 Cesare Cantù, *Storia d'Italia ne' suoi patimenti e nelle sue glorie raccontata ad uso del popolo e delle scuole* (Milan: Pagnoni, 1861).

52 Pietro Bolla, *Dell'amor patrio. Dialoghi per fanciulli ad uso delle scuole e delle famiglie* (Cremona: Tipo. Ronzi e Signori, 1864).

53 Giovanni Parato, *I doveri morali e civili. Insegnati ai giovinetti per via di precetti ed esempi* (Turin: Paravia, 1865).

54 Pierina Berra, *I redentori d'Italia, ossia la storia patria contemporanea narrata per bravi cenni ai giovinetti* (Turin: Tip. Unione dei Maestri, 1888).

55 S. P. Zecchini and A. Vianti, *Esempi della virtù italiana narrati da nostri classici storici* (Turin: Stamperia sociale degli artisti tipografi, 1843).

Giuseppe Pomba and Pietro Sella. The book closes with a call to arms aimed at the youth, who should 'learn to desire, learn to shun weakness, to shun frivolities and vanities; they should learn to turn their backs with disdain to their flatterers, who are more disgusting and vile than flatterers of Kings'.[56]

The task that Augusto Alfani set for his *The Character of the Italians* was more challenging. The volume included 278 dense pages of reflections on the nature of Italians, and advice on how to behave in the family, school and society as a whole. He wrote, for example, that:

> A strong, dignified and honest literature is necessary for the education of a strong national character. Bad books make corrupt men, and corrupt men make perverse nations. As Joubert once wrote, buildings are measured from East to West or from North to South; but books are measured from the earth to the heavens.[57]

Ignoring Lessona's suggestion to turn one's back on flatterers, Ernesto Montagnari heaped up such a quantity of historical, juridical and literary information to be able to give his book the title *We Are the Greatest: Towards a Vindication of Italic Superiority.* He maintained that:

> Our right has been established by our history, our greatness, our civic, moral and intellectual primacy. Away with looking at our defects, which are lesser than those of others. I fix my gaze upon our qualities. We have greater bearing than others. We must hold our heads up high, we who will instruct the modern world in everything, we who will be the precursors, the standard

---

56 Michele Lessona, *Volere è potere* (Florence: Barbèra, 1870), p. 488.

57 Augusto Alfani, *Il carattere degli italiani* (Florence: Barbèra, 1878), p. 211. The same series of *Opere popolari* included the following titles: Oreste Bruni, *La vera civiltà insegnata al popolo*; Giorgio L. Craik, *Costanza vince ignoranza, ossia la conquista del sapere malgrado gli ostacoli*; Sarah Stickney Ellis, *L'educazione del cuore.*

bearers, martyrs to every idea, every civil, social and political progress; for after Rome and the city states, there was nothing else, there is nothing new under the sun.[58]

Making the claim was exhilarating, proving it was more difficult. And indeed, the volume's 500 pages contain more hot air than facts, more delirious proclamations than truths. Lessona was not alone in warning against flatterers. In his *Thoughts on the History of Italy*, Cesare Balbo advised: 'nothing is to be gained from exaggeration and falsehood; such prejudices are, on the contrary, harmful, and is it extremely harmful to exaggerate their importance.'[59]

The instruments provided to Italians for their self-improvement, the betterment of their culture and the resolution of their practical problems included the *Biblioteca Hoepliana* for families, issued by the publisher Ulrico Hoepli, among which a special place was taken by Anna Vertua Gentile's *How Should I Behave?* As the editor specified:

This book is thus not simply a manual on good manners in the classical form of those by Castiglioni, Della Casa, Alberti or Gioia; nor does it follow modern examples; nor is it simply a formulary. It is what it says in the title: a practical and moral guide built on experience and compiled with a good conscience and a candid desire to be useful.[60]

The volume no doubt would make a reader laugh. For example, when it explains that 'a young woman ought never go to a beach hut on her own. The young woman must wear the most decent bathing costume

---

58 Ernesto Montagnari, *I più grandi siamo noi. Per rivendicazione dell'italica superiorità* (Rome and Milan: Mondadori, 1924), p. 23.

59 Cesare Balbo, *Pensieri sulla storia d'Italia* (Florence: Felice Le Monnier, 1858), p. 14.

60 Anna Vertua Gentile, *Come devo comportarmi?* (Milan: Hoepli, 1921), p. x.

possible, with a high collar, and the arms and legs as covered as possible.'[61] But other sections include tragic situations that still strike a chord today. Here is how Anna Vertua Gentile counselled the wives of men who returned from the slaughterhouse of the First World War:

> It is no doubt difficult the task of a wife whose spouse returns from the war ruined in his heath, mutilated or worse still, blind! Yet woe betide she who does not love her unfortunate partner with an intense, exclusive love that resists all! Woe betide her if commiseration [. . .] is followed slowly by indifference and therefore exhaustion.[62]

We should also recall finally the many novelists (all of whom we cannot cite) who attempted—or believed in all good faith to have attempted— to educate Italians through their works. We will select just one, Edmondo De Amicis, not because he excels especially, or because his message had a particular weight, but because of the extraordinary fortune experienced by his books, especially those which—in the author's mind—were meant to have a very precise educational purpose. Doubtless some of his lines, especially those in *Heart*, can make us laugh today, even more than the advice of Anna Vertua Gentile. And indeed, they provoked the indignation of Umberto Eco, who wrote an *Elogy to Franti*, in which he 'identified *Heart* as a filthy example of petty-bourgeois, classist, paternalistic and sadistically Savoyard pedagogy'.[63]

There can be little doubt that, on re-reading, De Amicis' works appear for the most part horrendously outdated, frequently maudlin, exaggerated or simply irritating. This is not only true for *Heart*; indeed, the most artificial, exasperating and unbelievable emotions are to be found in the sketches of *My Military Life*, his first book, published by

---

61 Gentile, *Come devo comportarmi?*, p. 175.

62 Gentile, *Come devo comportarmi?*, pp. 33–34.

63 Umberto Eco, *Il costume de casa. Evidenze e misteri dell'ideologia italiana* (Milan: Bomponiani, 1973), p. 89.

Treves in 1868, the work that propelled him into a celebrity. An officer who trained at the Academy in Modena and fought in Custoza, De Amicis clearly composed his sketches in order to communicate to the army and his superiors a feeling of respect and sympathy towards Italians. To achieve this aim (an extremely noble one, given that the army is equivalent to the *patria*), the Genovese writer made no half measures, even if his characters—officials, conscripts, invalids, mothers—end up seeming entirely fictitious. As an illustration, we can take the chapter entitled 'The Mother'. A woman who has not seen her son, a soldier, for four years, goes to visit him at his barracks. The reconnaissance officer—De Amicis—surveys the meeting from afar, and wonders:

> That soldier there, when in the field, will allow himself to be killed without fear, and will die with the name of his mother on his lips. Teach him what the fatherland is, make him understand that the fatherland is hundreds of thousands of mothers and hundreds of thousands of families like his own, and he will love the fatherland with fervour.[64]

Here, instead, is how De Amicis describes the conscript himself:

> And yet despite their lives of hardship and danger, the good soldier is composed of a good soul and never complains. If they can sleep, they are content; if not, they are patient; when there is bread, they celebrate; when there is none, they fast until necessary and hold no grudges. And you know why? Because they live among friends, among good comrades, and know they are performing their true duty.[65]

We then see the compensation obtained by a soldier who has lost his leg at Custoza. Returning, abject, to his home town, he does not know how to adapt to his new, debilitating condition. But one day—this is De

---

64 Edmondo De Amicis, *La vita militare* (Milan: Treves, 1868), p. 59.
65 De Amicis, *La vita militare*, pp. 221–22.

Amicis writing—he recalls his parents and friends and the assistance he received in hospital, and he rediscovers his happiness, he feels satisfied. Here is the relevant narration:

> And one day an old general arrived, his chest covered in medals, and all the officers behind him, and he comes over to my bed with his beret in his hands, and all the others have taken off their hats as well, and the general asks me how I am and where I've been wounded and how, and when I tell my whole tale to him—I can still see him now—he raises his eyes to the heavens, then he tightens his lips with a small sigh and says. 'Have courage my son.' And then he shakes my hand, you understand, the general himself.[66]

We could go on for pages and pages, the atmosphere is always the same: a forced, artificial pathos. It is a shame that, in those difficult years of nation-building, and of national and colonial war, the reality was very different indeed—as the following song testifies, once sung in the valleys of Antrona, which documents a very different yet common enough episode without frills and tears:

> I came back
> The war was over
> But at the window I did not see
> My beloved.
> I went back and forth
> But the window was closed
> I waited and she didn't come
> My beloved.
> I went to the church
> I went to the priest
> To ask where she had gone

---

66 De Amicis, *La vita militare*, pp. 271–72.

My beloved.
Go down there
Down by the cypress tree
There she lies in a grave
Your beloved.[67]

Building a nation, making Italians: to many, the undertaking seemed much harder than previously foreseen. To begin with, there was little agreement between the architects of Unification themselves. Once the exhilarating season of uprisings and victories was over, old divisions came to the fore and one sees increasingly recriminations by democratic, republican forces who had little tolerance for the fact that the process of Unification had been obtained through a manipulated conquest and a government of moderates. Nevertheless, we also find doubts about the possibility of an effective process of Unification arising from people like Massimo d'Azeglio, who had always waged their struggle under the flag of Savoy. In the introduction to his memoirs of 1865, he wrote:[68]

> For nearly a half century, Italy labours to become a people and a nation. She has regained her ground only in part. Her struggle against alien forces has found a good result, but this was not the greatest difficulty. The greatest, truest challenge—that which continues with greatest uncertainty and instability—is the struggle within. Italy's greatest enemies are not the Austrians, but the Italians. And why? Because the Italians wanted to make a new Italy, yet they remain the Italians of old, with all the ineptitude and moral poverty that has formed their heritage since ancient times [. . .]. The utmost need of Italy is that Italians come to be who are gifted with the highest and most noble

---

67 Loria Bonavia and Luca Bonavia, *Cantar storie. Un viaggio nel canto popolare tra i monti dell'Ossola* (Domodossola: Grossi, 1999), p. 21.

68 Massimo d'Azeglio, *I miei ricordi*, 2 VOLS (Florence: Barbare Editore, 1867).

characters; and yet every day the road takes us towards the opposite pole. Unfortunately. Italy has been created, but Italians are yet to be formed.[69]

Italy had been made, but it was a country deprived of a unified collective conscience, without which it would never be possible to create a modern national identity. Complaining of the lack of a civic spirit in Italy, Francesco De Sanctis wrote in 1869:

> The Italian race has still not been healed of its moral weakness, and still bears upon its forehead that mark of duplicity and dissimulation that has been impressed on her by history. This is man as he was through Guicciardini's eyes—*vivit, imo in Senatum venit*—one meets him on every corner. And it is this accursed figure who will block the way, unless we find the strength to cancel him from our minds.[70]

Yet the Italians were not only lacking in civic pride and moral conscience; they even lacked any interest in the nascent institutions of the state. In his speech in parliament of 17 May 1873, Sidney Sonnino treated the problem with an unusual vigour:

> The great majority of the population, more than 90 per cent [. . .], feel excluded from our institutions; they feel subjected to the state and forced to serve it with blood and money; but they do not feel that they are a living and organic part of it,

---

69 d'Azeglio, *I miei ricordi*, VOL. 1, p. 32.

70 Francesco De Sanctis, *Saggi critici* (Bari: Laterza, 1957), VOL. 3, p. 23. The Latin phrase ('Alive did I say? Not only is he alive, but he attends the Senate!') is a standard grammatical example taken from the Catilinarian Orations (Cicero, *In Catilinam*, I, 2). Here De Sanctis utilizes it to emphasize the endurance of the unhappy version of man as described by Guiccardini, which the former summarized as 'Each man for himself, against everyone else.' De Sanctis, *Storia della letteratura italiana* (Naples: Morano Editore, 1893), VOL. 1, p. 115. [Trans].

nor do they take any interest whatsoever in its existence and functioning.[71]

In 1878, Leone Carpi drew up a first account of Unification in his volume *Living Italy*,[72] offering an overall disturbing account. The rich lived in idleness preferring to hoard their capital in the banks rather than invest it in agriculture. The poor had abandoned the countryside to become poorer still, flowing into the cities. A few years later, in a letter to Bertrando Spaventa, Hegelian philosopher Angelo Camillo De Meis fully expressed his concerns:

> All our ancient aspirations, as audacious as they may have been, are as of now entirely behind us. Who could believe that we would see Italy forged, and all the insolvable questions resolved, those that had once weighed upon a nation from whom human history itself began? I know it, but it no longer moves me as it once did. It is certainly not the same Italy, but an insignificant one by comparison, as we had already begun to realize. Now there are no longer heroes, there are not even their epigones: there are merely do-nothings![73]

From his own corner, Giosue Carducci lamented the disappearance of great ideals and consolidation, instead, of a 'popular scepticism', writing in 1886: 'Italy no longer has any internal solidity, no more than it has any external strength; it is as corrupt within as it appears abject without [. . .]. The epic of the infinitely vast has been visited by the farce of the infinitely small.'[74]

---

71 Parliamentary speech, 30 March 1881. Cited in Domenico Settembrini, *Storia dell'idea antiborghese in Italia, 1860–1989* (Bari and Rome: Laterza, 1991), p. 37.

72 Leone Carpi, *L'Italia vivente. Aristocrazia di nascitia e del denaro, borghesia, clero, aristocrazie* (Milan: Vallardi, 1878).

73 Bertrando Spaventa, *Opere*, VOL. 1 (Florence: Sansoni, 1972), pp. 145–46.

74 Giosue Carducci, *Opere*, VOL. 25 (Bologna: Zanichelli, 1938), p. 35.

Everything was going slowly, faced with a thousand difficulties. Building a unified state meant, for a start, an administrative and legislative unification, which had to definitively overcome the regulatory residues of the pre-unification states. There was also the problem of scholastic unification, which we have already discussed, and—even more serious— the absorbing of the pre-Unification armies into a single national army, beginning with the Bourbon armies that had been defeated in the field in 1860 and still conserved a bitterness and humiliation that was difficult to set aside. And then there was always the need to disband Garibaldi's sections and, as far as possible, recuperate them.

Governments on both right and left dedicated special attention to strengthening the armed forces, and not only because—as with the schools—they represented an important mechanism for national unification, but also because the young nation's pride required that it maintain its place as the 'sixth great power'. This meant that, between 1862 and 1912, the army and navy received 18,250 million *lire*—23.7 per cent of the state's expenditure.

Despite this vast investment, the attempt to transform the army into a factory of heroes—as De Amicis so desired—and Carducci's constant fervour in claiming that 'Italy cannot defend herself save in offence',[75] the results were far from impressive. One defeat followed another. From Custoza to Vis, from Dogali to Adwa. The great Arab revolt of 1915 in Libya forced the Italians to almost entirely abandon the colony, with losses that outnumbered even those of Adwa. Not even the First World War, that great 'crucible of unity' managed to perform the necessary miracle.[76] Italy overcame the conflict as the victorious party—but at a

---

75 Giosue Carducci, *Contro l'eterno barbaro. Poesie e prose* (Florence: Società Dante Alighieri, 1915), p. 61.

76 The 'crucible of unity' (*crogiuolo unificatore*): Del Boca owes the phrase partly to Giulio Bollati, *L'italiano. Il carattere nazionale come storia come invenzione* (Milan: Einaudi, 1996), p. 45. [Trans].

cost of 650,000 dead, many of whom had no idea what they had fought for. Furthermore, it was Italian capital who won, and not the subaltern classes who had borne the brunt of the war.

There was also another Italy, albeit a minority, that had wanted the war, and even invoked it in the conviction that the conflict would have a purifying, sanctifying function. It was on this minority—comprised of nationalists, Futurists, D'Annunzio's legionaries, the 'arditi' of the Great War—that Benito Mussolini set his sights in the immediate postwar period.[77] The fact that he effectively managed to take power in less than four years demonstrates just how fragile the state structures had been, how fleeting democracy and how uncertain party ideologies. At Parma, the Arditi del popolo had fought fiercely and pushed back Italo Balbo's Fascist squadrons. But Mussolini no longer admired these men, even though he had fought side-by-side with them for socialist ideals in 1914. He was now thinking of a new Italy, one entirely regenerated by the trenches and flames of the Great War. On 3 October 1922, a few days following the March on Rome, in drafting the new ordinance for the Fascist militias, he expressed himself thus:

> The Fascist soldier must serve Italy with purity, with a spirit imbued by a profound mysticism supported by an unshakeable fidelity, dominated by an unwavering will, contemptuous of opportunism and caution as mere cowardice, decisive that sacrifice represents the very end of its faith, convinced by the burden of its tremendous mission to save the great Mother of all and give unto her both strength and purity.[78]

But this creed was not to be reserved only for the party's militia. It had to become the creed of all Italians, without distinction for class or age.

---

77 The arditi: literally, 'the fervent ones'. [Trans.]

78 Cited in Emilio Gentile, *Il culto del Littorio. La sacralizzazione della politica nell'Italia fascista* (Rome and Bari: Laterza, 1993), p. 39.

As Emilio Gentile—one of the sharpest scholars of the Fascist period—has written:

> [Mussolini's political movement] aimed to establish in the conscience of millions of Italian men and women a faith in the dogma of a new secular religion that sacralized the state, attributing it with a primary pedagogical function in order to transform the minds, characters and habits of the Italian people in order to create a 'new man', one who believed in and practiced the Fascist cult.[79]

If liberal Italy had limited itself to the two pillars of the school and the army in its failed attempt to make Italians into good citizens and good soldiers, Mussolini went further still, investing all of the country's resources and institutions in this radical transformation of values and habits.

As is well known, Mussolini did not have a high opinion of the masses. In a famous interview with Emil Ludwig conducted in 1932, he did not hesitate to claim: 'For me the masses are nothing more than a herd of sheep, until they are organized. I am not against them. I simply deny that they can govern themselves alone. But if one leads them, they must be guided with two reins: enthusiasm and interest.'[80] For the rest, he could draw on all available means of communication and information from across the police forces; he could also count on the best intellectual forces of the country, who were easily subjected and ready to develop myths, invent slogans and amplify the party's rituals and keywords.

We can look, for example, at the manipulation of the young generation in the schools, during the Fascist Saturdays, the school trips, camping outings, gym exercises, and even in their homes through the Italian Body for Radio Broadcasting. The Fascist Saturday, established in 1935

---

79 Gentile, *Il culto del Littorio*, p. *vii*.

80 Emil Ludwig, *Colloqui con Mussolini* (Milan: Mondadori, 1932), p. 121.

on the eve of the war in Ethiopia, saw the participation of nearly 8 million people, ranging from 6 to 28 years old. On Saturday afternoons—and often on Sunday mornings as well—the regime took over the lives of these young people, subjecting them to heavy doses of military and sporting exercises and Fascist rhetoric, usually at the barracks of the Gioventù italiana del littorio—the 'Italian Youth of the Lictors'—which, as Luca La Rovere has written, were meant to represent 'the true temples of our race'.[81]

For Mussolini, the 'new Italian' meant above all a new soldier, one more tenacious and aggressive—crueller even—who could take a rightful place next to the ancient Romans, and allow 'Little Italy' to put behind her the mediocrities and poor performances over the years. During the war on Ethiopia, Fascism's first military expedition, the volunteer-based army obtained a clear success. With only a few thousand casualties out of the 330,000 soldiers engaged, Badoglio and Graziani's troops demolished a millennial empire and a respectable army in merely seven months.[82] It should nevertheless be specified that Mussolini had personally presided over ensuring that the Italian armed forces had a clear superiority, in order to avoid any repetition of the disaster at Adwa.

The Italian intervention in the Spanish Civil War also began with great hopes. In the first few months, Italy proved the quality of its troops under Roatta's command, and above all the excellent performance of the Fascist air force. It was thus clear that, drawing on its totalizing mobilization, the regime had managed to perform the miracle of transforming mediocre fighters into ruthless tools of war. But the Duce's satisfaction was not to last long. On 8 March 1937, the four Italian divisions—around 40,000 men equipped with thousands of vehicles,

---

81 Luca La Rovere, *Giovinezza in marcia. Le organizzazioni giovanili fasciste* (Novara: Editoriale Nuova, 2004), p. 81.

82 For the crimes of the Italian generals Pietro Badoglio and Rodolfo Graziani, see Chapters 8 through 12.

flamethrowers, 230 canons and 250 tanks—launched an attack with the aim of taking Guadalajara and then moving on to Alcalá de Henares and finally Madrid. But they were immediately blocked by the Lìster Division alongside the Garibaldi Brigade, a battalion formed of Italian anti-Fascists. During more than a week of extremely violent fighting, the Republicans managed to put the Fascists to rout, inflicting 1,400 casualties and 4,500 wounded, as well as capturing 400 prisoners.[83] For Mussolini, Roatta's clear defeat represented a hard blow. Not only had his 'new Italians', forged by the regime, been incontrovertibly defeated, but also they had been defeated by other Italians who had not attended the Fascist Saturdays.

He would, nevertheless, have his revenge. On 15 March 1938, without even forewarning Generalìsimo Franco, Mussolini ordered General Valle of the Italian Royal Airforce to execute a terrorist bombing of Barcelona, inflicting thousands of deaths and thousands more injuries. When Italian diplomat Galeazzo Ciano communicated the criticism of Lord Perth, British Ambassador in Rome, Mussolini replied by claiming that the bombing was 'excellent for breaking the reds' morale while the troops were advancing on Aragona'. He also declared that he was especially 'happy about the fact that we are managing to arouse horror for [Italians'] aggression rather than pleasure for their mandolin playing.'[84]

Two years later, Mussolini entered the war alongside Hitler, with an entirely unmotivated army and armaments dating back to the First World War. He was quite aware of this and confided to Ciano that 'making a great people requires leading them into battle, and perhaps

---

83 For greater detail on the Battle of Guadalajara, see Franco Giannatoni and Fabio Minazzi, *Il coraggio della memoria e la guerra civile spagnola* (Varese: Edizioni Arterigere, 2000), pp. 347–51.

84 Galeazzo Ciano, *Diario 1937–1943* (Renzo De Felice ed.) (Milan: Rizzoli, 1980), p. 115.

getting a thrashing. That's what I will do.'[85] The lack of a national plan for rearmament and the Duce's decision to undertake a form of 'parallel war' in relation to Hitler's own—including absurd, senseless decisions like the invasion of Greece—could only lead to one disaster after another.

Following the news of the catastrophes in Albania and Libya, on 24 December 1940 a visibly depressed Mussolini revealed to Ciano that he was extremely irritated 'by the mediocre performance of the troops' and added: 'I should also note that in 1914 Italians were better than these ones of today. This is certainly not a good result for the regime, but that's the way it is.' The next day, looking out at the heavy snowfall from his window at Palazzo Venezia, he confided to his son-in-law: 'The snowfall and frost are an excellent thing, this way the weak will die off and this mediocre Italian race will be improved.'[86]

In March 1942, various Italian cities saw the first protests against the regime, due to bread rationing; Mussolini found nothing to say other than to insult the people: 'This war wasn't made for the Italian people. They have neither the maturity nor the conscience for such a challenging and decisive test. War is for the Germans and the Japanese, not for us.'[87]

With these words, he thus recognized the total failure of his own doctrine. Twenty years of the cult of heroes and martyrs, of exalting the sacredness of the nation, of glorifying the Italian flag and the Fascist rods, of devotion to Ancient Rome, of collective mobilizations for regime rituals, of mass sport and oceanic gatherings had not sufficed. It had all been for nothing. The same went for his own charisma, an attribute to which he had entrusted so much—that too turned out to be a mere bubble, one that popped on the night of 15 July 1943 during the final

---

85 Ciano, *Diario*, p. 418.

86 Ciano, *Diario*, p. 491, for both quotations. [For 'the weak', Ciano writes *mezze cartucce*—literally, 'half-cartridges'. Trans.]

87 Ciano, *Diario*, p. 598.

and most dramatic Fascist Council. And yet, according to Emilio Gentile, up until just a few months' earlier he had still represented

> the sum and summary of every form greatness of a man of thought and of a man of action that had ever appeared in any era: statesman, legislator, philosopher, writer, artist and universal genius but also a prophet, messiah, apostle, an infallible sage sent by God, chosen by destiny and a harbinger of destiny, as foretold by the prophets of Unification.[88]

Mussolini's opinion of the Italian people was extremely severe, and held back no punches. On the eve of war, well-informed of their pacifist spirit, he had declared: 'the Italian race is a race of sheep; 18 years are not enough to transform them, one needs 180 years, or perhaps even 180 centuries.'[89]

At the end of this marathon, in which we have spanned three centuries of Italian history, it seems correct to underline that Mussolini had neither right nor justification in issuing such a drastic judgement. To limit ourselves simply to the accusation of military incapacity, we can state that Italians have behaved as both heroes and cowards according to the circumstance. As Fabrizio Battistelli observes: 'more than the outcome of an innate military inability, the Italian's failures in war appear to be determined by the ineptitude of the ruling classes [. . .]; it has often been the case that irresponsible politicians and opportunist military leaders have dragged the country and its armed forces into engagements destitute of any rationality.'[90] When the circumstances were right, Italians have fought with the same fury and determination as any people renowned for their bellicose nature; we need simply note the Battle of Curtatone and Montanare in 1848, the victory of Garibaldi's troops at

---

88 Gentile, *Il culto del Littorio*, p. 271.

89 Max Gallo, *Vita di Mussolini* (Bari: Laterza, 1967), p. 249.

90 Fabrizio Battistelli, *Gli italiani e la guerra. Tra senso di insicurezza e terrorismo internazionale* (Rome: Carocci, 2004), p. 101.

Bezzecca in 1866, some of the episodes of the Battles of the Isonzo in the First World War, the battles of Lero and Cephalonia in the Second World War, or the defence of the Partisan Republics of Ossanam Carnia and Montefiorino.

As for the other judgements of the Italian people that we have collected, expressed by foreigners and Italians alike, some of them seem pertinent—to the extent that they appear to maintain some relevance down to today—while others simply communicate common tropes that are difficult to set aside. There can be no doubt that the processes of unification and of forming a national conscience have been slow and difficult, caught between raids by foreign armies and insufferable foreign rule. It is also true that the efforts to 'form Italians', i.e. to create a homogeneous national identity, have produced relatively modest results. Carducci's invective and appeals, De Amicis's model stories about fraternal solidarity and heroic self-sacrifice, Giolitti's plans for nationalizing the masses through liberal methods and institutions, two World Wars that mobilized the people, and the rituals and myths of Fascism—none of this was enough. Despite 145 years having passed since Unification, the anniversary is nevertheless being marked in a period of secessionist manoeuvres and grotesque inventions like Padania.[91] The opinion of a man from Piedmont, cited by René Bazin, still resonates today, pronounced in 1894: 'Our country is too long, Signore. Its head and tail will never touch each other. And if they try to, the head will bite the tail.'[92]

Everything is made more complicated in our country by that which Pierluigi Battista has called 'a myth of self-pity':

a self-image which the democratic Italians of the postwar period—
vaccinated against the nationalistic arrogance administered until

91 Padania: the name claimed for the area around the River Po by the local ethno-nationalist secessionist movement which found political representation in the Northern League (today simply the League). [Trans.]
92 Bazin, *Les Italiens d'aujourd'hui*, p. 98.

'overdose' by the previous regime—enjoyed spreading in politics and film, in fashion, cooking and behavioural models. Italians were *brava gente* they said. This claim represented a shield of good-naturedness, cheerfulness and a natural inclination to meekness, to being socially informal and agreeable, that was meant to defend us from any fierce hostilities, a comfortable cushion that might muffle the dramatic cries of history and cruelty.[93]

Battista's cutting analysis perfectly defines the myth of the Good Italian. Yet it needs to be both refined and broadened out. In truth, this myth was not created after the Second World War, but in the closing decades of the nineteenth century. And, contrary to Battista's claim, it did not dissolve in any way when the journalist Enzo Baldoni was murdered in Iraq in 2004. The myth lives on and indeed risks becoming part of our people's DNA.[94]

The myth of the *brava gente* began to impose itself with the colonial policies inaugurated by Pasquale Stanislao Mancini, Minister for Foreign Affairs. Italy arrived in Africa last, once the great slicing-up had already taken place; but, as Mancini underlined in a speech given on 16 June 1885, 'she could not remain an inert spectator of the battle between civilization and barbarians'.[95] Right from the start, equipped with few means or ideas, Italy tried to impose itself by exhibiting its own admirable past as a bearer of civilization, emphasizing its *difference* on all possible occasions. In other words, it wanted to establish that Italians

---

93 Pierluigi Battista, 'Italiani brava gente. Un mito cancellato', *La Stampa*, 28 August 2004, p. 6.

94 The freelance journalist Enzo Baldoni (1948–2004) was captured by a militia in Iraq demanding the withdrawal of the Italian troops engaged in the 2003 invasion; he was killed a week later. [Trans]

95 Cited in Angelo Del Boca, *Gli italiani in Africa Orientale*, VOL. 1 (Rome and Bari: Laterza, 1976), p. 191.

were different from other colonizers: more humane, more tolerant, more generous. Even if General Baldissera had employed harsh methods to conquer Asmara—to the extent that Filippo Turati accused him of having begun 'a period of terror in Africa' and defined him as 'Baldissera the dog'—the locution began to be spread in the colonies of the *italiano buono*, translated in the local language as *bono italiano*.

In 'The Slave of Somalia', a short story from 1903, adventure-novelist Emilio Salgari imagines a young African rescued from pirates by a group of Italian sailors who pays back his debt by showing them the way to Assab, and thus to salvation. 'Me love 'talians . . . yes, going with 'talians my benefactors. [. . .] 'talians are good.'[96] In only a few years, therefore, the phrase had already entered into popular fiction. There could be little doubt: those who governed Eritrea and Somalia were 'good folk'.

Even when, in the mid-1930s, Eritrea was invaded by hundreds of thousands of Italian soldiers and workers, to prepare for the formal invasion of Ethiopia, it was seen as imperative to maintain the fable that this was not the undertaking of an imperialistic colonial campaign but, rather, a generous engagement by Fascism in sending 'a whole army of workers to labour concretely side-by-side with the indigenous peoples, for the common good.'[97] The Italians were *brava gente*, therefore, even when tanks, canons, fighter planes, bombers, flamethrowers and hundreds of tonnes of arsenic and mustard gas were unloaded from the steamboats anchored in the port of Massawa. The belief in their radical 'difference' was so thoroughly consolidated in the minds of Italians themselves that even through the 1950s and 60s, when Eritrea was no longer under Italian rule, the *bono italiano* still enjoyed an important following

---

96 Guido Altieri [Emilio Salgari], *Lo schiavo di Somalia* (Palermo: Salvatore Biondo, 1903). Thanks are due to Felice Pozzo for the citation.

97 Vito Rastelli, 'La civiltà del lavoro verso l'impero', *Il Solco fascista*, 11 August 1935.

and wide circulation, as writer Erminia Dell'Oro—born and raised in Asmara—recalls.[98]

The myth of *Italiani brava gente* is a legend that refuses to die. To give one example: in 2003, Italy sent an expeditionary corps to Iraq, the Antica Babilonia, modestly armed and with scarce understanding of the situation. But the mission's architects entrusted in the fact that both their allies and their adversaries alike would have recognized the Italian soldier in his privileged status as the 'good Italian'. And when instead the guerrillas of Abu Omar al-Kurdi launched a violent attack against the Italian contingent, inflicting 21 deaths, the episode provoked not only pain but also—even more than comments condemning the action—surprise, as if al-Kurdi's guerrillas had broken some unwritten but well-understood pact.[99]

Behind this protective screen of ostentatious but false goodness, the very worst kinds of crimes have been committed over the last 150 years, in both Italy and the colonies. Our minds turn to the 100,000 Libyans killed between 1911 and 1932 in fierce combat, or in the hell of the concentration camps. One thinks of the three days of blood in Addis Ababa following the attempt on Graziani's life, on 19 February 1937. One thinks of the 2,000 priests and deacons assassinated in the convent-city of Debre Libanos, due to no more than the suspicion that they may have played a part in the plot against Graziani. One thinks of the 'ethnic cleansing' in the Balkans.

Over the following chapters, we will examine the cruellest of these episodes, beginning with the war on banditry, the very worst beginning that a newly unified Italy could have experienced.

---

98 Account provided to the author by Dell'Oro, 26 January 2005.

99 For the attack against the *carabinieri* in Nasiriyah, Iraq, in 2003 and on Italian involvement in Iraq more generally, see Paolo Rosa, *Strategic Culture and Italy's Military Behavior* (London: Lexington Books, 2016); and Olivier Schmitt, *Allies That Count* (Washington DC: Georgetown University Press, 2018). [Trans.]

TWO

THE WAR ON BANDITS

In the years between the annexing of the Southern regions (culminating in the defeat of the Kingdom of the Two Sicilies at Gaeta on 15 February 1861) and the terrible battle of Custoza on 24 June 1866, the newly unified Italy found herself fighting an unforeseen, insidious and seemingly interminable war. It was called—somewhat haphazardly and crudely—'la guerra al brigantaggio', the war on banditry.[1] But the actual bandits, while they had always existed in the South, in truth constituted an extremely insignificant minority, even if an aggressive and cruel one. The vast majority of those rising up against the new Italian state comprised at least 10,000 soldiers from the Bourbon army, who had taken up arms following the flight of Francesco II, the last King of the Two Sicilies.[2] These humiliated and broken soldiers were far from willing to enter into Savoyard armies from Piedmont in the north, and were soon joined by thousands of landless peasants and townsfolk who rejected military conscription and the tax hikes being imposed on them.

---

1 Another translation would be 'brigandry', but the importance and success of Eric Hobsbawm's treatment of the topic in his *Bandits* (London: Weidenfeld and Nicolson, 1969) has been decisive. [Trans.]

2 In general, see Lucy Riall, *The Italian Risorgimento: State, Society and National Unification* (London and New York: Routledge, 1994). [Trans.]

As historian Mario Isnenghi has rightly put it, this was 'a war with neither rules nor honour.'[3] It was also a colonial-style war that anticipated the unspeakable violence and total disregard for the enemy that were to characterize the wars fought in Africa. Indeed, it was General Enrico Cialdini, lieutenant to Vittorio Emanuele II, who declared when in Naples: 'This is Africa, never mind Italy! Compared with these hooligans, the Bedouins are milk and honey.'[4] He was not the only one to claim that the Italian South was an 'exotic region inhabited by a proud people who are so close to nature that they are almost on its same primitive level.'[5] Sixty years after these horrific events, Antonio Gramsci very accurately interpreted what the 'bourgeois propagandists' in the North thought:

> the Southerners are biologically inferior beings, semi-barbarians or total barbarians, by natural destiny; if the South is backward, the fault does not lie with the capitalist system or with any other historical cause, but with Nature, which has made the Southerners lazy, incapable, criminal and barbaric.[6]

It was widely believed among soldiers and politicians in Piedmont that the South was populated entirely by criminals such as Carmine *Crocco* Donatelli, 'the hook'; Luigi *Chiavone* Alonzo, 'the big key'; Cosimo *Pizzichicchio* Mazzeo, 'the grain-picker'—as well as Luigi Andreozzi,

---

3 Mario Isenenghi, *L'Italia in piazza* (Milan: Mondadori, 1994), p. 69.

4 Cited in Gigi Di Fiore, *1861: Pontelandolfo e Casalduni. Un massacro dimenticato* (Naples: Grimaldi, 1998), p. 33. For the role of the Bourbons and the Pope during the War on banditry, see Emidio Cardinali, *I briganti e la Corte Pontificia ossia La cospirazione borbonico-clericale svelata*, 2 VOLS (Livorno: Davilli e C., 1862).

5 Luigi Lombardi Satriani, *Menzogna e verità nella cultura contadina del Sud* (Naples: Guida, 1974), p. 124.

6 Antonio Gramsci, 'Some Aspects of the Southern Question' in *Selections from Political Writings (1921–1926)* (Quentin Hoare ed. and trans.) (London: Lawrence and Wishart, 1978), p. 444.

Nunzio Tamburrini, Luigi Croce Di Tola and hundreds of other battle-hardened bandits. And this belief led them to view banditry exclusively as a question of crime for which there could be no response other than the most immediate and harshest repression, in a manner potentially more spectacular than the original offense.

The execution of 'bandits' usually took place in the main squares of Southern towns, in front of terrified crowds. Yet murder was not enough; documents had to be produced for posterity. As Giulio Bollati observes:

> Normally entirely deprived of any imaginative powers, during the repression of the bandits in the years following Unification the soldiers proved to be in possession of a prodigious photo-graphic capacity. Gone is that cold, dispassionate, silent stare; the cadavers are brought out from hiding and put on display. Officials and soldiers collaborated in arranging the gunned-down bodies in front of the lens, organizing scenes in which the still-living recite the part of the bandit. In this macabre fashion, crowds of peasants from the Italian South thus peeped through at the history of the nation.[7]

The same gruesome spectacles, aimed at both education and dissuasion, are to be found throughout the history of the Italian presence in Africa, such as with the hanging of Omar al-Mukhtar in the concentration camp at Soluch, performed in front of 20,000 Libyans brought there by force from different camps; or the severed head of Degiac Hailu Kebede displayed on a pole in the market square at Quoram.

The Southern insurrection began in Basilicata in April 1861, and over the summer extended through to Irpinia, Sannio, Molise, Abruzzo, Puglia, Capitanata and the area around Naples (the 'land of labour', *la terra di lavoro*). According to some estimates, there were 400 gangs comprising 80,000 people at the peak of the revolt, while over 1,400

---

7 Giulio Bollati, *L'Italiano* (Turin: Einaudi, 1983), pp. 142–43.

towns were involved in the conflict.[8] The gangs, often led by former soldiers from the Bourbon army, were able to occupy villages and towns for days on end, assassinating or taking hostage those who espoused liberal ideals, waving the white flags of the Bourbons. While they did not fear conflict with regiments from the official army and the national guard, they were extremely capable at pulling back and taking to the woods.

In order to repress these uprisings, which put the government in Turin in great difficulty—already disturbed as it was by the death of Cavour—Giovanni Durando of the Sixth Corps was replaced as General by Enrico Cialdini, the man who had won the siege of Gaeta in 1860, and perhaps the most famous soldier in the Northern army. Immediately following this substitution, the number of soldiers engaged in the South rose from 15,000 to 50,000. Later, in 1863, the army amounted to 116,000 men.

Bringing together both military and civil powers, Cialdini reneged on his predecessor's policy of conciliation with the former Bourbonic soldiers, instead not hesitating to persecute them, arresting and expelling aristocrats, upper officers and even 71 priests, including Archbishop of Naples, Cardinal Sisto Riario Sforza. 'These ordinances,' notes Giorgio Candeloro, 'were military actions, effected without any respect for legality; they were not approved by Ricasoli [then President of Italy], who would have wanted a series of trials to be established.'[9] Completely unbending with the Bourbon diehards, Cialdini responded to the insurrectionary violence with unprecedented brutality, terrorizing the local populations who sheltered the outlaws, often burning

8 Taquino Maiorino, *Storia e leggenda di briganti e brigantesse* (Casale Mongerrato: Piemme, 1997), pp. 91–92. Other sources drastically reduce the number of insurgents to 6,000.

9 Giorgio Candeloro, *Storia dell'Italia moderna, Volume 5: 1860–1871, La costruzione dello Stato unitario* (Milan: Feltrinelli, 1968), pp. 168–69.

their villages and cottages, arriving even at firing-squad executions carried out with hasty sentencing issued by military courts in the field, or simply without any trial at all.

From their refuge in the papal state in Rome, the Bourbons themselves supplied the insurgents with arms (very few, truth be told) and excellent propaganda support, meaning that the echoes of these repressive acts crossed the borders of the realm and solicited the disapproval of various European governments. On 21 July 1861, for example, Napoleon III sent a telegram to his aide-de-camp, Emile-Félix Fleury:

> I have written to Rome to express my protest. The news that is arriving is of such a nature as to alienate all honest hearts from the Italian cause. Not only are poverty and anarchy at their peak, but the most unworthy crimes at daily occurrences. A general, whose name I forget, having forbidden them to go and work in the fields with foodstuffs, put a group of peasants before the firing squad, because they had been found with a few crusts of bread. The Bourbons never did as much.[10]

President of the Council, Ricasoli, quickly drafted an extremely long note for all the foreign diplomatic representatives, attempting (not without some confusion) to diminish Cialdini's responsibility, maintaining that the insurgents' 'ferocious acts' deserved a 'proportionate repression'; that banditry had not 'political claims'; and that the false news that was circulating had been issued by Rome, 'in the name of dynasties interested in the Divine Right and that of the Pope's temporal power'.[11] Again in haste, on 3 January 1862, he issued a second note to

---

10 Ministero degli Affari esteri [Foreign Office], *Documenti Diplomatici Italiani*, SERIES 1, VOL. 1, DOC. 231, NOTE 1, p. 269. The ban on bringing food into the fields was adopted due to the fear that the farmers would have passed vitals onto the insurgents.

11 Ministero degli Affari esteri, *Documenti*, DOC. 273, pp. 329–35. Dated 24 August 1861.

the diplomatic community, announcing 'The last residues of the bandits, supported through foreign gold and intrigue, have now been destroyed and the repressions against them are being willingly carried out not only by the National Guard, but the people themselves.'[12] But Ricasoli was wrong; the worst was yet to come. The war on banditry continued until 1865, and in some regions till 1870. It was only with the Capture of Rome in 1870 that everything came to an end.

Among the thousands of offensives that the regular army launched over the course of the war on banditry, nothing—in terms of ferocity and the number of victims—compares to the operation undertaken, with utmost premeditation, on 14 August 1861, against the citizens of two large rural towns in the area of Benevento: Pontelandolfo and Casalduni. We can draw on two important sources for the episode: the memoirs of Major Carlo Melegati, whose division participated in the massacre, and the patient reconstruction of the events carried out by historian Gigi Di Fiore.

A few days before the frenzied attack, Cosimo Giordano—a former corporal in the Bourbon cavalry who now led a band of 400 men, comprising former soldiers who had served under Francesco II, draft dodgers and peasants who had hoped in vain that Garibaldi was going to distribute the common land—decided to occupy the towns of Pontelandolfo and Casalduni in order to demonstrate his unrivalled authority and power to the people of Sannio and Matese, as well as other Piedmont invaders. When the news reached him, Lieutenant Colonel Pier Eleonoro Negri charged Lieutenant Augusto Bracci with leading three platoons of infantry to the occupied towns but to avoid any conflict and limit themselves to taking position. Lieutenant Bracci, however, did not respect his orders and entered into Pontelandolfo, which he believed to be empty. But this was not the case. Surrounded

---

12 Ministero degli Affari esteri, *Documenti*, DOC. 2, p. 4.

by Giordano's men, the soldiers took refuge in an old medieval tower, from which they attempted a sortie. They were all massacred.

The news of the conflict, which saw the death of an official as well as 44 soldiers from the 33rd infantry regiment, caused immediate agitation among the higher echelons of the command in Naples. General Carlo Piola Caselli sent for Major Melegari, exclaiming: 'No doubt you will have heard speak of the painful and terrible facts of Casalduni and Pontelandolfo; well, General Cialdini does not so much order for but strongly desires that of these two towns there remain not a single stone [. . .]. You are authorized to make use of every means.'[13] As Lieutenant Negri received the same orders, the next morning both he and Melegari left Sannio with 900 riflemen from the 18th Battalion, all of them deriving from the dissolved Tuscan army.

At dawn on 14 August, while Lieutenant Colonel Negri entered Pontelandolfo with 500 soldiers—after losing 25 in an ambush—Major Melegari and the other 400 men fell on Casalduni with no resistance. 'I called in the officers of the three companies—who were now amassed in the central square, and the mayor's house,' Melegari recalls, 'and I ordered them to break down the doors and set fire to the houses, beginning with the mayor's. Soon there were thick clouds of smoke bellowing through the sky and the flames were rising in different parts of the town.'[14]

At this point, the major's memories become a little vague, reticent. There is no word about the massacre of the helpless townsfolk, the acts of rape, the looting, the sacking of the church. His narrative pauses instead on how he had spared the life of a poor old man: 'He was so overcome by emotion [. . .] that he bent down with tears in his eyes to kiss my hand; I helped him up and told him to go with God.' The

---

13 Carlo Melegari, *Cenni sul brigantaggio. Ricordi di un anitco bersagliere* (Turin: Roux Frassati & C., 1897), pp. 12–13.

14 Melegari, *Cenni*, pp. 18–19.

major then gets into his carriage and makes for San Lipo, where he accepts the hospitality of the colonel of the National Guard. Entirely unmoved by the massacre that he has just overseen, he participates in a banquet, surrounded by his officers. 'During the dinner, which was fit for a prince,' he adds, 'we spoke lightheartedly about matters; at the fruit course, the colonel raised a toast to the riflemen and to the Army; I replied by thanking him and proposed a toast to the King of Italy, to the National Guard and above all to the Neapolitan legionaries.'[15]

It was thus while Major Melegari was proposing his hearty toasts that Colonel Negri finally reached the first available telegraph office, which happened to be at Fragneto Montforte, and sent the following dispatch to Cialdini: 'Thursday, 15 August 1861. Yesterday, at dawn, justice was carried out in Pontelandolfo and Casalduni. They are still burning.'[16] An overall account of the massacre has never been formed. The newspaper *Il Popolo d'Italia* reported the figure of 164 deaths, but this was a very low estimate, for certainly hundreds of people were killed and burnt alive. And yet the two architects of the massacres did not have any background as ruthless soldiers. It is true that Negri, following this, was promoted to Major General and thus commanded divisions in Ancona and Piacenza; and Melegari, who had served with Cialdini in the Crimea, rose up to the very highest ranks in the army. But the Tuscan riflemen who had spent the entire morning burning houses, assassinating helpless peasants, raping and pillaging were not— as far as we know—particularly wicked people. And probably none of them felt the weight of the crimes they had committed. Officers and soldiers alike had simply carried out their orders with extraordinary zeal, convinced that they were acting to the benefit of the fatherland, legitimately punishing bandits who were less than human. Given that no one was put on trial for the massacre, they did not even have the

---

15 Melegari, *Cenni*, p. 23 and p. 24, respectively.

16 Di Fiore, *1861: Pontelandolfo e Casalduni*, p. 125.

irritation of needing to entrench themselves behind the orders of their superiors (as was the case, instead, 80 years later, for those responsible for the killings in Oradour, Sant'Anna di Sazzema and Marzabotto).[17]

Three months after the massacre, the left-wing member of parliament, Giuseppe Ferrari—following a particularly arduous journey—finally arrived at Pontelandolfo. Only three houses remained of the town that had once housed 6,000 people. Listening to the few remaining survivors, Ferrari learnt that even the liberal supporters in the town had 'suffered the arson of their homes, the loss of their goods, the death of innocent friends and relations, and today are in a condition of poverty and nakedness, the unhappy victims of every kind of misfortune.'[18] On his return to Turin, Ferrari brought back to parliament the crimes and abuses committed by the Piedmontese army against the insurgents—who, as he specified, could certainly not all be described as 'bandits'. Nevertheless, he found support from only one other member of parliament, Francesco Proto, Duke of Maddaloni, who expressed his total disgust for what was taking place in the South: 'People of our country are put before the firing squad without any form of official trial, singled out as an enemy on the simple suspicion of having provided food or shelter to an insurgent.'[19]

Following the intervention, an official Commission of Inquiry was established to investigate the reasons that had led to the armed revolt in the South. But the Inquiry's results—even while reporting the deep suffering of the Southern population and suggesting a socioeconomic response—were not absorbed into the related legislation, which instead represented a substantially repressive and exceptionalist intervention, handing over an emergency solution to the military courts and firing

---

17 All massacres ordered by Nazi commanders. [Trans.]

18 Di Fiore, *1861: Pontelandolfo e Casalduni*, p. 131.

19 Di Fiore, *1861: Pontelandolfo e Casalduni*, p. 135.

squads.[20] No justice was given, therefore, to that part of the insur-gents—in all likelihood the majority—who had taken up arms to respond to old and new wrongs against them, who were desperate for land and had to make the hard choice between protest on the one hand and a one-way ticket to America on the other.

Once the war on banditry was over, the authorities and historians did everything in their power to cover over the dramatic episodes of the civil war. A mere few lines were included in the school textbooks, and all of them in defence of the repressive forces who had saved the country's unity. There was no remark on the great political alliance between the ruling classes in the North and the big landowners in the South, an alliance that only acted against the subaltern classes. We have to wait till 1945 and the publication of Carlo Levi's *Christ Stopped at Eboli* to read a calm and faithful view on the most tragic of all the Italian wars of unification. Recalling his year in imprisonment in the Southern region of Lucania and his encounters with the peasants of Gagliano, Levi tried to interpret the revolt that had taken so many years earlier but which was still an unforgettable part of local sentiment:

> Even the appearance of the peasants today recalls that of the
> bandits: they are silent, lonely, gloomy and frowning in their
> black suits and hats and, in winter, black top coats, armed
> whenever they set out for the fields with gun and axe. They
> have gentle hearts and patient souls; centuries of resignation
> weigh on their shoulders, together with a feeling of the vanity
> of all things and of the overbearing power of fate. But when,
> after infinite endurance, they are shaken to the depths of their
> beings and are driven by an instinct of self-defence or justice,
> their revolt knows no bounds and no measure. It is an unhuman
> revolt whose point of departure and final end alike are death, in
> which ferocity is born of despair. The bandits unreasonably and

---

20 Law n. 1409 of 1863, the so-called Legge Pica. [Trans].

hopelessly stood up for the life and liberty of the peasants against the encroachments of the state. By ill luck they were unwitting instruments of History, and History, quite outside their ken, was working against them; they were on the wrong side and they came to destruction. But through the bandits the peasants defended themselves against the hostile civilization that never understands but everlastingly enslaves them; instinctively, they looked on the bandits as heroes.[21]

How many victims did this insipid, fratricidal war claim? The statistics are scarce and doubtless incomplete. The most trustworthy data on losses from among the insurgents' ranks are those compiled by Franco Molfese, who calculates 5,212 shot or killed in the fighting, 5,044 arrested, and 3,597 who gave themselves up to the authorities, amounting to 13,853 people.[22] But these numbers only refer to the period

---

21 Carlo Levi, *Christ Stopped at Eboli* (Frances Frenaye trans.) (New York: Farrar, Straus and Company, 1947), pp. 139–40.

22 Franco Molfese, *Storia del brigantaggio dopo l'Unità* (Milan: Feltrinelli, 1964). There are hundreds of volumes available on banditry. We will limit ourselves to citing only a few: Carlo Angelo Bianco di Saint Jorioz, *Il brigantaggio alla frontiera pontifica dal 1800 al 1863* (Milan: Daelli and C., 1864); Angelo De Witt, *Storia politico-militare del brigantaggio nelle province meridionali d'Italia* (Florence, Coppini, 1884); Cesare Cesari, *Il brigantaggio e l'opera dell'Esercito italiano dal 1860 al 1870* (Rome: Ausonia, 1920); Marco Monnier, *Notizie storiche documentate sul brigantaggio nelle provincie napoletane* (Naples: Berisio, 1965); Francamaria Trapani, *Le brigantesse* (Rome: Canesi, 1968); Aldo De Jaco (ed.), *Brigantaggio meridionale. Cronaca inedita dell'Unità d'Italia* (Rome: Editori Riuniti, 1969); Gaetano Cingari, *Brigantaggio, proprietari e contadini nel Sud, 1799–1900* (Reggio Calabria: Editori Meridionali Riuniti, 1976); Alfonso Scirocco, *Il Mezzogiorno nella crisi dell'unificazione, 1860–1865* (Naples: SEN, 1881); Antonio Lucarelli, *Il brigantaggio politico del Mezzogiorno d'Italia dopo la seconda restaurazione borbonica (1815–1818) e il brigantaggio politico delle Puglie dopo il 1860* (Milan: Longanesi, 1982); Michele Topa, *I briganti di sua Maestà* (Naples: Fratelli Fiorentino, 1993); Carlo Alianello, *La conquista del Sud. Il Risorgimento nell'Italia meridionale* (Milan: Rusconi, 1994); Lorenzo Del Boca, *Maledetti Savoia* (Casale Monferrato: Piemme, 1998).

between 1 June 1861 and 31 December 1865, and do not count the losses suffered over the first months of 1861, nor those in the five years following 1865, when General Pallavicino was no less brutal than Cialdini in his own repressive operations. It would perhaps be closer to the truth to increase Molfese's figures by a third. With this retouching, we arrive close to the estimates provided by Giacinto de' Sivo, cited by Carlo Alianello: 9,860 shot, 10,604 wounded, 13,629 arrested. Another partial estimate, this time for July 1861–February 1863, compiled by Luigi Torres on the basis of documents conserved in the Archive of the Historical Office of the General Staff of the Army, provides the following figures: 1,765 shot, 2,343 killed in combat, 4,496 arrested, 3,083 surrendered.[23]

No figure, however, is available for the casualties suffered by the soldiers of the regular army and the National Guard during their repressive operations. It is also unknown how many losses there were among civilians who did not side with the insurgents. Leafing through the lists of the deeds of arms, along with the related numbers of casualties, one easily reaches the conclusion that the soldiers paid a very high price as well, perhaps quantifiable in the thousands, especially when one bears in mind that, over the first few months of the war, the military divisions launched infantry attacks and experienced the insurgents' superiority, almost all of whom were mounted and knew the terrain perfectly. To this should be added the fact that the soldiers from Piedmont, Tuscany and Modena had received no preparation at all for dealing with a guerrilla war, and were overcome by panic at the mere thought of being captured by the bandits. The macabre bent of Luigi Andreoti and his gang was a secret to no one: 'They show mercy to neither the wounded nor prisoners; they kill and slaughter them, massacring the bodies to shock the soldiers when they find them.

---

23 Luigi Torres, *Il brigantaggio nell'Abruzzo Peligno e nell'Alta Sangro, 1860–1870* (Alessandria: Majell, 2003), p. 286.

When a soldier fights, he always thinks about what awaits him if he is hurt or taken prisoner, and when he sees a bad end coming, he turns and runs.'[24]

We lack information about the morale among the troops engaged in the South, but it cannot have been particularly strong. The seven years of enforced conscription did not only weigh heavily on the conscript, but also on their family and community. It is no wonder that this song was sung in the countryside of Romagna:

Oh Vittorio, who commands the Kings of Kingdoms
How many men will you send to the slaughter!
If you want soldiers, make them out of wood
But leave that fair boy alone.[25]

What we do know with some precision, however, is that the soldiers engaged in the South, much of which was infested with malaria, did not enjoy good health. In 1864, '47,510 were admitted to hospital for 'fevers', which in more than a thousand cases concluded in their death. On average, each soldier engaged in the war on banditry spent 13 days in hospital.'[26]

Finally, we know very little about the losses suffered by the Bourbon army which, in this inter-Italian war, first opposed the regular army and Garibaldi's troops, and then provided an important contribution to the Southerners' struggle against Unification. In his speech in parliament on 20 November 1861, Francesco Proto, Duke of Maddaloni, spoke of 'the loss of 20,000 men, some in combat, some to the rifles as prisoners or suspects or those unjustly accused'.[27] If we do not know

---

24 Torres, *Il brigantaggio*, p. 134.

25 Lamberto Mercuri and Carlo Tuzzi (eds), *Canti politici italiani, 1793–1945* (Rome: Editori Riuniti, 1973), p. 185.

26 Maiorino, *Storia e leggenda*, p. 111.

27 Cited in Gigi Di Fiore, *I vinti del Risorgimento. Storia e storie di chi combatté per i Borbone di Napoli* (Turin: Utet, 2004), p. 3.

the exact number of dead, we do nevertheless know that of the prisoners and their tragic fate. Defined as 'lost' because they refused to join the regular army, more than 10,000 were deported to Northern Italy in cattle wagons, and distributed among different towns: Genoa, Alessandria, Bergamo. The most unruly were carried through the castle gates of Fort San Maurizio Canavese near Turin, of Castello Sofrzesco in Milan and Fort Fenestrelle in Piedmont—the latter of which was a tragic site of repression. In the words of Gigi Di Fiori:

> The weaker among those present, accustomed to the climate of the Two Sicilies, and now for the first time in their lives far from the land of their birth, simply collapsed [. . .]. For sanitary reasons, and for the evident difficulty in burying the cadavers, many of the bodies were thrown into a huge vat of quicklime, which is still visible behind the church at the fort's entrance.[28]

Farcical plebiscites, violent annexations that violated every norm of international law, the establishment of concentration camps, the pacification of the South realized through a state of permanent siege, military courts, summary executions: this process of Unification was far from representing a promising start for the new Italy. 'And yet,' as Di Fiori writes, 'there are those who continue to speak of the "good Italians" who came from the North to liberate their "brothers in the South" from foreign oppression.'[29] Indeed, the legend of the 'good Italians' had begun to circulate in the newly unified country, if we believe the account that Major Migliara, accusing the mayor of Cervinara of claiming to be a great patriot when he was in truth guilty of abusing his powers,

---

28 Di Fiore, *I vinti del risorgimento*, p. 250. Also see Fulvio Izzo, *I lager dei Savoia. Storia infame del Risorgimento nei campi di concentrameno per meridionali* (Naples: Controcorrente, 1999). See also the heated debate on the topic, especially Barbero, *I prigionieri dei Savoia*.

29 Di Fiore, *I vinti del risorgimento*, p. 5.

exclaimed: 'Listen up old Mayor, we Piedmontese are good folk, too good perhaps, but we're not the stupid fools you think we are!'[30]

One hundred and forty years after the deportation of 10,000 of Francesco II's soldiers to the North, a note by a certain Bruno Faccini was published in the letters section of the newspaper *Corriere della Sera* (a section previously curated by Indro Montanelli and then Paolo Mieli, now in the hands of Sergio Romano):[31]

> Don't you think the *Risorgimento* has a few skeletons in its cupboard that need to be brought out? Things need to be said! For example, take the moment when the poor defeated Bourbonic soldiers were left to die in the frozen winter of a Savoy fortress 1,800 metres above the sea, equipped with nothing but a Southern soldier's uniform. Why don't we care about, and almost never discuss, what happened at Fenestrelle?[32]

Mieli did not avoid the question, and responded amply, drawing on Gigi di Fiore's volume, *The Victors of the Risorgimento*, which includes an exhaustive chapter on the facts of Fenestrelle. Yet the issue, clearly still a hot question, triggered other letters to be sent to the newspaper, with further questions. Silvestro Acampora wrote:

> After more than 140 years, and with the Savoys removed from any influence over Italian affairs, surely the new generation of today should be taught history as it really was, and not according to a comfortable interpretation? Don't you think that the Italian Republic would come out stronger, if the Southern

---

30 Melegari, *Cenni*, p. 77.

31 The names are significant: Montanelli fought in the colonial invasion of Ethiopia (see Chapter Ten); Mieli was a student of Renzo De Felice, known for his sympathetic biography of Mussolini; Sergio Romano, a conservative, served as a diplomat to successive Italian governments. [Trans.]

32 Letters section, *Corriere della Sera*, 11 October 2004.

populations—who paid with thousands killed, imprisoned or deported—could finally be released from the label of bandits, and recognized instead for the rebels they were?[33]

The requests made by Faccini and Acampora seem legitimate to us, and not mere provocations. Above all, they cannot be accused of pro-Bourbon revisionism. It is extraordinary that serious and well-informed historians such as Ernesto Galli della Loggia[34] and Giovanni Russo[35] express their discomfort and concern every time some unorthodox piece of research is published in Italy, i.e. anything that does not conform to the canonical interpretation of the *Risorgimento*. Attempting to fill in the 'holes in collective memory', as Antonio Gambino puts it, does not equate to disrespect for Unification.[36] Those of us who have passed a good share of our lives filling in those 'holes' in our colonial past, and thus encountering more barriers than consent, know that it is not easy to swim against the current. It is, however, necessary—still more so today—that the inventories of documents concerning period of the war on banditry in the State Archives and in the Secret Vatican Archives are finally made available, as well as those in some Spanish archives. Alfonso Scirocco, who has been working on these new sources, correctly observes that 'we can now step aside from the approximations (perhaps desired, perhaps circumstantial) of the official publications'.[37] A systematic investigation of these archives will surely reveal many

---

33 Letters section, *Corriere della Sera*, 4 November 2004.

34 Ernesto Galli della Loggia, 'Il brigantaggio' in Giovanni Belardelli (ed.), *Miti e storia dell'Italia unita* (Bologna: Il Mulino, 1999), p. 47.

35 Giovanni Russo, 'I briganti sono meglio di Cavour?', *L'Indice* 6 (June 2004): 39.

36 Antonio Gambino, *Inventario italiano. Costumi e mentalità di un Paese materno* (Turin: Einaudi, 1998), pp. 120–30.

37 Alfonso Scirocco, 'Introduzione' in Renato Dentoni-Letta (ed.), *Guida alle fonti per la storia del brigantaggio postunitario conservate negli Archivi di Stato*, VOL. 1 (Rome: Ufficio Centrale per i Beni archivistici, 1999), p. *xxxv*.

surprises. On 27 January 1866, Stanislao Mancini exclaimed in parlia-ment: 'do not force me to make those revelations about which Europe would be so horrified';[38] in our opinion, he was not covering up the massacres at Pontelandolfo, Casalduni and the Fenestrelle camp alone.[39]

---

38 Camera dei Deputati [House of Deputies], *Atti Parlamentari, Discussioni*, 27 January 1866.

39 As Cesare Cesari rightfully notes, a swathe of decorations were awarded to cover over the massacres: 4 gold medals; 2,375 silver medals; and 5,012 honorable mentions. The awarded and promoted included Alfondo Del Boca, class of 1838. Having joined the civil war at the rank of captain in 1861, he obtained promotions in the field and eventually the colonel's cross 'for special merit'—rewards conceded only to those who had demonstrated particular zeal and few scruples.

THREE

THE HELL OF NOKRA

There was no real reason for Italy to participate in the scramble for Africa. They joined in, quite simply, for a question of prestige. The geographical societies, the arms industry, the shipyards and steelworks, the colonial clubs and their newspapers all egged on the enterprise, insisting on a Messianic conception of Italy's destiny, its mythic connection to Ancient Rome and the apparent need to find an outlet for the demographic leap—among the highest in Europe. Finally, on the eve of Tancredi Saletta's landing at Massawa on the Eritrean coast, even King Umberto I of Savoy himself put pressure on the government of President Mancini, claiming that the African expedition would restore glory to his dynasty.

Thanks above all to the meticulous offices of the British Empire, the events of how we arrived in Massawa in 1885 have been well recounted, if in a somewhat comic tone. The commander of the troops, Colonel Tancredi Saletta, quite candidly confessed in an official report to have never laid eyes on a map of Massawa up till the moment of the landing, and also to have learnt in that very moment that the artillery with which he was meant to then fight off the Egyptian canons was stuck under 600 tonnes of cargo in the hold of a merchant navy vessel, the *Gottardo*. Fortunately, in order to neutralize any possible offence, the British agents operating in the Red Sea took charge of matters; they had been ordered by London to facilitate the landing of the Italians at Massawa in every way possible.

Some years later, recalling the haphazard beginnings of the Italian expansion into the Horn of Africa, Ferdinando Martini wrote: 'Just as it is useful to ask why we had gone there, so too it is painful to remember how we did so.'[1] That is to say: without any idea of the locations, with few means and confused plans, with a total lack of logistical, strategic and political preparation, and an absolute ignorance of the customs and cultures of the indigenous population. All of this fatefully led to the development of unjustified prejudices and a widespread racialized disrespect for Africans. This was true to the extent that General Baldissera, the high commander of the troops in Eritrea, had no scruples in claiming in 1888 that 'Abyssinia must be ours because this is the fate of inferior races; Blacks will, little by little, disappear, and we must bring civilization to Africa not for the Abyssinians, but for ourselves.'[2] The hypothesis of substituting the 'subjected race' with the 'race of rulers', which implied the genocide of a whole people, was not an entirely new idea. As Nicola Labanca notes, 'it seemed that the great American myth had taken hold among the majority of the Africanists in the Italian ranks, that of the ferocious Indian wars, of a totalizing war and a totalizing victory, of the subjection and even extermination of an entire indigenous people.'[3]

It was in this unstable climate, and with ambitions that were entirely unmatched by the available means, that the Italians began to build their 'first-born' colony, using the same methods of repression that they had employed 20 years earlier in the war on banditry: the constant abuse of

---

1 *L'Eritrea economia* (Novara: Istituto Geografico De Agostini, 1913), p. 3.

2 Tenente Anonimo [Anonynous Lieutenant], *Campagna d'Africa. 1885–1896* (Milan: Ed. Agom, 1935), pp. 65–66, cited in Angelo Del Boca, *Gli italiani in Africa Orientale, I: Dall'Unità alla marcia su Roma* (Rome and Bari: Laterza, 1976), pp. 441–42.

3 Nicola Labanca, *In marcia verso Adua* (Turin: Einaudi, 1993), p. 182.

exceptionalist military courts, summary executions, secret repressive operations followed by disappearances, waves of imprisonment, deportations to Italy, and a total lack of respect for the laws that were meant to rule the colony itself. What was new, in relation to the operations in the Italian South, was the desire to keep the Eritrean population segregated in ignorance and misery. One can easily see the motivation for this brutal conduct from the official acts, newspapers and soldiers' letters. As it had been consolidated that the 'semi-barbarous' local population only understood force, then it was necessary to use punishments that inculcated terror. The day after Saletta's landing at Massawa, Francesco Crispi addressed parliament: 'What is our aim? It is but one: to underline the name of Italy in the African territories and demonstrate to the barbarians that we are strong and powerful! The barbarians cannot feel anything except for the force of cannon-fire; very well then, the cannon will sound at the right moment!'[4]

And if the moment had still not arrived in 1885 for the cannons to fire, it was always the right moment for rifles. As soon as Saletta had landed at Massawa, he realized that the city was swarming with the spies of Ras Alula Engida, Ethiopian governor of Asmara. Without losing a moment—and without even setting up a court—he issued a death sentence against a certain Nicolaus the Greek. Here is how his execution was described by a local gazette, sold at 5 cents per copy:

> The execution was very hurried: the Greek was too weak to stand on his own two feet, nor could he sit down; he was thus bound to the back of a chair brought in by a soldier; then the squad advanced a dozen steps and fired; the bullets of the 12 Vetterli rifles almost took the head off the condemned man. Two hospital-soldiers then approached with the coffin: they gathered up the body and threw it in, and took it near to the cemetery in a cart. Those present left in silence; an example

---

4 Giuseppe Piccinini, *Guerra d'Africa* (Rome: Perino, 1887), p. 981.

had been made. Two Abyssinians and another spy met the same fate shortly after.[5]

Spies, suspected moles, reticent informants, village chiefs fallen from grace: the smallest trifle was enough to send someone to the gallows or be crumpled under gunfire. The sheer frequency of the executions, which for the most part were not preceded by anything resembling a trial, eventually came to disturb the government in Rome, even more so once it seemed that the Italian governors in Eritrea—Baldassarre Orero and Antonio Balisssera—were directly involved in the violations. Yet an official request by the Prime Minister to render the inquiries public was blocked by King Umberto I. On 19 July 1891, the King wrote to him:

> First of all, in the interests of the country and of the army, it is close to my heart that the generals engaged in the Eritrean Colony—from Saletta to Baldissera and right up to Gandolfi and Driquet—be left outside all these impassioned discussions. If there have been errors, then these will be judged severely, with criteria upheld by honourable men in front of honoured officials, but without abandoning valiant soldiers—who are still fit to render service to the Fatherland—to the fleeting whims of those who make headway with views and considerations of an almost exclusively political nature.

The preamble complete, he then ordered Rudinì that the report from the official inquiry into the deeds attributed to Baldissera and Cossato 'must be—and remain—sealed' in order to 'regain the prestige of the Colony's administration'.[6]

---

5 Piccinini, *Guerra d'Africa*, pp. 983–84.

6 Archivio dell'Ufficio storico dello Sato Maggiore dell'esercito, Rome, *Carteggio Eritrea*, b. 118, f. 13, 19, 19 July 1891: Umberto I to Rudinì. Cited in Labanca, *In marcia verso Adua*, p. 81.

The facts investigated by the commission of the inquiry had taken place in Eritrea between 1888 and 1890. At the centre of the crimes were the manoeuvres of two colonial functionaries, and a trial against several indigenous persons. The two functionaries were the lawyer Eteocle Cagnassi, Secretary for Colonial Affairs, and lieutenant of the carabinieri, Dario Livraghi, chief of the indigenous police in Eritrea. The trial, on the other hand, concerned the accusation of high treason against a rich Muslim merchant called Hassan Mussa el-Akkad, filed against Kantibai Aman, the chief of the Habab, and against his secretary, Said Ali Safi. The trial concluded on 11 February 1980 with the issuing of a death sentence to the first two and life imprisonment for the third.

Francesco Crispi—then leader of the government—knew el-Akkad personally and refused to believe that he was guilty of 'enemy intelligence'. As soon as he heard about outcome of the trial, Crispi had the sentence suspended and entrusted Vincenzo Piccolo Cupani, one of the colony's three civil counsellors, with opening an inquiry. Within a few weeks, Cupani had decided that the three accused men were in fact innocent and, consequently, levelled very serious accusations against Cagnassi and Livraghi, not only for having falsified proof in order to send el-Akkad and the others to their death, but also for a series of other conspiracies. In April 1890, Cagnassi and Livraghi were arrested in Milan. The latter, however, managed to escape to Switzerland, from where he sent a letter of defence to the newspaper *Il Secolo*, which contained a set of terrifying revelations about the methods of 'justice' practiced in Eritrea.

While the editors of the Neapolitan newspaper had reservations about publishing the letter due to its explosive content, *La Tribuna* in Rome came out with the correspondence of Napoleone Corazzini from Massawa, which included devastating criticism of Lavraghi and Cagnassi, the latter accused of being the mastermind and the former his agent. The accusations spoke of the physical elimination for material gain of various Eritrean aristocrats, and of constant massacres of Abyssinian formations in Italy's pay. At the same time, the *Secolo* in Milan published the recollections of Livraghi, in which the lieutenant, even while attempting to lay the blame with his superiors, nevertheless provided an even more monstrous version of what had taken place in Massawa. Not only did he confirm the series of crimes reported by Corazzini, he also revealed the horrors of the Eritrean prisons in which the most atrocious acts of torture had been practiced to make the prisoners speak, and the death of a prisoner following torture had happened more than once. Yet the most serious accusation levelled by Livraghi related to the two governors, Baldissera and Orero, concerning the order to eliminate entire Abyssinian formations that had been put on Italian pay but were suspected of planning desertion. Livraghi claimed, furthermore, that the task of taking these 'undesirables' to the Ethiopian border—in other words, of assassinating these 800 'rebels'—was given to Adam Aga's men, the most amenable of the collaborating chiefs.[7]

Faced with the severity of the revelations contained in the articles in *Il Secolo* and *La Tribuna*, as well as the speech given by Napoleone Colajanni to parliament on 9 March, President Rudinì established the commission for an official inquiry, who immediately left for the 'first-born' colony. On 17 July, the commission was already prepared to present its report. In the meantime, General Baldissera, who was heavily cited by the report, decided to provide an interview in which he vehemently refused Livraghi's figure of 800 Abyssinians having been murdered: 'it is certainly true that I had 8 to 10 natives shot, without organizing a military court', and in his defence he underlined that he only had 6,000 men under his command. 'Having experimented uselessly with pardons', the general continued, 'it became necessary to change tack, revealing

---

7 Dario Livraghi, 'Gli assassini in Africa. 800 morti?', *Il Secolo*, 5–6 March 1891. [See Stephen C. Bruner, *Late Nineteenth-Century Italy in Africa: The Livraghi Affair and the Waning of Civilizing Aspirations* (Newcastle-Upon-Tyne: Cambridge Scholars Publishing, 2017). —Trans.]

the difference between tolerance and weakness. It was necessary to inculcate terror in order to keep those barbarians down.'[8]

In November 1891, the commission's report was made public, which journalist Achille Bizzoni immediately described as 'an incredible, medieval document that ought to have been seized as justification for criminal acts [. . .] a blatant defence of an assassin.'[9] In reality, the report was a masterpiece of reticence, ambiguity, subtleties, a defence of high command and military honour. The document's conclusions undermined all of Livraghi's accusations and tended to make him seem an exaggerator. It reduced the scandal to episodes of more humble proportions, justifying them all the same, as 'the colony's security was effectively under threat'. The number of assassinations cited by Livraghi were reduced from 800 to 16, and even these were justified. The blame for the few 'abuses' was entirely attributed to the Eritrean gendarmes, and to the victims themselves. Indeed, the report claimed that:

> The facts that really took place, if they were to be construed as an abuse of some kind, ought be attributed to the savage nature of the native soldiers, who necessarily need to be charged with following orders, as well as to those individuals who were the victims; it cannot be traced up to the High Command, nor to the colony's functionaries.[10]

---

8 Cited in Anonymous Lieutenant, *Campagna d'Africa* (Milan: Agom, 1935), pp. 65–66. The arguments provided by General Orero were not dissimilar from those provided by Baldissera. When questioned during the Livraghi trial about the fate of certain local chiefs, he claimed 'it was necessary for them to be secretly executed, while their families were allowed to believe that they had been deported to Italy'. Archivio storico del Ministero dell'Africa italiana, pos. II/3, f. 10, 28 March 1891, examination transcription n. 14; cited in Labanca, *In marcia verso Adua*, p. 285.

9 Achille Bizzoni, *Eritrea nel passato e nel presente. Ricerche, impressioni, delusioni di un giornailsta* (Milan: Zonzogno, 1897), p. 238.

10 Bizzoni, *Eritrea nel passato e nel presente*, p. 250.

Given the report's unashamedly forgiving tone, the case filed against Cagnassi and Livraghi could no longer arrive at a guilty sentence. Indeed, on 19 November, after 96 witnesses were paraded in front of the judges, the vast majority of whom testified in the accused's favour (with Saletta, Baldissera, Orero and Cossato in pride of place), the special court presided over by Colonel Cesare Tarditi exonerated the two Italians and issued extremely heavy sentences to Kassa and Abdel Rahman, two native police offices, thus turning on its head the entire responsibility for the massacres. The three generals involved in the scandal (Baldissera, Orero and Cossato) were exonerated by a jury comprised of Generals Mezzacapo, Pianell and De Sonnaz; it should be noted that they were not absolved of the crimes of which they were accused, but because they had not violated military discipline. The most heinous scandal in the history of nineteenth-century Italian colonialism was thus put to rest through two sentences that were, to say the very least, scandalous. More than one scholar has perceived, in the behaviour of the Commission of Inquiry, signs of pressure from King Umberto who held an audience with the Commission's seven members, no less, on the evening of their departure for Massawa on 2 April.[11]

Those among the 'ill-meaning and dangerous people' who were neither hanged nor shot ended up in prison. At the beginning of the 1890s, there were seven prisons in Eritrea: in Assab, Massawa, Asmara, Cheren, Adi-Ugri, Adi-Caie and finally in Nokra, on the Dahlak islands. According to the level of activities in the colony, the prison population varied from 500 to 1,500 detainees, a very large number once one considers that Eritrea was inhabited by less than 200,000 people at the time. Here we will concern ourselves only with the penitentiary at Nokra

---

11 For the Livraghi episode, see Del Boca, *Gli italiani in Africa Orientale*, VOL. 1, chap. 6, pp. 434–61.

which, in terms of the inhumane conditions in which the prisoners were forced to live, became a symbol of Italian colonial oppression.

Nokra is one of 209 hard coral islands in the Dahlak archipelago, about 55 km off the coast of Massawa. On this incomparable site of beauty, characterized by its pristine natural surroundings, man forged hell itself. General Saletta identified the island as an ideal location to build a prison, above all due to its distance from the mainland. This total isolation was not only intended to discourage any attempt at escape, but would also ensure the utmost secrecy regarding the violent methods used. The first building campaign to transform Nokra into a penal camp were completed by the end of 1887, to the cost of 6,500 *lire*, charged to the Interior Ministry. These were not, in truth, significant works: a brick building for the guards, lodgings for 200 prisoners (half tents, half haphazard *tukuls*), an excavation of eight deep trenches for the prison and the erection of a stage with two gallows.

Due to the hot climate, which could reach up to 50 degrees Celsius, there was a fundamental problem of water supply. The little garrison was to be supplied with drinking water by small barges that would make the journey from the mainland three times a week. For the prisoners, on the other hand, a well was dug to the depth of 10 metres, which provided brackish water, and even this in small quantities—to the extent that, in periods of drought, the water was rationed. The burning sun and the lack of water, in the minds of those who had chosen the place, constituted further instruments of punishment. Another such tool for violent re-education was forced labour in the stone quarries, the yield from which was loaded onto the ferries and brought to Massawa for roads and buildings.

There are only very few accounts of daily life on Nokra. The island almost always hosted political prisoners, and was rigidly off-limits to everyone. Captain Eugenio Finzi of the Italian Royal Navy visited it in 1902, and described the situation thus: 'The prisoners, covered in sores and insects, literally die from hunger, scurvy and other illnesses. With no doctor to assist them and only 30 cents spent on their sustenance, they are skeletal and filthy; most have lost the use of their legs, reduced as they are to living constantly chained to a metre-high board.'[12] Those who tried to escape this hellhole, who were almost always caught—as was the case with an attempted mass escape in 1893—were immediately shot.

Who were the unlucky detainees of Nokra? At the beginning they were common criminals. Then, from 1889, the political prisoners arrived, not only chiefs and important persons in tribes that did not accept Italian rule, but also spies or people presumed to be as such, treacherous collaborators, agitators, shamans and fortune tellers who preached the coming end of Italian presence. In 1892, during Oreste Baratieri's military and civil rule of the colony, the Nokra prison reached its full capacity of 1,000 detainees. We can provide the names of a few of them.[13] In September 1895, on the eve of the disaster at Adwa, 'Memer Walde Ananias, licce Wolde Yesus and Gherasmacc Sadur', three members of Tigrin nobility whose only crime was to have travelled to the military camp at Baratieri to begin peace negotiations on behalf of Ras Mengesha Yohannes.[14] Saur, already an old man, was unable to take the island's climate and the cruelty practiced there; he died in prison.

---

12 Cited in Marco Lenci, *All'inferno e ritorno. Storie di deportati tra Italia ed Eritrea in epoca coloniale* (Pisa: Biblioteca Franco Serantini, 2004), p. 37n112.

13 Archivio storico del Ministero dell'Africa italiana, pos. 12/3, f. 26, 21 December 1885, Genè to Robilant; cited in Labanca, *In marcia verso Adua*, p. 290.

14 'Memer', licce' and 'Gherasmacc' are noble titles, as Del Boca recognizes in the original text, italicizing the spelling. Here I have maintained General Genè's orthography, though we can confidently identify the third title as Gerazmač. See the appendix to Martha Nasibù, *Memorie di una principessa etiope* (Vicenza: Neri Pozza, 2005), and Tsehai Berhane Selassie, 'An Ethiopian Medical Text-Book', *Journal of Ethiopian Studies* 9(1) (1971): 95–180. [Trans].

The prison remained in use without pause from 1887 to 1941. From 1936, after the Italian occupation of Ethiopia, soldiers and functionaries of the deposed emperor, Haile Selassie, comprised the majority of the detainees—and, soon after, guerrilla warriors imprisoned during the various repressive operations, middling aristocrats, and priests and monks who had escaped the massacre at Debre Libanos. The prisoners' diet comprised of 300 g of flour, 10 g of tea and 20 g of sugar. Yet not even these miserable rations were necessarily provided every day.

One of the more noble justifications for Italian presence in Africa was its supposed capacity to civilize the country. Italy might have, therefore, performed an important role in the struggle against slavery, a campaign already begun in the Horn of Africa by Great Britain. On 14 September 1889, in fact, Crispi signed a convention in London against the trade; the document has 11 articles, the first of which declares:

> Her Majesty the Queen of the United Kingdom of Great Britain and Ireland and His Majesty the King of Italy engage to prohibit all Trade in Slaves, either by their respective subjects, or under their respective flags, or by means of capital belonging to their respective subjects; and to declare such Traffic piracy. Their Majesties further declare, that any vessel which may attempt to carry on the Slave Trade, shall, by that fact alone, lose all right to the protection of their flag.[15]

This humanitarian initiative was warmly welcomed in Italy. The newspapers and the popular press discussed it. Issue 26 of Giusepe Piccinini's now-famous *War in Africa* depicted the following poignant scene on the cover: an Italian soldier, his colonial helmet adorned with a plume of feathers, breaks the chains from the wrists of a busty, semi-naked

---

15 Statutory Instrument 1889/5018; Camera dei Deputati, *Tratta degli schiavi*, Session 17, December 1889.

native girl. The caption reads: 'Faced with the progress of our civilization and our weaponry, the chains will break and the slaves will arise from their centuries-long subservience.'[16] This was what was believed in Italy. In Eritrea, on the other hand, the governors (from Oraro to Gandolfi, from Balddisera to Baratieri) were much more cautious, and less motivated. As historian Nicola Labanca has observed: 'they feared that by engaging in the fight against slavery they might uproot traditional local society, with consequent dangers that were worse than the existing state of the colonial order.'[17]

Italy's contribution to the struggle against slavery, consequentially, had no impact whatsoever, even if, in 1890, Crispi's government had signed the final Acts of the Brussels Conference, imposing on all European governments the need to entirely abolish the trade. To provide an example of Italian inaction, we can note that General Baratieri knew perfectly well the routes used by the slave caravans in Eritrea. He also knew where the slave traders landed their boats to transfer their human commodities to the Arabian Peninsula. He was so fully informed—probably by the head of his Cabinet, Antonio Miani[18]—that in November 1892 he sent a weighty report to the Foreign Ministry entitled *Slavery in the Eritrean Colony in Relation to the Act of Brussels*. But he did not seem to be particularly interested in limiting the trade. He had other thoughts and plans in mind: first the occupation of Kassala, then the invasion of Tigray and its eventual annexing. The slaves could wait. And indeed, the slavers' *sambuks* continued to sail across the Red Sea for another 40 years, mocking the ships of the Italian Royal Navy.

The struggle against slavery in Somalia was entrusted, on the other hand, to a private company, the Benadir Society, since Italy had to wait

16 Piccinini, *Guerra d'Africa*, pp. 201–4.

17 Labanca, *In marcia verso Adua*, p. 256.

18 For the activities of General Miani in Eritrea, see Del Boca, *La disfatta di Gasr bu Hàdi. 1915* (Milan: Mondadori, 2004), pp. 29–36. [See also the conclusion to Chapter Six.]

till 1905 to assume direct management of the colony. Composed of around 20 Italian officials and functionaries, flanked by 600 Arab mercenaries, the Benadir Society was so incapable that it even overlooked 30 detainees in the *garesa* (the governor's residence) in Mogadishu. The Society was placed under indictment by parliament for its extraordinary inertia and for having tolerated—if not actively favoured—the practice of slavery, and was consequently investigated by three commissions of inquiry. The inquiry requested by the Italian Anti-Slavery Society was entrusted to celebrated journalist Luigi Robecchi Bricchetti who, between April and June 1903, produced an inquiry that is exemplary for its serious and meticulous approach, and which concluded that, under the watch of distracted or overly tolerant Italian authorities, slaves had been freely bought, sold, inherited, offered as gifts, exploited, chained and deported. Only on very rare occasions had they been freed, despite the impositions of the Brussels Conference.

Bricchetti went from door to door in three Somalian cities, compiling a painful census that led him to conclude that there were 2,096 slaves among the 6,695 residents in Mogadishu, 721 slaves in Merca and 829 in Brava. In the countryside, the number of slaves was even higher and their living conditions still worse. The Italian explorer reported that:

> They always have their heads bowed down to the earth while they await the most tiring of labours, with a fistful of ash or chalk on the back of their necks, set there by their masters to ensure that they do not shirk from the chore. If a slave lifts their head for an instant from the furrow that they plough, sow or work in some other manner, then the ash or chalk falls from their neck and they will soon feel the kurbash of the slave-driver across their shoulders.[19]

---

19 Luigi Robecchi Bricchetti, *Dal Benadir. Lettere illustrate alla Società antischivaista d'Italia* (Milan: La Poligrafica, 1904), p. 91.

There was worse still, as Bricchetti discovered when he began to examine the official acts kept in the residences of the governor, Emilio Dulio. Here he found contracts for the buying and selling of slaves, legally authorized with an Italian stamp and the then-necessary authentication process. The Society's treasurer, Mazzucchelli, received a contribution for every deal, as he had diligently noted in his records. Transcribing these deeds in his report—which were endorsed by Governor Dullio— Bricchetti commented bitterly: 'One's indignation is so intense that it is impossible to comment on such a monstrosity: we shall leave all judgement to posterity.'[20]

Nevertheless, the Italians in the colony felt comfortable with the situation throughout the entirety of the liberal period and even more so in the two decades of Fascism; they were not disturbed in any way by the orders they gave and received, which entailed the creation of a world that allowed the employment of drastic repressive measures, the con- struction of the cruellest of prison regimes, the practice of a criminal justice system that would have horrified Cesare Beccaria, and a tolerance for slavery—or even, as was the case with the Benadir Society, the active exploitation of it.[21] Instead of being repulsed by the unhuman universe they had created, they were proud of it, a pride that was associated with the belief that only Italians—due to their open, kind and tolerant char- acter—were able to raise the natives up to a superior level of civilization. The myth of the 'good', 'welcomed', 'not racist', 'accommodating' Italian thus soon re-emerged in Africa as well, imposing itself with vigour. This charitable, forgiving self-description explains the lack of scruples, the absence of remorse or concerns among the 1,500 officials and 70,000

---

20 Robecchi Bricchetti, *Dal Benadir*, p. 33. [The account of Italian enslavement of Somalians is continued in Chapter Seven.]

21 See Luciano Martone, *Giustizia coloniale. Modelli e prassi penale per i sudditi d'Africa dall'età giolittiana al fascismo* (Naples: Jovene, 2002).

soldiers who passed through Eritrea in the 11 years between the conquest of Massawa and the defeat at Adwa.[22]

Yet this myth of the 'good Italians' had to face up to another, equally widespread notion, of a ruthless people with no respect for the rules, who demonized their Black adversaries and treated them like animals. There is a totalizing disrespect contained in the famous line pronounced on the eve of the defeat at Adwa: *Ai butuma qua granade e a l'è faita*— 'Lob four grenades at them and the job's done.' Baldissera's behaviour during his periods in Eritrea recalls that of the American generals during the Indian Wars, who deliberately aimed for genocide. How else can anyone comment on the life of the explorer and army captain, Vittorio Bottego, who pushed through with a column of prisoners towards the Ethiopian south, who believed in no rules other than the law of the gun? He could have saved his life, and the scientific results of his expedition to Omo, if only he had surrendered to the functionaries in a country that he had swept through with murder and devastation. Yet the mere idea of giving himself in to the 'Black dogs', and recognizing that he had systematically violated the laws of a sovereign nation, drove him crazy, and he preferred to die on the hill of Daga Roba.[23]

In truth, as we have seen from the handful of episodes in this chapter, the myth of *Italiani brava gente* only served to cover up and excuse the true nature of a horde of unscrupulous conquerors engaged in mistaken operations, guided by crazed orders, and abandoned to their fate after a series of errors committed by Crispi and Baratieri.[24] Over a few hours

---

22 For an analysis of racism in the colony, see Nicola Labanca, *Oltremare. Storia dell'espansione coloniale italiana* (Bologna: Il Mulino, 2004), pp. 411–24.

23 See Del Boca, *Gli italiani in Africa orientale*, VOL. 1, pp. 746–49. In 1987, the supposed ruins of a monument to Bottego were photographed near Ghidami, close to the Sudanese border. See Antonio Mascolo, 'La spedizione Bottego ha conquistato il Daga Roba', *Gazzetta di Parma*, 5 December 1987. [Trans].

24 One of Baratieri's most serious errors was the administrative absorption of the best land in Eritrea, counting around 394,000 hectares. This large-scale looting

between the hills of Abba Garima and Saurìa, everything that had been built over 11 years of looting, violence and violations simply vanished into thin air. All that was left on the ground were 5,000 Italian soldiers mangled by Balcha's cannons and the Oromo cavalry. Another 2,000 were taken prisoner and deported to the Shewa. The first Italian experience in the Horn of Africa ended here. It could hardly have been more disastrous and humiliating—and yet the lesson went unheeded.[25]

provoked the rebellion of the *Degiac*, Bahta Hagòs, ferociously repressed on 18 December 1894.

25 See Paulos Milkias and Getachew Metaferia (eds), *The Battle of Adwa: Reflections on Ethiopia's Historic Victory Against European Colonialism* (New York: Algora, 2005). [Trans].

FOUR

UP AGAINST THE BOXERS IN CHINA

The lesson of Adwa, however, did not suffice. The sight of the battlefield glistening with the white bones of 5,000 bodies stripped bare by vultures and hyenas was not enough, nor was the ransom of 10 million lire paid to Emperor Menelik to free the prisoners, nor was the contempt of the other nations who underscored that this was the first time a European army had been so emphatically defeated by an African one. None of it was enough.

If prestige had been the basic reason for Italy's entrance into Africa—an attribute entirely lost at Adwa—then the main motivation to enter China was the hope of saving face, responding to Beijing having denied them a concession at Sanmen Bay.[1] These were the years of the great assault on the Qing Empire, whose Manchu dynasty was experiencing an unstoppable decline. The British, Russians, Japanese and Germans all aimed at snatching up concessions, zones of influence, mines and authorizations for buildings railways: a competition for partition. To many it seemed that China would now face the same fate as Africa. All that was lacking was a new Berlin Congress to codify the allotments; as

---

1 For the Sanmen Bay episode, as well as an overview of the Boxers in general, see Xiang Lanxin, *The Origins of the Boxer War: A Multinational Study* (London and New York: Routledge, 2003), pp. 79–102. [Trans.]

the nineteenth century came to a close, China was already host to 62 foreign 'settlements'.

A new and furious rush to slice up the country was triggered in June 1900, when the diplomatic quarter in Beijing was laid siege by the Boxer rebels (Yìhéquán, officially known as the Society of Righteous and Harmonious Fists) with support from sections of the Chinese army and the tacit consent of the Empress Dowager Cixi.[2] The Boxers were immediately demonized by diplomatic officials and newspapers the world over. They were, without doubt, responsible for killing missionaries and Chinese converts to Christianity, as well as for destroying their private property, but the ferocity with which they did so needs to be put in the context of that particular moment of extraordinary, world-shaking change.[3] The Boxers brought together landless peasants, artisans, rickshaw

2 On the Boxers and on China in general, see Victor Purcell, *The Boxer Uprising* (Cambridge: Cambridge University Press, 1963); Auguste Gérard, *Ma mission en Chine, 1893–1887* (Paris: Plon, 1918); Fernand Farjenel, *La Morale chinoise, fondement des sociétés d'Extrême-Orient* (Paris: Giard & Brière, 1906); Giuseppe De Luigi, *La Cina contemporanea. Viaggio e note* (Milan: Treves, 1912); Glauco Licata, *Notabili della terza Italia* (Rome: Cinque Luna, 1968) [which includes the memoirs of Salvago Raggi.—Trans.]; Mario Sabattini and Paolo Santangelo, *Storia della Cina. Dalle origini alla fondazione della Repubblica* (Rome and Bari: Laterza, 1986).

3 There are hundreds of volumes about the persecution of the Catholic clergy in China, published almost entirely by religious organizations. While not without value, they nevertheless nearly always omit the Chinese side of matters. See Luigi Crescitelli, *Vita del servo di Dio Padre Alberico Crescitelli, missionario apostolico nello Scen-si meridionale in China* (Avellino: Tipografia Gennaro Ferraro, 1914); Gerardo Brambilla, *La Chiesa di Cina e i suoi fasti* (Milan: Istituto delle Missioni Estere, 1917); Giovanni Ricci and Ercolano Porta, *Storia della missione francescana e del vicariato apostolico del Hunan meridionale dalle sue origini ai giorni nostri* (Bologna: Stabilimenti Poligrafici Riuniti, 1925); Giovanni Ricci, *Pagine di eroismo cristiano* (Lonigo: Tipografia Moderna, 1925); Giovanni Baur, *Il servo di Dio P. Giuseppe Freinademez* (Vienna: Tipografia missionaria San Gabriele, 1942); Lorenzo M. Balconi, *Trentatré anni in Cina* (Milan: Pontificio Istituto delle Missioni Estere, 1943); Giancarlo Politi, *Martiri in Cina* (Bologna: EMI, 1998); Amelio Crotti, *Noè Tacconi, 1879–1942. Il priimo*

and sedan-chair carriers, low-level functionaries and former soldiers who had watched in horror the expansion of the rail network, the construction of telegram lines, the appearance of steamboats on their rivers and the introduction of factory-made fabric and yarn. All this was new and—in the short-term, at least—meant unemployment.

Those who had brought these novelties were the foreigners, especially the engineers on the railroads and in the mines. Thus they were the targets of a ferocious hatred, along with another category of persons: the missionaries, Catholic and Protestant alike. A Chinese text produced during Mao Zedong's rule explained that 'the foreign missionaries, especially the Catholics, built churches by expropriating the land, threatening local functionaries, swallowing up the administration, intervening in trials, rounding up criminals and turning them into "converts" who they then utilized to oppress the masses. Of course, this way of behaving provoked the indignation of the Chinese people.'[4]

The source is doubtless not without bias. And yet Peter Fleming reached the same conclusions; indeed, he went further still, emphasizing that the secular interventions of the Catholic missionaries knew no bounds. In an imperial request presented on 15 March 1899, the missionaries demanded unconditionally the same political rights and privileges as high-ranking Chinese officials, i.e. for Christian bishops to be treated like governor generals. Fleming comments: 'The effect of this measure on Chinese opinion can approximately be gauged by imagining nineteenth-century British reactions to an announcement in the Court

---

Vescovo di Kaifeng (Cina) (Bologna: EMI, 1999). According to these authors, the total number of Christian victims of the Boxers shifts between 20,000 and 30,000.

4 Jian Bozan (翦伯赞), Shao Xunzheng (邵 循正) and Hu Hua (胡华), *Concise History of China*, 2nd EDN (Beijing: Foreign Language Press, 1981) [Del Boca consulted the Italian translation of 1960].

Circular that senior witch-doctors were to have equal precedence with Lords Lieutenant.'⁵

No one in Europe took the time to truly understand the situation before demonizing the Boxers. Commentators limited themselves to declaring that the rebels belonged to one of the many Chinese secret societies, that they wore blue shirts and blue trousers and tied red bands around their heads, that they claimed to be invincible to gunfire (of which even the Empress Dowager was convinced) and that their battle cray was *Sha! Sha!* (Kill! Kill!). It did not occur to anyone that the revolt, except in the most savage way, expressed an opposition to the increased foreign presence, and its resultant transformation of values and customs. It was with this hatred for the Boxers that Emperor Wilhelm II, in addressing the German contingent departing for China from Bremen on 27 July 1900, barked that:

> When you meet the foe you will defeat him. No quarter will be given, no prisoners will be taken. Let all who fall into your hands be at your mercy. Just as the Huns a thousand years ago, under the leadership of Attila, gained a reputation in virtue of which they still live in a historical tradition, so may the name of Germany become known in such a manner in China that no Chinaman will ever again dare to look askance at a German.⁶

The American, Austrian, British, French, Japanese and Italian contingents sailed out from different ports within a few days of one another, counting more than 20,000 soldiers in total. Their target was Beijing, where 473 foreign citizens, defended by 451 soldiers, were being besieged in their

---

5 Peter Fleming, *The Siege at Peking* (Hong Kong, Oxford and New York: Oxford University Press, 1986[1959]), p. 42. [The use of the fiercely British Fleming as a source—like Del Boca, a soldier, journalist, traveller and writer prior to historian—is meant to contrast with the previous Maoist quotation.—Trans.]

6 Reported in the *Weser Zeitung*, translation from the *London Times*, 30 July 1900. For the original, see Johannes Prenzler (ed.), *Die Reden Kaiser Wilhelms II* (Leipzig: Reclan, 1904), VOL. 2. pp. 209–12. [Trans.]

respective diplomatic quarters by thousands of Boxers. They also needed to provide support to Admiral Edward Seymour of the British Royal Navy, whose land force—following an unproductive attempt to march on the city—had been forced to retreat to Tianjin.[7] No time could be spared: not only was the Boxers' revolt extending across Northern China, but also, in the besieged neighbourhoods of Beijing, munitions and rations were starting to dwindle, including in the fenced-off zone around the Catholic cathedral of Beitang.

The new Chinese adventure did not raise any particular enthusiasm in Italy. The memory of Adwa and its 5,000 dead was still fresh. A year earlier, when parliament had discussed the proposal to request the government in Beijing to concede the Bay of Sanmen—coming in at the end of the 'scramble for concessions'—the opposition had reacted very negatively. In the session on 1 May 1899, Republican politician Salvatore Barzilai declared: 'After the disappointments and disasters in Africa, here we are being dragged away even further than the Red Sea, towards the Pacific. Now they tell us all of a sudden that Italy's true interests of lie in the Pacific Ocean, and all the ministers' trained parrots will now go on repeating this all about town.'[8]

In the same session, socialist Leonida Bissolati took the floor, claiming in turn:

> We've learnt a thing or two about these coastal occupations by now. Military reasoning would have it that, after the coast has been occupied, you go on to occupy a piece of the country inland; and this way the occupation expands out to include

---

7 On the disastrous expedition of Seymour's column, which saw 62 casualties and 223 wounded (of which 5 Italians dead and 8 wounded), see Eugenio Chiminelli, *Nel Paese dei Draghi e delle Chimere* (Perugia: Lapi, 1903), pp. 205–49; Ufficio Storico della Regia Marina, *L'opera della R. Marina in Cina* (Florence: Vallecchi, 1935), pp. 71–97.

8 Salvatore Barzilai, *Vita internazionale* (Florence: Quattrini, 1911), p. 15.

large tracts of land, as was the case at Massawa [. . .]. Today's Chinese expedition is being planned, organized and executed all while our country is only just coming out of a terrible crisis of poverty, and while law and order is still under a state of permanent siege [. . .]. We socialists will give this policy neither man nor penny.[9]

In 1899, thanks above all to Beijing's blanket refusal to concede the Bay of Sanmen to Italy, the Chinese expedition was cancelled. But just one year later, despite the barrage of criticism from the parliamentary opposition—and despite the fact that the Left had obtained an extraordinary result in the 1900 elections—the new government's line prevailed (overseen by new conservative president, Giuseppe Saracco). In the session of 6 July, Republican MP Napoleone Colajanni, known for his moral stature and for exposing a banking scandal in Rome, aimed his provocative words at the government benches, albeit in vain: 'What would you say if tomorrow some foreigner said "I rather fancy the port of Messina" and then took it? And if he then did the same with Naples? This is exactly how the Europeans are operating in China!'[10]

The contingent was waved off from Naples on 19 July by Umberto I himself. The King (who would be assassinated 10 days later by anarchist Gaetano Bresci) was not the kind of man who could have delivered a speech like Wilhelm II's on the Huns. He limited himself, instead, to specifying that the troops were departing to defend 'a humanity that has been trodden underfoot, and the people's sacred rights', inviting the soldiers to 'remember the prestige of the Italian army and honour our country'.[11] Vittorio Emanuele III, who succeeded to the throne on 30

---

9 Leonida Bissolati, *La politica estera dell'Italia dal 1897 al 1920* (Milan: Treves, 1923), p. 36 and pp. 49–50.

10 Cited in Ferdinando Fontana, *In viaggio per la Cina* (Milan: Tipograifa Nazionale di V. Ramperti, 1900), p. 275.

11 Cited in Raffaele Ciasca, *Storia coloniale dell'Italia contemporanea* (Milan: Hoepli, 1940), p. 339.

July, would probably have been far more laconic given the same occasion. He did not share his father's enthusiasm for the Chinese expedition. Indeed, writing in a letter sent on 9 September to his old governor, General Egidio Osio, he noted: 'when we finally make China pay the significant costs of this expedition, we must conclude the whole Chinese adventure and let private initiatives do what they can over there. One should not send soldiers before sending merchants. In brief, one should not set about making a second Africa.'[12]

The main body of the Italian mission comprised one infantry battalion, another of rifles, a battery of machine gunners, a mixed detachment of engineers and a field hospital. All together this amounted to 83 officials, 1,882 soldiers and 178 quadrupeds. This command was assumed on 16 July by Colonel Vincenzo Garioni, who years later would become the governor of Tripolitania. The contingent left Naples on 19 July on board three steamboats (the *Singapore*, the *Giava* and the *Marco Minghetti*), and arrived at the bay of Taku at dawn on 29 August. One reads in the official report from the Italian Ministry of War that 'due to inconveniences deriving from the hurried departure and confused loading,'[13] the corps arrived at their destination in a pitiful state. The damp had almost completely destroyed the food supplies, especially the flour and sugar. Pulling no punches, the report continues: 'The humidity produced serious damage to nearly all the items loaded on board: the weapons were rusty, the leather mouldy, even the clothes the officers had packed away in their trunks had grown damp.'[14] And though relatively and luckily contained, the lack of space on board the *Giava* had also contributed to an outbreak of typhoid.

---

12 Cited in Giovanni Artieri, *Cronaca del Regno d'Italia. Da Porta Pia all'Intervento* (Milan: Mondadori, 1977), p. 805.

13 Amedeo Tosti, *La spedizione italiana in Cina, 1900–1901* (Rome: Provveditorato Generale dello Stato, 1926), p. 63.

14 Tosti, *La spedizione italiana*, pp. 60–61.

Yet the worst was to come when the contingent disembarked at the port of Tongku. Unlike the other European powers, Italy had no Chinese concessions, meaning that the landing had not been officially authorized. Colonel Tommaso Salsa expressed his full shock and rage in a letter he penned to his mother back home:

> It is painful to say it, but our Navy has been witness to such unbelievable improvidence here—and, indeed, everywhere. Not even the smallest landing craft had been procured to unload the steamboats at Taku, nor a strip of land for the troops or warehouses, not a single gangway [. . .]. And so we ended up making a terrible impression, having to continuously go and beg for this or that from the other nations [. . .]. I don't know if these facts will come out, but I think it will be difficult to keep them hidden. I can tell you that I am truly very ashamed of our country.[15]

In another letter, Salsa gave his opinion on the causes of the Chinese crisis:

> To tell the truth, the principal reason for the current actions against foreigners should be sought in the intolerance and intrigues of every kind enacted by the missionaries, who use the severity of religion for political and earthly ambitions. I believe it would be a good thing if, for a few decades and perhaps more, missions from whatever religion or nation were not to set foot in China.[16]

---

15 Emilio Canevari and Giovanni Comisso, *Il generale Tommaso Salsa e le sue campagne coloniali. Lettere e documenti* (Milan: Mondadori, 1935), p. 329. The letter is dated 6 September 1900, Tianjin.

16 Canevari and Comisso, *Tommaso Salsa*, p. 327. Letter dated near Ta-Ku, 30 August 1900.

Salsa had participated in the invasion of Eritrea, and in in the construction of that cruel universe we have already described above. He had even witnessed the devastation at Adwa. Nevertheless, when he arrived in Tianjin, he was horrified by the wreckage he encountered: 'Bridges destroyed, cannons dismantled, trains bombed, entire wagons burnt down to their iron bones, like the skeletons of giants. Tianjin is a heap of ruins, everything has collapsed beneath the devouring power of flames and the destructive power of modern artillery.'[17]

Luigi Barzini, in Tianjin as a correspondent for the *Corriere della Sera*, wrote in similar tones:

> There is not a house still standing. The trees have been slashed and sliced by the hurricane of lead that exploded across the city for eight days. You walk across rubble [...]. There is desolation and poverty everywhere. Tianjin, the most densely inhabited city of Northern China, its blossoming metropolis, is no more. [...] The Peiho Bridge, across from the French concession, has been destroyed. Now you have to make the crossing over some boards which only just about stay afloat. The swirling water is putrid with cadavers, carrying the carcasses of animals and Boxers, swollen and bruised, their skeletal hands at the waters' edge. You hear nothing but the marching of soldiers, the noise of carts, the barking of commands.[18]

On 8 September, the news arrived that the Boxers had gathered in the village of Duliu; a large mixed contingent of foreign troops was formed, led by General Arthur Dorward of the British Army. Lieutenant Colonel Salsa took part in the action, but was less than enthusiastic about the results. Indeed, he wrote again to his mother:

---

17 Canevari and Comisso, *Tommaso Salsa*, p. 332. Letter dated 6 September 1900.

18 Luigi Barzini, *Avventure in Oriente* (Milan: Mondadori, 1959), p. 18.

But when the nets were finally pulled in, not even the smallest fish had been caught in the trap. The Boxers had disappeared— if indeed they had ever existed—and not a single shot was fired. But the English employed their methods, which meant sowing the destruction of the city at fault, and after it had been completely abandoned to looting, it was burnt to the ground with a scientific methodicism. We also took some things, rather than letting the others get everything, but to see all these Indians, Cossacks and Americans, what a race of thieves! [. . .] Once the troops had left, the city was finally set alight by a detachment of the English genius, who didn't leave a single house standing. And just to think that we supposedly came here to bring civilization![19]

Salsa was not alone in complaining about the conduct of the campaign. A medical officer, Giuseppe Messerotti Benvenuti, wrote to his mother from Tianjin on 2 October: 'Our coming here, in terms of the humanitarian aim, has been perfectly useless. It is quite clear by now that the stories about the war were exaggerated, and that Minister's tales of massacres were almost entirely fabricated by those who had an interest in sending a large expedition to China.'[20]

In the following letter, he confirmed Salsa's criticisms, writing in no uncertain terms that 'it seems that the only reason we came here was for plunder'. He also wrote of Italian officers and soldiers 'who have made small fortunes for themselves', in particular a medical officer in the navy who 'looted so much, and with such little care, that they punished him with immediate expatriation'.[21]

---

19 Canevari and Comisso, *Tommaso Salsa*, pp. 336–37.

20 Giuseppe Messerotti Benvenuti, *Un italiano nella Cina dei Boxer. Lettere e fotografie, 1900–1901* (Nicola Labanca ed.) (Modena: Associazione Giuseppe Panini Archivi Modenesi, 2000), p. 24.

21 Messeroti Benvenuti, *Un italiano*, p. 27. Letter dated 10 October 1900.

For his own part, Luigi Barzini underlined the continuous series of pointless massacres that represented nothing other than taking potshots at the Chinese:

> Every limit has been outrun; one might say that the human beast overtook mankind. Not a single home nor fugitive has escaped assassination, looting and arson. The French as much as their friends the Cossacks, the Germans as much as the Japanese, everyone has fallen into this race for criminality without exception. In such a moment as this, one must lower the flag of civilization. [. . .] A German artillery officer told me that he used to kill one Chinese a day, to keep up the troops' morale.[22]

In one of his last letters from China, Salsa—who 12 years later would be awarded a gold medal for his part in the Battle of Ettangi, in Libya—gave a wholesale criticism of the expedition: 'Overall, there is very little that satisfied me about this Chinese campaign, where there is little military honour for us to gain and no practical aim either, given that our government, as usual, has no actual plan and simply advances by bouncing between opposing interests.'[23]

While a section of the troops, as we have seen, tried to clear out pockets of rebellion around Tianjin, massacring civilians when the Boxers themselves gave them the slip, the 'liberating forces' led by Major General Alfred Gaselee of the British Army left Tianjin and marched on Beijing, encountering little resistance.[24] On 13 August, the troops amassed under

---

22 Barzini, *Avventure*, pp. 22–23.

23 Canevari and Comisso, *Tommaso Salsa*, p. 339.

24 The Chinese resistance would have been quite different if the two divisions led by the governor of Shandong, General Yuan Shikai [袁世凱], had been engaged—which had been armed and trained to a European level. He was sharply opposed to the Boxers and had murdered several to show how baseless was the legend of their

the city walls; and the following day, the Japanese, American, French, Russian and British soldiers, subdivided into four columns, launched their final attack, preceded by open fire from the combined artillery.[25] With the final resistance defeated, they entered the capital and liberated the besieged international legations and the Cathedral of Beitang, while the Empress Dowager and her followers fled, disguised as peasants.[26]

The Boxer siege of the legations had lasted 55 days. Over the course of the fighting, 76 foreigners had been killed and another 150 wounded. The balance of losses within the Cathedral perimeter was heavier, where 3,500 Chinese Christians had taken refuge, against whom the Boxers had launched 2,500 rounds of cannon fire. Immediately after the liberation of the siege, the international forces proceeded to divide up the capital, and it was in this phase, according to all of the sources, that the victors' behaviour scaled new peaks of cruelty. Historians Marianne Bastide, Marie-Claire Bergère and Jean Chesneaux describe the situation thus:

---

invulnerability. See the portrait in Jerome Ch'en [陳志讓], *Yuan Shih-k'ai, 1859– 1916. Brutus Assumes the Purple* (London: George Allen and Unwin, 1961).

25 On the attack on Beijing, see Colonel Edouard de Pélacot, *Expédition de Chine de 1900* (Paris: Charles-Lavanzelle, 1901). The copy in my possession bears the following dedication by the author: '*à sa Majesté Victor Emmanuel III, Roi d'Italie. Hommage de profond respect en souvenir de la collaboration des détachements Italiens et Francais pour la defense du Pe-tang (1900), Tananarive, le 16 février 1904*'. The book also bears the ex libris of the King and the words: '*Proprietà privata di Sua Maestà il re Vittorio Emanuele III*'.

26 On the Empress Cixi [慈禧太后] and her court, see John Ottway Percy Bland and Edmund Trelawny Backhouse, *China Under the Empress Dowager* (London: Heinemann, 1910); Princess Der Ling, *Two Years in the Forbidden City* (New York: Moffat, Yard and Company, 1911); Daniele Varè, *Yehonala. Storia dell'imperatrice Tzu Hsi e del trapasso dalla vecchia Cina alla nuova* (Florence: Bemporad, 1933); Carlo Dragoni, *La meravigliosa vita di Tzu Hsi, imperarice* (Milan: Mondadori, 1943).

The systematic slaughter and plunder which then began far surpassed the worst excesses committed by the Boxers. In an orgy of cruelty, the foreign troops massacred thousands of men in Beijing; women and whole families committed suicide rather than survive the dishonour; the whole city was sacked. The imperial palace was occupied by foreigners and stripped of most of its treasures.[27]

Celebrated writer Pierre Loti, on mission for the French newspaper *Le Figaro*, wrote of the 'madness of murderous rage and destruction' wreaked upon the cursed 'City of Purity':

> The Japanese soldiers arrived, little heroic soldiers of whom I do not wish to speak ill, but who destroy and kill like the barbarian hordes of another era. I have still less desire to criticize our Russian friends, but they sent Cossacks here from the Tartar regions, half-Mongolian Siberians, all of whom are very capable at shooting but who still wage battle in the Asian manner. And then the ruthless Indian cavalry arrived, sent by the British. America sent her own mercenaries. When the Italians, Germans, Austrians and French arrived after the first great excitement of revenge against the Chinese atrocities, they found that nothing had been left intact.[28]

General Adna Chaffee of the United States Army, for his own part, told journalists that one could correctly claim that 'where one real Boxer has been killed since the capture of Beijing, fifty harmless coolies or laborers on the farms, including not a few women and children, have been slain.'[29]

---

27 Marianne Bastide, Marie-Claire Bergère and Jean Chesneux, *China from the Opium Wars to the 1911 Revolution* (Anne Destenay trans.) (New York: Pantheon Books, 1976), p. 334.

28 Pierre Loti, *Les Deniérs jours de Pékin* (Paris: Calmann-Levy, 1901), pp. 75–76.

29 Fleming, *The Siege at Peking*, p. 253.

The sacking of Beijing, with its long list of gratuitous killings, lasted for many months, as each foreign contingent accused the others of looting, all while maintaining a part that would leave their own consciences clean. Italy passed the buck no less than the others, as is quite clear from the official report redacted by the Ministry of War, as well as from journalistic commentary and even from letters sent home by soldiers. In the official report, Amedeo Tosti claimed: 'For its conduct, its demonstrable qualities and the behaviour of its commanders, our contingent was consistently viewed well and with a generalized benevolence.'[30]

Barzini, even while emphasizing the extraordinary deficiencies of the Italian contingent—feeling both pity and disgust at the sight of the riflemen's ragged uniforms[31]—nevertheless wrote in his dispatch for the *Corriere della Sera*: 'Our soldiers are well-meaning, adaptable, jovial and disciplined; their comfort has been reduced to the absolute minimum but they do not complain.'[32] Mario Vallu was more explicit in describing the apparently excellent qualities of the Italian soldier and his total extraneousness from any pillage and massacre:

> We cannot ignore the fact that the Italian soldier, due to his meekness, is generally averse to acts of violence. A brutality that leads to murder, a taste for torturing the harmless, the drive to do evil for mere pleasure—all these wayward instincts, which emerge so easily when a mass of men has snatched victory, belong to the worst kind of delinquency, revealing the innermost character, and do not pertain to our soldier. There lies within

---

30 Tosti, *La specizione*, p. 83.

31 Barzini, *Avventure*, p. 60. This is how he describes the gunners uniforms: 'Their berets had been so long in use that they now displayed a whole array of shades, from crimson to black; their uniforms, dappled with stains, were covered with hardly concealed patches, darned "with a soldier's touch"; their bags, their sagging, threadbare straps, were all held together by string carefully dyed black.'

32 Barzini, *Avventure*, p. 54.

him instead, one might say, a basic goodness of the soul—and even if he is capable of villainous acts through lack of education, it is difficult for him to arrive at such excesses of cruelty.[33]

This shameful discursive game was drastically concluded by Field Marshall Alfred von Waldersee, commander of the German contingent, with a cutting joke: 'Every nationality accords the palm to some other in respect to the art of plundering, but it remains the fact that each and all of them went in hot and strong for loot.'[34] The Italian troops took part in the massacres, looting, arson of homes and public beheadings of Boxers— or people assumed to be as such—along with all the other contingents. The official report of the Ministry of War did not, for example, cover up the fact that the expedition to Baoding, 'one of the heaviest retaliations effected by the allies against the Chinese population' earned the Italians $26,000 in spoils.[35] The one aspect that set them apart was that only the Italians had the problem of trying to appear to be *brava gente*.

The final mass theft carried out by those allied powers in China that participated in the expedition was the imposition of damages for the costs of the war. The figure provided presented an absurd millstone: 450 million maritime tael—the equivalent of 18,000 tonnes of silver. Of this, Italy was due 26,617,000 tael—amounting to 99,813,769 Italian lire.[36] King Vittorio Emanuele II perhaps expected a little more, but the division

---

33 Mario Valli, *Gli avvenimenti in Cina nel 1900 e l'azione della R. Marina italian* (Milan: Hoepli, 1905). Cited by Nicola Labanca in his introduction to Messerotti Benvenuti, *Un italiano*, p. *vii*.

34 Cited in Fleming, *The Siege of Peking*, p. 242, note.

35 Tosti, *La spedizione*, p. 74 and p. 73, respectively.

36 For the treaty signed in Xinchou by 13 plenipotentiaries on 7 September 1901, see Fleming, *Siege of Peking*, pp. 250–51. [The maritime or Haikwan tael [海關兩] was a diplomatic version of the Chinese silver currency. See Frank King, *Money and Monetary Policy in China* (Cambridge: Harvard University Press, 1965).—Trans.]

had been determined according to the number of men sent by each nation.

Furthermore, China was to recognize Italy's 'settlement' at Tianjin, i.e. Italy's outright possession of a piece of land measuring 46 sq. km and inhabited by 17,000 people, situated in the city suburbs between the Russian and Austrian concessions. This was, however, largely swampland, with a village at the centre comprising 700 mud huts. It never brought in a single lira to the treasury; instead, in order to reclaim the marshes and build decent buildings on the site, Italy had to make deposits and anticipate loans reaching the not-insignificant figure of 400,000 lire.[37]

Thus, with a clear loss, ended the Chinese adventure. Perhaps the only person who made himself useful during his long period in the Qing Empire was the medical officer Messerotti Benvenuti. Not only because he eased the sufferings of people in the field hospitals, but also because he brought back to Europe a few hundred photographs he had taken with his Kodak Cartridge. Far from amateur works, these images taken by a simple doctor from Modena depict the ruins of Tiajin, the walls of Beijing, the Imperial Winter Palace, the largest bell in the world, the Empress' bed, the Cathedral of Beitang, Chinese citizens in the stocks, blind musicians, groups of Italian officers, a Mandarin's family. The cruellest photographs were those taken in Beijing on 22 December 1900, a series showing the decapitation of a Chinese man suspected of involvement in the assassination of an Italian soldier. The doctor's comment to the five images reads: 'Perhaps I have a bad soul, but I can assure who that, even though effected in the barbarous manner of the Chinese executioner and his assistants, the sad spectacle did not shock me in the manner that I feared it might have. Perhaps because I was

---

37 See Vincenzo Fileti, *La conessione italiana di Tien-Tsin* (Genoa: Barabino e Gravese, 1921).

convinced of the individual's guilt and the correctness of the punishment.'[38] Among the souvenirs he brought back to his home in Villanova, there was the following small poem. Although it represents a trivial work, it says much about the most generalized activities among the Italian troops:

Se vogliamo confessarci
andiam dal bonzo nella pagoda
Se non troviamo nulla da razziare
noi gli rubiamo i cristi sull'altare.
Ciascuno è convinto di far la sua parte
seguendo un istinto: l'amore per l'arte.

If we want to go to confession
let's go to the little Buddha in his pagoda
And if we don't find anything to loot there
we can go get the Christs from the altar.
For each man knows he's just doing his part
by following an instinct: the love of art.[39]

---

38 Messerotti Benvenuti, *Un italiano*, p. 49. On this topic, also see Michele Smargiassi, 'L'italiano che fotografo l'orrore. Pechino 1901 sembra Bagdad', *Repubblica*, 23 May 2004.

39 Benvenuti, *Un italiano*, p. 56.

FIVE

SHAR AL-SHATT: MASSACRES AND DEPORTATIONS

The pointless, shameful campaign in China should have warned Italy's governments to stay away from undertaking new adventures far from home. Adwa and Beijing should have been enough to demonstrate that this was not the road to regaining prestige for a young nation that not only still needed to prove its presence along its natural borders, but also was discovering new and urgent problems to resolve every day. But the louse of imperialism had already begun to dig down into the new government, despite the stature of its leadership under Giovanni Giolitti.

This time around the goal was Libya. For years it had been common enough to hear that in order to re-establish an equilibrium in the Mediterranean, it would be absolutely necessary to take hold of the two Ottoman provinces (the *vilayetler*) of Tripolitania and Cyrenaica—above all, since the French had occupied Tunisia, a country that Italy had also been eyeing up.[1] The task of convincing public opinion that an occupation of the 'fourth bank' fell into both the inviolable rights of Rome and the indelible plans of destiny was left to political nationalists and the press. From 1903, the nationalists began to hope for the creation of an 'energetic' Italian society, soliciting a reprisal of colonial expansion; they railed

---

1 For Italy's complex relation with Tunisia in the late nineteenth century, see Mark I. Chaote, 'Tunisia, Contested: Italian Nationalism, French Imperial Rule, and Migration in the Mediterranean Basin', *California Italian Studies* 1(1) (2010). [Trans.]

against pacifism, humanitarianism, socialism and internationalism, invoking war—any war whatsoever—'in order to revitalize Italy, condemned to the basest existence by the material poverty of her emigrants and the moral poverty of her politicians'.[2]

Aside from the leaders of the Italian Nationalist Association—such as Enrico Corradini, Luigi Federzoni, Maurizio Maraviglia, Francesco Coppola and Roberto Davanzati—there was a significant group of writers and journalists who had no qualms about fabricating the most spurious stories about Libya's riches. We can turn to Enrico Corradini's words, for example, following his visit to a few gardens in the oasis of Tripoli: 'Such dense olive groves, dark and unpruned, wild and full of olives! Vines that trail on the ground for the weight of their grapes. This is no desert! We are in the promised land.'[3] For his part, Giuseppe Bevione truly knew no bounds, reaching a climax in this frenetic declaration:

> I saw mulberry trees as thick as beeches, olives more gigantic than oaks. The alfalfa can be harvested a dozen times in a single year, while the fruit trees develop in a spectacular manner. In an average year, the grain and melic provide three or four times the yield of the best and rationally cultivated earth in Europe. The barley is world-renowned, bought up entirely by England for its beer [. . .] The grape vines are of an incredible girth, twenty to thirty kilos per tree. The dates are the sweetest and most lustrous that Africa produces.[4]

Wise figures such as Luigi Einaudi, Edoardo Giretti, Gaetano Mosca, Pio Schinetti, Guido Miglioli and Arcangelo Ghisleri came out against the Libyan engagement, noting the dangers and economic burden that would interrupt Italy's path towards modern industrial civilization—

---

2 Pier Ludovico Occhini, *Corradini* (Florence: Rinascimeno del Libro, 1933), p. 213.

3 Enrico Corradini, *L'ora di Tripoli* (Milan: Treves, 1911), p. 74.

4 Giuseppe Bevione, *Come siamo andati a Tripoli* (Turin: Bocca, 1912), p. 171.

and indeed setting it in reverse, as Giretti maintained, pushing it 'towards a backwards kind of barbaric-militaristic society'.[5] Ghisleri—a geographer and historian—contested Libya's supposed agricultural wealth with the authority of someone who had undertaken important research on the North African country: 'According to the studies that I have made of the argument in various aspects, whatever the infatuated and colonizing may write and fantasize from improvised erudition, we believe that one can entirely exclude the idea that Tripolitania could ever become a "populizing colony" for Italian farmers'.[6] Gaetano Salvemini, finally, defined Libya as a 'vast abyss of sand' that would swallow up men and money for years on end.[7]

There was no justification to go to Tripoli, just as there had been none to go to Massawa or Beijing. There was simply the desire for a brawl, to make war, to impose one's will on others, to loot and destroy. Joseph Conrad's lines in *Heart of Darkness* are extraordinarily pertinent. Here is Captain Marlow, describing to his sailors the Roman legions who made their way up the Thames on fragile wooden boats:

> They were no colonists; their administration was merely a squeeze and nothing more, I suspect. They were conquerors, and for that you want only brute force—nothing to boast of, when you have it, since your strength is just an accident arising from the weakness of others. They grabbed what they could get for the sake of what was to be got. It was just robbery with violence, aggravated murder on a great scale, and men going

---

5 Edoardo Giretti, 'A proposito della Tripolitania. Ottimismo o pessimismo coloniale?', *La Riforma sociale*, December 1911.

6 Arcangelo Ghisleri, *Tripolitania e Cirenaica dal Mediterrano al Sahara* (Milan and Bergamo: Società Editoriale Italiana–Istituto Italiano d'Arti Grafiche, 1912), p. 99. 178.

7 Gaetano Salvemini, *La politica estera dell'Italia, 1871–1914* (Florence: Barbera, 1944), p. 178.

at it blind—as is very proper for those who tackle a darkness. The conquest of the earth, which mostly means the taking it away from those who have a different complexion or slightly flatter noses than ourselves, is not a pretty thing when you look into it too much.[8]

It really was no pretty thing at all. The men comprising the Italian expedition about to land in Libya were not very different, and certainly no better, than the Roman legionaries who had sailed up the Thames to invade Britain. The ultimate motivation, for the former as for the latter, was the same: a long and drawn-out act of theft.

The Italian Prime Minister, Giovanni Giolitti, did not believe in the fairy tale of the 'promised land'. Since he was by character contrary to undertaking risky engagements, and known for always letting politics at home take precedence, everyone was surprised when he agreed to the intervention. People tried to discover the reasons for his about-face. It was said that he was trying to create an outlet for rampant nationalist tendencies; and by offering them Africa, he was providing them with a diversion away from their more dangerous ambitions—those that looked beyond Italy's Northern borders and towards the Balkans. It was said that he was driven by the search for a better balance in the Mediterranean, or that he had fully signed up to the program presented to him by Foreign Minister Antonino di San Giuliano. Yet in the end it was Giolitti himself, at the Regio Theatre in Turin, who explained the real reasoning behind his decision, in a speech delivered on 7 October 1911. It was an extraordinary act of justification, uncharacteristic of this cold and cynical, impassionate man:

> There are facts which impose themselves with historical fate upon us, which no people can avoid without irreparably tearing

---

8 Joseph Conrad, *Heart of Darkness* (New York: Barnes and Noble, 1994), pp. 9–10.

themselves away from their destiny. In such moments, government has a duty to assume full responsibility, for any hesitation or delay can signal the beginning of a political decline, producing consequences that a people will then deplore for many long years to come—or even for centuries.[9]

These read more like the words of Corradini than those of the then Prime Minister. Shifting from the realm of politics and the economy to those of the irrational and the supernatural, here Giolitti proves himself as having identified and grasped in the correct moment the irrefutable goal indicated by fate. But what Giolitti probably thought—and could certainly not have revealed at Turin—was that the Libyan expedition would soon be over after a brief martial 'walk in the park', and that the other European powers, as Antonino di San Giuliano theorized, would find themselves 'with a *fait accompli*, almost even before being able to discuss it'.[10] Giolitti based his assuredness on the information that he continued to receive from the consul in Tripoli, Carlo Galli, who not only minimized the dangers in the landing phase, but above all excluded any possibility of collaboration between the Arabs and the Ottomans. Nor was there any fear of the call for a holy war: the coastal populations simply would not have agreed, and 'those tribes that perhaps might give heed to such an appeal are nevertheless poor, unarmed, or too far away to provide any cause for concern'.[11] Finally, Galli assured Giolitti that the Arabs would in fact welcome the Italians as liberators, as they were tired of Ottoman rule.

9 Cited in Nino Valeri, *Giolitti* (Turin: Utet, 1971), pp. 218–19. For Giolitti's about-turn, see Brunello Vigezzi, *L'Italia unita e le sfide della politica estera. Dal Risorgimento alla Repubblica* (Milan: Unicopli, 1997), pp. 83–103.

10 Giovanni Giolitti, *Quarant'anni di politica italiana. Dalle carte di Giovanni Giolitti, Volume 3: Dai prodromi della Grande guerra al fascismo, 1910–1928* (Claudio Pavone ed) (Milan: Feltrinelli, 1962), p. 53.

11 Archivio centrale dello Stato, Rome: Carte Giolitti, b. 22, f. 59, telegram n. 1059/449.

On the basis of this information, Giolitti acted without delay. On 26 September, he sent an ultimatum to the Ottoman Empire which, through its brutal and unjustified tone, was equivalent to a declaration of war. The document, as a French scholar noted shortly after, 'did not contain the vaguest kind of grievance that might constitute a *casus belli*'.[12] As soon as the ultimatum ran out on 3 October, Vice-Admiral Luigi Faravelli moved in on the Libyan coastline with 20 vessels, including battleships, cruisers and destroyers, and opened fire on the old forts of Tripoli (which were defended by old-fashioned canons). The landing took place two days later without incident, and within a couple of weeks the entire expeditionary force, commanded by General Carlo Caneva and counting some 34,000 men and 72 cannons, took possession of Tripoli and Homs in Tripolitania, and of Bengasi, Derna and Tonruk in Cyrenaica.

The Italians did not find it easy, however, to take possession and install themselves across the board. In Derna, Bengasi and Homs, they met with serious fighting; in the last of these locations, Galli's thesis on the impossibility of an alliance between the Ottomans and the Arabs fell to pieces when 1,000 Arabs came to the aid of 500 men in the Ottoman garrison—and proved to be excellent fighters as well. This new and unforeseen fact should have acted as a warning to the high command, but they were deaf to it. As Giorgio Rochat has rightly observed:

> Yet again, a colonial war was undertaken by a completely unprepared force. The only thing that might diminish any of the high command's responsibility is the mechanism of nationalist propaganda, which was as furious as it was deprived of any real sense, leading to an underestimating of the difficulties involved in the expedition and the local population's ability to resist.[13]

---

12 'R. L', 'La Guerre de Tripoli et l'esprit public en Italie', *Chronique sociale de France*, March 1912, pp. 81–82.

13 Giorgio Rochat and Giulio Massobrio, *Breve storia dell'esercito italiano dal 1861 al 1914* (Turin: Einaudi, 1978), pp. 157–58.

On the evening of 22 October 1911, Carlo Caneva, General of the Armed Forces in Libya, led some 22,500 men arranged along a fairly narrow perimeter around Tripoli, ranging from the village of Shar al-Shatt to al-Ras al-Ahmar.[14] While the defences along three-quarters of the line, from the west to the south, were easy enough to organize (because the trenches had the desert in front and a wall of palm groves behind), the eastern line, from Fort Mesri up to the sea, passed through a series of oases and two million palm trees, a veritable labyrinth of incised pathways and clay walls, well covered in obstacles such as palms, olives, thick shrubbery, houses, tombs and wells.

The first attack arrived with the dawn of 23 October, hitting to the right of the line. An hour later came the second attack, to the centre. At 7.45 a.m. the third and decisive assault struck to the left, in the heart of the oases, between Fort Mesri and Shar al-Shatt. Right from the start, the Italians realized that the Arabs were fighting alongside the Ottomans, and that these were not only the guerrillas that had come from inland but also the inhabitants of Tripoli and from the oases themselves. This was, essentially, that generalized insurrection which the consul, Galli, had rejected as a possibility. Indeed, a widespread revolt was underway, involving everyone, men and women, old and young, and like all such rebellions, it was inspired not only by xenophobia but also a religious fanaticism.

In the labyrinth of the oases near Shar al-Shatt, two rifle companies from the 11th Regiment were surrounded and annihilated in the space of a few hours. Surrender was futile, as the Arabs did not take prisoners. One of the few soldiers who escaped the disaster reported: 'Our dead at Shar al-Shatt are scattered everywhere, unburied; many are nailed to the date trees like Jesus Christ. Some had their eyes sewn together; others

---

14 Del Boca gives 'Ras Lamhar'; this must be الرأس الأحمر, i.e. the Red Cape. The location was to the east of the old Ottoman fort; see the map in Angelo Del Boca, *Gli italiani in Libia. Tripoli bel suol d'amore, 1860–1922* (Rome: Laterza, 1986), p. 103. [Trans.]

were buried up to their necks in the earth, so that you can only see their heads; a great many had their genitals cut off.[15] By the end of the day of fighting, the final count was extremely serious: 21 officials and 482 soldiers killed, to which needed to be added those who had been assassinated within the walls of Tripoli, where the revolt had reached by midday.

The Arab-Ottoman attack of 23 October, involving perhaps 8,000–10,000 well-armed and fiercely driven men, and concluding with episodes of unspeakable brutality, provoked an equally charged counter-reaction. Over the course of the repression, a thousand Arabs were indiscriminately killed (some of the Libyan sources, and a few European ones, claim as many as 4,000 dead),[16] driven by the irrational but nevertheless widespread

---

15 Felice Piccioli, *Diario di un bersagliere* (Milan: Il Formichere, 1974), p. 26. As Major Braganze wrote in his historical diary for his section: 'The horrendous ferocity was driven by the fact that the riflemen, more enterprising than the infantry, had not resisted from harassing the Arab women, despite our very rigid orders and surveillance.' Guido Valabrega, 'Il servizio trasporti e tappe nella guerra libica, *Africa* 3 (1984): 442.

16 'The defeated occupying troops reacted by massacring the neighbourhood of al-Manshiyyah in Tripoli, where no less than 4,000 people were killed, and countless Beduin villages burned to the ground, along with their tents and herds.' [Muhammad 'Abd al-Nabî al Daqâlî, 'Gli esiliati libici nell'arcipelago delle Termiti. Una pagina drammatica' in Francesco Sulpizi and Salaheddin Hasan Sury (eds), *Gli esiliati libici nel periodo coloniale* (Rome: IsIAO Centro Libico per gli Studi Storici, 2003), p. 119.] The same figure is of 4,000 deaths is provided by Paolo Balera in his well-known report: 'The English and German journalists have returned their press cards to General Carlo Caneva in protest against the massacre of the Arabs. Everyone saw the horrific sight. The correspondent for the *Westminster Gazette* claimed that out of the 400 bodies of women, girls and boys, and those of the 4,000 men cut down with showers of lead, no more than 100 could be defined as guilty.' [Cited in Romain Rainero, *Paolo Vaera e l'opposizione democratica all'impres di Tripoli* (Rome: L'Erma di Bretschneider, 1983), p. 99]. The same figure is also given, finally, in Mahmud Edeek, 'Les Dimensions politiques, économiques et sociales de la conquête italienne en Libya' in Anna Baldinetti (ed.), *Modren and Contemporary Libya: Sources and Historiographies* (Rome: IsIAO, 2003), p. 93.

conviction that the Arabs of Tripoli had 'betrayed' the Italians. The newspapers fomented the theory of this supposed betrayal through barbed summaries abundant with words such as 'traitor', 'trickery', 'insidious', 'sneaky', a 'vile' or 'conspiratorial' attack—an act that everyone feared calling by its true name: rebellion. The only figure who did not talk of betrayal was Luigi Barzini, who instead admitted a whole series of errors: 'We came here without preparing either the terrain or ourselves. [. . .] that's how Shar al-Shatt came about. Our self-delusion was so great that we got there without heeding the countless signs which should have set us on our guard.'[17] An image remained from those days of horrific repression that can be considered symbolic of that cruel and unjust war: the gallows erected in Tripoli (at Piazza del Pane), where 14 Arabs were hanged in one go. The vision of those bodies lined up, stiff with rigor mortis, their necks broken and twisted, their clothes ragged and torn, was meant to serve as a healthy warning for the 'rebels'.[18] As we shall see, from that point on, the gallows sprung up across Libya like an unstoppable weed, inspiring Giuseppe Scalarini to sketch a series of horrifying satirical drawings that firmly pinned the responsibility on Giolitti and his circle.[19]

Nevertheless, the worst was still to come. The 4,000 dead in the manhunt that swept through the streets of Tripoli, tracking down the 'treacherous' Arabs, was not enough, nor were the collective hangings in the Piazza del Pane. The day after the Battle of Shar al-Shatt, at 4.45 p.m., Giolitti sent the following telegram to General Caneva:

---

17 Luigi Albertini, *Epistolario, 1911–1926*, VOL. 1: *Dalla guerra di Libia alla Grande Guerra* (Milan: Mondadori, 1968), pp. 74 and 46–48.

18 For photographs of the war in Libya, see Nicola Labanca (ed.), *Un nodo. Immagini e documenti sulla repreessione coloniale italiana in Libia* (Manduira: Lacaita, 2002) and Alberto Angrisani, *Immagini della guerra di Libia* (Nicola Labanca and Luigi Tomassini eds) (Manduria: Lacaita, 1997).

19 For these political cartoons and their creator, see Mario De Micheli, *Scalarini. Vita e disegni del grande caricaturista politico* (Milan: Feltrinelli, 1978). [Trans.]

YOU WILL SEND ARRESTED REBELS NOT SHOT ON SITE TO THE TREMITI
ISLANDS IN THE ADRIATIC FOR FORCED CONFINEMENT. YOU SHALL
DIRECT THEM THERE ADVISING ME OF DEPARTURE. THE TREMITI
ISLANDS CAN HOLD OVER FOUR HUNDRED PRISONERS. I AM SENDING
THE INSPECTOR GENERAL FOR PUBLIC SECURITY TO ADMINISTER THEIR
ARRIVAL.[20]

The Arabs that Caneva embarked for Italy between 25 and 30 October,
however, counted many more than 400. The number was perhaps closer
to 4,000, meaning that they were also sent to Ustica, Ponza, Caserta, Gaeta
and Favignana. Just as is the case with the number of people killed during
the repression, no official document tells us how many there were; unfortunately, Libyan historians, despite meticulous work over the past 20 years,
have still not been able to assist further. What was the criteria according
to which the Arabs were chosen for deportation? An eye-witness, journalist
Giuseppe Bevione, wrote: 'There are men of all ages: men with long beards
and clean-chinned youngsters; Black men with horrid faces and Arabs
with purer profiles. They carry nothing with them save for the scrap of
cloth that covers them.'[21] They were made to walk through the night,
escorted by soldiers who pointed their bayonets at them, driven towards
the castle's quay, the ships' lights cutting across them. Bevione continues:

> The Arabs walks with the soldiers in total silence, without even
> allowing their bare feet to make a noise, like shadows. They stick
> close together, the one behind holds onto a scrap of tunic of the
> man before him. Departing for the unknown, they feel the need
> to forge a single block, to submerge themselves into an unfeeling
> mass, a herd, a storm.[22]

---

20 Archivio centrale dello Stato, Rome: Carte Giolitti, b. 22, f. 58, telegram n. 27979
(24 October 1911).

21 Bevione, *Come siamo andati a Tripoli*, p. 371.

22 Bevione, *Come siamo andati a Tripoli*, p. 371.

A few ferries brought them to the anchored steamboats: the *Nilo*, the *Serbia*, the *Molfetta*, the *Minas* and the *Rumania*.[23]

Some of the deportees had been captured bearing arms, but the majority had been arrested in their streets and houses without even a shred of proof regarding their guilt. They were not even identified at the quay, which explains the great uncertainty about their precise number and destinations. Giolitti and Caneva were only concerned with removing the pressure of local resistance movements from Tripoli and, at the same time, imposing a striking demonstration of force. The report for the commission on prisoners, drawn up for the Ministry of War, recognized that the arrests had often been arbitrary and the naval departures chaotic:

> The arrests that preceded the forced transfers took place in haste: the arrestees are a mix of beggars, rich land owners, workers, fruit sellers, merchants and peasants; they are the elderly, women, children and young people; their names have not been recorded on any lists other than after their arrival in Italy; the Italian authorities in Libya made no attempt at this, given the speed with which the deportees were made to alight on the ships.[24]

There is no document that could better depict the atmosphere of fear, decisional ineptness and disorientation that inflicted Giolitti, Caneva and their collaborators. 'The ships that brought the first waves of prisoners

---

23 On Shar al-Shatt and the subsequent deportations, see Rainero, *Paolo Valera*; Angelo Del Boca, *Gli Italiani in Libia. Volume 1: Tripoli bel suol d'amore, 1860–1922* (Rome and Bari: Laterza, 1986), pp. 96–156; Lino Del Fra, *Sciara Sciat. Genocidio nell'oasi: l'esercito italiano a Tripoli* (Rome: Datanews, 1995); Simone Bernini, 'Documenti sulla repressione italiana in Libia agli inizi della colonizzazione, 1911–1918' in Labanca (ed.), *Un nodo*, pp. 117–202. [Also see Francesca Di Pasquale, 'The "Other" at Home: Deportation and Transportation of Libyans to Italy During the Colonial Era (1911–1943)', *IRSH* 63 (2018), pp. 211–31.—Trans.]

24 Cited in Habîb Wada'ah el-Hasnawî, 'Effetti psico-sociali delle operazioni di deportazione dei libici nelle isole italiane sugli esiliati e i loro parenti in epoca coloniale, 1911–1943', in Sulpiz and Sury (eds), *Gli esiliati libici*, pp. 31–32.

were so full that they shook dangerously across the Mediterranean Sea,' writes Libyan historian Habîb Wada'ah el-Hasnawî, whose description cannot but bring to mind the shoddy vessels that continue to arrive at Lampedusa, with their human cargo of the poor and the dead. 'Those who drove the boats seemed to take no interest in the future of those desperate souls, held prisoner on the icy, uneasy ships, who did not know that the places to which they were being taken would be worse still— colder and wetter, surely places not appropriate for human habitation.'[25]

After four days of navigation, the steamboats set down anchor in the Tremiti Islands or at Ustica, once those who had died during the journey had been thrown overboard. Then the real Calvary began.

As the prefect of Palermo emphasized in his report, many of the detainees reached the penal colonies in 'filthy rags', while others already displayed symptoms of infectious diseases including typhoid, smallpox and cholera. The scarce and unhealthy food they received, along with the harsh climate, the revolting hygienic conditions, their degrading lodgings in freezing bunkers or even in caves on the island of San Nicola, did the rest. 'On the Tremiti Islands on 9 January 1912,' Claudio Moffa notes, '198 prisoners were recorded dead, including two children of 10 years of age, 35 people between 60 and 70 years, 7 between 70 and 80, and one over 90. On 10 June, the total number of dead had risen to 437, representing 31 per cent of the original mass of exiles.'[26] Tremiti was not the only site of such deaths, however. Between 29 October and 31 December 1911, 69 people aged 16 to 60 died on Ustica; at Gaeta, 62 deaths were counted between January and July 1912; on Ponza, for the same period, 13 deaths.

'On 31 January 1912,' Simone Bernini recounts, 'these were the presences in the different penal colonies: 654 deportees at Gaeta, 136 on Ponza,

---

25 Wada'ah el-Hasnawî, 'Effetti psico-sociali', p. 33.

26 Claudio Moffa, 'I deportati libici della guerra del 1911–1912 alle Tremiti', in Sulpiz and Sury (eds), *Gli esiliati libici*, p. 67.

1,080 on the Tremiti, 834 on Ustica and 349 on Favignana.'[27] To this total of 3,053 detainees, one must add the number of dead, around 600–700, which brings us close to the figure of 4,000 deportees in total, as indicated by many scholars. While it is true that 917 Libyan exiles were repatriated over the course of 1912, the deportations continued for years, with significant peaks in 1915 following the Great Arab Revolt. Today, nearly a hundred years after the Battle of Shar al-Shatt, there are still families in Libya who would like to know where their relatives are buried.[28]

From his detention on Favignana, in the Egadi Islands, Misratan poet Fadil Hasin ash-Shalmani raised a voice of fierce protest. Before being woken each day for forced labour, he was examined by a 'Christian chief' and treated like 'a sheep in the hands of a merchant.' Sentenced by a court in Bengasi to 25 years of detention under accusations for which there was no proof, he served seven. His extreme suffering is contained in the following lines:

We are in small cells, pressed together
without the light of day.
Doors closed with thick irons.
And everywhere I might look, I see nothing but Italians.[29]

It is after Shar al-Shatt that you begin to see the elegy of the gallows, in Italy as much as in Tripoli, as a useful weapon and deterrent. According to Ezio Maria Gray, who participated in the manhunt through the streets of Tripoli on 23 October, the wave of repression had been too mild, the hatred too watered-down: 'Were we too harsh?' he asked himself in his memoirs, *La Bella Guerra* ('the beautiful war'). 'We daren't even ask the

---

27 Bernini, 'Documenti sulla repressione', p. 128.

28 On the basis of a joint statement issued on 4 July 1998, Italy and Libya agreed to undertake research into the deportations of Libyans to Italy. [For the text, see Gianluigi Rossi, 'La collaborazione culturale tra l'Italia e la Libia oggi', *Rivista di Studi Politici Internazionali*, 266 (2000): 295–97.]

29 Cited in Wada'ah el-Hasnawî, 'Effetti psico-sociali', p. 45.

question! This sentimentalism is a typical and torpid sickness of our race, which poisoned our defensive reaction even on that day itself. [. . .] We only split the blood that it was essential to spill, and not even that. Any renewed act of treachery would have provoked the utmost severity.[30] Poet Filippo Tommaso Marinetti was also particularly critical: 'We have suffered the fatal results of our stupid colonial humanitarianism.'[31] Had massacring 4,000 Libyans and deporting the same number again truly been a sign of sentimentalism, of humanitarianism, of weakness? Was it the case then that in Libya the Italians had been too good, too tolerant, too much the *brava gente*?

On 18 October 1912, a year into the war in Libya—during which Italian soldiers had made little progress into the inland territory, despite the corps now counting the respectable figure of 100,000 men—the diplomatic representatives of Italy and the Ottomans signed a peace treaty in Ouchy, Switzerland. The military 'walk in the park' might have cost Italy 3,431 casualties and 4,220 wounded, but the 'promised land' was by now at an arm's reach, no longer defended by Ottoman soldiers. It was a shame then that the 'box of sand' was still infested by Arab guerrillas who, after Italy's annexation of Libya, turned into 'rebels' to all effect, for whom the main response had to be the gallows.

Once peace had been concluded, the next task was conquering the inland area of the country, representing around 90 per cent of the territory. The mission seemed more feasible in Tripolitania where, after the Battle of al-Asaba and the defeat of the Berber leader Sulayman al-Baruni, it had been possible to occupy the gebel (i.e. the plateaus) from Tarhuna to Nalut and even right across to the oasis of Ghadames. Following this, in 1914, Colonel Antonio Miani was able—through a bold and even reckless

---

30 Ezio Maria Gray, *La bella guerra* (Florence: Bemporad, 1912), pp. 14–15.

31 Cited in Sergio Romano, *La quarta sponda. La guerra di Libia, 1911–1912* (Milan: Bompiani, 1977), p. 165.

campaign—to bring over to Italian rule the immense region of Fezzan.[32] Yet occupying such territories with any stability required troops and equipment that Rome could not concede, given that in Europe another war had opened up and it was unclear for how long Italy could remain outside of it.

The situation in Cyrenaica was worse still. At the end of 1913, General Giovanni Ameglio was still not very far from the coastline. The stably occupied territories were limited to a few ports, like Bengasi, Tocra, Derna and Tobruk. They were opposed by an extremely respectable adversary, Grand Senussi Ahmed Sharif as-Senussi, who led 18,000 men and 15 cannons.[33] Notwithstanding Ameglio's success over the first half of 1914 in destroying some of the main Senussi camps in western and central Cyrenaica, in truth he had only taken the smallest fragment of the old Ottoman *vilâyet*. Determined to crush the Senussi resistance, the Sicilian-born general decided to again rely on the gallows as a tool of repression and intimidation. He even established that when the natives refused to play the part of hangman, the Italian soldiers could execute the role.

The scandal exploded when, on 5 December 1913, the Italian newspaper *Avanti!* published a series of six photographs depicting Italian soldiers as they hanged a group of Arabs. Railing against these horrors in the parliamentary session of 18 December 1913, Filippo Turati claimed that:

> A few days ago, I heard the King say that Italy's acquisition of Libya represents a great mission of civilization, and that our first goal must be to make friends with the people there, with respect

---

32 See Angelo Del Boca, *La disfatta di Gars bu Hàdi. 1915: il colonnello Miani e il più grande disastro dell'Italia coloniale* (Milan: Mondadori, 2004).

33 Among other accounts of the Senussi, see Edward Evan Evans-Pritchard, 'The Sanusi of Cyrenaica', *Journal of the International Africa Institute*, 15(2) (1945): 61–79; Nicola A. Ziadeh, *Sanusiyah: A Study of a Revivalist Movement in Islam* (Leiden: Brill, 1958). [Trans.]

for their religion, property and family, and make them understand the benefits of civilization. But I see the shadow of the gallows extending everywhere across your undertaking! [. . .] Every soldier who carries out the noble function of the hangman receives a reward of 5 francs from the *carabinieri* [. . .]. I cannot but help ask myself whether we are still in Italy, and whether the government knows that a certain Cesare Beccaria was born here.[34]

This harsh interventions against General Ameglio, first by the Minister for the Colonies, Pietro Bertolini and then by his successor, Ferdinando Martini, did not obtain the desire results. Martini in particular expressed his doubts and criticisms about the extreme ease with which capital sentences were being issued and executed. On 24 August 1914, he wrote to Ameglio in relation to a certain Mohammed bu Kraim being sentenced to death: 'One can see that the sentence is sloppy and almost without justification, and the punishment seems excessive given that the crime is the suspicion of collaboration with the rebels, about which there is a near-total lack of evidence.'[35] A few months' later, Martini reiterated the point, this time in relation to the sentencing of 27 Arabs: 'It is my profound belief, upon reading all of the trial documents, which I have done here with great conscientiousness, that these verdicts are not only excessive but inappropriate.'[36]

The governor of Cyrenaica, who had to answer his critics several times over his two years in the post, declared in his defence that:

---

34 Camera dei Deputati, *Atti parlamentari*, XXIV legislature, Session I, 18 December 1913, pp. 555–57. [Beccaria is the founding figure of liberal Italian jurisprudence.— Trans.]

35 Archivio storico del Ministero dell'Africa italiana, Rome: Libya, pos. 114/1, f. 4 (letter dated 24 August 1914).

36 Archivio storico del Ministero dell'Africa italiana, pos. 114/1, f. 4 (letter dated 15 February 1915).

I do not doubt that the carrying out of capital punishment might have a less than favourable echo in Italy, but I am also deeply convinced that this echo would be quite different if, along with the news of the firing squads, it was also made known that these are effected against traitors who, after having been welcomed into our troops, later run off with our arms and then aim them at the breasts of our soldiers with no reason other than the most fanatical hatred.

Cutting the discussion short, he brusquely concluded: 'I thereby, in full conscience, assume all the responsibility that is due to me in carrying out this painful duty.'[37]

Martini, however, was not the kind of minister to allow himself to be awed by the manoeuvres of a soldier, even one of Ameglio's stature.[38] A few weeks later he replied:

Doubtless one cannot but recognize the need to punish with a sentence of death crimes as serious as those of treason in the context described by Your Eminence; but I cannot, nevertheless, deny that there remains within me the lively concern that a

---

37 Archivio storico del Ministero dell'Africa italiana (report n. 82, highly reserved, dated 1 May 1915).

38 General Giovanni Ameglio had participated in all of the Eritrean colonial campaigns, as well as having led the Italian contingent in China in 1902. Over the course of the Italo-Turkish war he occupied Rhodes and the Dodecanese. While he did not employ the same methods in the Aegean that were ruthlessly engaged in Libya, the Italians nevertheless did not leave behind a positive legacy. See above all the works of Jack Nicolas Casavis: *Italian Atrocities in Grecian Dodecanese* (New York: The Dodecanesian League of America, 1940) and *The First Day of the Occupation of the Dodecanese Islands by Italy* (New York: The Dodecanesian League of America, 1935). See furthermore Nicholas Doumani, *Una faccia, una razza. le colonie italiane nell'Egeo* (Bologna: Il Mulino, 2003) and Ettore Vittorini, *Isole dimenticate. Il Dodecaneso da Giolitti al massacro del 1943* (Florence: Le Lettere, 2004).

too-frequent use of such radical decrees of repression might not damage the cause of pacification.[39]

The dispute between the Minister for the Colonies and Governor Ameglio on the abuse of capital punishment certainly stands in Bertolini and Martini's favour. Nevertheless, it does not absolve them from the accusation of complicity with the soldiers. Whether people were effectively hanged or shot by Libyan or Italian staff did not fundamentally worry either of the ministers. They were concerned that the sentences should be issued in the correct way, respecting procedural norms after a clear and exhaustive trial. Neither Bertolini nor Martini—both of whom were extremely well-educated and important statesmen—were even minimally disturbed by doubts or regrets. It would only be in 1915, when he was forced to gaze on helpless at the crumbling of Italian rule in Libya, that Martini would finally realize that you cannot pacify a colony by waging genocide against its people.

The Libyan Calvary was not, however, comprised only in the issuing of hundreds—perhaps thousands—of arbitrary death sentences. There were also thousands of Libyans who continued to suffer in the Italian concentration camps. In Ustica alone, in March 1916, there were 1,300 Arabs in confinement. The combination of violence, the lack of respect for Libyan traditions, culture and religion, the denial of every kind of legal right—including those which had been promised—in the end could only lead to a general revolt. On the night of 28 November 1914, an attack was launched at al-Gahra in Sabha, leading to the destruction of the garrison and beginning that which would come to be called the Great Arab Revolt, eventually setting alight across all of Libya and pushing the Italians back to the sea.[40]

---

39 Archivio storico del Ministero dell'Africa italiana, Rome: Libya, highly reserved letter n. 4701 (29 May 1915).

40 On the Arab Revolt, see Rashid Khalidi (ed.), *The Origins of Arab Nationalism* (New York: Columbia University Press, 1991). [Trans].

According to calculations made by General Lentini, from January 1915—i.e. from the hasty retreat from Fezzan—till July that year, when the final inland defences were evicted, 55 officers were killed, 483 national soldiers and 894 askaris. The missing numbered 29 officers, 1,951 'metropolitan' soldiers and 159 'coloured' soldiers. Furthermore, 52 officers, 1,278 Italian soldiers and 130 askaris were counted as having fallen into enemy hands. The total number of losses was thus 5,031 men.[41] Estimates by the Ministry of War elevated the number to 5,412. Finally, the Minister for the Colonies in 1920, Meuccio Ruini, declared that 'the retreat signalled the death of 10,000 men in the colonial desert.'[42] This thus represented a loss of human life superior even to that at Adwa. If we take into consideration the material loss, then there is simply no comparison. The rebels' booty comprised 37 cannons, 30 machine guns, 9,048 rifles (other sources put this number at 23,205), 28,031 shells, 6,185,000 cartridges for those rifles and machine guns, 37 trucks and 14 radio stations—an arsenal fit for an army.[43] Indeed, those arms allowed the Libyan resistance to continue operations up to 1932.

The thousands of dead had not been enough, nor was the agony of the frantic retreat and the humiliation of being chased into the sea in pitiful conditions. In drawing up his report for General Santangelo, entitled, *The Spirit of the Officers and Troops*, Colonel Gherardo Pàntano claimed:

> It is not rare, unfortunately, to hear distinguished and generous officers espouse the most ferocious and reactionary theories, such as the usefulness of suppression against all of the Arabs in Tripolitania. They recount with pleasure, and as good, useful

---

41 Archivio storico del Ministero dell'Africa italiana, Rome: Libya, pos. 122/9, f. 74, telegram n. 4720 (26 November 1915).

42 Meuccio Ruini, *L'Islam e le nostre colonie* (Città di Castello: Il Solco, 1922), p. 77.

43 Archivio storico del Ministero dell'Africa italiana, Rome: Libya, pos. 122/9, f. 74, telegram n. 4724 (26 November 1915).

engagements, the most shocking of things: Arabs found seriously wounded who are then soaked in petrol and set alight; others thrown into and walled up in wells; others gunned down for no other reason than savage wickedness. *Some officers personally take charge of such executions*, and even brag about it. Others systematically plunder *non-rebellious* towns, thus creating the best possible propaganda for the Senussi. [...] How our officers have discovered such blind savagery, such bloodthirstiness, such fine-tuned cruelly, I truly cannot say.

With officers such as these, Pàntano continued, it was all too easy to imagine what the troops might do, incited by their superiors' words and deeds. The truth, the Colonel concluded—who would soon lead operations from the Karst Plateaus of Isonzo—was that 'we avenge the Arabs for our own mistakes, our retreats, the looting we have suffered; not for their abilities, but for our ineptitudes. Indeed, not being able to take revenge on our enemies who have obtained such extraordinary results with such little means, we have taken out our humiliation on the weak and helpless.'[44]

The first attempt to occupy Libya thus ended in blood and shame. It had lasted four years. Finally occupying the whole of the 'fourth bank' would take another 17 years and the annihilation—in combat and in extermination camps—of an eighth of the Libyan population.

---

44 Archivio storico del Ministero dell'Africa italiana, Rome: Libya, pos. 122/9, f. 74, letter n. 224. The Minister for Colonial Affairs, Martini, fully confirmed Pàntano's complaint [Archivio storico del Ministero dell'Africa italiana, Rome: Libya, pos. 127/1, f. 5, highly reserved letter to General Amgelio, n. 820 (1 February 1916)].

SIX

THE CRIMES OF
GENERAL CADORNA

Following a year of neutrality—and beginning talks with both Vienna and London, at one point even at the same time—Italy entered the war on 24 May 1915, siding with the Allies. This extremely important decision was not taken by parliament following an exhaustive debate but by three men alone: Antonio Salandra, President of the Council; Sidney Sonnino, the Foreign Minister; and King Vittorio Emanuele III. The majority of the country was against the war, beginning with the women of Italy, though they still did not have the vote. And who had even thought to ask the masses of peasant farmers, who still lived in ignorance and poverty? Nevertheless, it was they who would be called on to bear the greatest burden of the war, in total passivity and resignation.

The talks in Vienna had continued until 11 May 1915, even though Sonnino had already signed a pact in London on 26 April. While it is true that Austria was agreeing to concede only Trentino (and not even all of the province), as well as part of the Adriatic coast and full autonomy for Trieste, Italy's requests had gone far beyond 'national aspirations', aiming at imperial objectives entirely outside the conflict's nationalist vision. For example, initial requests included the annexation of areas inhabited by important German, Slovenian and Croatian minorities, running the risk of soliciting irredentist struggles against Italian rule.

Instead of an agreement with Vienna—that over time might have improved and would not have involved the sacrifice of a single soldier—they chose a war that would cost 652,000 lives, with 450,000 people wounded and a financial burden of 157 billion lire, gifting the Italian state with a public debt of gigantic proportions. Italy's entrance into the war brought further sacrifices and disasters as well, beginning (in Giorgio Rochat and Giulio Massobrio's words) 'with the destruction of the gains of the trade unions and an intensified exploitation of the proletariat both in the factories and in the trenches'.[1]

With little gravitas, and by creating a myth of a 'patriotic war', Italy entered into a conflict that had already dragged on for more than a year, and of which everyone could already see all the atrocious novelties. Humankind's first World War was a war without proportion, mercy or honour. It was a war that introduced new murderous weapons, such as aeroplanes, tanks, flamethrowers, hand grenades, air-bombings, mustard gas and tear gas. It introduced the inferno of the trenches, where millions of men rotted away while waiting to be burnt to death. By the end of this exterminating bloodbath, 10 million soldiers had been killed on both sides, and another 8 million wounded. To this should be added the 5 million civilians who died through enemy occupation, bombings and generalized suffering.[2] Another million victims, from 1917 onwards, were taken by the Spanish Flu pandemic.[3] Nor should it be forgotten

---

1 Giorgio Rochat and Giulio Massobrio, *Breve storia dell'esercito italiano dal 1861 al 1943* (Turin: Einaudi, 1978), p. 177.

2 Countless books have been written about the First World War, and more are still being written. Not even the Second World War—far more bloody and extensive—has stimulated such interest. We will therefore limit ourselves to highlighting some of the most important titles: Basil Henry Liddell Hart, *The Real War (1914–1918)* (London: Faber & Faber, 1930); Martin Gilbert, *The First World War: A Complete History* (New York: Henry Holt, 1994); Mario Isnenghi and Giorgio Rochat, *La grande guerra, 1914–1918* (Florence, La Nuova Italia, 2000); Niall Ferguson, *The Pity of War* (London: Allen Lane, 1998); Ian Ousby, *The Road to Verdun* (New York: Anchor Books, 2002); Emilio Faldella, *La Grande Guerra* (Chiari: Nordpress, 2004).

that the vast disturbances of the World War provoked the birth of all forms of totalitarianisms, from Fascism to Nazism and Bolshevism.

The role of leading the Italian army was given to Luigi Cadorna, General of the Armed Forces as well as Senator, who from 27 July 1914 became Chief of Staff. Despite the fact that he had never experienced battle, he had built a rapid career and was considered a brilliant tactician. Of a cold and reserved temperament, he was authoritarian with his subordinates, did not tolerate dissent and was extremely sure of himself. 'The unappealing Cadorna represented much of the bad side of the Italian officer corps,' notes American historian John R. Schindler. 'He was undoubtedly an unfortunate choice to lead Italy in the greatest war ever seen.'[4]

Cadorna entered the conflict with an army that was unprepared for long-lasting and extremely intense operations. He could draw upon 2,000 guns, between howitzers and field cannons. The heavy artillery was composed of 112 pieces, while the machine guns—which were to have a determining role in the war—counted no more than 618, which equated to two for each infantry regiment. The reserves did not possess enough Model 1891 rifles, uniforms or mess tins. The army was also lacking officers, to the tune of 10,000.

These deficiencies could not be compensated for by the enthusiasm of volunteers, who nevertheless represented an insignificant minority, nor by Ardengo Soffici's insults against the 'slobbering, cancerous, repugnant mob in the Senate',[5] nor by a young Benito Mussolini's incitements: 'We will fight alongside the French, the Belgians, the English and the Russians: with our intervention we will forge a ring of iron and fire

---

3 The Spanish flu was an epidemic that spread across all regions and continents, running rife through Europe in 1918–1920, frequently and fatally leading to a form of polyencephalitis.

4 John R. Schindler, *Isonzo: The Forgotten Sacrifice of the Great War* (London: Praeger, 2001), p. 14.

5 Ardengo Soffici, 'Sulla soglia', *Lacerba*, 15 May 1915.

around the imperial powers responsible for the European conflagration; we will shorten the duration of the war, we will be victorious [. . .]. Italian bayonets: our steel is being entrusted with the destiny of Italy and of all the peoples of Europe.'[6] But more than chatter was needed to re-enforce an army that had vanished in Libya.

Cadorna's plan, on paper, was the very best one could imagine. The General began from the observation that in one year of war, the Austrians had already lost 800,000 men, that they were exhausted and on the brink of collapse, and would find great difficulty in sustaining the burden of a third front. Based on these premises, he proposed to give a powerful 'shove' to the weakened enemy forces (25,000 men and 100 cannons) just beyond Isonzo, employing the 3rd Army to push through the Isonzo line from Gorizia to Plezzo. According to his predictions, the undermining of this front would be extremely rapid, requiring no more than one week. Following this, the 3rd Army would take possession of Trieste while the 2nd Army would push right through to Ljubljana, precipitating the collapse of the Hapsburg Empire.

This plan would, in all likelihood, have worked if Cadorna had been capable of attacking immediately after the declaration of war. But even if preparations had secretly been underway for months, he still needed 30 days to bring the two armies to the front and complete some scouting missions beyond the Isonzo line. These 30 days proved to be fatal, because they allowed the Austrian Chief of Staff, Franz Conrad von Hötzendorff, to move the 15th and 16th corps from Serbia to Isonzo, and to form a new force—the 5th Army—which he entrusted to General Svertozar Boroević von Bojna, the man who was to become, for nearly three years, Cadorna's extremely effective and unwavering adversary. Another negative element, which Cadorna surely must have taken into consideration, was the Austrian's morale. Not only did they feel insulted by the treachery of

---

6 Benito Mussolini, *Scritti e discorsi, Volume 1: Dall'intervento al fascismmo* (Milan: Hoepli: 1934), pp. 40–41.

their former allies, who had abandoned them for the Triple Entente, but— for the Croatian and Slovenian soldiers above all—they also feared Italian sights being aimed on the coastline and Dalmatia. The Isonzo line became for them, therefore, the national bulwark to be defended at any cost.

At the moment of the attack on 21 June, the Austrians—according to Cadorna himself—had 'overall an important numeric inferiority in relation to the 35 divisions of our own army, but largely compensated for this through the greater abundance of artillery of every calibre, machine guns, the natural strength of the terrain, the power of the fortified lines and their experience of ten months of war'.[7] Cadorna's two armies, therefore, immediately encountered extremely strong resistance, failing to improve their positions; the 'march to Ljubjana' was very quickly transformed into the butchering of 30,000 Italian soldiers.

Cadorna did not assume any responsibility for this reasonably pre- dictable failure. Attributing it instead to the lack of munitions, the problems with the vehicles, 'the slowness with which the Ministry organized the arrival of supplies', the majority 'of the firearms of medium calibre' explod- ing 'due to imperfections in the bullets'. Finally, accused in both Austrian and Italian newspapers of having lost time and not profiting from the initial weak phase in the enemy's ranks, Cadorna responded with a line that only Jacques de La Palice could otherwise have pronounced: 'It is nevertheless true that the eruption into enemy territory in the first days of the war only came to a halt when faced with the impossibility of advancing any further'.[8]

Right from the start of taking command, General Cadorna proved himself to be particularly stubborn, incapable of self-criticism, unmoved

---

7 Luigi Cadorna, *La guerra alla fronte italiana* (Milan: Treves, 1934), pp. 127–28.

8 Cadorna, *La guerra*, p. 146, p. 146 and p. 129, respectively. ['Jacques de La Palice': an early modern French officer and nobleman, whose epitaph—'if he were not dead, he would still be alive'—gave rise to the term *lapalissade*, referring to a banally obvious truism. Del Boca is also playing with a similarity between the two military men, both of whom fought against the Hapsburgs, albeit 400 years apart.—Trans.]

by human loss—even of vast proportions—and indifferent to the suffering and morale of his soldiers. He also demonstrated an attitude of spectacular snobbery in relation to the great mass of soldiers who were essentially peasant farmers. A convinced practitioner of the most severe military discipline, he was determined to win out against what he believed to be the chronic indiscipline of the Italians, making use of firing squads and the barbaric practice of decimation. He was extremely severe even with his officers (of all ranks) if they did not meet his expectations to the full. This was the form of authority he claimed to embody when, in the first two months of the war, he removed 27 generals from their posts and a similar number of lower-ranking officers.

He not only engaged in constant argument with the government, who he did not believe to be up to the challenge of the difficult period the nation was going through, but was also hostile to the entire political class, as well as a sworn enemy of the socialists who he accused of undermining the army's morale. As Ernesto Ragionieri has rightly noted: 'Cadorna's presumption that he could impose himself over political power, not only in terms of military operations but also of the direction the country was taking, found objective grounds in the government's prevarications and deficiencies. This went to accentuating his aggression in relation to any political or social force that hesitated even minimally in the face of the war effort.'[9]

Convinced that a parliamentary democracy could not function in periods of emergency, he believed that political action needed to be exercised by a single figure—and in clarifying that this figure ought to be 'a man superior in both intelligence and character', it seemed he was indicating himself. 'A dictator not by right, but by default,' he continued.[10] A fervent catholic, he seemed to receive orders from God

---

9 Ernesto Ragionieri 'La storia politica e sociale', in Ruggiero Romano and Corrado Vivanti (eds), *Storia d'Italian Einaudi, Volume 4: Dall'Unità d'Italia a oggi* (Turin: Einaudi, 1975), p. 2007.

10 Cadorna, *La guerra*, p. 38.

alone, with whom he conversed in a daily mass given by his private chaplain.

Unlike other military chiefs (such as Caviglia, Pecori Girardi, Di Giorgio or Diaz), who were highly respected and even venerated, Cadorna not only failed to earn any respect from his soldiers—he was actively hated by them. He repaid them by minimizing or simply ignoring their sacrifice in his memoirs: while he remarks on the number of the enemy's dead at every battle, he makes no mention of the deaths on his own side, as if this were a small detail that could be passed over. He did not only ignore his own dead but also the crimes committed under his command. For example, in the fighting in June 1915 for the conquest of the Black Mountain, sections of the 4th Corps, frustrated by their repeated defeats, vented their anger on the Slovenian locals, burning six villages to the ground. In the same area, on the slopes of the Mrzli, dozens of Slovenian civilians were put to the firing squad on suspicion of having killed some wounded Italian soldiers.[11] And while Cadorna was not directly named by the anonymous author of the protest song *Gorizia*, everyone knew that it was he who held a burning passion for the city, a passion so great that he grabbed it back from the Austrians after six battles and a vast scale of death.

O Gorizia, you are accursed!
So many hearts without any thought
My departure was so painful
And for many there was no return.

O dear treacherous officers
Who wanted the war so badly
Mockers of sold human flesh
And the ruin of our youth.[12]

---

11 Schindler, *Isonzo*, p. 49.

12 Lamberto Mercuri and Carlo Tuzzi, *Canti politici italiani, 1793–1945* (Rome, Editori Riuniti, 1973), p. 257.

The 100,000 soldiers who took part in the first Battle of Isonzo also included my father, Giacomo. A hotelier, class of 1878, he passed his life between the hearth, the mineral waters of Crodo and the slopes of Mount Cistella. Already advanced in years, he was not sent to participate in the bayonet attacks against the Austrian trenches, but after the final wave—his arms bathed in blood up to the elbows—he was tasked with separating the dead from the wounded.

I was around six when my father began to talk to me about the Great War and General Cadorna. The conflict had only concluded a dozen or so years before, and his recollections of the massacre were incised in his memory, to the extent that, whenever he touched on the topic, I was submerged in a flood of words, images and suggestions. I was too young to understand what drove my father to confide his memories and anxieties in me. But there was one thing that I did understand: his stories were not to be confused with the fairy tales that my sisters told me at bedtime, to help me sleep. These stories were true and tragic—stories that my mother refused to listen to.

Our encounters usually took place in the shed he had built in the garden, behind our house in the working-class neighbourhood of San Rocco, in the suburbs of Novara. We sat around a stone table, where I usually did my homework; as if there were some kind of agreement between us, my father would open his book of memoirs—which was sometimes mixed with those of this brother, Enrico, who had earned in the field the rank of Sergeant Major. I do not know how many stories were recorded there, but I know there were a great many. I recall a dozen episodes very well, the merit of which is surely due to my father, who was an extraordinary storyteller, as well as to the peculiarity of the facts that he narrated.

Let us take the example of attending to the cable car, surely the most nerve-racking of the tasks he was entrusted with. The cable car had two functions: to send supplies, arms, munitions, boards and sandbags to the front line; to receive, on the return journey, the dead and wounded. My father recalled:

> It was worse than living in the trenches. You began to hear the screams of the wounded from far away, half-way through the journey. Some of them had such terrible mutilations that they died in your arms while you unloaded them from the cable car. I preferred to deal with the dead, because at least they stayed quiet. But even they made problems sometimes, because the bodies were so destroyed that you couldn't put them together. In the end, there were always extra legs and arms that we couldn't match up with a body. In one single day, after a furious battle, we divided up 700 people between the dead and the wounded.

Transferred from the Isonzo line to Trentino in 1916 on the eve of the Strafexpedition, he remained on the slopes of Mount Corno for nearly a year. His main recollections of this period were connected to the desperate struggle against the mice that had invaded the trenches that they had dug out of the rock. My father told me:

> They were famished, stubborn and fearless. They would throw themselves into a pile of empty tins and clean them all up in a flash. We killed them by the dozen with spades, but the next day they would come back in even great numbers. They attacked you in the night, aiming for your throat and face. Then there was the problem of where to throw the carcasses, which soon started to give off an intolerable stench.

The conflict was not, therefore, only with the Austrians. They fought every day with mice, lice, bedbugs and every other kind of insect that feeds off human blood. There was also another enemy in the trenches: the mud. As my father told me:

> The base of the trenches wasn't able to absorb the rainfall. After only a couple of hours, it turned to mud. It would rain for two

days in a row, and the mud rose up to your heels, and you had to dig it out over the sandbags. In the end, you were covered with mud and there was no way to clean yourself. The mud stank of everything: of dead mice, of our excrement, of rotten food and of the latest Austrian gas attacks.

Almost every time, at the end of his stories, my father would say, enunciating very clearly, so that the words remained impressed on my mind: 'And remember one name: Cadorna. He was our true enemy. Not the Austrians.' My father blamed all the horrors of the trenches on Cadorna, as well as the mass deaths. Over and again he would show me a postcard depicting the monument to the fallen of Boca, our town, saying: 'There are twenty-five names engraved on this stone. Twenty-five names in a town of one thousand people. Four of them bear our own name, while another eight are relatives. Now do you understand why I hate Cadorna?'

When my father expressed all of his rancour for General Cadorna, I was certainly not able to evaluate his claims. But several decades later, with a historian's experience, I was; and it turned out that—even without feeling his same anger—I could not contradict him. There is not the slightest doubt that Cadorna held the sole and direct responsibility for the massacre on the Isonzo line. The fact that other generals in other countries—Foch, Joffre, Haig, Conrad, Hindenburg, Ludendorff—did the same on their own fronts does not redeem him. The truth is that the Cadorna plan was completely erroneous, and re-proposing it 11 times over was simply criminal. It was based on the idea of a gradual attrition of the enemy, to be effected through continuous 'pushes', each one heavier than the former. He was certain that by applying this strategy he would eventually break through the Austrian defences and be able to march on Ljubljana and Vienna. Yet if the Isonzo Valley was surely the shortest road to reaching the final objectives, it was also notoriously the most favourable for its defenders, even if they were constantly struck by a hurricane of fire.

Cadorna was perfectly aware that his plan to break through the Isonzo line was not shared by everyone. The Duke of Aosta himself, whose 3rd Army had suffered the greatest losses, no longer had any faith in the General's strategic project. At the meetings of the high naval command, he had twice suggested an alternative to the 'pushes': organizing a landing behind Austrian lines, between Aurisina and Prosecco, protected by the fleet's cannon. But Cadorna rejected it.

A form of paranoia emerged from within his plan. So long as the country continued to concede to him young lives to throw into the furnace, and industry continued to procure artillery and munitions, he would not give up on his project of opening up a gap in the enemy lines. The first battle of Isonzo involved just over 500 cannons; the eleventh, 5,200. With this leap, he would demolish every part of the defence—even if Boroević's engineers excelled at reconstruction. It mattered little to him that in the 11 battles of Isonzo he had lost nearly 800,000 men between casualties, the wounded, the missing and those taken prisoner. There was still the class of 1899 to call up to the front, and even the teenagers of 1900.

Nothing dented this certainty in a final victory. Cadorna did not ignore the fact that the soldiers were launching attacks because they feared the repercussions of refusal—from imprisonment to summary executions and decimation—rather than strong morale. If the Austrians, with German support, had not attacked on 24 October 1917, breaking into fragments the Italian defences at Caporetto and striking through to Germona and Cividale, Cadorna would have prepared to the smallest detail his twelfth battle, with still more battalions, more cannons, more bombardments, always pushing forward with his insane project. Instead, the twelfth battle of Isonzo was led by a German General, Otto von Below, who caught the Italians by surprise, despite their having lived in that position for 29 months. The rest is sadly well known: Cadorna's army lost 700,000 men in the retreat, between casualties, wounded, prisoners and those given up for lost, as well as 3,150 cannons of every calibre, 1,732 mortars, 3,000 machine guns and 300,000 rifles. By comparison, the disasters at Custoza, Lissa and Adwa fade from view.[13]

Relieved of his post by Vittorio Emanuele III on 8 November 1917, Cadorna refused to accept his dismissal on principle, almost as if he felt himself superior even to the King. He then rejected every accusation, laying all blame for the disaster on the 'deficient resistance of several divisions, some of which surrendered without honour, others of whom ran away in cowardice.'[14] In his memoirs, he pointed a stern finger at the country and at the government, who were guilty—in his view—of not having 'been able to sustain the troop's spirit. Having failed at this task of theirs, the consequent disaster was inevitable.' He repeats these accusations on the following page, describing the 'mistrust of an official Italy closed off from the military spirit, incapable of believing in the heroic virtues of a people in arms, ignorant of the deepest levels and healthiest aspects of the Italian people.'[15]

Who knows with what sentiment he dared to formulate these sentences, the man who had turned the 'Italian people' into cannon fodder, who had 'sustained the spirit of the troops' by denying them permissions, rest, every form of moral assistance, providing them with miserable rations and pay, forcing them into combat under threat of death.

Cadorna exited from the drama, but one of his cursed decisions—which was shared, it should be noted, by Sonnino—had not been excluded by

---

13 Custoza and Lissa were the sites of important land and sea battles, respectively, in the Third War of Independence in 1866. [Trans].

14 See Paul Allard and Frédéric Drach, *Images Secrètes de la guerra* (Paris: Les Illustrés Francais, 1933).

15 Cadorna, *La guerra*, p. 577 and p. 580, respectively.

Orlando's new government: the high command's approach in relation to the Italian prisoners of war, who by the end of 1917 counted 600,000 people. Over 100,000 would die from disease and, above all, hunger. As Giovanna Procacci has importantly revealed: 'the mass death of soldiers taken prisoner was provoked—and to a large extent even desired—by the Italian government, above all by the high command. Italy thus transformed the problem of prisoners of war, a problem that all of the warring states had to face with urgency, into a veritable case of collective extermination.'[16]

Unlike other countries in the war, the Italian state's refusal to organize the transport of assistance (food and clothes) to the soldiers detained in the Austrian concentration camps derived from a very decisive intention to dissuade the soldiers at the front from surrendering. In other words, this refusal—which was publicized, along with descriptions of the horrors of the Austrian prisons—was part of the cruel packet of edicts that was meant to impede desertion, rebellions, self-harming, feigned madness and suicides. The type of soldier that Cadorna hoped for was the exact copy of the soldier without qualities, without temptations, described by Agostino Gemelli:

> The best quality in a soldier in a long-lasting mass war is precisely the absence of every kind of quality: he must be rough, ignorant and passive. Only this kind of soldier can be fully transformed so that he can adapt to the trenches and the attack, so that he can become that highly manipulable material that is a perfect piece of the war machine. [. . .] The soldier ceases to be mother, husband, citizen—he becomes only a soldier.[17]

---

16 Giovanna Procacci, *Soldati e priogionieri italiani nella Grande Guerra* (Turin: Bollati Boringhieri, 2000), p. 175.

17 Cited in Antonio Gibelli, *L'officina della guerra. La Grande Guerra e le trasformmazioni del mondo mentale* (Turin: Bollati Boringhieri, 1991), pp. 91–92.

Because the prisoner gradually and definitively loses all of these characteristics of the mass soldier and cannot be used for the furnaces of war, both Cadorna and Sonnino—finally in agreement on one matter—assumed the responsibility of ignoring the prisoners' fate. The only exception was made for officers, who could receive assistance through the Red Cross. Yet even these supplies were suspended after Caporetto and during the battle of Piave. The living conditions in the Austrian camps where catastrophic, to say the least, especially in Sigmundsherberg where 180,000 Italians were held. The diary entry of Lieutenant Giuseppe Leonida Capobianco for 18 November 1917 reads: 'The insufficient food, the lack of fire, the cold weather and the constantly overcast sky force us to meditate on this terrible trial we are facing, reserved for us by a cruel and mocking fate.' Nevertheless, the officer—who, due to his rank, enjoyed better treatment than the privates—was concerned for those who 'have had no bread *for five days*. The officers have formed a kind of charity commission to assist the soldiers, but what can we do, with the few coins we have available?'[18]

The prisoners' tribulations continued even after the end of the war. After being stopped at the borders on their return, they were then detained in concentration camps that differed little from the Austrian ones. Lieutenant Capobianco recalled: 'It is insufferable that [General] Petitti di Roreto insults half a million Italian citizens and soldiers by forcing them to die of hunger, fenced up and under the watch of other Italian soldiers, the beardless youngsters of 1900!'[19] Observing that the French authorities regularly provided supplies for their own prisoners and thus—for the same number of detainees—recorded 20,000

---

18 Giuseppe Leonida Capobianco, *Impressioni e ricordi della prigonia di guerra in Austria* (Naples: Federico & Ardia, 1928), p. 46. In accordance with international conventions, officers received a salary from the host country. A lieutenant, for example, received 6.11 corone per day, which corresponded to 2.44 lire.

19 Capobianco, *Impressioni*, p. 155.

deaths rather than 100,000, Mario Isenghi and Giorgio Rochat bitterly concluded that:

> Sonnino and the high command, along with the collaboration of various governments, not only substantially blocked the provision of government aid (which was the only serious way to assist the prisoners) but did all they could to sabotage the work of the Red Cross and the pressure of the prisoners' families. [. . .] This behaviour represents the lowest point in the moral and professional conduct of the Italian government and military commanders during the Great War.[20]

As fate would have it, I was to meet once more with General Cadorna. Two years ago, the family of General Antonio Miani entrusted me with their relative's archive, in the hope that I could shed some light on the reason for which he—and only he—had been made the scapegoat for the Libyan disasters of 1915. The archive proved to be extraordinarily dense and important. Aside from original copies of all the operational telegrams that the General sent to Tripoli while he was concluding the conquest of Fezzam, it also includes correspondence with a range of high-ranking army officers as well as politicians.[21]

Between 13 March and 2 September 1926, General Miani sent around 30 letters to these figures in the hope of obtaining some form of justice. He did not succeed nor, following his death, did his courageous wife. But there was one result which he did achieve: putting Cadorna (now field marshal) in a corner and forcing him to admit that he had,

---

20 Isenghi and Rochat, *La grande guerra*, p. 342.

21 These included Field Marshall Luigi Cadorna, the military generals Guglielmo Pecori Girardi and Gaetano Giardino, the general (and secretary to the Interior Minister) Attilo Teruzzi, general and senator Carlo Porro di Santa Maria, the Minister for the Colonies Prince Lanza di Scalera, and the Minister for War and Head of Government—Benito Mussolini.

perhaps, made a mistake, and extracting from Cadorna the promise to restore his name. Miani had two good reasons to detest Cadorna and request reparation. To begin with, in August 1917, when Miani was in command of the difficult operations in Vallarsa, Cadorna had suddenly removed him from office and put him in reserves without any explanation. This practice of 'shelving' his under-officers was an almost daily occurrence for Cadorna: from May 1915 to the battle of Caporetto, he removed 807 officers from command, including 217 generals and 255 colonels.

The second reason was much more serious however, because Cadorna had publicly criticized Miani's military qualities and his honour. In a book called *Further Pages on the Great War*, Cadorna had dedicated an entire chapter to the disastrous events in Tripolitania over 1914–15, and did not hesitate to define the conquest of Fezzan—an operation of which Miani was extremely proud—as 'the most reckless and untimely undertaking in the colonial history of any country'. He concluded by minimizing the campaign with a summary that was intentionally brief and superficial: 'During the march, Miani encountered a few hundred armed rebels who blocked the road, defeating them in three engagements.'[22] Furthermore, he attributed to Miani the entire responsibility for the disaster at Gasr Bu Hàdi and the losses that followed.

This was simply too much for Miani. In a letter dated 5 April 1926, he wrote to Cadorna with a particularly bitter tone:

> I have been able to read that which Your Eminence has written
> regarding the events that took place in Tripolitania in 1914 and
> 1915, which—I will permit myself to inform you frankly—
> represents an accumulation of imprecisions and serious errors,
> both in terms of a historical exposition of the facts and therefore
> in its judgements on the events, which I can demonstrate with

---

22 Luigi Cadorna, *Altre pagine sulla Grande Guerra* (Milan: Mondadori, 1925), p. 48.

great ease by use of a collection of telegrams exchanged with the government in Tripoli.[23]

Cadorna's reply to this letter and those preceding it was unusually brief, in a diplomatic and sober tone. Even though he lied when sustaining that he had not 'any impression of having treated you with such severity' when he had relieved him 'of the command with which he had been charged' in Vallarsa, his tone changed when discussing the Libyan question and the harsh judgement he had made of Miani in his book:

> I cannot do otherwise than state that if I too freely judged the Fezzan engagement as 'reckless', it is a judgement that should be laid on the Minister of the Colonies, who ordered it; the engagement itself was led well. As far as your own actions as a soldier are concerned, not even the smallest doubt can be expressed, as your previous engagements and decorations duly demonstrate.[24]

This correction, while substantial, was not enough for Miani. In a following letter, in a still more bitter and desperate tone, he wrote:

> Once the facts have been gathered from the official documents that I can produce in my defence, Your Eminence might want to revise and correct that which You have espoused in your book, which has damaged my honour and seen that I have been unjustly and excessively stricken off, my career cut short despite the countless recognitions that I had believed to have secured; which has impeded me from effecting my duty to my fatherland, denying me the possibility to take part in the war.

23 Angelo Del Boca, *La disfatta di Gasr bu Hàdi. 1915: il colonnello Miani e il più grande disastro dell'Italia coloniale* (Milan: Mondadori, 2004), p. 116.

24 Del Boca, *La disfatta di Gasr bu Hàdi*, pp. 116–17.

In a following letter, Miani contested all of Cadorna's claims on the events in Libya point by point, using that tactic of continuous 'pushing' so dear to the general of Isonzo.[25]

Despite the aggressions he received—which certainly did not put him in a good light—Cadorna responded immediately with an incredibly moderate and conciliatory tone. He began by suggesting that the Ministry of War be requested to establish an official inquiry into the Libyan episodes, which he would warmly support because 'I love nothing but the truth, and I will be pleased to see it re-established in the case that there has been an undesired error.'[26] During a meeting in Rome between the two officers, Cadorna went further still, promising to revise the incriminating chapter of the book and make the necessary changes. The promise, however, could not be kept: Cadorna died in 1928. In 1933, Miani also passed away, without ever obtaining the rehabilitation for which he had fought so passionately.

I have brought this little-known episode to the reader's attention above all to highlight Cadorna's strange and unusual behaviour, equivalent to an unconditional surrender. At this point, we are forced to ask ourselves: how come there was so much submission, conciliation, almost self-flagellation in a man who we know as hard, indifferent to the lives of others, always convinced of his own infallibility and being in the right? Cadorna had been the undisputed leader of Italy for 29 months. No one before him or after—including Mussolini—had enjoyed such power over life and death of everyone in the peninsula. He had at his disposal one of the most powerful armies in the world, constantly revitalized through mass blood transfusions. He organized his own military courts, which imposed *his* law. Through a military censorship, he cast silence over both combatants and civilians. Without batting an eyelid, and with Sidney Sonnino's complicity, he decreed a sentence of death by

---

25 Del Boca, *La disfatta di Gasr bu Hàdi*, p. 118.

26 Del Boca, *La disfatta di Gasr bu Hàdi*, p. 119.

famine over 100,000 prisoners. He was a man, finally, who did not suffer the smallest embarrassment in draughting directives of the following kind: 'Every soldier must be certain that, should the need arise, their superior will act as both father and brother; but he must also believe that his superior possesses the sacred power to pass cowards and weaklings before the firing squad without hesitation.'[27]

This man who had lived in a delirium of omnipotence for 29 months could not be the same who gave in to Miani so easily, a middling general who had made some serious errors at Gasr Bu Hàdi. There was something that we had not grasped, something that the epistolary correspondence between Cadorna and Miani did not reveal. Some form of deep change had clearly overcome the general if, after his meeting with Miani in Rome, the latter was able to confide in his wife, Laura: 'He was extremely courteous with me, and expressed his sympathies [. . .]. He assured me that he held my expedition in Fezzan in high esteem.' Cadorna even promised to support his appeal to the Ministry of War and, 'if necessary, to Mussolini himself.'[28]

Without further documents, we do not feel capable of advancing hypotheses regarding this radical change in Cadorna's character. An investigation into the meandering paths of the psyche is not the historian's task. What we can say, however, is that Miani could not have hoped for a better treatment from the *generalissimo*. There was all the more reason for this because he was not, as it happened, his real enemy. It is true that Cadorna had removed him from command in Vallarsa, and harshly criticized his African campaign. But it had not been Cadorna who had declared the end of Miani's career and laid the blame for all of the Libyan disasters upon him. Miani died without learning the truth. He had, however, nurtured some suspicions: in 9 March 1914, he had made the governor in Tripoli, General Vincenzo Garioni, aware of a group of

---

27 Cited in Rochat and Massobrio, *Bbreve storia dell'eserico italiano*, p. 120.

28 Del Boca, *La disfatta di Gasr bu Hàdi*, p. 120.

officers who, in his view, were impeding the Fezzan expedition. 'It is necessary to purge our surroundings of a group of freemasons from Rome who do not have our country's interests at heart and indeed are impeding the campaign for the sake of deluded personal ambitions.'[29]

It was to be precisely this structure of freemasons, working at the very highest level, that isolated Miani, discrediting him as a witness and burying him beneath absurd accusations in order to block the opening of an inquiry that would surely have dragged them in. These were 'the figures right at the top' who even Mussolini felt he could not deal with, even if he promised Miani's widow his utmost support. But that is another story.

---

29 Del Boca, *La disfatta di Gasr bu Hàdi*, p. 70.

SEVEN

THE SLAVES OF
WEBI SHABEELLE

The yield of hatred and violence sown by Cadorna and his lieutenants was harvested at the end of the war. The unrepeatable climate of tension was exploited by D'Annunzio and Mussolini, the former to march on Fiume, the second to rule over Italy. By 16 January 1919, Mussolini was already attacking the government of Vittorio Emanuele Orlando for its indifference to the fate of the war veterans in an article entitled 'For Those Who Return':

> They return in small huddles. No one has even the aesthetic and spiritual satisfaction of being received in triumph, as soldiers who have literally demolished 'one of the most powerful armies in the world' ought be. [. . .] It is still more infinitely sad that these men who were ready to die cannot find that which is necessary to live, now that the Patria has been saved.[1]

Mussolini was to make this very real negligence by the government one of his battle cries. He knew that, with this protest, he could count on millions of demobilized soldiers who—despite repeated promises to the contrary—had no pension or support. He extended his concern to the rejected former prisoners-of-war as well, who he recognized—during

1 Benito Mussolini, *Scritti e discorsi, Volume 1: Dall'intervento al fascismo* (Milan: Hoepli, 1934), p. 368.

a rally in Piazza San Sepolcro—as the signatories to Fascism's birth certificate, people who had entirely fulfilled their duty: 'If this were not the case, well, then, we would need to undermine Cesare Battisti and many other valiant, brilliant officers and soldiers who had the misfortune to fall into enemy hands.'[2]

Many other factors contributed to creating and consolidating the Fascist movement, but there is no doubt that Mussolini's first move—proclaiming himself the defender of those who had experienced the horrific experience of the trenches—secured him an immediate consensus and a significant space for manoeuvre. He knew that when the time would come (which was not far off) for him to decide to cut short his road to the conquest of power, he could draw on the perfect kind of manpower. For example, there were the arditi ('the audacious ones') waiting in the wings—15,000 men who had gone to war with no more than knives and hand grenades, and proven themselves during the battle of Bainsizza and, on 4 September 1917, during the surprise attacks on San Gabriele. These shock troops went to work between 1919 and 1922 in Trieste, Bologna, Sarzana, Novara, Magenta, Ravenna and Parma. But in Sarzana and Parma they came off the worst.

In the chaos of the postwar period and on the fragile foundation of liberal democracy, once the road of violence had been taken, it could only lead to the conquest of power. Mussolini enacted this conquest with only 25,000 men—all extremely driven but badly armed and clumsily led. Indeed, the March on Rome could have easily been thwarted and blocked on the edge of the city if the King had had the courage to do so.

The rise of Fascism and the use of violence reframed the entire approach to the Italian colonies. Aside from Eritrea—which had not been struck by the upheavals of the war, leaving the colonial territory intact—the

---

2 Mussolini, *Scritti e discorsi*, p. 373.

other two pre-Fascist colonies were standing on the brink of crisis. Libya had been almost completely reconquered after the success of the Great Arab Revolt amid failed attempts to reach an agreement with the Emir of Cyrenaica, Mohammed Idris, and his representative in Tripolitania, Ahmed el-Mràied. And while Somalia was not in the same catastrophic condition as Libya, the government in Mogadishu had for years lost all authority over the sultanates in the north, which was equivalent to around half the colony.

When he came to power, Mussolini had still not developed his own ideas about the colonies, nor had he drawn up a map of demands. It was nevertheless clear in 1922 that he intended to adopt new methods that would be decidedly opposed to those used in the past. There were no longer to be compromises or torturous appeasements in either Libya or Somalia. Fascist Italy would have free reign, it would be decisive in crushing its enemies instead of trying to earn their friendship.

At the moment of Fascism's establishment, the governor of Somalia was Carlo Riveri, a disciple of Giolitti 'who governed with a sage and serene humility, working indefatigably without waking the trumpets of celebrity'.[3] An accomplished administrator and prudent politician, Riveri made every effort—with the few economic resources available to him— to maintain the 'Cinderella' of the Italian colonies,[4] and did not even remotely consider initiating a campaign for the northern sultanates, especially given the fact that a limit on the excessive autonomy of the sultans (Ali Yusuf and Osman Mahmud) could probably be achieved through new and effective agreements.

---

3 Associazione italiana per il controllo democratico, *Il governo fascista nelle colonie. Somalia, Eritrea, Libia* (Milan: Corbaccio, 1925), p. 11.

4 See Douglas Jardine, 'Somaliland: The Cinderella of the Empire', *Journal of the Royal African Society*, 24(94) (1925): 100–09. [Trans].

The new governor, Cesare Maria De Vecchi—one of the *quadrumviri* of the March on Rome—held a diametrically opposed view.[5] He arrived in the colony on 8 December 1923 along with a small court of relatives and armed henchmen from Turin. Eight days into his stay, he already felt able to state that 'everything had to be done or re-done' in Somalia.[6] As he saw it, the political situation was 'intolerable and dangerous, because the entire population under direct rule were armed, and those protected by the Sultanates enjoyed absolute independence'. He thus alerted the Minister for the Colonies, Ferdezoni, that given the Somalians had 16,000 rifles and his own forces only 2,500, he would proceed without any hesitation and 'with every means available for the disarming of the local population'.[7]

In truth, De Vecchi's bellicose attitude concealed a deep, burning irritation. The governorate of Somalia was not, for De Vecchi, a reward or promotion, but a deliberate and humiliating punishment inflicted upon him by Mussolini for a period of at least five years. Relations between De Vecchi and Mussolini had never been good even before the March on Rome, and afterwards had only worsened. In a letter from 18 December 1922, having accused De Vecchi of recklessness and calumny, Mussolini added: 'I'm sure you would then add that the merit for the March on Rome is all yours, while I was in Milan trying on black shirts. But this is completely untenable, because you know full well that the March on Rome was my idea, that I pushed for it and that in the end I made it happen.'[8] De Vecchi responded to these criticisms by denying everything—but also by stepping down from his position as undersecretary

---

5 *Quadrumviri*: literally, the 'four men', a term from classical Rome reprised during Fascism to refer to the four members of the party's secretariat. [Trans.]

6 Cesare Maria De Vecchi, *Orizzonti d'impero. Cinque anni in Somalia* (Milan: Mondadori, 1935), p. 12.

7 De Vecchi, *Orizzonti d'impero*, p. 10 and p. 14, respectively.

8 Achivio centrale dello Stato, Rome: Segreteria particolare del duce, Carteggio riservato, b. 4/47, f. De Vecchi.

for war pensions. Mussolini nevertheless kept him under a watchful eye and had him tracked by the prefect of Turin, Enrico Palmieri.

Mussolini's telling-off clearly was not enough for De Vecchi; during a fiery speech at the Alfieri Theatre on 22 April 1923, he launched an appeal for Fascists to clear Italy of the 'filth' that had remained after October the year before: 'If necessary—and it certainly will be, I believe, to fully establish a new order and to reach the supreme goal—we might need to engage in half an hour of fighting and a minute of gunfire. That would probably do the job.'[9] This was too much for Mussolini. De Vecchi has challenged him publicly to make the Fascist revolution real—a revolution that in his opinion had been left incomplete—and, if this task were not immediately undertaken, to complete the revolution himself with 'a minute of gunfire'.

In order to make sure that De Vecchi could not do any further damage, the Minister for the Colonies suggested to Mussolini that he could be sent as far away as possible, for example: to far-flung Somalia. The Duce immediately seconded the suggestion. No one could have foreseen the cost to the Italian state of a governor whose powers were little more than those of a viceroy. No one could have suspected that the *quadrumviro* would end up launching costly, blood-soaked, gratuitous military campaigns. When the accounts were closed, the colony's expenses had increased eight times over, and Somalia—which had never created significant problems before—had become a land of insecurity.

De Vecchi certainly could not have opposed Mussolini's decision to confine him to Somalia. But he could transform his punishment into a positive fact—if only by demonstrating to the Duce that he was capable in the military sphere. Already a captain of the *arditi*, the holder of six medals for military valour, an organizer of the violent squads in Turin and Piedmont, commander general of the volunteer corps and seriously

9 Benito Mussolini, *Corrispondenza inedita* (Milan: Edizioni del Borghese, 1972), p. 203.

wounded in 1921 during a punitive expedition against the socialists of Casale Monferrato, De Vecchi had certainly already demonstrated that he was a practical man with neither scruples nor mercy. As he travelled to Mogadishu, he did not remotely think of himself as defeated; instead, he wanted to use his new engagement and experience as best he could. 'I am a veteran of the war, and of the fight against the socialists,' he confided in some friends. 'All I can do therefore is to continue the war in order to continue my journey.'[10]

De Vecchi wasted no time. At the beginning of January 1924, he ordered the disarmament of all the inhabitants of southern Somalia. The commissar of the Shabeelle region, Major Dell'Era, tried to explain to the new governor that the arms in circulation were bolt-action rifles that had never been used against the colonial government but, on the contrary, had been employed in its defence during the Derwish revolt.[11] Ignoring the invitation to proceed with caution that arrived from the Minister for the Colonies as well, and without any justification whatsoever, De Vecchi authorized the commander of the troops, Lieutenant Colonel Mario Re, to invade the lands of the Gaalje'el, Bersane and Badi Adde clans.[12] For several days at the end of March, the regions inhabited by these unlucky people were submitted to lead and steel, their herds annihilated, several villages bombed and set alight, and dozens of villagers paraded before the firing squad. 'The fires in the abandoned settlements which soon followed in the wake of our marching troops'—a pleased De Vecchi reported—'served as a healthy warning to encouraged the submission of the local population. They soon came to ask for mercy.'[13]

---

10 Associazione italiana per il controllo democratico, *Il governo fascista nelle colonie*, p. 14.

11 For the Derwish revolt, see 'Abdi Sheik-'Abdi, *Divine Madness: Mohammed Abdulle Hassane* (London: Zed Books, 1993) [Trans.]

12 Del Boca gives 'Galgial Bersane' and 'Badi Addo'; I have followed the spellings in Mohamed Haji Mukhtar, *Historical Dictionary of Somalia* (Maryland: Scarecrow Press, 2003) [Trans.]

This, however, was nothing more than a very modest taster of his overall program, a simple test of Mussolini and Federzoni's mood. De Vecchi's ambitions were quite different. His intention was to repeat the disarmament operation in the protected sultanates of the North, knowing full well that this would entail an actual war, a couple of years of full-scale police operations across the colony, and the necessity to conquer vast and inhospitable territory inch by inch. Since no explicit orders against this arrived from Rome, he sent about dedicating his entire attention to re-organizing and re-enforcing the colony's military forces, increasing the number of soldiers from 3,000 to 12,000, supported by 16 reconnaissance planes and a naval division under the command of Admiral Ugo Conz.

With the preparations complete, on 1 October 1925 the expedition corps established by De Vecchi invaded the Sultanate of Obbia, occupying it within less than a month and without a single Italian casualty. Matters did not go quite so smoothly, however, in Majeerteen. Both Sultan Osman Mahmud and his son, Erzi Bogor, refused to hand over their weapons, giving De Vecchi the motivation he needed to launch an offensive. As Mario Giovana has noted, this was not so much a traditional war as it was 'a colonial re-edition of the punitive expeditions by Fascist thugs'.[14] In other words, terrorist surprise attacks. And as always, ten against one.

De Vecchi personally took command of the operations in Majeerteen; but, instead of 'pacifying' Somalia, he managed to transform it into a single, immense battle field. While his attacks against Osman Mahmud came to nothing, behind him in the Sultanate of Hobyo—which De Vecchi believed to be already 'pacified'—a lieutenant called Omar Samantar led an attack on the garrison at El Bur, killing its commander, Captain Franco Cariolei, around 60 askari, and taking hold of an

---

13 De Vecchi, *Orizzonti d'impero*, p. 37.

14 Mario Giovana, *L'avventura fascista in Etiopia* (Milan: Teti, 1976), p. 31.

enormous arsenal. The episode was too serious to not solicit concerns in Rome. As De Vecchi himself recalled in his memoirs, Marshall Badoglio, then Chief of Staff

> first proposed that I should be removed from command, then insisted that I should be left only to handle civilian affairs [. . .]. His attempts led to nothing, but he did not give up. He compiled a report on the situation and described it in such catastrophic terms that the Minister for the Colonies trembled in fear. [. . .] With a passionate telegram I cut the discussion short and, ignoring the Marshall's orders, set upon relaunching the offensive.[15]

Employing a policy of terror, in the span of two years De Vecchi managed to stamp out outbreaks of rebellion in North Somalia, but the definitive count he himself provides was not insignificant. Three Italian officers had been killed, four Italian soldiers, 97 askari and 449 dubat,[16] while the wounded numbered 341. In the enemy camp, the dead numbered 1,236 and the wounded 757.[17] From these figures one can deduce that the entire bloody tribute was paid for by Somalians in an essentially fratricidal war, while the colonialists had so finely-tuned their methods— naval and air assaults, as well as an extensive use of mercenaries—that they did not lose more than seven men.

Concluding the narrative of his mission in Africa, De Vecchi claimed that:

> With the visit of His Royal Highness, Principe Umberto, Somalia—from Cape Kamboni through to the Gulf of Aden—

---

15 Cesare Maria De Vecchi, *Il quadrumviro scomodo. Il vero Mussolini nelle memorie del più monarchico dei fascisti* (Milan: Mursia, 1983), p. 115.

16 *Dubat*: literally, 'white turbans' (العمائم البيضاء). Name given to members of irregular soldiers employed by the Italian colonial troops in Somalia [Trans].

17 De Vecchi, *Orizzonti d'impero*, pp. 280–81. These are obviously unverifiable figures; in our view they do not include the losses suffered by the civilian population.

received the consecration of its new life and greater prosperity, and the Governor, following five years of effort and the execution of his program, requested the Head of Government to be relieved of office, a request which was conceded to him. He returned to Italy on 4 May 1928.[18]

In truth, Mussolini had already decided by the second half of 1927 that De Vecchi should be replaced. This was not only because he had become known as the 'butcher of the Somalians' in a moment in which Fascism was seeking to create a human face across Europe, but also because the costs of the military operations had exploded (62 million lire in 1927 alone), precisely when the regime was heavily engaged in re-stabilizing the currency. Finally, by authorizing a raid on Gorrahei in order to punish Somalian rebels who had taken refuge in Ethiopian territory, De Vecchi risked sabotaging the treaties that Rome and Addis Ababa were desperately trying to agree upon to ensure 20 years of friendship. All of this meant there was a certain urgency in disavowing and repatriating him.

There is an episode in the war waged by De Vecchi against the Somalians that not only reveals the typically thuggish Fascist methods utilized but also demonstrates how, faced with an emergency, he used the Fascist henchmen he had brought with him from Piedmont in order to crush his enemies.

The enemy in question was Sheikh Ali Mohamed Nur, owner of the mosque of Eli Hagi on the outskirts of Merca. He was suspected of nurturing overly hostile feelings to Italian domination, and of being the leader of a large mass of resistors, in particular the 7,000 farmers forced to work in the land reclamation project in Genale, managed by concession to a group of Italians. There was no real evidence, but it was believed

---

18 De Vecchi, *Orizzonti d'impero*, p. 292.

that the Sheikh could potentially organize a guerrilla attack against the Italians in the Benadir at the same time as the offensive Osman Mahmud was preparing in the North. In order to clarify matters, on 28 October 1926, the Commissar of Merca requested Ali Mohamed Nur's presence, but the Sheikh twice rejected his invitation. When the Marshall of the carabinieri, Aldo Fiorina, finally went to the mosque with a small escort and a warrant to bring the Sheikh to Merca by force, he was attacked and killed by a group of the holy man's followers.

De Vecchi was informed of the episode the same night, and immediately sent Captain Giuriati to Merca with 230 askari and zaptiè, as well as a section of mountain artillery.[19] The column, however, had to cover 150 km between Mogadishu and Merca; so they arrived at the destination not before dawn on 30 October, much too late to encircle the mosque of El Hagi and block the rebels' flight. De Vecchi thus decided to make use of the Italians managing the project at Genale, who in truth were a group of Fascist thugs that had followed him for the Somalian mission. 'I gave you the canal so you could irrigate your bananas and native shamba. I made the whole district of Genale rise out of nothing, 120 km from Mogadishu. It represents your future wealth. Now lend me your rifles—do not forget that you were once victorious soldiers of the Great War.'[20]

For this horrendous episode, we can draw upon the testimony of former colonialist Carlo Vecco, who was the deed-holder, along with his friend Mario Chiamberlando, for a concession of 325 hectares in Genale:

> There were around 50 of us who responded to the governor's appeal. So as not to lose any time, we cut off the road and took

---

19 *Zaptiè*: the term used for Somalians enrolled into the carabinieri, deriving ultimately from Arabic (ضبورية), i.e. policeman [Trans].

20 Cited in Ernesto Quadrone, *Pionieri, donne e belve. Uebi Scelebi, Giuba* (Milan: Agnelli, 1934), pp. 34–35. [*Shamba*: a Swahili word for cultivated land.—Trans].

the paths between the dunes. The road was not easy, but the moon was bright and in less than three hours we were in sight of Merca. We were armed with muskets and shotguns. Some had hand bombs and knives in their knapsacks. I led a squadron of around 20 men; another 30 were under the command of Cesare Buffo, the political secretary of Genale. With him there were also Benvenuto Bordone, Giovannini and Gariglio.

It seemed that the old days of guerrilla fighting against the socialists had returned, the gang skirmishes of Brandimarte, the assault on the labour building in Turin. This time, however 8,000 km from Italy, and without any uncomfortable witnesses and under De Vecchi's protection, the game was far more easy. Ali Mohamed Nur's followers were armed with nothing more than large sabres, knives and a few rifles acquired after the attack on Marshall Fiorina's escort. It was like participating in a hunt for big game, but more exciting and less dangerous. Vecco recalls:

> The most merciless among us were determined to liquidate all the natives in the area. There would never be an occasion like this again, Cesare Buffo underscored, and indeed he shot down the first 13 Somalians that he came across on the dunes. Once we had arrived in the city, we cleaned up a few wards by forcing people towards the El Hagi mosque, then we laid siege to it. If someone tried to run away, we put them down with a musket blast. When Captain Giurati arrived with his troops at dawn, we pulled back, because we felt we had finished our task. And in fact the governor never forgot our contribution, even mentioning it in his book, *Horizons of Empire*.[21]

---

21 De Vecchi recalled the intervention of 'fifty Fascists' (*Orizzonti d'impero*, p. 245). Carlo Vecco's account was recorded in Turin on 21 October 1977; but we met with him on many occasions between 1955 and 1965 at his concession in Genale, where we were able to see for ourselves that the way he treated the local labourers left much to be desired.

After putting the cannons in position and firing some warning shots, Captain Giurati demanded that the rebels surrender—but only 200 women and children exited the mosque. The men had decided to resist. This is how De Vecchi describes the operation:

> The artillery began another round, and a first assault was ordered, which was pushed back with great skill. [. . .] The next day the shots were better aimed and the mosque was occupied. More than 70 people lay dead on the ground, and the few defenders who had survived were shot. Sheikh Ali Mohamed Nur, however, had managed to escape. [. . .] He was surrounded in Fidarat on 7 November, and killed along with his followers. Between 28 October and 7 November, the operation cost us 8 dead and 20 wounded, as well as the life of an Italian, the marshal of the Royal Carabinieri—but more than 200 rebels met their death. On the government's order, all of them were shot.[22]

We might well ask ourselves today, as was asked at the time in government circles, what the reason was for so much ferocity. The official documents are silent about the episode, but in truth it is not difficult to understand the motivations for De Vecchi's rage. Badoglio had already asked for his head following the disaster at El Bur: if the governor had not immediately stamped out the rebellion at Merca, in all likelihood Badoglio would have reiterated his criticisms and had him removed from office as unfit for the role. It was not difficult to explain the cruel behaviour of the concessionaires either. As Buffo specified—a Fascist through and through—Merca presented a long-awaited chance to remind the Somalians (especially those working in the new district of Genale) that the men who had arrived with De Vecchi were completely new Italians, who had nothing in common with the natives and did not intend to

---

22 De Vecchi, *Orizzonti d'impero*, p. 246.

either. They wanted to demonstrate that they were extremely demanding masters who would not tolerate rebellion, apathy or idleness on the job. The gunfire that exploded around the El Hagi mosque represented an edict that no authority had ever issued but which from that point on would function admirably and would be tacitly accepted. From that moment until 1926, the Somalians of Benadir would be further enslaved—if this were possible; they would become objects even more, registered in batches along with camels, goats and cows.

We have seen how the colonialists of Genale organized a manhunt in Merca; now we will go and visit them in their kingdom, the land-reclamation district along the banks of the river Webi Shabeelle. Created by De Vecchi from the ashes of the experimental but failed Genale 'company', the district included an imposing dam and 54 km of canals, incorporating 18,000 hectares subdivided into 83 concessions, varying from 100 to 1,000 hectares each. The main products of the district were cotton, castor, corn, sugar cane, bananas, incense and kapok. The labour was provided by 7,000 natives, who De Vecchi defined as 'good, serious and faithful working masses'.[23] In truth, this was a completely wayward description, and the governor knew it. Aware of the vast number of violations, he was forced to send the concessionaires an official note, stating for example that:

> the organization and employment of the government's—and the governor's—impressive influence over the native peoples has the humanitarian, disciplinary, Fascist objective of the gradual introduction of labour among those peoples; it is not that of a random coercion that would create a pseudo-slavery or serfdom, and even less of a simply use and abuse in the interest of private persons.[24]

---

23 De Vecchi, *Orizzonti d'impero*, p. 321.
24 De Vecchi, *Orizzonti d'impero*, pp. 326–27.

The local peasants were protected in theory by the 'Bertello' farmworkers' contract, but the concessionaires interpreted the terms very liberally, turning it in their favour.[25] In truth, in the hands of the greedy concessionaires—who had almost no agricultural experience—the peasants had become slaves to all effects. Their working conditions did not improve either when Guido Corni, a noted colonial functionary, took over from De Vecchi. Corni's main task was to set the colony in order after years of guerrilla fighting and the frenetic, chaotic governance of the *quadrumviro*—who had left the coffers empty as well. Maurizio Rava, who replaced Corni in turn in 1931, was also unable to resolve the question of the enslaved peasants. Ceding to the pressure of the concessionaires—who constituted the largest, strongest, most homogenous and most Fascist group in the colony—Rava was not only forced to back them by halving their export tax and rewarding them with supportive prizes, he also had to close an eye to their continued labour violations.

In the end, in a tone that brings to mind the abolitionist cries of Gustavo Chiesi or Robecchi Bricchetti, the waywardness was criticized by the most unlikely of persons: Marcello Serrazanetti, Federal Secretary for Somalia, i.e. the highest Fascist authority in the colony. A close friend of Leandro Arpinati, with whom he had founded the Fascio of Bologna, and just as fiery, antagonistic a critic as his spiritual leader, Serrazanetti arrived in Somalia in 1929; over the following years, he sent three long reports to Mussolini and to Parliament that described all the colony's problems—and first and foremost that of forced labour. Printed in very few copies, these reports represent the only public document over the two decades of Fascist rule that question the organization of the colony and its abysmal relationship with the indigenous population.

Serrazanetti knew that there would be explosive consequences to sending such reports to the highest levels of the regime. The accusations

---

25 See Angelo Del Boca, *Gli italiani in Africa Orientale, Volume 2: La conquista dell'impero* (Rome: Laterza, 1979).

and revelations did not only relate to Corni and Rava, but also involved the Ministers for the Colonies and Foreign Affairs, and even the head of government himself in the final instance. Let us examine, for example, how he introduced the problem of forced labour. Having established that 'it would be naive to consider the colonization as a purely philanthropic expansion' and that, faced with the urgency of making the colony profitable, it was possible to 'make use of forced labour', considered as 'a harsh initial necessity', Serrazanetti noted that this should nevertheless be 'limited to the execution of works of public utility' and never for 'private utility', and never accompanied by 'abuse and maltreatment'.[26]

On the contrary, the Federal Secretary observed that:

the form of forced labour that has been imposed on the Somalian natives for years—futilely and cynically concealed since 1929 by a work contract—is far worse than true slavery, because over there the indigenous labourer has been robbed of that valid protection enjoyed by the slave, which was constituted by his market value, a protection that ensured him at least a minimum of care, the kind that even the worst cart driver has for his donkey, knowing that he must buy another one if it dies. In Somalia, however, when an indigenous worker assigned to a concessionaire dies or is unable to work, he simply asks the governor's office for a substitute, who sends one over for free.[27]

Serrazanetti then progressed to examining the most unsettling details of the situation, beginning with the fact that the workers were not freely recruited but conscripted by force 'from those *qabiil* that are perceived to be the most devoted and docile', often with the complicity of some waged local authority figures.[28] The rows of deportees were then sent to

---

26 Marcello Serrazanetti, *Considerazioni sulla nostra attività coloniale in Somalia* (Bologna: Tipografia La Rapida, 1933), pp. 5–9.

27 Serrazanetti, *Considerazioni*, p. 10.

28 *Qabiil*: the Somali word for 'clans', ultimately from the Arabic (قبيلة). See Ioan

a destination under armed guard, sometimes even chained together to impede any escape, sometimes covering hundreds of miles. Once they arrived at the concession, the new recruits were told to sign a contract (the meaning of which they could not possibly understand) with their fingerprint, and thereby began the job—for 10 hours a day and under the strict surveillance of either gangmasters of the concessionaires themselves. In many concessions it was normal that if the labourers failed to provide the expected yield, whether due to health reasons or due to their broken spirit, their food rations would be either halved or even suspended, in the hope that hunger would drive them towards greater activity.[29]

In this inferno, the hardiest managed to adapt themselves to the new environment, albeit slowly; others fell ill and died; others still attempted to flee and resigned themselves to living in the hostile bushland. Serrazanetti recalled that 'in 1929, a few hundred of them were picked up at Juba, around 400 km from Genale.' If an enslaved person refused to work or rebelled against the concessionaire, he would be reported to the colonial authorities, who would punish him harshly, usually with a series of lashings or, in the worst cases, a few months of prison. Serrazanetti added:

> I will not continue at length, exposing other episodes such as the dead found in the fields or by the road, or the sick and dying abandoned to their fate with no assistance of help, of workers who have died after beatings from the concessionaires they depended upon, because hunger had driven them to steal a few husks of corn from the field, or finally of those individuals who, sent to work in the concession, preferred suicide—an

Myrddin Lewis, *A Pastoral Democracy* (Oxford: Oxford University Press, 1961), p. 133 [Trans].

29 Serrazanetti, *Considerazioni*, pp. 11–12.

extremely rare occurrence among the Somalians—opening their veins with their own knives.[30]

The overview sketched out by Serrazanetti in 1933 was confirmed for us by Vecco in 1977, who also provided us with details that render the situation more murky still. For example, he admitted that the workers spent 11 or 12 hours in the fields, and that beatings were constantly used. As a rule, discipline and punishment were delivered by Marshal Avella of the carabinieri in Genale, but the concessionaires often reverted to performing their own 'justice'. Vecco told us quite calmly, without any embarrassment, that one day after receiving a slap from a Bimal-clan Somalian, he dragged him to the barn and almost beat him to death in front of the other workers. He then tied him up and sent him to Avella to get what was due to him.[31]

Every now and again someone raised their voice in defence of this unfortunate mass; Commissar Pietro Barile, for example, who denounced the violations and maltreatment, calling on the concessionaires to be more humane. But these were isolated voices with no influence. The standard practice was quite different. As Serrazanetti recalls: 'To shore up the constant diminishing productivity of the workers, the local authorities intensified the application of corporal punishment. During a meeting of the concessionaires called by him at Vittorio d'Africa last summer, His Excellency Maurizio Rava declared that he would personally assume the moral responsibility for corporal punishments inflicted.'[32]

Aside from the concessionaires' brutality and greed, and the governor's open complicity, what irritated Serrazanetti was the 'poetic, pastoral, Olympian' framing that was expressed in relation to Genale by Italian scholars and politicians who were invited to Somalia. He accused them of fabrication and short-sightedness, even of impeding the colony's

---

30 Serrazanetti, *Considerazioni*, p. 14.

31 Account provided to the author by Carlo Vecco.

32 Serrazanetti, *Considerazioni*, p. 18.

development through their comments. His own proposal was to abolish forced labour 'which maintains 6,000 or 7,000 Blacks in a state of slavery', to strengthen the indigenous economy, and to protect the Somalian people without delay, who had mourned 60,000 dead in the famine of 1932 alone.[33]

To lay the basis for these policies and find the necessary funds, Serrazanetti suggested cutting back the stellar salaries and perks enjoyed by the governors, saving on public works that represented pure prestige as well as on the frequent and costly official receptions. He concluded thus: 'In order to rip open the diaphragm that distorts the truth before it arrives up top, it might be necessary to offer up one those people who, in other times, we called fools when they were sent over the top to an enemy trench; well, then, as a Fascist I am proud to offer myself up, entrusting myself to the judgement of the Duce and to posterity.'[34]

Mussolini did not mete out the judgement he deserved. On the contrary, he first removed him from the role of federal secretary, entrusting it to Maurizio Rava—who thus, without precedent, embodied the offices of both governor and secretary. Later, in 1933, Serrazanetti was called back to the Patria and charged with the more modest role of vice-secretary to the Fascist federation of Bologna. In 1934, when Leandro Arpinati was arrested and accused of treason, Serrazanetti fell from grace along with his spiritual leader, and was sent to the penal colony in Sardinia for five years. The *quadrumviro* Emilio De Bono also had him in his crosshairs, writing to Mussolini on 30 November 1934 that: 'the question of indigenous labour has been resolved, which is now sufficiently and correctly paid. Serrazanetti's libellous accusations have been clearly

---

33 Marcello Serrazanetti, *La politica indigena in Somalia* (Bologna: Tipografia La Rapida, 1934), pp. 4–11, p. 20 and p. 24, respectively.

34 Serrazanetti, *La politica indigena*, p. 32. The third part of Serrazanetti's memoirs was entitled *Basi economiche della Somalia Italiana* (Bologna: Tipografia La Rapida, 1930).

dismantled by the facts observed in the field with absolute objectivity.'[35]

In truth, that which Somalians called 'white slavery' was not officially suppressed until February 1941, when the British occupied the country. Even then, it was not entirely stamped out: in 1948, one of the 23 conditions established by the Conference of Somalia in order to accept the Trust Territory of Somaliland under Italian Administration was the abolition of the forced labour.[36] The horrendous practice was only finally wiped out when the last concessionaire left Somalia. The era of whips and bananas was finally over.[37]

---

35 Achivio centrale dello Stato, Rome: Segreteria particolare del duce, Carteggio riservato, b. 224, sf. De Bono.

36 Pietro Beritelli, *L'amministrazione municipale di Mmogadiscio negli anni dal 1941 al 1949*, p. 207). [The work is a typewritten MS, a copy of which is deposited in the Fondo Bruno of the historical archives of the Ministry for Italian Africa.—Trans.]

37 For a more detailed account of the events described in this chapter, see Angelo Del Boca, *Gli italiani in Africa Orientale, Volume 2: La conquista dell'impero* (Rome and Bari: Laterza, 1979), pp. 50–93 and 198–216.

EIGHT

IN SULUQ AS IN AUSCHWITZ

While Cesare Maria De Vecchi, *quadrumviro* and Count of Val Cismon,[1] cleaned the rebels out of Northern Somalia and enlisted a gang of Fascist thugs to liquidate a hostile holy man—remunerating them by permitting the most abject form of slavery—in Libya, another young colonel, Rodolfo Graziani, a man who was destined to become the most celebrated—and hated—of all colonial officers, was consolidating his fame.

Graziani himself revealed the secret to his own success. Openly arguing against the 'regressive and stagnant theories' of the old colonial officers, he outlined a strategy that aimed more at the enemy's death rather than at occupying their territory. His strategy utilized all the modern technology available (radio, reconnaissance planes, air bombings, tanks, armed cars), relying not so much on the number of soldiers deployed but on the speed of the strikes. Graziani also utilized 'the essential character of the Eritrean and Libyan troops, which till now has been greatly repressed by our tactical designs, tactics are too rigid and slow to deal with contingencies.'[2] Removing these limitations from the 'barbaric hordes', Graziani transformed the indigenous troops into a horrific instrument of death, on the basis of which he built his rapid career and spectacular fortune.

1 Count of Val Cismon: an honorific title De Vecchi was awarded by the King in 1925 in recognition of the eponymous battle of 1918. [Trans.]

2 Rodolfo Graziani, *Pace romana in Libia* (Milan: Mondadori, 1937), p. 32 for both quotations.

Finally, Graziani claimed that he and his officers were of a character very different from that demonstrated by the officer class operating in Libya since 1911:

> The Arabs understood that they were facing a new enemy, one with a new soul born from the great victory on the European front, one that was using new methods; the enemy no long froze at the first sounds of gunfire, he was no longer concerned by the torrid heat and merciless climate, he no longer showed his cards but instead attacked immediately, furiously, on the flank, the rear, the front, without respite or mercy.[3]

In a report dated 18 June 1922 about the occupation of Al Jawsh, Graziani added further remarks on his constant success: 'I impose my will on the adversary, engaging in combat when and where I wanted it, instead of being prey to his own will.'[4]

The arrival of Fascism impressed a decidedly more accelerated rhythm on the operation to reconquer Libya, which had already begun under the watch of the previous liberal governments. This aligned with Graziani's hopes, who had often criticized the hesitation and pauses of the past. He had still not acquired any fame back home, but his name was widely known among his troops, who followed him with great fidelity. Indeed, he himself ensured the expansion of his own reputation, which clearly pleased him. In his book he refers to the fact that, on more than one occasion, he had listened to a song sung in his honour around the campfire:

> If you don't know us, they know us well on the uplands
> We're the hardened soldiers of General Graziani
> *bon, bon, bon* to the sound of the cannons![5]

---

3 Graziani, *Pace romana*, p. 32.

4 Archivio centrale dello Stato, Rome: Carte Graziani, b. 1, f. 3, sf. 1.

5 Graziani, *Pace romana*, p. 58.

Over the years, servile journalists and writers competed with each other in constructing Graziani's persona, attributing him with virtues of heroism and charisma, making him into a living legend, even comparing him to the Ancient Roman general Scipio Africanus. He was also meant to be an intellectual—even if in truth his excessive and error-riddled prose was intolerable. It was Graziani himself who supported the myth of his vast learning: 'If it befall me some time to feel my powers awavering, I love to sip from the great source of classicism next to which, on the question of colonial conquests, life itself has no more to teach us. Caesar, Livius, Tacitus and Sallustus are my lords and masters.'[6]

At the same time, however, he was also consolidating his infamy as a cruel and pitiless soldier. It was not only the relatives of his victims who labelled him the 'butcher of the Arabs' but also those among his colleagues who did not share his merciless methods. This negative publicity did not, however, seem to disturb him:

> I have frequently examined my own conscience in relation to these accusations of cruelty, atrocities and violence that have been attributed to me. I have never slept so well as on those nights when it has been necessary to undertake such reflections, for I know from the history of all epochs that nothing new can be built without destroying, in part or entirely, a past which can longer handle the present.[7]

---

6 Paolo Orano, *Rodolfo Graziani, generale scipionico* (Rome: Pinciana, 1936), p. 17.

7 Orano, *Rodolfo Graziani*, p. 16. In truth, not even his closest collaborators held him in high esteem. The Duke of Aosta told the Minister for Italian Africa: 'I have known Graziani since I was a major *meharista* and followed his orders. I have always seen him betray his superiors, with the exception of General De Bono, because he let him do whatever he wanted. If I were to welcome him as a colleague, it would simply end with him betraying me.'—Alessandro Lessona, *Un ministro di Mussolini racconta* (Milan: Edizioni Nazionali, 1973), p. 169.

A military man of such a character naturally appealed to Mussolini, who had dreamt of a 'new Italian' from the very first years of his regime. Graziani did not let him down. Immediately after the March on Rome, he demonstrated that he was the most Fascistic among all the higher-ranking officers. Here is how he described his own march, on Yafran, which magically coincided with Mussolini's on Rome:

> Destiny would have it that the fighting took place around the ancient mausoleum of Suffit, and that I should find, among its ruins, a very ancient coin depicting the figure of Rome Imperious on one side and that of an Emperor on the other, a coin that I had the occasion later to present to the Duce. Destiny would have it that my troops would display their victorious arms on the advent of Fascism and would glorify our great victory, finally won and redeemed, to the four winds and under the desert's watch, bringing the greatest auspices for Italy's prestige in the land of Africa.[8]

Between 1922 and 1932—the year in which Libya was fully re-occupied—the only pauses in the fighting were due essentially to financial problems, and never to doubts or wavering of a political nature. With the support of a strong government, Governor of Tripolitania, Giuseppe Volpi, could steam ahead with his program of reconquest without needing to take account of public opinion, answering only to the young Minister of Colonies, Luigi Federzoni. Thus, as soon as the political and military situation in Yefren was stabilized, Volpi decided to give the rebels no respite and proceed without delay to reoccupying the Jebel and Garian mountains. On 6 February 1923, Tarhuna was taken. On 27 December, Ben Walid fell. On 15 June 1924, Mizda; on 23 November, Sirte; on 5 February 1925, the far-flung oasis of Ghadames was conquered. In practice, with only 20,000 men, Volpi had

---

8 Graziani, *Pace romana*, p. 52.

managed to reoccupy almost all of Tripolitania. Over the course of this operation, Graziani distinguished himself as the most audacious and successful of officers, earning himself a promotion to the rank of brigadier general.

When the operations recommenced in January 1928, Graziani had already set off, commanding group 'A' which, combined with other forces, was meant to operate across the 29th parallel, thus connecting Tripolitania to Cyrenaica. Following four heavy bombardments of phosgene—which sowed panic and death among the Mogarba er-Raedat—Graziani's column occupied Houn on 14 February and stormed Zella on the 22nd.[9] On the 25th, he recommenced the campaign with the aim of arriving at the wells of Tagrift, in the Tagrift Basin. However, in this particularly challenging terrain, which was perfect for ambushes, Graziani's column of 1,500 men was suddenly attacked by Aulad Soliman and warriors from other clans, whose number equalled that of the Italian-Eritrian forces. At Tagrift, they finally fought with even numbers, rifles against rifles, bayonets against sabres. The mujaheddin fought impressively in this context, taking aim above all at the officers, killing or wounding 11 of them.

Despite the danger of being encircled, Graziani managed to repel the attacks and rout his enemies, who were under the command of two brothers, Ahmed and Abdel Gelil Sef en-Nasser.[10] Graziani doubtless overcame this formidable test, but the final balance of losses was not insignificant. On the Italian side, 5 officers and 54 men had been killed; 6 officers and 156 wounded. The mujaheddin, on the other hand, had lost 247 men on the battlefield, while another 50 had been shot by the platoons of spahis during the retreat.[11]

---

9 *Mogàrba er-Raedàt*: Potentially the Magarha. [Trans].

10 For the brothers, see Angelo Del Boca, *A un passo dalla forca* (Milan: Mondolibri, 2007). [Trans].

11 *Spahi*: locally recruited light cavalry, from the Farsi sepâhi, 'soldier'. [Trans].

Reflecting on the mission, Graziani commented with his usual modesty:

> At 8 a.m. on the 3rd of the month, our column finally entered the basin of Nufilia and laid battle, after a periplus of *c*.2,000 km through steppe and desert zones, surely to be counted among the greatest challenges that were overcome by anyone in the entirety of the colonial campaigns, and in which the power and maturity of our preparation and organization, as well as the tactical abilities of the commanders and troops, appeared in the greatest brilliance, so as to make us proud of the labours carried out and sure in being able to imagine still more arduous and difficult undertakings.[12]

The attempt to mimic the classics is all too visible in his halting Italian prose—but, as General De Bono made clear, the encounter at Tagrift, for all its importance, did not deserve such hyperbolic praise. In his *Diary*, De Bono dealt with the episode in these few words: 'Yesterday Graziani gave fight a little to the north of Tagrift. The rebels defended the wells fiercely. Was he taken by surprise? On our own side the losses are significant.'[13]

At the beginning of 1929, Mussolini decided to entrust the government of Tripolitania and Cyrenaica to a single figure. For this task he chose Pietro Badoglio, *maresciallo d'Italia*, who maintained—by his own expressed will—this role as the military chief of staff. Badoglio reached Tripoli on 24 January 1929; on the very same day he issued two edicts. The first generic proclamation was direct to the Italians. The second— brutal and threatening in tone—was for the Libyans:

---

12 Graziani, *Pace romana in Libia*, p. 52.

13 Archivio centrale dello Stato, 'Diario De Bono', VOL. 11, p. 65.

All of you, whether you live in Tripolitania or Cyrenaica, have known the Italian government for years, and you know that it is just and benevolent towards those who submit to its laws and orders with a pure heart; it is unwavering and merciless, on the other hand, towards those few ill-meaning persons who believe, in their madness, that they can oppose Italy's invincible strength.[14]

Badoglio's message had the contrary effect however. Instead of repenting, the 'ill-meaning persons' congregated in West al-Shatii and decided to organize a new offensive against the Italian garrisons. Between March and May, the chiefs of the Tripolitanian resistance launched their final attacks, commencing from distant bases. Thus while Saleh el-*Atèusc* descended from the mountains of Harugi es-Soda to hit out with raids between en-Nufilia and Agedabia, Ahmed Sef en-Nasser and Mohammed ben Hag Hassen brought their mehalla forces into the Ghibla,[15] slicing between the Italian outposts on the uplands. Graziani's reaction was immediate, effective and relentless. In three victorious battles, he pushed back the mujaheddin, decimating their ranks.

'Following the brilliant political-military success of the first half of 1929,' Graziani reported, 'the mirage of Fezzan, a far-off dream even if already connected to the fortunate events of 1915, fascinated everyone's hearts and minds. [. . .] The order to advance was thus awaited by all with an unparalleled anxiety and enthusiasm.'[16] Once Mussolini had given his consent, Badoglio and Graziani completed the logistical preparations over November, aiming for a full occupation of the region. The plan reprised that of the unlucky colonel Miani, and included an

---

14 *Rivista delle colonie italiane*, 3 (March 1929): 296.

15 *Mehalla*: a section of armed men, from the Arabic word (محلة), 'neighbourhood'; Ghibla: locality to the south of the Green Mountains. [Trans].

16 Graziani, *Pace romana*, p. 142.

initial manoeuvre with a single mass of troops and vehicles along the axis of Shweref-Brak-Sabha-Murzuq. Even if at the peak of its force the column did not count more than 4,000 men, all of them were equipped with either armed cars or cavalry. The column was to form a wedge between the rebel regiments, which were apparently imbalanced on the East and West, and whose forces were evaluated as no more than 1,500 men. This was still a significant force, but after eight years of uninterrupted guerrilla warfare, they were in fragments and exhausted.

On the eve of the operation's commencement, Graziani called the officers together at Shuwairif and explained to them the basic outline of his plan:

> This will not be a simple campaign of territorial occupation but one of a dynamic motion that goes right to the end, right up to the extreme limits of the refuges that the enemy erroneously believes to be inaccessible to our military capabilities. He will be taken by surprise and defeated due to this very miscomprehension. An unforgettable and, we might say, Biblical march across the desert looms before us. We will overcome everything with our usual energy, in the spirit of our motto: *Usque ad finem*. The campaign will last three months.[17]

Graziani remained faithful to the strategy he had developed with Badoglio's assistance. On 5 December 1929, he occupied Brak. Ten days later, Sabha fell without casualties. Then, instead of continuing to Murzuq, Graziani decided to curve to the left and engage the Sef en-Nasser in combat at their stronghold at Wawa al Kabir, a good 360 km from Sabha. This extremely risky operation did not achieve its aim, because the brothers decided to avoid the engagement, withdrawing to the far-off oasis at Kufra. Nevertheless, it represented a success:

---

17 Graziani, *Pace romana in Libia*, p. 153. Also printed in *L'Oltremare*, 3 (March 1931): 105.

with the Sef en-Nasser out of the way, the Italians no longer had to fear any threat from the east.

Murzuq, the capital of Fezzan, fell on 21 January 1930. On 28 January, Graziani reached Awbari and learnt that the last cells of the mujaheddin were trying to reach Algeria to save themselves. A fragmentary force of around a thousand fighters, slowed down by families and livestock, their only source of sustenance. Examined objectively, they did not represent any real danger, given their decision to cross over to Algeria, where the French would have disarmed them in haste. Another commander, such as Miani, would have given up the chase, contenting themselves with having ridden Libya of rebel leaders of the calibre of Abd en-Nebi Belker, Mohammed ben Hag Hassen and Hamed ben Hassen ben Ali. But Graziani was too acrimonious, too vengeful to let his prey escape, and immediately launched two full columns in pursuit. He learnt a few days later that the offensives had come to nothing, and that, from 8 February, the rebels had already begun to cross the border.

Irritated at the lost opportunity for combat, he launched all the air units available at the fleeing mehella. For two days, 13 and 14 February 1930, a fleet of Romeo Ro. 1 and Caproni Ca. 73 light bombers—which could hold up to a metric ton of incendiaries—alternated attacks on the border, with bombardments and machine guns. As journalist Sandro Sandri, an eye-witness recalled, the attacks fell on 'a human herd that, aside from armed men, was composed of a multitude of women and children. Behind them, the cattle: a Biblical vision of an exodus caused by the stubbornness of a few criminal chiefs who dragged the poor people with them in their flight.'[18] Sandri and other witnesses to this exodus—which culminated in a massacre— had no doubt about who to condemn. Not a single one managed to

18 'Le ultime marce all'inseguimento dei ribelli', *Il Regime fascista*, 8 March 1930.

grasp the greatness and nobility of the drama that was unfolding before their eyes.

Many of the mujaheddin had taken up arms eight years' before; for eight armed years, they had lived in one of the most inhospitable countries in world. For eight years, they had fought against a vastly strong and merciless enemy, occasionally managing some lucky strikes, but more often receiving devastating losses. They had left behind pieces of their flesh and blood on the Mediterranean shores and right through to the most southern extremes of Libya, along 1,500 km of dunes, serir and desolate mountainscapes. They had abandoned their country only when they had felt their enemy on their heels. Abd en-Nebi Belker had crossed the Algerian border on 12 February, presenting himself to the French authorities at Fort Chalet, in the oasis of Janet. The majority of the rebels, along with their families and herds—around 2,800 people and 6,000 camels—took the crossing further north, followed by a hurricane of gunfire; the survivors gave themselves up at the French garrison of Fort Tarat.

This absurd, futile massacre—of which one reads almost nothing in the official documents, and of which Graziani himself, usually so ready to underline his brutal successes, makes no mention in his book *Pace Romana in Libia*—brought the Fezzan campaign to a close. Before taking the plane to Tripoli, Graziani applauded his troops, who had allowed him to leap from one victory to another over the previous nine years. He concluded by addressing Uaar, his 'noble steed', with a monologue that expresses a boundless vainglory through the most hackneyed romanticism:

> Together we overcame Gefra, the Jebel, Ghibla, the Hammada, the desert of Sirte, Fezzan; I led you to every well of which to drink, and you carried me to quench my unquenchable thirst for conquest. [. . .] Your hard saddle was my cushion, your blanket my mantle, in the frozen camps that breathed the

danger of an inimical surprise. [. . .] But this is our kingdom no more! We shall return melancholically to the sea Uaar, for upon this long enterprise, which we have dreamed, led and accomplished together, a beautiful but terrifying word is about to fall: end.[19]

The occupation of Ghibla and Fezzan, completed in only three months, represented the productive result of the alliance between Badoglio and Graziani. Badoglio was the brains, Graziani the brawn. Both were boundlessly ambitious, stubborn, merciless and indifferent to the suffering of the people of Libya, for whom they held a demonstrable contempt. Of the two, Badoglio was the greedier; despite the dire financial situation of the country, he managed to extract an annual salary of 698,000 lire.[20]

At the end of 1930, Badoglio and Graziani reunited, this time to definitively liquidate the Senussi resistance in Cyrenaica. Badoglio maintained his role as the single governor of all of Libya, while Graziani—who had received an ovation from parliament and Mussolini himself during a rapid visit to Rome—installed himself in Benghazi as vice-governor of Cyrenaica. In his first speech from the balcony of the governor's residence, he announced: 'my government's actions will be faithfully formed according to the directives of the Fascist government, because, as a general of a military division in active service, I feel it is important to declare my clearly Fascist principles.'[21] This was the first time, since Fascism had risen to power, that an army general had made a public declaration of faith of this kind. By proclaiming himself a Fascist, Graziani intended to communicate that his governmental activities

---

19 Graziani, *Pace romana in Libia*, pp. 182–83.

20 Archivio centrale dello Stato, 'Diario De Bono', VOL. 13, p. 104. For the sake of comparison, the annual salary of an elementary school teacher was 300 lire.

21 The complete text of the speech was published in *Rivista delle colonie italiane*, 5 (May 1930): 428–29.

would differ from those of the past, that there would be a new 'dynamic and powerful' approach.[22]

As soon as he assumed the role of vice-governor, Graziani began to put in practice a series of 'protective measures' that affected military, judiciary and administrative spheres. To begin with, he reduced the corps from 23,000 to 13,000 soldiers, removing the indigenous Libyan battalions and the irregular troops who he no longer trusted. At the same time, he began the total disarmament of the Libyan population, which possessed 7,000 rifles and 250,000 cartridges. He hardened sanctions against deserters and punished the crime of living with the enemy with the death sentence. He can also be attributed with the creation of the 'flying court', i.e. a special military court that moved quickly from one location to another in the colony, in order to provide an image of efficient, effective and permanent justice.

But when in June Graziani set his renewed military machine in motion—following a visit to Bengasi by Badoglio and the Minister for the Colonies, De Bono—enacting a vast raid on the Fayed, he only obtained very modest results, just as the governors before him—who he had publicly criticized—had done. The main reason for his lack of success was due to the presence of Omar al-Mukhtar on the battlefield, representative of Idris es-Senussi, who had been successfully waging a guerrilla war against the Italians for nine years.

In his memoirs, Graziani provided a reductive and, in some aspects, patently false sketch of the old Ikhwan:

> It ought not be believed that Omar al-Mukhtar was a man of any superior intelligence, or gifted with exceptional virtues, as has often been said, simply because he was able, by his cunning, to give our command the slip for so long. He was a Bedouin like the others, without any education or idea of civilized life.

22 *Rivista delle colonie italiane*, p. 5.

He was a fanatic. And he was ignorant: he could only just about write his name.[23]

In truth, Omar al-Mukhtar was extremely educated. Before taking to the hills, he had taught for decades in a Koranic school. Furthermore, he held an extraordinary influence over the peoples of Cyrenaica, to the extent that he had asked them to make the greatest of sacrifices for years. The losses among his own small army (he never led more than 1,500 men) were continuously compensated by new and highly motivated recruits. Finally, he possessed a genuine gift for guerrilla strategy. He had managed to keep forces ten times superior to his own in a stalemate for nine years. He would strike with ferocity and then speedily retreat from the enemy's jaws before they closed in on him.

Graziani knew perfectly well that he was facing a worthy adversary, otherwise he would not have issued two extremely difficult ordinances in preparation for his (eventually unsuccessful) June offensive: expropriating the Senussi zawiyas of all of their goods and property;[24] and the forced resettlement of the local, indigenous population in the proximity of the Italian garrisons.[25] In doing so, Graziani attempted to deprive the rebellion of the direct help of the local population and of

---

23 Graziani, *Pace romana*, p. 243. Badoglio's own judgement of Omar al-Mukhar was quite different: 'The rebellion is being carried forward by a man who enjoys complete prestige and authority. Omar al-Mukhar shares his power with no one. He has only the most devoted and disciplined of lieutenants. [. . .] In every situation and moment, his strong will is law. He is extremely capable as both commander and as organizer.' Archivio centrale dello Stato, Carte Graziani, b. 1, f. 2, sf. 2, report by Badoglio to De Bono, 1 July 1930.

24 *Zawiya*: Sufi religious monuments, including mosques and tombs. From the Arabic (زاوية), 'corner'. [Trans.]

25 The 33 religious leaders of the Senusite zawiyas were boarded on the Italian destroyer *Stocco* on 28 September 1930 and deported to Ustica. They were repatriated on 15 August 1933 (Ministero per Affari Esteri, Affari Politici, b. 7, f. 1).

the Senussi confraternity. It was not, however, meant to be a permanent operation. Badoglio and De Bono alike had a much more vast and radical intervention in mind, entailing the total eviction of Jebel Akhdar and Marmarica. Graziani's ordinance was simply the dress rehearsal for the mass deportation which would finally be enacted between July and December 1930.

Angered by Graziani's failure in the Fayed, Badoglio sent him a long letter on 20 June in which he harshly criticized his efforts and gave him the following new and terrifying orders:

> To begin with, we need to create a broad and well-defined territorial break between the rebel units and the subjected population. I will not conceal the grave consequence of this order, which will effectively mean the ruin of the so-called subjected population. But at this point the road has been shown to us, and we must follow it right to the end, even if the whole population of Cyrenaica should perish.[26]

Five days after writing this letter, which would lead to the deportation of 100,000 Libyans from Jebel Akhdar and Marmarica, Badoglio met with Graziani to map out the method by which to carry out an operation which had no precedents in the history of modern Africa. They were not, however, the only figures responsible for his infamous undertaking. The Minister for the Colonies, De Bono, had long requested this kind of extreme measure, and there is certainly no evidence that Mussolini had any qualms in approving it.

The total eviction of the uplands of Cyrenaica began on 27 June 1930 and continued for several weeks. But effecting the eviction of the Marmaricans and Abeidats would require covering more than 1,000 km, lasting several months. The documentary material on the deportations from Cyrenaica is extremely scarce, and the little that is

---

26 Archivio centrale dello Stato, Carte Graziani, b. 1, f. 2, sf. 2.

conserved in the state archives is vague. We can, however, make use of a full and detailed report on the exodus of the Awagir. This represented the eviction of several thousand people, the vast majority women, children and the elderly. Right from the first days of the march, the old and weak were gradually left behind:

> Delays were not allowed during the stations. Anyone who hesitated was immediately shot. Such a draconian approach was taken through necessity, given that the population was reticent to abandoned their lands and goods. Even the animals that were not physically able to keep up with the march were immediately put down by the light cavalry of the irregular police force, who had been given the role of protecting and safeguarding them.[27]

The different columns were then taken to concentration camps located across South Bengasi and Sirte, in other words: in the most torrid, inhospitable zones of Libya. According to a report by Graziani from 2 May 1931, i.e. once the transfers had been completed, the largest camp was at Marsa Brega, which housed 21,117 inhabitants from Abeidat and Marmarica. After this came Suluq, with 2,123 people from Awagir, Abid, Orfa, Fawakhir and Mogarba; then Sidi Ahmed el-Magrun, with 13,500 people from Braasa and Dorsa; el-Agheila, with 10,900 people from Mogarba and Marmarica, as well as relatives of armed rebels; Agedabia, with 1,000 people from unspecified tribes; el-Abiar, with 3,123 Aughiri. In all, the six camps contained 78,313 people from across Cyrenaica.[28] To this figure we must further add the 12,448 people held in the smaller camps at Derna, Apollonia, Barce, Driana,

---

27 Archivio storico del Ministero dell'Africa italiana, Inventari e supplementi, VOL. 5, *pacco* 5. Commissariato regionale di Bengasi, *Relazione sugli accampamenti*, 8 July 1932, p. 4.

28 Archivio storico del Ministero dell'Africa italiana, Libia, pos. 150/22, f. 98, Graziani to De Bono, report n. 1058, 2 May 1931.

Sidi Chalifa, Suani el Teria, en-Nufilia, Bengasi, Coefia and Guarscia, bringing the total to 90,761 detainees.[29] We then need to take account of the people who were killed during the great march, and those who died in the camps over the first few months of their imprisonment through malnutrition, sickness and during attempts to escape. The total number of deportees thus amounted to no less than 100,000 people.

This figure represented exactly one half of the population of Cyrenaica, if we are to trust the Turkish census of 1911, which described a population of 198,300 people. When the Italian authorities completed the first census undertaken with modern techniques on 21 April 1931, they discovered that the indigenous inhabitants numbered only 142,000. In other words, the population of Cyrenaica, over a period of 20 years, had been reduced by 60,000 people: 20,000 during the exodus to Egypt, and 40,000 through the trials of war, deportation and imprisonment in the camps. No other Italian colony reached the level of repression effected in Cyrenaica, which had the character and dimensions of a genocide.

One of the very few functionaries who tried to limit Graziani's destructive fury was Commissar Giuseppe Daodiace. Requesting that Daodiace be sent back to Italy, Graziani wrote to the Minister of the Colonies: 'The honourable Daodiace's *forma mentis* was formed in the old systems, and he had always been shocked by myself, given that I follow new ones. Naturally, I have never spoken of the great effort expended, on my own part, in directing the functionary's will in terms of the new methods I have realized, and of which he does not approve.'[30] Daodiace himself wrote to Giuseppe Brusasca—Under-Secretary to the Minister for Italian Africa—on 7 January 1951:

---

29 Rodolfo Graziani, *Cirenaica pacificata* (Milan: Mondadori, 1932), map on p. 104.

30 See Angelo Del Boca, *Gli Italiani in Libia*, p. 183.

That I did not approve [of his methods] is clear from my many and repeated protests, both spoken and in writing, especially the fact that when there was fighting between our troops and the rebels, not only did they never take prisoners, but *they shot women and children as well*. I cannot recall in exactly which year, but a group of indigenous police, who had been ordered to shoot 36 women and children in a tent site, came to me in protest, explaining to me that, if they were given another order of this nature, then they preferred desertion.[31]

What was life like in the concentration camps? Let us listen to the accounts of some of the eye-witnesses. 'They have us very little to eat,' recalled Reth Belgassem, detained at el-Agheila. 'We had to try and survive on a fistful of rice or flour, and often we were too tired to work.' 'I remember the poverty and the beatings,' recounted Mohammed Bechi Seium. 'Every day someone got their ration of beatings. As far as food is concerned, I remember that we received a crust of hard bread, about 150 grams, or 200 at the most, which had to last the whole day.' As if hunger and epidemics were not enough, the guards practised every form of violence on the prisoners. Reth Belgassem recalled: 'Our women had to keep a container in their tents for when they needed to relieve themselves. They were too scared to go out; outside, they risked being abducted by the Ethiopians or the Italians.'[32]

Any attempt at escape, any act of rebellion, even returning late to the camp was punished by death. 'The executions always took place at midday, in a clearance in the middle of the camp, and the Italians brought people to watch,' Reth Belgassem continues. 'They forced us to watch while our brothers died.' 'Fifty corpses left el-Agheila every

---

31 Archivio Giuseppe Brusasca, Casale Monferrato: b. 44, f. 236.

32 Eric Salerno, *Genocidio in Libia* (Milan: Sugarco, 1979), p. 90, p. 99 and p. 91, respectively. The account refers to the askari recruited in East Africa, who included no small number of Ethiopians from the northern regions.

day,' Salem Omran Abu Shabur recalled. 'They were buried in mass graves. Fifty bodies a day, every day. We always counted them. People who were murdered. People hanged or shot. Or people who died from hunger and disease.'[33]

The detention in the camps lasted around three years. The final sites were dismantled in September 1933. Of the 100,000 Libyans who had left Jebel Akhdar and Marmarica, only 60,000 made their way back. Perhaps fewer still.

The deportation of the inhabitants of Cyrenaica, and their internment in concentration camps, removed from Omar al-Mukhtar the support that he had always received from them. Furthermore, in order to block any aid that might have arrived from Egypt, within only six months Graziani had built an unscalable fence spanning 270 km from Port Bardia to Jaghbub, which cost 20 million lire. Deprived of supplies and ammunition, and with only a small, diminishing army (he had no more than 700 followers left), al-Mukhtar's days were numbered.

On 11 September 1931, his camp of Braasa and Dorsa clans was spotted in Wadi Bu Taga. Having escaped from the clutches of his hunters a hundred times in the past, this time the old warrior was shot in the arm, after which his horse was killed. It was over; he did not even reach for the musket slung over his shoulder. He got up from the

---

33 Salerno, *Genocidio in Libia*, p. 90 and p. 95, respectively. Despite the regime's censorship, the crimes committed in Libya were well known and the press—especially the Arab press—did not fail to provide cutting commentaries. The European papers also expressed strong criticisms, for example the leading article in *Jugoslavenski List*, the daily paper of Sarajevo on 26 September 1931: 'General Graziani has spent the past three years destroying the Arab population with unprecedented ferocity, in order to make space for Italian colonies. While it is true that other peoples have not operated with kid gloves against the rebels in their respective colonies, the Italian colonization has beaten a bloody record.'

ground and tried to run into the woods. But he staggered as he ran. Perhaps he did not realize it, but he was 73 years old, 10 years of which he had passed in the most tiring of battles, without relent. The savari were soon on top of him, ready to finish him off, as they had already done with 11 of his companions.[34] But one of them recognized him, and spared his life. As soon as Captain Bertè understood the importance of his catch, he called off the chase, mounted Omar on a horse and escorted him as far as Suluntah. From there he was transferred to the nearest port, in Apollonia, and immediately put on board the destroyer *Orsini*. By the evening of 12 September, he was already in Benghazi prison.

Before the show trial could take place, with a sentence predetermined in Rome, Graziani interrogated al-Mukhtar. On one side of the table is a young, arrogant, self-impressed general. On the other, a 73-year-old man, bound in chains, dressed in a white barrakan, his feet swollen with gout and his voice hoarse; he could barely speak. During the interrogation, al-Mukhtar felt he was about to faint (remember that he was also wounded in the arm). He turns to his interrogator and says, 'I am old, let me sit.' It is only at this point that the general offers him a chair.

Graziani first played the card of intimidation, and then of persuasion, to convince al-Mukhtar to use his authority to end the guerrilla war. When he realized that he would obtain nothing from him—neither information nor favours—he quickly dismissed him. 'He tried to offer me his wounded hand,' Graziani recalls, 'but he could not, he was unable to. As for myself, I would not have touched him. He shuffled out of the room, as he had entered. The drama of Cyrenaica was over.'[35] If Graziani intended to render Omar detestable through this account of the interrogation, then he calculated badly: the old, fallen, swollen

---

34 *Savari*: cavalry (Farsi). [Trans].

35 Graziani, *Cirenaica pacificata*, p. 271.

Omar who drags his feet is at the same time clear-headed, proud and unwavering, appearing as a giant by comparison. In his boundless arrogance and egoism, Graziani the Übermensch cannot understand that he has gifted us with an intact, credible, inspiring portrait of the rebel leader.

Al-Mukhtar's attitude during the final hours of his life was similarly proud and dignified. As soon as the interpreter, Nasri Hermes, finished translating the death sentence, al-Mukhtar simply said: 'We have come from God, and to God we must return.'[36] The following day, 16 September 1931, he was taken to the concentration camp at Suluq, and hanged at 9 a.m., in front of the local leaders imprisoned at Benina, as well as 20,000 Libyans forced to attend from the local camps. 'The effect was very powerful indeed,' Graziani reported. 'The body was taken to Benghazi and buried in the Sabri cemetery. With the passing of the leader of the Cyrenaica rebellion, a new life began for that colony which so passionately desires works of peace.'[37]

The final insult to Omar al-Mukhtar occurred in more recent times, with Italy's banning of the film *The Lion of the Desert*, which narrated the epic life of the resistance leader. Adjudicated 'damaging to the honour of the Italian army', the film—a work by Syrian-American director Moustapha Akkad—still today can only be watched in hiding in private film clubs. The stubborn ostracism of Akkad's film is part of

---

36 Cited in Enzo Santarelli, Giorgio Rochat, Romain Rainero and Luigi Goglia, *Ommar al-Mukhtàr e la roconquista fascista della Libia* (Milan: Marzorati, 1981), p. 268.

37 Graziani, *Cirenaica pacificata*, p. 273. On the reconquest of Libya, see Alessandro Cova, *Graziani. Un generale per il regime* (Rome: Newton Compton, 1987); Giuseppe Mayda, *Graziani l'Africano. Da Neghelli a Salò* (Florence: La Nuova Italia, 1992); Romano Canosa, *Graziani. Il Maresciallo d'Italia, dalla guerra d'Etiopia alla repubblica di Salò* (Milan: Mondadori, 2004); Giambattista Biasutti, *La politica indigena italiana in Libia. Dall'occupazione al termine del governatorato di Italo Balbo, 1911–1940* (Pavia: Università degli Studi di Pavia, 2004).

a much longer and underground campaign of mystification and disinformation, one that attempts to conserve a romantic, mythical and radiant version of our recent colonial history. That is, a false one.[38]

38 On Akkad's film and its censorship in Italy, see Enzo Magri, 'Garibaldi della Libia', *Oggi*, 10 August 1979; Aldo Ricci and Roland Giglio, 'Sconfitto, mma nella leggenda', *Il essaggero*, 6 February 1981; Angelo Del Boca, 'Chi ha paura di Omar?', *Il Messaggero*, 14 March 1983; Roberto Silvestri, 'Il "Leone del deserto" come la "Battalia di Algeri"', *Quaderni internazionali*, 1 (1987): 113–18; Enrico agrelli, 'C'è uno scheletro nel deserto', *Panorama*, 18 September 1988; Paolo d'Agostini, 'Noi colonialisti diventati censori', *Repubblica*, 20 September 1988; Claudio Tosatto, 'Un film e la storia. Lion of the Desert, 1982', *Studi piacentini*, 36 (2004): 173–88. [The film was finally broadcast by Sky Italia in 2009.—Trans.]

NINE

STORMS OF MUSTARD GAS

Mussolini had considered taking revenge for the searing defeat at Adwa right from the outset of his government. Already in 8 July 1925, he wrote to the Minister for the Colonies, Pietro Lanza di Scalea, advising him: 'Prepare yourself both militarily and diplomatically, and take advantage of any possible chink in the Ethiopian empire. In the meantime, work in silence, where possible collaborate with the English, and apply a little chloroform to the official Abyssinian world.'[1] In August 1926, Mussolini—who was also Minister for War—posted General Giuseppe Malladra to Eritea and Somalia to examine the materiel in the two colonies and prepare them for a war against Ethiopia.

There was, however, a series of political and economic events and factors that dissuaded him from taking such a burdensome and serious decision. The regime still lacked any solid basis, and public opinion— not yet sufficiently controlled by the new tools of communication— would certainly not appreciate any new African enterprises. It would be preferable to wait for a better moment, and in the meantime continue that policy of 'applying a little chloroform' that had begun to show its first results. Indeed, this anaesthetizing approach would eventually lead to a 20-year treaty of friendship which the two sides signed in 1928,

---

1 Archivio storico del ministro degli Affari esteri, Fondo Guerra, Ethiopia, b. 5, f. 3, pos. 1. Mussolini underlined the word *militarily* three times.

even if with scant enthusiasm, each party attempting merely to earn some time.

The ink had not yet dried when Governor of Somalia, Guido Corni (with the consent of the Minister for the Colonies, De Bono) sent Captain Roberto Asinari di San Marzano to south Ethiopia, tasked with fomenting the local population and organizing military espionage activities. A similar underground operation was effected by Baron Raimondi Franchetti in the empire's north. He not only managed to form agreements with Ras Hailu Tekle Haymonot—the great rival to the reigning Ras, Tafari Makonnen—but also laid the basis for the treachery of the Azebo and the Raya Galla, two of the most bellicose tribes in the country. Finally, the former governor of Eritrea, Jacopo Gasparini, transformed his farm in Tesseney into a hub of spying and subversion, even managing to undermine the imperial fealty of one of the most prestigious of local leaders, degiac Ayalew Birru, the future commander of one of the Abyssinian armies.

There were enough reasons to turn the treaty of friendship to dust. Indeed, in 1932, Ras Tafari Makonnen—who in the meantime had become emperor, taking the name Haile Selassie I—began to acquire arms on the European markets, convinced that, sooner or later, Fascist Italy would invade his country.[2] Contemporaneously, the Italian commanders began to work out their plans in detail. The most insistent among the military men was General Emilio De Bono, who presented Mussolini with his own strategic plan in early December 1932, managing to secure the promise that, if war were declared on Ethiopia, he would be entrusted with the high command.

---

2 Among many other titles in English, see Angelo Del Boca, *The Negus: The LIfe and Death of the Last King of Kings* (Anthony Shugaar trans.) (Addis Ababa: Arada Books, 2012[1995]) and Harold G. Marcus, *Haile Selassie I, My Life and Ethiopia's Progress* (Edward Ullendorff trans.) (New York: Frontline Books, 1999). [Trans.]

De Bono's project, however, would later be scrapped, judged as being too superficial and 'brigadieresque', and replaced with other plans. By this point, however, it was no secret that Fascist Italy was preparing to attack the thousand-year-old Abyssinian Empire. For example, on 22 February 1933, Brigadier General Ferdinando Cona gave a talk at the military college entitled 'Some Ideas on the Engagement of Troops in the Eritrean-Ethiopian Theatre', in which he concluded significantly:

> The colonial question today can no longer be considered as merely accessory to the life of the nation, of interest only to specialists and enthusiasts. For it is in Africa—which by now everyone understands to be deeply connected to the life of a tormented Europe—that, through political and military action, we will need to search for solutions to many of the problems that disturb the daily life of the peoples of Europe.[3]

Mussolini was simply waiting for an excuse to attack. The banal border incident at Welwel, which in any other moment would have been resolved peacefully, provided the excuse he needed. On 24 December 1934, the Duce sent Emilio De Bono to Eritrea. On the 27th, he ordered the mobilization of the troops in Somalia, and a partial mobilization of the Eritrean forces. On 3 October 1935, with preparations finally complete, the invasion of Ethiopia began, Japanese-style, without any official declaration of war.[4]

While the idea of taking revenge for the defeat at Adwa was doubtless a significant motive behind Mussolini's decision to drag Italy into war—and as a direct result of this, into the effects of heavy sanctions imposed

---

3 Scuola di Guerra, *Alcune idee sull'impiego delle truppe nel teatro d'operazione eritreo etiopico* (1933), p. 21.

4 Del Boca's reference is to the Japanese attacks on Lüshun (Port Arthur) in 1904 and on Pearl Harbor in 1942, both of which occurred several hours *before* the official declaration of war. [Trans.]

by the League of Nations—there were other reasons too. One was his repeated promise of providing the Italian people 'a place in the sun', i.e. to finally take possession of a country that was rich and fertile, not simply an assemblage of deserts: fruitful land for those who had none, space for those who felt that Italy was overcrowded and provincial, and a new frontier for the adventurous.

In Mussolini's eyes, the planned conquest of Ethiopia would also have redeemed a situation of profound injustice: the fact that Italy did not possess a colonial empire worthy of the name, as France and Great Britain did. Mussolini had underscored this injustice during his globally broadcast speech on 2 October 1935, only a few hours after the attack:

> When Italy threw her lot in with the Allies and confused her destiny with theirs, how much was our courage lauded and how many promises were made to us! But around the odious table of peace that followed our shared victory—a victory to which Italy made the utmost contribution of 670,000 dead, 400,000 invalids and a million wounded—our country received mere crumbs from the rich colonial spoils.[5]

There was another reason still that drove Mussolini into Africa: he wanted to verify whether 13 years of his regime had given birth to a new kind of Italian. He could only discover this in the furnaces of a real war, the type of war that he envisaged waging on Ethiopia; not in the modest Libyan and Somalian conflicts of the past, in which the lion's share of the burden had weighed upon the mercenary troops. The new Fascist soldiers would prove—on the very same plateaus that had seen Baratieri's soldiers defeated—whether they had truly absorbed the doctrines of Fascism and the religion of the fatherland during the Saturday assemblies, at their school desks and in the gym halls, which ought to have rendered them invincible. This test was so important to Mussolini that he had no

---

5 Benito Mussolini, *Scritti e discorsi*, VOL. 9 (Milan: Hoepli, 1935), p. 218.

hesitation in sending his own sons, Bruno and Vittorio, into battle, along with his son-in-law, Galeazzo Ciano.

When, with shame and repulsion, we re-read some of the witness accounts of the Italo-Ethiopian war, such as *Desperate* by Alessandro Pavolini, *Wings Above the Ambas* by Vittorio Mussolini, Giuseppe Bottai's *African Notebook*, or *The Twentieth Eritrean Battalion* by Indro Montanelli, we can see that these authors shared features that were the product of the very worst of Fascism's lessons: disregard for the enemy, a complete mercilessness, support for extermination and the general exaltation of death.[6] Was this the new Italian for whom Mussolini had hoped, a puppet with no soul, no future, animated by the most primordial and homicidal instincts?

Alessandro Pavolini, who would later establish and lead the Black Brigades during the Republic of Salò (the utmost expression of hatred and cruelty), was part of *La Disperata*, the 15th air bombers' squadron under Galeazzo Ciano's command. One of the constant, almost obsessive motifs in his account is the manhunt for Abyssinians, perceived as prey, as animals, not as a legitimate adversary and certainly not as human beings. This is how he described the Ethiopian withdrawal after the Battle of Amba Aradam (1936): 'The aviation was conceived of as pursuit cavalry. What was to all effects a charge of vehicles swooped along the caravan, forcing the fugitives into the low waters, dispersing their columns, picking off the stragglers with machine guns and carbine rifles.' Pavolini omitted a not-irrelevant detail here, which was then supressed through censorship of other accounts: 60 tons of mustard gas were dropped during the pursuit. A few days later, Pavolini flew his Caproni bomber into another furious, merciless hunt: 'This final operation, in

---

6 Alessandro Pavolini, *Disperata* (Florence: Vallecchi, 1937); Vittorio Mussolini, *Voli sulle ambe* (Florence: Sansoni, 1937); Giuseppe Bottai, *Quaderno affricano* (Florence: Sansoni, 1938); Indro Montanelli, *XX Battaglione eritreo* (Milan: Panoramma, 1936).

the woods, gorges and caverns of Tembien, again brought to mind images of big game hunting. It was like a gigantic flushing out. [...] Military history has certainly seen many other slaughters, and on a much greater scale. But seldom has the killing been so concentrated in time and in so restricted a space. [...] As if struck down by lightning, a generation lay strewn across the dirt tracks of the highlands.'[7]

Vittorio and Bruno Mussolini fought with the 14th Squadron, *Qui sum leo* ('Here I am the Lion'). In his own account of the war, *Wings Over the Ambas*, Vittorio also felt the pressing need to describe his hunting in detail: 'An Abyssinian with a rifle ran southwards. A nice swoop and the Abyssinian was on the ground. It was thus a lone manhunt, as usual, and every unit took it upon himself to search every hole, sniffing out the Abyssinian.' More enjoyable still was setting light to villages and farms with incendiary devices: 'It was extremely fun work and had a tragic but beautiful effect. [...] There was a big hut, surrounded by high trees, that I couldn't strike. You had to take aim at the straw roof, and I only managed it on the third try. The wretches inside saw the roof burning and jumped out like they were possessed.' But there was a prize for all of this. Vittorio recognized that he had 'graduated as a human being. War educates and tempers you, and I advise it to everyone; I believe it is a man's duty to participate in at least one.'[8]

Having volunteered in the war at the age of 40, Giuseppe Bottai, unlike Pavolini and Vittorio Mussolini, could not call upon his young age and lack of education as attenuating factors. He had already been Minister for Corporations, Governor of Rome and Editor-in-Chief of *Critica Fascista*. Even in the eyes of his political enemies, he seemed to constitute the very best that Fascism had produced. Nevertheless, his *African Notebook* contains racist regurgitations and vileness that become all the more intolerable given that they issued from someone of such

---

7 Pavolini, *Disperata*, p. 243, p. 254 and p. 266, respectively.

8 Mussolini, *Voli sulle ambe*, p. 52, p. 78 and p. 150, respectively.

high culture. For example, here is how he describes the village of Doghea, which was destroyed by the Italians:

> The ruins of the village, picked out by a few trees, the walls of its hovels torn down by our artillery and flamethrowers, cause no shame. They do not pull at one's heart strings, because the ruins are too similar to how these villages usually look, the result of the tragic horror of broken lives and empty hearths. In a catastrophe of this kind, four houses in Fruili or Venice take on an air of grandeur, because they were once *houses*, i.e. civilization, an idea, a tradition, that had been overturned.[9]

Just as Bottai made no effort to understand that the Abyssinians' houses, their poverty notwithstanding, had their own history and dignity, so too he denied that his adversaries were qualitatively human, even in death. Leading a battalion in the assault on Amba Aradam, Bottai saw Black and White fall. But while he describes the dead Italians as 'serious, pallid, ponderous', he shows no regard for the 'Black people's cadavers. They do not move you. It is a death that seems masked by colour.'[10]

For his own part, Indro Montanellli went to Africa 'not in search of 'colour' but 'to find a human conscience there'. The future prince of Italian journalism believed to have found this conscience while leading a group of Eritrean askari in the early operations on the northern front. Here is how he describes the attack on an Ethiopian village: 'The expedition went well: 67 for sure. The askari spread out among the tukul huts and razed them to the ground; and these served as the last sacraments for anyone holed up in some hiding place, who flung out their last pangs of death.' In other words: 67 certain deaths, during which the Eritrean soldiers were authorized to destroy homes and slaughter the wounded. One cannot help but wonder how Montanelli thought he could form a

---

9 Bottai, *Quaderno affricano*, p. 40.

10 Bottai, *Quaderno affricano*, p. 70 and p. 73, respectively.

conscience through this spiral of extreme violence. And yet he thanks Mussolini for providing him with such an experience: 'This war is like a long and beautiful holiday conceded to us by Father Christmas as a reward for 13 years of school. And, between you and me, it was about time.'[11]

The soldiers' own respectability, both humble and potent alike, fades in significance next to the importance of Mussolini's relations with Africa. This Mussolini is little known in Italy, and the historian who has recently brought him to light, Renzo De Felice, is generally ignored by historians, including those outside Italy who are yet to form any opinion of his work. On the other hand, this Mussolini is very well known in Africa, where his orders meant nothing but violence and extermination, from the Gebel of Cyrenaica to the bare mountains of Majeerteenia, from the roads of Addis Ababa to the convent city of Debre Libanos. If Africa had been able to demand her own Nuremberg, if it had had the power to put on trial the crimes committed against her, then this African Mussolini would have found no salvation.

There was only one time, in his long career as a politician and states-man, that Mussolini took Africa's side: in 1911, when Giolitti went to Libya. On that occasion, he criticized the colonial enterprise, defining it an acts of international banditry. He also boasted, in those years, of sup-porting the Arabs and sharing in their suffering. This was, however, false—because Mussolini was, by character and culture, irremediably racist. His constant, almost obsessive anxiety about the 'empty cots' was not dictated by any Malthusian concerns, but by the fear of the 'Yellow and Black races' making progress 'in number and extension', suffocating 'White man's civilization'. He raised the first cry of alarm in a speech in 1926; eight years later, in an article written for *Universal Service*, he returned to the argument and claimed that demographic policies are,

---

11 Montanelli, *XX Battaglione eritreo*, p. 9, p. 196 and p. 226, respectively.

'for Italy and for all countries inhabited by the peoples of the White race, a question of life or death.'[12]

In Libya and Somalia, Mussolini had let his generals conduct the campaigns, limiting himself to encouraging them and signing off the most serious decisions, but in the Italo-Ethiopian conflict he took the lead, as Vittorio Emanuele III recognized by awarding him the highest military honours of his kingdom: 'As Minister of the Armed Forces, he prepared, led and won the greatest colonial war recorded in history.'[13]

To begin with, down to the smallest detail, it was Mussolini who constructed the enormous war machine that was to destroy the Ethiopian armies in only seven months. Mindful of the defeat at Adwa and to avoid any repetition of the catastrophe, Mussolini did not skimp on men and weapons, doubling and even tripling the requests sent by high command. Between March and September 1935 alone, the port of Massawa disembarked 177,431 well-equipped soldiers, 24,531 steed, 4,278 vehicles and 548,659 tons of materiel.[14] There was a constant influx of reinforcements over the course of the conflict, to the extent that, in May 1936, the Italian command could deploy 17,959 officers, 476,543 privates and minor officers,[15] 102,582 horses, 18,932 vehicles, 1,542 cannons of every calibre, 492 tanks, 350 air planes, 513,276 rifles and muskets, 14,570 machine guns, 850 million cartridges for light arms and 4,197,936 artillery projectiles.[16]

---

12 Mussolini, *Scritti e discorsi*, VOL. 9, p. 117 and p. 122, respectively.

13 Royal Decree 7 May 1936 (Year 14), conferring the rank of Knight of the Great Cross of the Military Order of Savoy. See *La Legislazione fascista nella XXIX Legislatura. 1934–1939* (XII–XVII), VOL. 1 (Rome: Tipografia della Camera dei fasci e delle corporazioni, 1939), p. 15.

14 Fidenzio Dall'Ora, *Intendenza in A.O.* (Rome: Istituto Nazionale Fascista di Cultura, 1937), p. 101.

15 This figure includes 87,000 askaris.

16 Ministero per la Guerra, *Relazione sull'attività svolta per l'esigenza A.O.* (Rome: Istituto Poligrafico dello Stato, 1936), attachment n. 76.

From 3 October 1935 onward, it was Mussolini who decided on the sites to be conquered, choosing the dates in accordance with his unscrupulous diplomatic game. He sent telegrams almost daily to De Bono (and, later, to Badoglio) on the northern front, and to Graziani on the southern line, with precise orders that were not to be discussed. When his generals found themselves in difficulty because the enemy was stronger or more audacious than foreseen, and had broken through the northern line, invading Eritrea, it was Mussolini who conceded the use of weapons banned under the Geneva Convention: murderous toxic gasses. In order to carry out these chemical aggressions, he had authorized the secret landing in Eritrea of 270 tons of gas for close application, 1,000 tons of aerial bombs (filled with mustard gas) and 60,000 artillery grenades (filled with arsine). He maintained full rights over these totalizing weapons. The order to use them—as well as any calling-off of that order—could come from him alone, the supreme and exclusive dispenser of death; and yet again, the use of chemical warfare was employed in harmony with his moves on the European chessboard. There were days in which he could spread death as he pleased, others when it was necessary to make a show of a deep humanity.[17]

The first general authorized to use the gas was Graziani. On 27 October 1935, as he was about to attack the stronghold of Gorahai, he received the following telegram from Mussolini: 'Good for action on 29th. Use of gas authorized as final means to suppress enemy resistance or in case of counter attack.'[18] In the end, chemical attacks were not used in the operation at Gorahai, because 6 tons of traditional explosives were enough to ensure that the base collapsed. On 15 December, however,

---

17 For an analysis of the systematic use of gas during the Italo-Ethiopian conflict of 1935–36 and during the counter-insurgency operations of 1936–40, see Angelo Del Boca, *I gas di Mussolini. Il fascismo e la guerra d'Etiopia* (Rome: Editori Riuniti, 1996).

18 Documents on Ethiopia from the author's archive.

having learnt that Ras Desta Damtu and his army were closing in on the Italian fortifications at Dolo, Graziani requested 'free hand in employing gas for asphyxiation'[19] in order to slow down the enemy's advance. Mussolini's positive reply came immediately: 'OK for use of gas in case Your Eminence believes it necessary for utmost reasons of defence.'[20]

Graziani wasted no time. On 24 December, he sent three Caproni 101b's to fly over Areri—the town where Desta, his army and caravan of animals had paused their advance for sustenance—and spray them with mustard gas and phosgene. These aerial attacks were repeated on 25, 28, 30 and 31 December, with a total of 125 bombs launched. On 10 January 1936, Graziani telegraphed Bernasconi, commander of the aviation brigades in Somalia: 'Recent completed actions have demonstrated the efficacy of the use of gasses. In daily telegram n. 333, the Head of Government authorized me to use them in the current conditions, a defining battle situation with the army of Ras Desta.'[21]

Gas was used on the northern front from 22 December 1935, after Ras Imru's advance units had massacred the irregular forces led by Major Luigi Criniti. In his efforts to block the Abyssinian offensive in Shire, Marshal Badoglio launched all the Eritrean aviation units over the crossings of the Tekeze and Golima rivers, the town of Mai Timchet and the Agumserta Pass. For the first time in the Ethiopian campaign, type C-500 T bombs were dropped on the Abyssinians while on the move; the bombs contained 212 kg of mustard gas which, with the aid of a timing mechanism, opened 250 m above ground, creating a mortal rainfall.

19 Comando delle Forze Armate della Somalia, *La guerra italo-etiopica. Fronte Sud. Relazione*, VOL. 3, p. 274, telegram n. 1457.

20 Documents on Ethiopia from the author's archive, secret, maximum precedence, telegram n. 14551, response to n. 1475.

21 Commando delle Forze Armate della Somalia, *La guerra italo-etiopico*, attachment n. 313, p. 401.

Between 22 and 27 December 1935, 74 such bombs were launched, and a further 117 between 2 and 7 January 1936.

To understand the effects of this prohibited weapon, we can turn to the eye witness account of Ras Imru himself:

> It was a terrifying spectacle to behold. It was only by chance that I escaped death myself. It was the morning of 23 December, and I had only just crossed the Tekeze when a few air planes appeared in the sky. We weren't too alarmed by this because by then we were used to the air bombings. That morning they didn't launch bombs, but instead these strange stalks that broke apart as soon as they touched land or water, shooting out a colourless liquid. Before I could understand what was happening, a few hundred of my men had been hit by the mysterious liquid and were crying out in pain, and their naked hands, feet and faces were covered in blisters. Those who had been drinking from the river writhed in pain on the ground, in an agony that lasted for hours. There were also farmers who had brought their herds to the river among those struck down, and people from the nearby villages. In the meantime, my captains surrounded me and asked my advice, but I was struck dumb, I didn't know how to respond, I didn't know how to fight this rain that burned and killed.[22]

On 5 January 1936, Mussolini telegraphed Badoglio to 'suspend the use of gas until the Geneva meeting, unless it is absolutely for reasons of defence or offence. I will provide you with further instructions on this matter.'[23] Badoglio ignored the Duce's request to suspend the deployment of C-500 T bombs, and used them again on 6 and 7 January, spraying a

---

22 Account provided to the author by Ras Imru Haile Sellasie in Addis Ababa, 13 April 1965.

23 Documents on Ethiopia from the author's archive, secret telegram to Badoglio, Mekelle.

torrent of mustard gas on the citizens of Abiy Addi, as well as over the Segalò and Rassi fords. But he was forced to interrupt the bombings and even received a strong reproach from Mussolini for 'the serious failure by which, up to today, the Ethiopians have manage to take and hold every operational engagement on our right flank.'[24] Unable to receive criticism lightly, Badoglio looked for the support of the Minister for the Colonies, Alessandro Lessona, sending him the following telegram: 'Use of mustard gas has proved extremely effective especially in the area around Tekeze. Terrified rumours abound because of the gas. Suspension is certainly to our serious disadvantage.'[25] Then, without waiting for any further authorization from Mussolini, he recommenced the bombings, launching a further 76 C-500 T's between 12 and 18 January. It was only on 19 January that permission finally arrived: 'I authorize Your Excellency to use all means of war, and I mean all, from earth and sky. Maximum decision.'[26]

From 21 January onward, during the furious First Battle of Tembien, mustard gas was deployed on a daily basis. Overall, between 22 December 1935 and 29 March 1936, 1,020 C-500 T bombs were dropped on the northern front, representing 300 tons of gas. Between 24 December 1935 and 27 April 1936, 95 such bombs were dropped on the southern front, as well as a further 186 bombs containing 21 kg of mustard gas and 325 bombs full of 41 kg of phosgene, totalling 44 tons. During the Battle of Amba Aradam, Badoglio authorized the use of 1,367 rounds of artillery packed with arsine, bringing the total tonnage of chemical weapons to 350. The military 'Chemical Service' was especially positive about the use of these arsine ballistics: 'The atmospheric conditions

---

24 Documents on Ethiopia from the author's archive, secret telegram to Badoglio, Mekelle, 6 January 1936.

25 Cited in Giorgio Rochat, 'L'impiego dei gas nella guerra d'Etiopia 1935–36', in Del Boca (ed.), *I gas di Mussolini*, p. 65.

26 Documents on Ethiopia from the author's archive, maximum precedence.

mean that their use is extremely effective, to the extent that it even penetrated the protective masks (perhaps an old model) with which a few chiefs and commanders were equipped, leading to the legend that the Italians used gas from which no protection existed.'[27]

Despite their devastating, terrifying effects, at a certain point the gas weapons were not enough for Mussolini. In order to liquidate his enemies even more rapidly (whom he defined as either 'Amharan slavers', 'savage raiders' or 'Abyssinian head hunters') when matters were going badly for Badoglio at the end of 1936, who was about to order the retreat from Mekelle under the pressure of Ras Kassa's armies, Mussolini thought of utilizing germ warfare, even while perfectly aware that no country in the world had ever deployed such weapons. Though the new plague was never utilized, this was only due to Badoglio, who expressed a 'clearly negative view', specifying that the use of new and horrific chemical attacks would have alienated Italy from any support among the peoples of the Horn of Africa, and would have had enormous and disastrous repercussions on the international stage. On 20 February 1936, Mussolini replied to Badoglio with the following message: 'I am in agreement with Your Excellency's views on the use of germ warfare.'[28]

Relying on all possible tools of censorship, the Fascist regime managed to conceal from the people of Italy that forbidden weapons had been used in Ethiopia, shamelessly and readily denying any news that appeared in the international press about the use of gas. The silence imposed over one of the worst of Fascism's crimes was to last for a long time—indeed, for decades, long into the democratic period. Once the censorship had been lifted, the central tactic was to simply deny what had been done and to attempt to silence anyone who raised any

---

27 Del Boca (ed.), *I gas di Mussolini*, p. 62.

28 Documents on Ethiopia from the author's archive, secret telegram to Badoglio, Mekelle.

doubts as 'anti-Italian'. Indro Montanelli, one of Italy's most highly respected opinion makers for over 50 years, led the group of deniers. He had been in Ethiopia, and was sure to use his platform in an authoritative manner. His testimony was that of a combatant who had always been on the front line with the advanced troops—and he swore to have never seen an Abyssinian killed by gas, to have never smelt the unmistakeable smell of mustard gas. Whoever maintained the contrary opinion was simply a liar.

On 7 February 1996, i.e. 60 years after the war, Italian Minister of Defence General Domenico Corcione replied to a series of questions in parliament and finally admitted that 'the Italo-Ethiopian war had seen use of aerial bombings and artillery ballistics filled with mustard gas and arsine, and that Marshal Badoglio was in full knowledge of the use of such gas, signing off several reports and communications on this matter.' Six days later, Montanelli recognized in his widely read column that 'the documents proved him wrong'. Referencing a polemic between us that had lasted 30 years, he wrote: '[The documents] say that these gases were effectively used, as you have written in your historical reconstruction of that engagement.'[29] The public apologies followed soon after.[30]

Mussolini was less interested in winning the war than exterminating his enemy. This is why he raged against the helpless populations, authorizing the use of mustard gas against not only them but, consequentially, also their animals, harvests, rivers and lakes. This is why he ordered the insignia of the Red Cross to be ignored, allowing 17 medical stations to be destroyed, including the field hospitals at Mela Dida,

---

29 Del Boca (ed.), *I gas di Mussolini*, p. 40 and p. 43, respectively.

30 For the long polemic with Montantelli, see Del Boca (ed.), *I gas di Mussolini*, pp. 28–48.

Ambra Aaradam and Quoram.[31] This is why he allowed the Muslim Libyans in the Libyan Division, led by General Guglielmo Nasi, to launch themselves against Coptic Ethiopia.

By sending these Libyan troops—all of whom were of the Islamic faith—to the southern front, to fight a majority Christian enemy, the Fascist regime committed a new and extremely serious crime: allowing the Libyans to avenge themselves for the violence that they and their families had suffered for 20 years at the hands of the Amhara-Eritrean battalions, they committed perfidy. Engaging in action on 15 April 1936, the Libya division took part in Graziani's final and decisive offensive at Ogafen, which was meant to uproot the defensive line prepared by the Turkish general Wehib Pasha and the degiac Nasibu Zamanuel in order to protect the cities of Jijiga and Harar. As Graziani himself recognized, the Libyans were always at the front, in the midst of the fighting. Their battle cry—*Uled*! *Uled*!—rose over the din of war and filled the Ethiopian units with terror, who fought 'proudly, nimbly exploiting every imbalance in the terrain', as Nasi wrote in his final report.[32]

The most bloody fighting took place along the Wadi Korak, an area full of hidden caves which the aviation units and artillery shot at futilely, but were devastated by flamethrowers and mustard-gas ballistics. The final ferocious resistance was broken by the Libyans of the 1st and 7th battalions, who managed to cross the Wadi after it had been filled by rainfall, blocking their enemy's exit and wreaking havoc. Three thousand Ethiopians lay dead on the ground afterward, but the

---

31 On the attacks on the Red Cross camps, see Rainer Baudendistel, *Between Bombs and Good Intentions: The International Committee of the Red Cross and the Italo-Ethiopian War, 1935–1936* (Oxford and New York: Berghan Books, 2006).

32 Guglielmo Nasi, *Relazione sulle operazioni effettuate per l'occupazione di Harar* (Commando delle Forze Armate della Somalia, *La guerra italo-etiopico*, VOL. 4, attachment n. 488), p. 277.

body count was tragic for the invaders as well. Twenty officers were killed or wounded, 11 Italian soldiers and 707 African soldiers, for the most part Libyan. Graziani ended his balance sheet with a chilling reflection: 'Few prisoners taken, according to the customs of the Libyan troops.'[33] The massacre was of such immense proportions that General Nasi—more humane than Graziani—offered the Libyan askaris an award of a hundred lire for every prisoner that they took alive.[34]

By now, however, it was too late to stop the religious hatred in which the Italian army had put its trust with such wreckless determination. The slaughter of the prisoners continued at the wells of Birkuta, in Segag, in Dagamedo, in Dagahbur. Nasi's promise of offering recompense for every living Ethiopian prisoner did, however, provide some results: 'In the fighting at Gianagobo,' he recalled, 'the Libyan Division captured 500 Ethiopian prisoners, who were sent to a concentration camp in Mogadishu, where they were treated well and released a year later.'[35] The massacre of the prisoners continued, nevertheless, even after the war, during the vast colonial police operation in Bale and Harayno against what remained of Haile Selassie's army.

---

33 Telegram by Graziani n. 4924/30, sent to the Minister for the Colonies, Lessona, and to Badoglio (Commando delle Forze Armate della Somalia, *La guerra italo-etiopico*, VOL. 4, p. 187).

34 Guglielmo Nasi, *Venticinque anni in Africa*, unpublished diary, pp. 46–48 (archive of the Nasi family).

35 Guglielmo Nasi, *L'azione di comanda politico militare in AOI dal 1936 al 1941 del generale Guglielo Nasi* (Rome, February 1950) in Archivio Giuseppe Brusasca, Casale Monferrato: b. AI/2, p. 16. We harbour serious doubts about the claim that the prisoners were 'treated well' in the concentration camp at Danane. Of the 6,500 Ethiopians and Somalians who were interned there between 1936 and 1941, 3,175 died through malnutrition, malaria, enterocolitis, the poor climate and poor hygiene in general. See Angelo Del Boca, *L'Africa nella coscienza degli italiani* (Rome and Bari: Laterza, 1992), pp. 41–57.

Following the Second World War, in an attempt to limit his responsibility, Nasi wrote:

> While bearing in mind an objective understanding of the character of the war, one should also recall that the Libyan askaris had old scores to settle with the Ethiopians, whose mixed battalions (Amharan-Eritrean) had left a terrifying impression in Libya between 1919 and 1931. [. . .] These were native troops, anyway, who are not easy to change in their instincts and traditions.[36]

Further on in his text he repeats the point: 'Native troops, including in the regular forces, do not take prisoners, instead executing anyone who is captured, without exception, not even for the wounded, because they do not share that sentiment felt by civilized peoples for whom the wounded are sacred.'[37]

It is not likely that a military man as intelligent and, indeed, insightful as Guglielmo Nasi—an excellent administrator and among the most valiant of soldiers (he was the last to lower the Italian flag at Gondar in 1941), really lay the blame with the Libyan askari for actions that derived from the Italians, who systematically exploited the ethnic and religious hatred of the populations they subjected. It is particularly unlikely given that Nasi could draw on a double experience: that of leading the assault by the Christian Amharan-Eritrean battalions in Libya against the Muslim mujaheddin, as well as then commanding the entirely Muslim Libyan division against Coptic patriots in Ethiopia. It is impossible that Nasi did not connect these two experiences, and did not understand the lowliness of turning religious hatred into a weapon—indeed, into a final solution.

---

36 Nasi, *L'azione di comando politico militare*, p. 16.
37 Nasi, *L'azione di comando politico militare*, p. 21.

Nasi's final, supremely dishonest attenuating factor is similarly unacceptable. 'The colonial history of all countries is, unfortunately, a history of horrors; but we must recognize that Italian colonial history is certainly that which contains the least.'[38] Yet again, here in the reflections of one of the highest ranking officers of the Italian army, we have the myth of the Italian as different, more tolerant, more kind. Yet again the Italian puts himself, in the great classification of peoples, in a privileged and protected position. Yet again we see that usual, knee-jerk, nonchalant, almost natural self-absolution.

---

38 Nasi, *L'azione di comando politico militare*, p. 14.

TEN

DEBRE LIBANOS:
A FINAL SOLUTION

On 5 May 1936, Marshal Pietro Badoglio entered Addis Ababa without a single casualty. Emperor Haile Selassie had abandoned the city three days earlier, taking the last train for Djibouti and the road of exile. On 8 May, General Graziani occupied Harar, and the following day took Dire Dawa. The 'seven-month war' was over. At 10.33 p.m. on 9 May, Mussolini appeared on the balcony at Palazzo Venezia in Rome and announced to the crowd below that 'the land and people who once belonged to the Ethiopian Empire are now under the full and entire sovereignty of the Kingdom of Italy.'[1] Raffaele Carrieri, a journalist loyal to the regime, commented on the important announcement: 'A world has collapsed, another rises. We see it arise in this magnificent silence like a dawn issuing from the words of the Duce. After 15 centuries, Mussolini has finally returned to Rome her immortal Empire.'[2]

In reality, the situation in Ethiopia was less clear. Almost two thirds of the vast country still needed to be occupied, and remained under the control of the Negus's chiefs and functionaries. Furthermore, the residue of the Imperial army—around 100,000 men—was still active in Sidamo, Bale, Gojjam, Jimma and Hararghe, led by extremely capable commanders

---

1 Benito Mussolini, *Scritti e discorsi*, VOL. 10 (Milan: Hoepli, 1936), p. 118.

2 Raffaele Carrieri, 'La più bella notte d'Italia', *Illustrazione italiana*, 17 May 1936. [The quote is also significant because Carrieri, much like Montanelli, continued his journalist career long after the war.—Trans.]

such as the Ras Desta Damtu and Imru Haile Selassie, and the degiacs Beyene Merid, Gabre Mariam and Makonnen Wosenie. Finally, the 10,000 soldiers who were holding Addis Ababa were essentially besieged by the armed forces led by the sons of Ras Kassa.

Sensing danger and impatient to cash in his gifts (the prebendaries and positions that had been promised to him, including a noble title and 3 million lire with which he would construct an opulent villa on Via Bruxelles in Rome), Badoglio returned to Italy and passed his post to the ever-ambitious Graziani, who had in the meantime been promoted to 'Marshall of Italy'. Invested on 20 May with the triple role of Viceroy, Governor General and High Commander of the troops, Graziani was simultaneously shocked by orders arriving by telegram from Mussolini, which were unreasonable to say the least. Pretending to ignore the news that the new Viceroy was practically trapped in Addis Ababa, on 21 May the Duce wrote to him: 'There is to be no more delay in advancing in the direction of Gore, where, according to a letter published by the *Times* in London by the former Ethiopian minister, there is a provisional Abyssinian government. This is a blister no doubt, but it is best to burst it.'[3]

Graziani tried in vain to explain to an impatient Mussolini that while he was more than ready to recommence the advance, the rainy season was blocking any movement along the roads and even made it difficult for supplies to reach the capital where, furthermore, they were impeded by rebel incursions. Mussolini wanted no excuses and bullied the Viceroy with telegrams such as: 'All the rebels taken prisoner should be executed.'[4] 'To finish off the rebels, as was the case at Ankober, use gas.'[5] 'Once more I authorize Your Excellency to lead a systematic policy

---

3 Documents on Ethiopia from the author's archive, telegram n. 5810 to Graziani, Addis Ababa.

4 Documents on Ethiopia from the author's archive, telegram n. 6496, secret, 5 June 1936.

of terror and extermination against the rebels and the collaborating population. Without the rule of cutting back ten-fold, the plague cannot be stopped in good time. I await your confirmation.'[6]

Graziani had amply demonstrated that he needed little encouragement to use an iron fist. Under his command, the counter-guerrilla actions would continue for 20 months, utilizing merciless methods that violated all the rules of war—but with scarce results. As soon as one outbreak of revolt was stamped out, another immediately flared up, each time larger and more complicated. Despite the continuing summary executions, the reprisals with chemical weapons (552 bombs of mustard gas and phosgene, totalling 60 tons), the burning down of villages and their churches, the deportation of entire communities, the construction of new concentration camps, Ethiopia seemed unconquerable and inhospitable. What was meant to have been a colony for repopulation, the promised land for Italian colonists (the idea had been to export between 1 to 10 million farmers), in truth it never hosted more than 3,500 families over the five years of Fascist occupation, distributed over no more than 114,000 hectares. These colonists hardly had time to till the black earth of Jimma, Kerker and Wogera before the first cannon blasts of the Second World War wrenched them away from their dreams.

The end of the rainy season and the arrival of important reinforcements in Addis Ababa allowed Graziani to loosen the rebels' grip on the capital and pass over to the offensive. Through a series of 'large-scale police operations', his generals managed to defeat the residual forces of the Ras Desta Damtu, Imru Haile Selassie and of the Kassa brothers. In March 1937, the occupation of the Empire was complete. In little more than 10 months—four of which were irrelevant due to the rains—the

---

5 Documents on Ethiopia from the author's archive, telegram n. 6595, secret, 6 June 1936.

6 Documents on Ethiopia from the author's archive, telegram n. 8103, secret, 8 July 1936.

columns that left Addis Ababa, Negelli and Harar had occupied more than 600,000 sq. km of territory, silencing the Negus's army and capturing 140,000 rifles, 450 machine guns and 50 mortars.[7] This vast operation, which relied on no less than 200,000 soldiers, cost the Italians their allies a relatively low number of casualties: 45 officials, 207 Italian soldiers, and 1,200 Libyan, Eritrean and Arab-Somalian soldiers.

Breaking every rule of war, Mussolini and Graziani decided to consider the leaders and fighters they had taken prisoner not as soldiers in a regular army—and therefore to be saved—but as armed rebels who therefore needed to be executed. On the basis of this absurd and criminal criteria, the three Kassa brothers were put before the firing squad, as were the bishops (or abuna) Petros and Micael. Not even the Emperor's son-in-law, Ras Desta Damtu, escaped the massacre. On 12 February 1937, while the Ras' remaining forces were being surrounded and decimated at Gogetti, Graziani sent the following telegram to General Geloso, commanding the operations: 'I bring to Your Excellency's attention the order from the Head of Government that all the armed leaders and combatants who have been captured, of whatever rank, are to be executed.'[8] Ras Desta managed once more to give the Italians the slip, along with 40 followers, and take refuge in his home village of Maskan. But he was tracked down, captured and delivered to Captain Bernardo Tucci, who sent Graziani the following telegram: 'Today on the 24th, at 6 a.m., my column took Ras Desta Damtu prisoner. In accordance with the orders of His Excellency the Head of Government, at 17.30 he was executed.'[9]

---

7 Fabrizio Serra, *La conquista integrale dell'impero* (Rome: Unione Editoriale d'Italia, 1938), p. 138.

8 Archivio storico del Ministero per Africa Italiana, Africa Orientale Italiana, pos. 181/40, f. 195.

9 Governo Generale dell'Africa Orientale, Stato Maggiore, *Il 1° anno dell'Impero* (Addis Ababa: Tipo-litografia dell'Ufficio superiore topocartografico, 1939), telegram n. 750/24, attachment 1157, p. 377.

The Italian newspapers announced the murder of the Emperor's son-in-law with page-width headlines, and the vice-secretary of the Fascist University Groups, Guido Pallotta, whose job was to interpret the feelings of the nation's most authentically Fascist stratum, wrote: 'And from the roar of the firing squad reverberated an ostentatious Fascist laugh in the face of the world, the most burning challenge to the sanctionist affronts. In true Fascist manner, Captain Tucci has served a magisterial slap to the bedaubed face of the Genevan whore.'[10] Pallotta was right, however, that Fascist Italy had taken a leap forward. By this point, there were no norms, laws, customs or moral judgements that could stop them. The Italian Empire of Ethiopia was proving itself to be a gigantic laboratory in which a supposedly civilized people were demonstrating their basest instincts and experimenting with the techniques of genocide.

Just nine months after Mussolini had nominated Graziani as Viceroy of Ethiopia, the climate in Addis Ababa had become particularly heavy, and the instability was palpable. The capital was home to several thousand Ethiopians who were mourning their loved ones killed in the 'policing operations'. Many others feared for the lives of their relatives who had simply disappeared, who likely found themselves in the Italian prisons. The manhunt for the cadets from the military college in Oletta continued without pause, as well as for the Ethiopians who had graduated abroad, in relation to whom Mussolini had issued the followed sentence on 3 May 1936, against 'all of the so-called Ethiopian youth, cruel and pre-

---

10 *La Gazzetta del Popolo*, 24 February 1937. Pallotta was poorly informed. Ras Desta was not short at Buttagera, but hanged, as was recounted to us by an eye-witness to his execution, Andrea Callisto Scotti: 'Ras Desta was hanged then left on the gallows for a whole day. A took a photo of the scene.' (Account provided to the author in Brescia, 10 February 1980). ['Genevan whore' is a reference to the League of Nations, which placed sanctions on Italy for its aggression against Ethiopia from October 1935.—Trans.]

tentious barbarians, moral authors of pillage.'[11] Finally, news was arriving from the surrounding regions where a resistance was being mounted by the *arbegnoch* (patriots) to the attacks, massacres and raids, the arson of whole villages and the systematic use of gas.

All the necessary elements were present for the triggering of a revolt or, at the very least, a desperate act of protest. With the complicity of Semeon Adefres, a taxi driver from Harar, and Fikre Mariam, one of the rebel leaders, this act of extremism was eventually delegated to two young Eritrean students, Abraham Deboth and Mogus Asghdom, who practised by throwing hand bombs off the slopes of Mount Zuqualla in the days running up to their attempt on Graziani's life. On 19 February 1937, taking advantage of a ceremony being held in the courtyard of the governor's palace (known as Piccolo Ghebì) to celebrate the birth of Prince Umberto of Savoy's son, the two Eritrean students slipped passed the guards, walked into the palace, went up to the first floor and out onto the balcony which looked out over the entrance steps where all the officials were assembled. It was around midday when the they hurled eight Breda hand grenades onto Viceroy Graziani and the Italian and Ethiopian authorities around him. The death count was serious: seven dead and fifty wounded, including Graziani himself; Vice-Governor General Petretti; Generals Liotta, Gariboldi and Amando; Colonels Mazzi and Amantea; Governor of Addis Ababa Siniscalchi; Fascist Inspector of Work for Italian East Africa Fossa; Federal Secretary Cortese; Bishop Cirillo; and *degiac* Haile Selassie Gugsa.

Taking advantage of the general chaos, the two young Eritreans— following a well-studied route—managed to escape and jump over the palace fence. Semeon Adefres was waiting for them in his Opel, and took them to safety in the convent city of Debre Libanos. From here they managed to reach Ras Abebe Aregai's partisan units, with which

---

11 Documents on Ethiopia from the author's archive, telegram n. 5007, secret, encrypted.

they were active for a time. Later they decided to make for Sudan but were killed during the journey under circumstances that remain unclear. Semeon Adefres, on the other hand, disappeared from Addis Ababa for a few days but was then reported to the city's political office, who arrested him and tortured him to death. His body was recovered by his sister and is laid to rest in the Church of Saints Peter and Paul.[12]

As soon as he learnt of the assassination attempt, Mussolini sent the following telegram to Graziani—who was recovering in hospital, having been hit by 350 pieces of shrapnel: 'I do not attribute the episode with any importance greater than that which it effectively has. But I believe it must be taken as a sign to begin that radical clean-up which, in my view, is absolutely necessary in the Shewa.'[13] The man who took the initiative in dispensing an unforgettable lesson to the Ethiopians was not, however, Graziani—who limited himself to transforming the hospital into a bunker—but Fascist Federal Secretary for Addis Ababa, Guido Cortese.

The reprisals kicked off almost immediately in the afternoon of 19 February itself. Journalist Ciro Poggiali made an entry in his secret diary:

> All the civilians in Addis Ababa have assumed the task of revenge, to be carried out speedily with the systems of the most authentic Fascist thuggery. They walk about with clubs and iron bars, slicing down as many natives as they can find in the street. [. . .] I saw a driver who, having killed an old negro with a swoop of his club, stabbed his head repeatedly all over with his

---

12 See Richard Pankhurst, 'Nuove rivelazioni sull'attentato alla vita di Graziani del 19 febbraio 1937', *Studi piacentini*, 36 (2004): 141–44. Until 2004, Semeon Adefres' name had never been mentioned.

13 Archivio centrale dello Stato, Fondo Graziani, *I primi venti mesi dell'Impero*, telegram n. 53956, 19 February 1937.

bayonet. It is futile to note that this havoc is being wreaked on people who are innocent and extraneous.[14]

Antonio Dordoni, another eye-witness who knew the Italian community in the city very well, reported:

> In the late afternoon, after they had received orders from the Fascist office, several hundred squads made up of blackshirts, drivers and Libyan askaris poured into the natives' neighbour-hoods and let loose the most frenzied 'black hunt' ever seen. They set light to roundhuts with petrol and finished off those who tried to flee with hand grenades. One of them boasted of having 'done ten huts' with a single flask of petrol. Another complained that his right arm was tired from lobbing so many grenades. I knew many of these frenzied men. They were shop-keepers, drivers, functionaries, people who I had believed to be calm and entire respectable persons. They were people who had never shot a single bullet throughout the war but who now revealed an entirely novel layer of rage and violence. The fact is, they had absolute impunity. The only risk they ran was earning themselves a medal. As far as I am aware, the police only inter-vened once, in order to stop the arson of the shops belonging to an Indian man called Mohamed Ali.[15]

We have three photographs of this horrendous massacre, taken by a young Alberto Imperiali, who—along with his father—was in touch with the Ethiopian resistance. The images are clear, terrifying and unequivocal, taken in the area of Gullale, between the Church of Saints Peter and Paul and the residence of Ras Hailu Tekla Haimanot. The bumpy earth is literally covered with strips of white cloth. This is not,

---

14 Ciro Poggiali, *Diario AOI. 15 giugno 1936–4 ottobre 1937* (Milan: Longanesi, 1971), p. 182.

15 Account provided to the author by Antonio Dordoni, in Addis Ababa, 26 March 1965.

however, the scene of an immense indigenous laundry, but of cadavers wrapped in white foutas, probably unloaded from armed cars en masse. Here and there a head or an arm emerges from the heap of white fabric, confirmation that we are looking at one of history's most abhorrent massacres. We can try and count the victims: one hundred, two hundred . . . It is impossible to continue.[16]

The interior of the Church of Saint George was also set alight, originally constructed by the engineer Sebastiano Castagna under the reign of Menelik I—a detail which probably evaded Cortese, who gave the order himself for the building to be burnt down. It was only the intervention of a colonel from the grenadiers that stopped around 50 deacons from being beaten into the flames with whips.[17] While the civilians were organizing the attacks against an unarmed and population entirely extraneous to the attacks, the soldiers were carrying out mass arrests, herding more than 4,000 Ethiopians into improvised concentration camps. The retaliations, however, took on genocidal dimensions in the agglomerations of roundhuts along the rivers Ginfile and Gilifalign, which cut across the city from north to south. Attacked and set alight in the late evening, they burnt throughout the night, illuminating the immense forest city in the morning.

'Very few roundhuts remain between Piazza Cinque Maggio and the American hospital,' Alfredo Godio recalled, who walked through the neighbourhood the next day. 'There were mounds of burnt bodies among the ruins. Later, on the road to Ambo, I saw a great number of 634-type armoured cars go by, upon which the bodies of dozens of murdered Abyssinians had been stacked up in a horrible tangled mess.'[18]

---

16 Copies of these photographs were provided to me by Alberto Imperiali in 1980 and are conserved in my photographic archive.

17 Poggiali, *Diario AOI*, p. 183.

18 Account provided to the author by Alfredo Godio, in Borgosesia (Vercelli) on 13 November 1979.

'The chaos lasted three days,' recounted Dante Galeazzi, an actor who had travelled to Ethiopia on the wings of adventure. 'No Abyssinian in sight had any way out over those three terrible days in Addis Ababa, a city of Africans where, for a while, you could not lay your eyes on a single one.'[19] On 21 February, concerned by the fact that the foreign diplomats in the capital might walk around armed with cameras and photograph the cruel sight of the massacre, Graziani authorized Colonel Mazzi to deliver the following phonogram by hand to Cortese: 'His Excellency the Viceroy requests that reprisals come to an immediate halt.'[20]

Cortese consented, and had a flyer distributed the next morning, printed on glossy paper, 20 cm x 30 cm, with the stamp of the Fascist Federation, Addis Ababa section. It read:

> *Camerati*! I order that from 12 midday, today 21 February, Year XV, that every act of reprisal should cease. At 9.30 p.m. all Fascists must return to their own houses. There will be VERY SEVERE repercussions for any transgressions. All public and private cars, including trucks (aside from those employed by the Government and Military) must cease circulation from 9 p.m. The Federal Secretary.[21]

Ciro Poggiali's diary entry was succinct: 'Clearly there was neither poultry nor coin left to loot.'[22] Dordoni's own comment revealed a profound sense of indignation: 'I read it and re-read it. I couldn't believe my eyes.

---

19 Dante Galeazzi, *Il violino di Addis Ababa. Uomo sulla soglia* (Milan: Gastaldi, 1959), p. 105.

20 Archivio centrale dello Stato, Fondo Graziani, b. 33, phonogram n. 2296.

21 An example of this flyer is conserved in the Fondo Graziani. [*Year XV* refers to the Fascist calendar.—Trans.]

22 Poggiali, *Diario AOI*, p. 186 [Poggiali writes 'talleri' for coin, referencing the Austrian Maria Thesera Thaler, currency still in use in Ethiopia at the time.—Trans.]

I couldn't believe that, after that type of massacre, documents of this kind could circulate, ones that clearly admitted their responsibility.'[23]

Wanting yet again to demonstrate that he was more stubborn than anyone else, on 21 February 1937 Mussolini sent the following telegram to Graziani: 'None of those arrested, or who will be arrested, are to be released without my order. In any case, all of the civilians and clerics under suspicion are to be executed without delay. I await your confirmation.'[24] Military lawyer Bernardo Olivieri presented Graziani with a report on an apparent conspiracy according to which the assassination attempt had been planned by students of the military college in Oletta (we now know that it was planned and carried out by only three people); consequentially, on 26 February, the Viceroy sent the following despatch to Mussolini: 'Duce, this morning 45 of the leaders and their followers have been executed, all of whom were clearly guilty of the assassination attempt on the 19th. Around 250 leaders and representatives of the clergy remain detained at the palace, in relation to whom I will make suggestions forthwith.'[25]

Despite the ease of access to the Italian and Ethiopian archives, it remains impossible to establish the exact number of victims over those three days of repression. The memo presented by the Ethiopian government to the Council of Foreign Ministers of the victorious powers (who met in London in September in 1945) cites '30,000 killed during the massacre of 1937.'[26] This figure probably includes the successive killings

---

23 Account provided to the author by Antonio Dordoni, in Addis Ababa, 26 March 1965.

24 Archivio centrale dello Stato, Fondo Graziani, *I primi venti mesi dell'Impero*, telegram n. 93980, 21 February 1937.

25 Archivio centrale dello Stato, Fondo Graziani, b. 48.

26 A part of the memorandum, including the numbers of people killed by the Italians in Ethiopia between 1935 and 1941, and the requests for reparations, can be found in Angelo Del Boca, *La guerra d'Abissinia, 1935–1941* (Milan: Feltrinelli, 1965), pp. 283–84.

of the 'patriots', clerics, fortune tellers, folk singers and hermits who were somehow connected to the attempt on Graziani's life.[27] The English, French and American newspapers of the time provide figures that move between 1,400 and 6,000 dead. For his own part, Graziani provided this preliminary and extremely reductive account for Mussolini on 22 February:

> Over the past three days, I have carried out searches throughout the city, with the order to execute anyone in possession of instruments of war, and that the relevant houses should be burnt down. A thousand people have thus been executed and as many houses burnt.[28]

There was, however, no vast and extensively planned conspiracy behind the assassination attempt of 19 February 1937, despite Olivieri's assertions to the contrary. His hasty and incorrect version was useful for Graziani, however, who needed to conclude that 'radical clean up' that Mussolini had ordered, and which he himself, for that matter, had suggested. As we have seen, on 26 February he had 45 'leaders and their followers' shot, 'all of whom were clearly guilty'.[29] Another 26 were assassinated over the next four days. As a result of these executions, Graziani effectively liquidated a part of the Ethiopian intelligentsia: high-ranking state functionaries, young officers, close collaborators of the Emperor and a swathe of young people who had only recently graduated from universities in Britain, France and the USA under the sponsorship of Haile Selassie.

27 Archivio centrale dello Stato, Fondo Graziani, b. 33, telegram n. 9170 [Trans: the fortune tellers and singers probably refer to the *debtera*, itinerant magical healers who were part of Ethiopian coptic culture.]

28 Archivio centrale dello Stato, Fondo Graziani, b. 33, telegram n. 9170.

29 Archivio centrale dello Stato, Fondo Graziani, *I primi venti mesi dell'Impero*, telegram n. 9894, 26 February 1937.

This was only the beginning of the repression. Graziani's proposals to Mussolini include that of 'razing the old native city to the ground and moving the entire population into a concentration camp'.[30] For once, Mussolini opposed such a monstrous project, not because it repulsed him but because it 'would provoke a very unfavourable impression internationally, and would not achieve its aim.'[31] He approved, on the other hand, of the Viceroy's proposal to deport to Italy those leaders who were still detained under the palace. Transferred by plane to Asmara, on 7 March 1937, 187 men, 8 women and 2 children were boarded on the *Toscana* at Massawa. Over the following months, four steamboats deported a further 200 aristocrats to Italy, bringing the total to 400 people.[32] 'The less important but nevertheless toxic elements',[33] on the other hand, were sent to concentration camps in Nokra (Eritrea) and Danane (Somalia), where around half died of disease or malnutrition.[34]

With the problem of the treacherous Shewan nobility finally resolved through deportation, Graziani could dedicate himself to the 'radical clean up', i.e. the elimination of every form of opposition—real, presumed

---

30 Archivio centrale dello Stato, Fondo Graziani, *I primi venti mesi dell'Impero*, telegram n. 10362.

31 Archivio centrale dello Stato, Fondo Graziani, b. 34, telegram n. 54599, 1 March 1937.

32 On the deportation of the Ethiopian nobility to Italy, see Archivio storico del Ministero per gli affari esteri, Africa Orientale Italiana, pos. 181/54, f. 250; Archivio centrale dello Stato, Fondo Graziani, b. 34; Alberto Sbacchi, 'Italy and the Treatment of Ehtiopian Aristocracy, 1937–1940', *The International Journal of African Historical Studies*, 10(2) (1977); Paolo Borruso, *L'Africa al confino. La deportazione etiopica in Italia, 1937–39* (Manduria: Lacaita, 2003); Martha Nasibù, *Le memorie di una principessa etiope* (Milan: Neri Pozza, 2005).

33 Archivio centrale dello Stato, Fondo Graziani, b. 34, telegram n. 20650, 18 April 1937, Graziani to General Santini.

34 On the Danane concentration camp, see Matteo Dominioni, 'Le fotografie di Danane nel contesto dell'immagine coloniale', *Studi piacentini*, n. 35, 2004, pp. 213–26.

or otherwise. The shocking episode of the massacre of fortune tellers and folk singers is illustrative. On 19 March, Graziani notified Alessandro Lessona, Minister for the Colonies, that the police had 'unanimously reported' to him that 'the most dangerous disturbers to public order' were to be found among the folk singers, fortune tellers, witches and hermits who skilfully spread false or catastrophic information, such as the imminent collapse of Italian rule in Ethiopia. 'Convinced of the need to radically unroot this unhealthy plant,' Graziani continued, 'I ordered that all folk singers, fortune tellers and witches in and around the city be arrested and executed. At the time of writing, 70 have been rounded up and eliminated.'[35] 'I approve of what has been done about the witches and rebels,' Mussolini was quick to reply. 'It should continue until the situation is radically and definitively calm.'[36]

Graziani was not to disappoint him. 'From 19 February till today,' he reported to Mussolini on 21 March, '324 summary executions have been carried out, always with certain and proven culpability. I repeat, 324, without of course including in this figure the repressions of 19 and

35 Archivio centrale dello Stato, Fondo Graziani, *I primi venti mesi dell'Impero*, telegram n. 14044.

36 Département de la Presse et de l'Information du Gouvernement Impérial d'Ethiopie, *La Civilisation de l'Italie fascite en Ethiope*, VOL. 1 (Addis Ababa: Berhanena Selam, 1945), p. 64: telegram n. 27/M, secret, 20 March 1937. This document represents the most detailed accusation against Fascist Italy. The first volume, comprising 144 pages, includes the operative telegrams that certify the arrests, repressions and killings. The second volume, comprising 62 pages, presents the horrific photographs of the mass executions, grave pits full of bodies, the gallows for multiple executions and the ostentatious exhibition of severed heads. There are very few lines of commentary: 'We have decided to withhold from annotating these documents. They stand by themselves as witness to that which the Ethiopian people suffered at the hands of Fascist Italy. We submit them, in all their starkness, to the judgement of honest minds, effecting our sacred duty, in the name of all the innocent victims, to ask that the guilty parties be punished.'

20 February.'[37] On 30 April, the 'rigorous actions' had risen to 710.[38] On 5 July, to 1,686.[39] On 25 July, to 1,878.[40] By 3 August, to 1,918.[41] At this point, the Viceroy's macabre and repulsive counting ceased, but from other sources we know that the executions did not. They were effected in the most total illegality, without either inquest or trial, often without even the most minimal of proof, sometimes out of pure revenge, at other times in order to cover up theft and burglary. From a report made by Colonel Azolino Hazon, we learn that the carabinieri alone executed 2,509 Ethiopians between February and May 1937.[42]

Analysing the despatches exchanged between Mussolini, Graziani, Lessona and Cortese (as well as the documents drawn up by the army's lawyers, Olivieri and Franceschino, and by Colonel Hazon) and reflecting on their language, in which the most recurrent expressions are 'execute', 'liquidate', 'clean up' and 'reprisal', one asks oneself what kind of Ethiopia they were building, and to whom they thought they would hand over this vast cemetery. If a governor, such as General Nasi, attempted to limit the massacres, he would be immediately beaten back by Graziani, who found the indulgence of his underling intolerable. 'I order that the 54 elements, cited in the first paragraph, are to be put before the firing squad, without delay. [. . .] Similarly, all of the fortune tellers and

---

37 Archivio centrale dello Stato, Fondo Graziani, *I primi venti mesi dell'Impero*, telegram n. 14440.

38 Archivio storico del Ministero per gli affari esteri, Africa Orientale Italiana, pos. 181/56, f. 267: Graziani to Lessona, telegram n. 2583, secret.

39 Archivio storico del Ministero per gli affari esteri, Africa Orientale Italiana, telegram n. 33911, secret, 7 July 1937.

40 Archivio storico del Ministero per gli affari esteri, Africa Orientale Italiana, telegram n. 36920, secret, 27 July 1937.

41 Archivio storico del Ministero per gli affari esteri, Africa Orientale Italiana, telegram n. 37784, secret, 4 August 1937.

42 Archivio centrale dello Stato, Fondo Graziani, b. 30, f. 6, document from 2 June 1937 entitled: *Statistica dell'attività dell'arma dell'AOI nel 1° anno dell'Impero.*

witches are to be shot. [. . .] Please assure me of this with the word "liquidation".[43]

Yet the worst was still to come.

Having wreaked his revenge on the Amharan nobility, on prominent members of the Ethiopian intelligentsia, on the cadets of the Oletta military college, on an anonymous and wretched mass of fortune tellers, folk singers, witches and hermits, over the last 10 days of May 1937, Graziani focused his crosshairs on the Christian Coptic clergy, in particular on the monastery-city of Debre Libanos. The task of imparting this new lesson was entrusted to General Pietro Maletti who—unlike Nasi—executed his orders to the key. He left Debre Berhan on 6 May 1937 and crossed Mens, where the resistance was led by the degiac Auraris Dullu. He swept across like an Atilla reborn. If we are to believe the reports he drew up, over two weeks his troops set fire to 115,422 huts, three churches, the monastery of St Michael (after executing the monks) and exterminated 2,523 arbegnuocs. The terror that Maletti spread was to a degree that the entire population of Mens fled.[44] 'Not a single person came to give homage', he reported to Graziani. 'All the non-combatants had fled with their herds and goods, taking refuge in the valleys, in the region's many creeks, ravines and caves. With their churches despoilt, the priests have defrocked and hidden among the population.'[45]

For the operation against Debre Libanos, which he surrounded on the evening of 19 May, Maletti decided to no longer make use of the Eritrean battalions (which were majority Christian), instead utilizing

---

43 Archivio centrale dello Stato, Fondo Graziani, *I primi venti mesi dell'Impero*, telegram n. 6246.

44 Mens: probably the locality of Mendida. [Trans.]

45 Archivio centrale dello Stato, Fondo Graziani, *Il 2° anno dell'Impero*, b. 60, part 6, chapter 2, p. 12.

the Libyan and Somalian askaris, who were not only Muslim but also—in his words—'ferocious mounted castrators from Mohamed Sultan's gang: 1,500 men armed with daggers, lances and old rifles, as agile as monkeys, free of any formal strategy, led only by their infallible instincts.'[46]

Located to the north of the Shewa region, the important monastery of Debre Libanos was founded in the thirteenth century by the Tigryn saint Tekle Haymanot, and included two large walled churches, a thousand huts inhabited by monks, priests, deacons, theology students and nuns, and a hundred tombs of important Abyssinian leaders, watched over by the monks and priests. While Maletti completed his occupation of the holy city, he received the following telegram from Graziani:

THE MILITARY LAWYER TELLS ME IN THIS PRECISE MOMENT HE HAS FOUND THE DEFINITIVE PROOF AS TO COMPLICITY BETWEEN THE MONKS AT DEBRE LIBANOS AND THOSE WHO CARRIED OUT THE ASSASSINATION ATTEMPT. EXECUTE ALL THE MONKS WITHOUT DISTINCTION, INCLUDING THE VICE-PRIOR. PLEASE PROVIDE INSURANCE BY COMMUNICATING THEIR NUMBER. PUBLICIZE THE UNDERLYING REASONS OF ORDER.[47]

In truth, the evidence discovered by Major Franceschino was extremely vague, and at the very most would have implicated a few of the monks, but certainly not the entire community. The Viceroy, however, had been convinced for some time that the monastery was 'a cove of assassins, BANDITS and monks who are completely hostile to us'.[48] He had no scruples in ordering their extermination.

---

46 Fondo Graziani, *Il 2° anno dell'Impero*, p. 14. [For 'mounted' troops, Maletti writes 'galla', referring to the Oromo light cavalry. —Trans.]

47 Département de la Presse et de l'Information du Gouvernement Impérial d'Ethiopie, *La Civilisation de l'Italie fasciste en Ethiope*, p. 128: telegram n. 25876.

48 Fondo Graziani, *I primi venti mesi dell'Impero*, telegram from Graziani to Lessona, n. 23260, 21 May 1937.

Graziani had assured Minister for the Colonies Lessona that 'the executions carried out as a consequence of the aforementioned assassination attempt will be effected in isolated locations and no one—I repeat: no one—will witness them.'[49] Maletti thus began on 19 May to look for an appropriate location for the massacre. He found it a few kilometres from Debre Libanos, on the plain of Laga Wolde, closed in on the western side by an amphitheatre of five hills and to the east by the river Fiche Wenze flowing into the gorge of Zega Wedem. The site was perfect because it was uninhabited and, more importantly, accessible to the armed cars needed to transport the victims.

After a few hasty checks, and the separation of the clerics from the occasional pilgrim, on 21 May the general had the selected monks transferred to the plain of Laga Wolde. In their detailed reconstruction of the facts, scholars Ian L. Campbell and Degife Gabre-Tsadik write:

> The victims were pushed off the trucks and quickly lined up, with their faces to the north and their backs towards the askaris. They were forced to sit in a line along the southern edge of the river, which in that period of the year was extremely dry. The askaris then took a long sheet, prepared specifically for the occasion, and put it over the prisoners like a tight curtain, forming a hood over their heads.[50]

They then proceeded to shoot the clerics. While an Italian officer would shoot at point blank in the head, near to the ear, the askaris removed the black cloth from the corpses so as to use it for the following group of victims. It was all over by 3.30 p.m., and Graziani wrote to Rome saying

49 Ministry of Justice, *Documents on Italian War Crimes Submitted to the United Nations War Crimes Commission by the Imperial Ethiopian Government, Volume 1: Italian Telegrams and Circulars* (Addis Ababa, 1949): telegram from Graziani to Lessona, 19 March 1937 (document n. 28).

50 Ian L. Campbell and Degife Gabre-Tsadik, 'La repressione fascista in Etiopia. La ricostruzione del massacro di Debrà Libanòs', *Studi piacentini*, 21 (1997): 100.

that 'today, at 13.00', General Maletti 'handed over 297 monks to the firing squad, including the Vice-Prior and 23 lay persons suspected of conspiracy. The young deacons, teachers and other members of the order have been spared, who instead will be taken to and detained in the churches of Debre Berhan. The monastery has, by consequence, been definitively closed.'[51]

Three days later, however, the Viceroy changed his mind—perhaps by suggestion of Ras Hailu Tekla Hamaynot, the most well-known and merciless of the collaborationists among the aristocracy—and sent Maletti the following order: 'I confirm in full the responsibility of the monastery of Debre Lebanos. All the deacons are to be immediately executed. Please confirm with the words "complete liquidation".'[52] With his usual zeal, General Maletti immediately began to dig two big pits near Engecha, a few kilometres from Debre Berhan, and on the morning of 26 May had 129 deacons machine-gunned, young martyrs that Christianity neither remembers nor mourns because they were African, because they were different. Graziani concluded: 'So the number of executions rose to 449.'[53]

The real number of assassinations was much higher, at least three times this estimate. Between 1991 and 1994, the two scholars already mentioned above, Ian L. Campbell from the UK and Degife Gabre-Tsadik from Ethiopia, undertook expansive and detailed research in the area around Debre Libanos, interviewing monks, priests and civilians, some of whom had witnessed phases of the massacre. From their accounts it emerged that the number of people murdered at Laga Wolde did not

---

51 Fondo Graziani, *I primi venti mesi dell'Impero*, telegram from Graziani to Lessona, n. 23260, 21 May 1937.

52 Département de la Presse et de l'Information du Gouvernement Impérial d'Ethiopie, *La Civilisation de l'Italie fasciste en Ethiope*, VOL. 1, p. 132: telegram n. 26609.

53 Fondo Graziani, *Il 2° anno dell'Impero*, part 4, chapter 3, p. 29.

count 320 but between 1,000 and 1,600. Following this, between 1993 and 1998, Campbell continued the investigations in the region of Debre Berhan, searching for information about the massacre at Engecha. Not only did he manage to locate the two mass graves that contained the bodies of the 129 deacons, but was also able to collect two oral accounts of people who had witnessed the massacre from beginning to end. Campbell's research revealed, furthermore, that Graziani had not told the truth when he had reported the elimination of the deacons to Lessona, because not only had he ordered Maletti to effect the 'complete liquidation' of the 129 deacons but also requested the killing of 276 other Ethiopian citizens, including teachers, theology students, monks and priests who pertained to other monasteries and had nothing at all to do with Debre Libanos. The death count at Engecha thus rose to 400 victims[54] and the overall count for the reprisal against the convent city of Debre Libanos, according to the two researchers, is somewhere between 1,423 and 2,033 people.[55] No religious community had suffered an extermination of such proportions in all of African history.

In relation to other massacres, Graziani would try and lay the blame on Mussolini and Lessona, or alternatively on his inferiors; the killings at Debre Libanos and Engecha, however, did not disturb him. He assumed full responsibility for them and, even if he lied about the number of deaths, he wore them as a badge of honour. He wrote in his memoirs:

> It is not mere bragging if I take full responsibility for the important lesson given to the entire clergy of Ethiopia through the closure of the monastery at Debre Libanos, which had previously been reckoned invincible by everyone, and for the summary justice applied to all of the monks following the evidence that revealed their guilt. Indeed, I take pride in this title, in having had the

54 Ian L. Campbell, 'La repressione fascista in Etiopia: il massacro segreto di Engecha', *Studi piacentini*, 24–25 (1999): 23–46.

55 Campbell and Gabre-Tsadik, 'La repressione fascista in Etiopia', p. 111.

strength of will to carry out an order that then rumbled in the bowels of the entire clergy, from the bishops down to the very last priest and monk, who in that moment finally understood that they needed to put an end to their hostility towards us if they wanted to avoid being radically destroyed.[56]

If Graziani was counting on this a harsh and unforgettable lesson to the Ethiopian population through the savage repression between February and May 1937, then he miscalculated. The indiscriminate violence obtained the opposite effect, pushing underground anyone who felt threatened in any way, ending any compliance and encouraging the peasantry to join the ranks of rebels, who mourned the constant arson of their villages. New leaders and new adepts meant that the resistance also radically changed its methods of struggle. It was Graziani himself who noted this qualitative leap:

> The rebel units are better organized than the regular Abyssinian military regiments that took part in the war. An iron discipline has been established and even light infractions of negligence or disobedience are punished by death. [...] The rebels' tactic is to avoid being blocked by our troops, leading a guerrilla campaign across all regions of the country with the aim of demonstrating that Ethiopia has not been completely conquered.[57]

The largest and most insubordinate revolt was organized in Lasta. Over the second half of August 1937, the former governor of Wag, degiac Hailu Kebbede, called upon the entire regional population to wage a 'holy war' against the Italians, and over a few days managed to annihilate the garrison at Amba Work and other bases nearby. The task of breaking the degiac fell to Colonel Tosti, who was given the following severe

---

56 Fondo Graziani, *I primi venti mesi dell'Impero*.

57 Fondo Graziani, *Il 2° anno dell'Impero*, part 7, chapter 2, telegram from Graziani to the Minister of Italian Africa, n. 32841 (no date).

orders by General Pirzio Biroli: 'First of all, capture the rebel leader Hailu Kebbede, dead or alive, hanging him in the square in Sokota; execute the secondary leaders; raze to the ground those towns that have found common cause with the rebels.'[58] In the meantime, Mussolini was furious. The empire that he had so tenaciously desired, and which was threatening to capsize state finances due to its astronomic costs, was perennially in revolt, disturbing his plans for Europe. On 15 September, he sent Graziani a telegram with a threatening, irritated tone: 'I have no problem with sending battalions and air planes but the revolt needs to be stamped out with the greatest energy and in the briefest period of time possible. No more time is to be wasted.'[59]

On 19 September, more than a month after the beginning of the insurrection, Graziani managed to finally complete the muster and invaded Sokota with 13 battalions of soldiers (both Italian and Eritrean) supported by 10,000 irregular troops. Following intense combat and a failed attempt to break the encirclement, Hailu Kebbede—attacked by over 20,000 men with both ground and air support, including mustard has from the 63rd air squadron—was captured by the Wollo cavalry under the command of Colonel Raugei, and immediately executed. He was not put before the firing squad, as Mussolini erroneously communicated to the King. Kebbede met a brutal end, which Mussolini knew very well because Graziani described it to him with macabre meticulousness in a despatch. The degiac was beheaded (even though the surgeon, Giuseppe Rotolo, had refused to perform the task),[60] and

58 Fondo Graziani, *Il 2° anno dell'Impero*, part 2, chapter 3, p. 39: telegram n. 4450, 30 August 1937.

59 Fondo Graziani, *Il 2° anno dell'Impero*, part 2, chapter 3, p. 72: telegram n. 69335.

60 Account provided to the author by Giuseppe Rotolo, in Milan on 20 April 1984. Four images of the broken body of the *Degiac* Hailù Kebbede, taken by the photographer Angelo Dolfo, can be found in Angelo Del Boca, *I gas di Mussolini. Il fascismo e la guerra d'Etiopia* (Rome: Editori Riuniti, 1996), pp. 113–16.

his head was hoisted on a pike, displayed in the market place first in Sokota and then in Quoram.

With this barbaric spectacle—which would have sufficed, on its own, to demolish the regime's political and military respectability—Graziani's reign as viceroy of Ethiopia came to an end. On 11 November 1937, Mussolini sent him a long telegram that began thus: 'Dear Graziani, with the liquidation of the attempts at revolt in Amhara and Shewa finally secured and lasting, I believe your task is complete.'[61] Before leaving Addis Ababa for Italy, the marshal sent Mussolini his final report, in which—for the first time—he told the truth about the empire's extremely high cost in terms of men and means: 'The intensity of the struggle waged over the last 18 months since the occupation of the capital [. . .] can be understood from the 13,000 men we have lost, between Italians and colonial troops, and the 250 officers, three times the losses of the war itself.'[62]

Mussolini replaced Graziani with Amedeo of Savoy, Duke of Aosta, a man of a very different character. Right up to the end, Mussolini was unsure whether or not to maintain his faith in the man he recognized as the new Italian—passionate, unwavering, merciless. Their long-lasting bond was forged through a shared disregard for Africans and their complicity in the most execrable crimes. Mussolini's continued esteem for Graziani is the only way to explain why he recalled him in 1940 and entrusted him with the defence of Libya, and why—after his clamorous failure through the fighting in North Africa—he was then made Minister for War in the Republic of Salò.

Yet here too he was to be disappointed by the new Italian. Instead of joining Mussolini in his flight towards Switzerland—and therefore in

---

61 Fondo Graziani, *I primi venti mesi dell'Impero*, telegram n. 72058, secret, 11 November 1937.

62 Documents on Ethiopia from the author's archive, telegram n. 58999, 21 December 1937.

what would be his death—Graziani slipped away from the column of escapees, handing himself in to Captain Emilio Daddario, the American Chief-of-Staff at Cernobbio, saving his own life. Throughout his trial, there was no mention of the crimes he had committed in Africa. The Ethiopian government requested his extradition in vain. In his home town of Filettino, he is still venerated like a saint today.[63]

---

63 For an overall account of Graziani, see Angelo Del Boca, 'Rodolfo Graziani', in *Dizionario biografico degli italiani*, VOL. LVIII (Rome: Istituto della Enciclopedia Italiana, 2002), pp. 829–35. See also Imani Kali-Nyah, *Italy's War Crimes in Ethiopia, 1935–1941* (Chicago: The Ethiopian Holocaust Remembrance Committee, 2001).

ELEVEN

SLOVENIA:
AN ATTEMPT AT
ETHNIC CLEANSING

We have seen the new Italian at work: in the Libyan deserts, on the Ethiopian plateaus, along the rivers of Somalia. We have seen him chase groups of Abyssinians and spray them with mustard gas. We have seen him wield the final blow to 2,000 monks in Debre Libanos. We have seen him beat a Somalian slave within an inch of his life, due to a lack of respect.

Clearly not all the Italians in the overseas territories pulled a trigger, enslaved people or practised torture. But they could have, every single one of them, without distinction, for the simple reason that the upper ranks of the regime, as we have seen, did not prohibit such violence. On the contrary, they encouraged it, and guaranteed impunity to those who practised it. As Antonio Dordoni recalled in his account of the massacre of Addis Ababa, 'the only risk anyone ran was that of earning a medal'.[1]

Even those who came out on the other side of the African adventure unstained, blameless, without regrets, they too lived within an atmosphere of violence and illegality. Furthermore, they could not have known how to reject it, because everything around them strove to convince them that Fascist Italy was in the right. The proof of this widespread and almost total complicity can be seen in the photographic archive in

---

1 Account provided to the author by Antonio Dordoni, in Addis Ababa, 26 March 1965.

Addis Ababa, which contains tens of thousands of images found in the archives of the Italian government offices that survived the war, and in the pockets of the 90,000 Italian soldiers taken prisoner by the Ethiopians following the collapse of the Fascist empire.

This is an unusually shocking and horrific photographic documentation. First there are images—by the hundred—of gallows of every type, whether refined or ramshackle, with one or more bodies hanging from them. The Italian perpetrators often had themselves photographed in front of the gallows, or holding up the severed heads of the Ethiopian patriots by their hair. In some of the photos, the torturers raise up the heads impaled on pikes. In others they are made to roll out of a barrel. In others still, they are displayed on a sheet, like objects at a market stall. An awkward, unsure smile rests on the faces of these soldiers who have been praised by Fascist propaganda as harbingers of civilization and prosperity. Yet what takes one most by surprise is the full consent expressed by the faces that surround the perpetrators, as if this macabre spectacle constituted a daily ritual, something natural, taken for granted. The cruel and horrendous exhibitionism of these displays demonstrates above all a total disregard for the indigenous people, who were held to be socially and culturally inferior. The comforting justification that other colonial nations incriminated themselves in Africa and Asia with analogous acts does little to excuse such horrendous savagery.

While in Ethiopia and later in Spain, the Fascist regime was carrying out the dress rehearsal for a war of very different proportions—one which at this point seemed inevitable, pitting Fascist civilization against a democratic, communist and Jewish one—in Italy, instead of arming the country with the weapons necessary for this coming aggression, it was the Fascistization of the masses that accelerated, along with their totalizing control by the police. Thus while on the one hand they tried to forge a new Italian, the supreme vessel of all of Fascism's values, on the other hand this new Italian was encouraged to become a spy and informer. As Mimmo Franzinelli rightly recalls:

> informing was an expression of civic spirit according to the principle that, in Fascist Italy, the opposition had no right to citizenship; Benito Mussolini had made this official in parliament on 26 May 1927, in an epoch-defining speech: 'There is no room in Italy for *anti*-Fascists; there is only space for Fascists, and perhaps for *non*-Fascists so long as they are honest, exemplary citizens.' In this view, spying responded to the needs of political protection.[2]

Despite the beating taken at the Warieu pass in Ethiopia[3] and at Guadalajara in Spain, Mussolini remained convinced that only a real, total war could carry out the miracle of completely and definitively transforming the Italians, drawing above all on that killing instinct that they had so clearly revealed in suppressing the Libyans, Ethiopians and the Spanish communists. Consequentially, on 10 June 1940, Mussolini entered into the war at Hitler's side. Two years' earlier, through the 'provisions for the defence of the Italian race', he had provided the tools to foment hatred of the Jews. As Enzo Collotti has observed: 'The struggle against the Jews bore Mussolini's personal touch. Its insertion into the rhetoric against the Italian bourgeoisie—who he considered lazy, cowardly and unfit for the tasks that Fascism foresaw, above all Italy's imperial destiny—was meant to galvanize a people who had still not fully become aware of their imperial expansion.'[4]

---

2 Mimmo Franzinelli, *Delatori. Spie e confidenti anonimi: l'arma segreta del regime fascista* (Milan: Mondadori, 2001), p. 23. See also Mauro Canali, *Le spie del regime* (Bologna: Il Mulino, 2004).

3 On 23 January 1935, shortly after leaving the redoubt at Warieu, a column under the command of General Diamanti was attacked and half-destroyed by the Ethiopians. Nineteen officers and 245 blackshirts were killed in the retreat.

4 Enzo Colloetti, *Il fascismo e gli ebrei. Le leggi razziali in Italia* (Rome and Bari:

With the conquests obtained over the first year of the war, when the course of the global conflict (despite the errors of the 'parallel war' that Mussolini had pushed for) was still uncertain, the Italian Empire had reached respectable dimensions.[5] Aside from the regions in the Horn of Africa and Libya, King Vittorio Emanuele III now ruled over the Aegean, Albania, Kosovo, Debar, Struga, the Slovenian province of Ljubljana, Dalmatia and part of the province of Fiume. Italian troops were also garrisoned in Montenegro, parts of Bosnia, Croatia and Greece, a part of Southern France and Corsica and some areas of the USSR. At the end of 1942, by which point Italian East Africa had been lost, there were nevertheless 1,200,000 men dispersed across various foreign fronts.[6]

In the Balkans alone, where we will now focus our attention, there were 650,000 soldiers, divided into 10 moderately armed corps. Above all they lacked vehicles, especially modern armed cars, and individual automatic firearms. They had the tools necessary for a static garrison when they should have been provided with the arms necessary for a counter-guerrilla operation. These problems did not concern Mussolini too much however, in part because in Rome the Balkan front was considered a secondary operation. Galeazzo Ciano's diary entry for 29 April 1941 reads: 'Buffarini and I are preparing the political roadmap for the occupation of Ljubljana province. It is inspired by very liberal concepts. It will find support in Germanized Slovenia, where the worst abuses [of

---

Laterza, 2003), p. 79. On this topic, also see 'La difesa della razza', *Il Ponte*, 11–12 (1978); Valentina Pisanty, *Educare all'odio. 'La difesa della razza', 1938–1943* (Rome: Nuova Iniziativa Editoriale, 2004).

5 'The parallel war': the Italian invasion of Greece in October 1940. The offensive was a spectacular failure. [Trans.]

6 For Fascist Italy's loss of the East African colonies in the Second World War, see MacGregor Knox, *Mussolini Unleashed. 1939–1941. Politics and Strategy in Fascist Italy's Last War* (Cambridge: Cambridge University Press, 1982) and Anthony Mockler, *Haile Selassie's War: The Italian-Ethiopian Campaign, 1935–1941* (New York: Random House, 1984). [Trans].

power] are being reported.'[7] In one of his regular press statements, on 2 May 1941, Minister for Popular Culture, Alessandro Pavolini, suggested paying careful attention to the Italian annexation of Ljubljana: 'It will become our Province, with a great deal of autonomy. It is necessary, therefore, to provide the Slovenians with a proper satisfaction for their provincial and national pride, in a certain sense, while also understanding the importance of the city, and the level of civilization it has achieved.'[8]

While in Rome 'very liberal' projects were underway for Ljubljana province, praising its autonomy, in reality the annexation was proceeding in a manner that was anything but serene. Military minds and functionaries on the ground were aiming above all at an accelerated Fascistization of the region, even if they were not offering the local population even full Italian citizenship, instead providing the ambiguous certificate of 'citizen by annexation.' When the first fires of revolt began to light up in Slovenia (as they would in Dalmatia, Montenegro and Croatia), the repression was immediate and inexorable.

Many of the soldiers and civil servants posted in the Balkans had already cut their teeth in Libya, Ethiopia and Spain, and considered the Slavic peoples to be only one level up from Africans. One of these was general Alessandro Pirzio Biroli, who had managed to gain the admiration of Graziani himself when governor of Amara, for having ordered the hanging of 20 civilians in Quorata and the shooting of 4 priests. In a telegram from 27 July 1937, the Viceroy had praised him thus: 'His Excellency Pirzio Biroli did well in following the example of Debre Libanos, which was very good for the clergy of the former Shewa, because the priests and monks behave well now, a wonderful outcome.'[9] Pirzio

---

7 Galeazzo Ciano, *Diaio, 1937–1943* (Milan: Rizzoli, 1980), p. 506.

8 Nicolo Tranfaglia (ed.), *Ministri e giornalisti. La guerra e il Minculpop, 1939–1943* (Turin: Einaudi, 2005), p. 129.

9 Matteo Dominioni, 'La repressione italiana nella regione di Bahar Dar', *Studi piacentini*, 33 (2003): 159–70.

Biroli had also covered up the secret killings of a handful of village chiefs, who had been thrown into the waters of Lake Tana with a millstone around their necks.

Even though Fascist Italy was present in the Balkans for just over two years, the crimes committed by the occupying troops—both in terms of their number and ferocity—were superior to those committed in both Libya and Ethiopia. In part this is because, in the Balkans, there were no Amaran-Eritrean battalions to carry out the dirty work, nor the 'castrators' of Mohamed Sultan. In the Balkans, the dirty work was carried out entirely by Italians, following very precise directives from the most important figures among the central military clique.[10]

In February 1945, the state commission of Yugoslavia, presided over by Dusan Nedeljkovic, was already in a position to present the United Nations War Crimes Commission in London with the first four reports concerning Italian war crimes. The reports concerned Dalmatia, Montenegro and Slovenia, and more or less followed the same model. They began with the identification of the main perpetrators of the crimes, then moved on to an examination of the methods of death employed: sentences by special courts, massacres during round-ups, episodes of torture, deportations to concentration camps and other forms of repression.

The accusations were extremely serious, up to the point of hypo-thesizing an attempted genocide and the practice, in some cases, of ethnic cleansing. 'From the following material, which has only partly been gathered', we read in Report no. 1 (Dalmatia), 'one can see very

---

10 Generals Mario Roatta, Mario Robotti, Gastone Gambara, Taddeo Orlando, Alessandro Maccario, Vittorio Ruggero, Guido Cerruti, Carlo Ghe, Renzo Montagna, Umberto Fabbri, Gherardo Magaldi, Edoardo Quarra-Sito. We can add to these the governors of Dalmatia, Giuseppe Bastianini and Francesco Giunta; the High Commisar for the Province of Ljubljana, Emilio Grazioli; and the governor of Montenegro, Alessandro Pirzio Biroli.

clearly how the Fascist criminals began the programmatic extermination of our people, destroying and evacuating what they called *Dalmazia Nostra*.[11] Report no. 4 (Slovenia) begins in this terrifying manner:

> During the occupation between 11 April 1941 and 8 September 1943, the Italian invaders shot 1,000 hostages and treacherously murdered a further 8,000 in the province of Ljubljana alone,[12] including people found guilty by the infamous military court of Ljubljana. They burnt down 3,000 homes, deporting more than 35,000 people to the Italian concentration camps, men, women and children alike, and completely destroyed 800 villages. Tens of thousands of Slovenians passed through the Ljubljana police station, subjected to the more horrific torture; the women were raped and mistreated to death. The Ljubljana military court issued a great number of life sentences and other forms of detention, to the extent that in the camp of Arbe alone more than 4,500 people died of hunger.[13]

In other words, in the arc of just over two years, over 50,000 Slovenians either lost their lives or were subjected to extremely violent actions by the occupying troops.

These figures for Ljubljana province were not only confirmed but actually expanded by more recent extensive research. Particular reference should be made to two investigations published in 1999: Tone Ferenc's scholarly study,[14] and the criminal accusation presented by the lawyer

---

11 The four reports have been published by Costantino Di Sante in *Italiani senza onore. I crimini in Yugoslavia e i processi negati, 1941–1951* (Verona: Ombre Corte, 2005), pp. 55–107. The quote is from p. 59.

12 The administrative province of Ljubljana, annexed by Italy, numbered 330,000 inhabitants in 1941.

13 Di Sante, *Italiani senza onore*, p. 103.

14 Tone Ferenc, *'Ubija se premalo': Obsojeni na smrt—Talci—Ustreljeni v Ljubljanski pokrajini 1941–1943: Dokumenti* (Ljubljana: Inštitut za novejšo zgodovino, 1999);

Dušan Puh in Portorož against a group of Italian war criminals.[15] This latter investigation provides a total figure of 12,807 murders, divided thus: 1,500 hostages shot; 2,500 civilians assassinated during the spring offensive; 84 civilian deaths as a result of torture; 103 civilians burnt alive or killed in other ways; 900 partisans captured and sentenced to death; 7,000 dead in the concentration camps.[16] For his own part, Ferenc provides very detailed information about the activates of the military court in Ljubljana. Presided over by Colonel Antonino Benincasa and, following him, Ettore Giacomelli, colonel of the carabinieri, the court oversaw 8,737 cases in relation to 13,186 people, sentencing 83 of them to death, 434 to life sentences, and 2,695 to sentences between 3 and 30 years of imprisonment, for a total of 25,459 years.

The fact that, in Ljubljana province, there was an attempt not so much at a rapid, coercive Italianization but an operation of ethnic cleansing is confirmed not only by the extremely high number of killings and deportations, and the statements of the officers themselves (General Robotti: 'Too little killing!'; Major Agueci: 'The Slovenians should all be killed like dogs, with no mercy'),[17] but also by a document shuffled among the papers, the infamous *Note n. 3C* from 1 March 1942, along with its attachments from 7 April, signed by General Mario Roatta. The official note, which established the method for opposing and liquidating the

---

'*Si ammazza troppo poco*': *Condannati a morte—ostaggi—passati per le armi nella provincia di Lubiana, 1941–1943: documenti* (Ljubljana: Inštitut za novejšo zgodovino, 1999).

15 The Slovenian lawyer Dušan Puh formally presented the criminal accusations to the district court of Ljubljana on 26 May 1999, acting on behalf of the Opinion Movement for Slovenian Istria, 11 patriotic veteran organizations, and 128 Slovenian citizens. There were 53 Italians named in the accusations, first and foremost General Mario Roatta, commander of the Second Army; Sergeant Foi's name closed the list.

16 Puh, criminal accusations of 26 May 1999, pp. 52–53.

17 Ferenc, '*Si ammazza troppo poco*', pp. 153–61 and p. 20, respectively.

rebels in Slovenia and Dalmatia, not only ordered the 'disowning of the negative qualities included by the phrase *bono italiano*', but also proposed the arson of houses and entire villages, the execution of hostages, and the deportation of questionable civilians. Point IV establishes that 'the treatment of rebels ought not be summarized as 'tooth for a tooth' but instead as 'head for a tooth!'.[18] Inspired by the note's words, the governor of Monetnegro—Pirzio Biroli—had 180 hostages shot in June 1943, justified as an act of reprisal against the killing of 9 officers from the 383rd Infantry regiment.

This incitement to hatred, and disregard for human life (it was widely believed among occupying troops that the Slavs were subhuman barbarians), ended up encouraging the Italians to reveal their worst instincts. In two 'highly reserved personal reports' from 30 July and 31 August 1942 sent to the High Commissar for Ljubljana province, the Civil Commissar for the Logatec district, Rosin, provided a truly disastrous snapshot of the soldiers' conduct:

> Arrests, arson and shootings take place without any real reason. [. . .] There are truly horrific, pitiful scenes in the towns of women, men and children dragging themselves on their knees before our soldiers, begging them, with their hands clasped together, to not set fire to their houses and to leave their loved ones alive. [. . .] The random mass shootings and the burning down of towns, undertaken simply through a taste for destruction (and our grenadiers have conquered a sad first-place in this field), have certainly imbued the people with a religious fear, but they have also eliminated a great deal of goodwill and trust, to the extent that it is clear to everyone, unless he is blind, that our soldiers wreak upon the helpless all that anger which

---

18 The note is extremely long, numbering 15 dense printed pages. It can be found in Massimo Legnani, 'Il 'ginger' del generale Roatta', *Italia conemporanea*, 209–10 (1998): 155–74.

they have not been able to wreak upon the rebels. [...] The line 'the Italians have become worse than the Germans', which you hear whispered all about, summarizes how the Slovenians feel about us.

Commissar Rosin concluded his reports with a severe and decisive accusation of the military authorities who, convinced 'that every Slovenian is an enemy, encourage the soldiers to commit massacres and destroy goods, with disastrous effects, especially in political terms: lacking rebels, the troops dedicated themselves to the purge without worrying about the details. The motto they have been taught is: 'Kill and loot everything, because where you're taking it from has already been taken.'[19]

Commissar Rosin's criticisms were confirmed by letters from Italian soldiers to their families, intercepted by resistance units. Lorenzo Tamburini of the 25th infantry regiment wrote to his wife Antonia, in Viterbo, in a letter dated 8 July 1942:

Cara Tota, I'm going to tell you yet again about the damage we're doing here. Today we went back to the camp where we were a few days ago, because we were sent by train to burn down two rebel villages, again. I can't describe to you the butchery that we committed, and the booty of civilians' clothes we took away. I was loaded up like a mule, I had two ski jackets, a pair of knickerbockers, three bedsheets, two pillows, a new school bag, women's shoes that will fit you very well, a pair of women's galoshes, a pair of women's boots, two table cloths and a dozen big silk headscarves. I've sold some of them, because I couldn't carry everything. [...] In three days' time we're going to attack some other village and I'll have to sell the things I've got anyway. I can't even send you a parcel. The officers also

---

19 Ferenc, '*Si ammazza troppo poco*', pp. 153–61.

have sacks full of merchandise, but they're officers so they have mules to carry it all.[20]

Another soldier, Giuseppe Cherubini of the 52nd infantry regiment, wrote the following letter to Giulia Luzzitelli:

> *Mio carissimo amore*, I'm back from the round-up. We were 80 km from here, near to Postumia. As soon as we got there, they shot around 20 times and then they fled. We found a lot of animals, cows and horses, and we took everything, wine, ham, chickens, potatoes, and we cooked all night, and then in the morning we went back to the camp, were the grenadiers were. On the third day we went to another nice village, where we found every kind of good made by God. [. . .] We began to shoot with our 41 and 84 mortars. They ran away during the night and only the women were left. First we took everything from the homes and then we burnt them down, even though there were still a lot of clothes, bedsheets and sewing machines inside. In brief, it all went up in flames.[21]

On 16 July 1942, General Mario Robotti made an appeal to these soldiers who, when not called upon to act like assassins, had been transformed into a bunch of chicken thieves by a miserable series of orders:

> Today we will begin our beautiful march through the fields and forests of Italian Slovenia, which a group of communist thugs, in the pay of anti-Italian money, foolishly thought to remove from Italian soldiers. Our goal in this advance is to catch and punish these traitors who have murdered our comrades. [. . .] Yet again, you represent the legionaries of civilization, of the highest intelligence in Rome, and you will bear the characteristics of the Italian citizen and soldier through decisive, bold action

---

20 Puh, criminal accusations of 26 May 1999, pp. 15–16.
21 Puh, criminal accusations of 26 May 1999, pp. 15–16.

against a lurid enemy, you will help and assist the weak who
have been caught up in the storm through no fault of their own,
through forbearance towards those who change their mind and
lay down their arms. The prestige of the Italian name and of the
army comes above all else.[22]

Once again, the Italian soldier—the very same who we have seen raze
Slovenian villages to the ground—is described by General Robotti as a
'legionary of civilization', ready to assist the weak, concerned above all
to maintain the high-standing of Italy's name and army. The other side
of the coin, however, lay in the declaration addressed to the Slovenians
themselves, which was pasted on the walls on the very same day, at the
beginning of the 'beautiful march through the fields and forests of Italian
Slovenia.' It read:

From today, throughout the entire province of Lubiana, the following persons will be shot: anyone who commits hostile acts
towards the Italian troops and authorities; anyone who is found
in possession of arms, munitions and explosives; anyone who
aids the rebels in any manner; anyone found in possession of
forged identity cards, passports or travel documents; all able
males who are found in the combat zones without justification,
whatever their behaviour.[23]

The 'beautiful march' through the fields and forests of Slovenia lasted
almost five months, and never was such an operation more methodical,
more ferocious, more destructive. The partisans killed in combat numbered 1,807; those shot after being taken prisoner, 847; the civilians
killed, 167, including 11 women. This horrendous balance sheet should

---

22 The document of the 11th Army can be found in Ferenc, 'Si ammazza troppo
poco', p. 181.

23 Ferenc, 'Si ammazza troppo poco', p. 182. The proclamation bore the signature of
General Robotti and the high commissioner Emilio Grazioli.

give us little cause for surprise, given that in the conclusive phase of the preparations for the offensive, General Robotti had stated his true intentions very clearly to his officers: 'Italian domination and prestige must be established at all costs, even if that means shooting all of the Slovenians and destroying all of Slovenia.'[24]

In a disturbing manner, these threats strongly recall Badoglio's order to Graziani on the eve of the deportation of the entire population of Cyrenaica. The two generals use almost the same words, the same images of death and destruction. On 23 July 1942, a reliable eye witness, the military chaplain Pietro Bignoli, attached to the 2nd regiment of the Sardinian Grenadiers Infantry Division, described the attack on the town of Kotel—and the subsequent executions and looting—thus:

> How we left that cursed town! We left it with a haggle of old men without sons, women without husbands, children without fathers, all powerless people, the majority of whom had been deprived of their houses, which had been burned down, and completely deprived of any means of subsistence (stables, crops, fields—everything had been sacked). We left them there naked, to die of hunger.[25]

Not all the superior officers, however, were ready to follow Robotti's criminal orders obediently. Robotti himself, in a telephone message given to the command of the 'Alpine Huntsmen' infantry division, reveals:

> On the afternoon of 23 July, a lieutenant, apparently interim command of your regiment, when speaking with an officer 'M', said: 'They want me to be a hangman. When I put my stars on,

---

24 Ferenc, 'Si ammazza troppo poco', p. 26 and p. 22, respectively.

25 Ferenc, 'Si ammazza troppo poco', p. 204. Don Pietro Birgnoli has published a diary of his bitter experience: Santa Messa per i miei fucilati. Le spietate rappresaglie italiane contro i partigiani in Croazia dal diario di un cappellano (Milan: Longanesi, 1973).

I thought I was going to be a soldier. But if that is what they want, then OK.' Such expressions are not acceptable, as they go against the explicit orders of the upper command and indicate a mentality that is inadequate for the current situation. Proceed with the necessary checks and report back to me in a complete and exhaustive manner.[26]

We will never know the name of this officer who dared to discuss Robotti's order. We do not believe, however, that he would have been the only one. There was a vast abyss between what was taught in a military academy—even a Fascist one—and the orders that arrived during a rounding-up operations from officers like Robotti, who had lost all respect for the uniform they wore and made declarations such as 'wherever we are, it is we who dispense justice'.[27]

It was no secret among the high command that, in order to 'pacify' Slovenia, a plan had been conceived of to deport one part or all of the population. General Roatta had approached the topic on 23 May 1942 during a meeting with Mussolini in Fiume. On that occasion, he had limited himself to proposing the internment of 20,000–30,000 Slovenians, claiming that it was urgently necessary to set up concentration camps for this number of people. A decade earlier, Mussolini had acted upon Badoglio's proposal to imprison 10,000 people from Cyrenaica in the camps; once again, he praised Roatta's policy; and on 30 July, in a meeting in Gorizia with Roatta, Cavallero and Ambrosio, he stated: 'I am convinced that the partisans' 'terror' must be met with iron and fire. We must do away with the common belief that Italians are inept and sentimental, incapable of being tough when truly necessary. [. . .] Do not worry yourselves about the population's economic woes. They asked

---

26 Ferenc, 'Si ammazza troppo poco', p. 196.
27 Puh, criminal accusations of 26 May 1999, p. 9.

for this. [...] I would have no problem with the mass transfer of the population.'[28]

The deportation of Slovenians from Ljubljana province began on June 1942. According to Slovenian sources, less than 35,000 people were deported, around 10 per cent of the province's population, and would have continued if the armistice on 8 September 1943 had not radically altered the Balkan situation. Fully aware that Mussolini approved of his plans, Roatta fine-tuned them, for example: deciding to hand over all of the property that once belonged to murdered rebels' or deportees to the families of Italians killed in battle.[29] He then went further, communicating to the high command on 8 September 1942 that 'internment can be extended [... to facilitate] the eviction of entire regions, such as Slovenia. This would involve transferring sections of the population en masse, and relocating them within the Kingdom, replacing them with the Italian population.'[30] A project of 'cultural genocide' and 'ethnic cleansing', a vision shared by Robotti and Grazioli, was thus taking shape precisely at the time that the concentration camps were being established in Dalmatia and Italy alike.

The early estimates provided by Tito's government in 1946 indicated 67,230 deportations in the province of Ljubljana alone. This figure, however, was later revised and almost halved; the latter version is shocking nevertheless. In the first phase, the aim of internment was to weaken the Osvobodilna Fronta, the resistance fighters, but in a second phase, as we have seen, internment aimed at emptying out the province of the

---

28 See Ugo Cavallero, *Comando Supremo. Diario 1940–43 del capo di stato maggior generale* (Bologna: Cappelli, 1948), pp. 298–99.

29 Cavallero, *Comando Supremo*, pp. 298–99.

30 Puh, criminal accusations of 26 May 1999, p. 8. Also see Carlo Spartaco Capogreco, *I campi del duce. L'internamento civile nell'Italia fascista, 1940–1943* (Turin: Einaudi, 2004), p. 69, note 47.

majority of Slovenians in order to replace them with Italian families.[31] The largest deportation operations took place at the same time as the round-ups of July-November 1942, one of the largest acts of repression in the history of the Balkans, which saw the engagement of 60,000 Italian soldiers.

While the partisans taken prisoner were invariably executed on the spot, civilians—sometimes entire families, at others entire villages— were rounded up (after being robbed of all their goods) and taken to the barracks and subjected to interrogations and hasty checks. Following this, whether they had collaborated with the partisans or otherwise, they were taken to the concentration camps. The largest and sadly infamous of the camps was on Rab, an island just off the Dalmatian coast. The Slovenians were detained in another five camps across Italian territory: Gonars and Visco in the province of Udine; Monigo and Chiesanuova, in the area around Venice; and Renicci, in the province of

---

31 On anti-Slav racism, the project to eliminate the Slavic people from Venezia-Giulia and the attempt at ethnic cleansing in the province of Ljubljana, see Paolo Parovel, *L'identità cancellata. L'italianizzazione forzata dei cognomi, nomi e toponimi nella Venezia Giulia dal 1919 al 1945* (Trieste: E. Parovel, 1985); Elio Apih, *Italia, fascismo e antifascismo nella Venezia Giulia, 1918–1943* (Bari: Laterza, 1966); Rodolfo Ursini-Uršič, *Attraverso Trieste. Un rivoluzionario pacifista in una città di frontiera* (Rome: Studio i, 1996); Enzo Collotti, 'Sul razzismo antislavo' in Alberto Burgio (ed.), *Nel nome della razza. Il razzismo nella storia d'Italia, 1870–1945* (Bologna: Il Mulino, 1999); Tone Ferenc, *Rab, Arbe, Arbissima. Confinamenti, rastrellamenti, internamenti nella provincia di Lubiana, 1941–1943. Documenti* (Ljubljana: Inštitut za novejšo zgodovino, 2000); Boris M. Gombac and Dario Mattiussi (eds), *La deportazione dei civili sloveni e croati nei campi di concentramento italiani. 1942-1943. I campi del confine orientale* (Gorizia: Centro isontino di ricerca e documentazione storica e sociale 'Leopoldo Gasperini', 2004); Alessandra Kersevan, *Un campo di concentramento fascista, Gonars 1942–1943* (Udine: Kappa Vu, 2003); Maico Trinca, *Monigo. Un campo di concentramento per slavi a Treviso, luglio 1942–settembre 1943* (Treviso: Istresco, 2003); Brunello Mantelli, 'Gli italiani in Yugoslavia, 1941–1942. Occupazione militare, politiche persecutorie, crimini di guerra', *Storia e memoria*, 1 (2004).

Arezzo. According to a report that Robotti sent to Cavallero on 16 December 1942, the Slovenians in internment at that point numbered 19,405, and were divided thus: 6,577 in Rab, 2,250 in Gonars, 3,884 in Renicci, 3,522 in Chiesanuova, and 3,172 in Monigo. According to Slovenian estimates, on the other hand, by the end of 1942 26,000 people had already been deported, 15,000 of whom were detained in Rab.

Franc Potočnik, detained at Rab, described it thus: 'Up to eight people were crammed into simple tents, and often forced to lie naked on the ground. The hygienic conditions were horrendous: the latrines were simply holes in the ground, in the open air, and three water taps had to make do for 20,000 people; there was water for only six hours each day, and often it was closed off as a method of punishment.'[32] The food was always insufficient. According to the investigation undertaken by Carlo Spartaco Capogreco, a scholar who dedicated 20 years of his life to exploring the universe of Fascist concentration camps, food was always reduced by one quarter before it even got to the detainees, due to a whole series of petty thefts:

> In truth, the rations provided for by the Royal Army were already 'hunger rations' from the start: the relevant instructions planned 877 calories per day for the 'repressed' and 1,030 calories per day for the 'protected'. In terms of the minimum requirements of a resting individual, these rations lacked at least 1,000 and 900 calories respectively. In the very best hypothesis, therefore, the Yugoslavian detainees received daily rations corresponding to half of their calorific minimum.[33]

---

32 Cited in Maico Trinca, 'Donne e bambini sloveni nei campi fascisti, 1941–1943', in Bruna Bianchi (ed.), *Deportazione e memorie femminili, 1899–1953* (Milan: Unicopli, 2002), p. 321. For Franc Potočnik, see *Il campo di sterminio fascista. L'isola di Rab* (Turin: ANPI, 1979).

33 Capogreco, *I campi del duce*, pp. 142–43.

In these inhumane conditions—the very same that had been seen in the 15 camps in Sirta, under Graziani and Badoglio's orders—'people literally died in the mud and in their own filth [. . .]. The conditions clearly demonstrated a certain desire for ethnic cleansing in Ljubljana province.'[34] The death rate in Rab was 19 per cent, i.e. the same as that in an extermination camp, and higher than even that recorded in the Nazi camp at Buchenwald (calculated at 15 per cent).[35] It has been possible to provide a name to 1,495 of the victims, but Slovenian sources state the dead as numbering 3,500 or even 4,500.

Women and children suffered the most in Rab. We can read the account from 1944 of Ivan Stimec, 12 years old at the time:

We were in Rab. We lived in a tent near the sea. We slept on the bare ground. One night, while we were sleeping, there was a strong wind and it started to rain. The tide came up and the water got in the tents, right up to our knees. We were crying and calling for help. We wanted to run away but the guards didn't let us through the fence. The sea kept rising, many children drowned.[36]

The commander of the camp and garrison on the island of Rab was the lieutenant colonel of the carabinieri, Vincenzo Cuiluli, probably the most hated man in all of Slovenia. He was arrested after 8 September 1943 by the camp's underground resistance group and taken to Crikvenica prison, where he was sentenced to death. He killed himself the night before the execution was to take place.[37]

---

34 Puh, criminal accusations of 26 May 1999, p. 37.

35 Capogreco, *I campi del duce*, p. 270.

36 Trinca, *Monigo*, p. 346.

37 Capogreco, *I campi del duce*, p. 270.

Lieutenant Colonel Cuiuli was probably the only one of these war criminals to have paid with his life for his actions. All the other officers who had committed the most heinous crimes were not only not handed over to those countries who asked to put them on trial, but they were not even tried in Italy, despite the evidence relating to their guilt. Thus, just as Haile Selassie had asked in vain for Badoglio to extradite Graziani to Ethiopia,[38] so too Tito attempted in vain for 729 Italian soldiers and civilians held responsible for the worst of the crimes (an earlier list had included 1,200 names) to be handed over to Yugoslavia.

The history of the denial, guilty silences and rhetorical acrobatics necessary to avoid the obligation of consigning these criminals to the hands of justice does not put Alcide De Gasperi and his government in a good light. Yugoslavia's extradition requests began in February 1944; the same request was presented to the United Nations War Crimes Commission exactly one year later. In July 1945, the Allies sent a list of the suspected war criminals to Rome, by request of different countries (Yugoslavia, Greece, Albania, Ethiopia, Great Britain, France and the USSR), to be handed over to the UN.[39] Italy ignored these repeated requests for at least three years, adopting an ambiguous strategy that aimed at gaining time. This was not all however. As Filippo Focardi has demonstrated, the Foreign Minister gathered 'counter-documentation', the aim of which was not only to 'ascertain the responsibility of those persons accused by Yugoslavia, but also to gather evidence relating to their innocence and re-direct the accusations at the Yugoslavian partisans. [. . .] The Foreign Ministry also drew up a "counter-list" of Yugoslavian war criminals with around 200 names. Tito topped the list.'[40]

---

38 Selassie also requested the extradition of generals Pirzio Biroli, Geloso, Nasi, Gallina and Tracchi, of the Miniser for the Colonies, Lessona, and of the Federal Secretary, Cortese the man who had ordered the massacre in Addis Ababa on 19 February 1937.

39 Yugoslavia requested the consignment of 729 suspected criminals, the Allies 833, Greece 180, Albania 140, France 30, the USSR 12 and Ethiopia 10.

It was only in April 1946, under threat that the Allies themselves would arrest Italian war criminals to hand them over to Yugoslavia, that President De Gasperi announced the forming of commission for an official inquiry within the Ministry of War, led first by Alessandro Casati and, later, by Luigi Gasparotto, whose extremely slow work concluded in 1949. However, even though 39 people suspected of war crimes were referred to the military prosecutor, the trials never took place; in 1951, drawing on a legislative loophole, the military judiciary shelved all the accusations and the commission for the official inquiry was dissolved. And so the chance to carry out an 'Italian Nuremberg' vanished, a trial that might have brought out to the open the long series of crimes committed by Italians in the African colonies, the Balkans and the Soviet Union.[41]

Having taken the reprehensible decision to not extradite potential war criminals to other countries, Rome—save for a small handful of figures—also reneged on asking Germany to hand over those Nazis who had contributed a series of massacres that took place in Italy between 1943 and 1945.[42] As Focardi rightly underlined, along with Lutz Klinkhammer: 'The Italian government and its diplomats decided to limit their claims over German war criminals because they were scared that a decisive action against the Germans would end up damaging Italy herself, who was invested in protecting her own citizens purported to be war criminals by other foreign states (first and foremost Yugoslavia).'[43]

40 Filippo Focardi, 'I crimini impuniti dei 'bravi italiani', *Storia contemporanea*, n. 2, 2005, p. 330.

41 Michele Battini, *Peccati di memorie. La mancata Norimberga italiana* (Rome and Bari: Laterza, 2003).

42 On the massacres carried out by the Nazis in Italy during the closing phase of the war, see Lutz Klinkhammer, *L'occupazione tedesca in Italia, 1943–1945* (Turin: Bollati Boringhieri, 1993); Lutz Klinhjammer, *Le stragi naziste in Italia. La guerra contro i civili, 1943–1944* (Rome: Donzelli, 1997).

43 Filippo Focardi and Lutz Klinkhammer, 'La questione dei 'criminali di guerra' italiani e una Commissione d'inchiesta dimenticata', *Contemporanea*, 3 (2001): 499.

Not only did Rome refuse to hand over to Belgrade people about whose guilt there could be no doubt but, in a few cases, even promoted them to the highest level. The unstoppable rise of General Taddeo Orlando is exemplary, a figure well known in Slovenia for having led the 21st Division of Sardinian Grenadiers, and who distinguished himself for cruelty during the round ups of summer 1942. In February 1944, Badoglio had chosen him as Minister of War. Later, he was made general commander of the carabinieri. Finally, in November 1947, De Gasperi promoted him to Minister of Defence. General Gastone Gambara, on the other hand—who had replaced Robotti as commander of the 11th Armed Corp in Ljubljana—was chosen by Badoglio as the first governor of Brindisi.

The most clamorous example, however, was that of General Mario Roatta, whose name is to be found at n. 105 on the list of Italian criminals presented by Belgrade to the UN. On his return to Italy from Slovenia, he was named by Mussolini as the army's Chief of Staff, a position he maintained, extraordinarily, after the fall of Fascism. Furthermore, it was he who repressed the joyous demonstrations at the end of the regime, deploying the army. Indeed, he ordered his troops to form up against the demonstrators 'in combat formation', 'as if proceeding against the enemy', and to 'open fire at a distance, including with mortars and canon, without notice', finally adding: 'do not fire into the air, shoot as if in combat'.[44] It was by following Roatta's orders that, in the five days following

---

As is tragically well-known, all of the documentation of the massacres ended up in the 'closet of shame' and remained there for decades. On this almost unbelievable episode, see Mimmo Franzinelli, *Le stregi nascoste. L'armadio della vergogna: impunità e rimozione dei crimini di guerra nazifascista, 1943–2001* (Milan: Mondadori, 2002); Franco Giustolisi, *L'armadio della vergogna* (Rome: Nutrimenti, 2004).

44 See Roy Palmer Domenico, *Processo ai fascisti, 1943–1948. Storia di un'epurazione che non c'è stata* (Milan: Rizzoli, 1996), p. 21; 'Mario Roatta', in Victoria de Grazia and Sergio Luzzatto (eds), *Dizionario del fascismo*, VOL. 2 (Turin: Einaudi, 2003), pp. 532–33.

25 July 1943, there were 93 casualties, 536 people wounded and 2,276 arrests.

After 8 September, Roatta followed the King and the Prime Minister, Badoglio, to Brindisi—but he had been too closely connected to Fascism to maintain the role of the army's Chief of Staff and, on 12 May 1943, was forced to step down, as was Vittorio Ambrosio, the general chief of staff. Exactly one year later, when the High Commission for Purging began to function under the leadership of Carlo Sforza,[45] Roatta was arrested and imprisoned at Boccea Castle—but, it should be noted, not for the crimes he had committed in Yugoslavia but for the terrorist methods he had used to protect the Fascist regime when he was head of military intelligence. Even so, while the trial was underway (which concluded in a sentence of life imprisonment) he managed to break out of prison and reached Spain, where he enjoyed extremely strong protection as the former commander of the volunteer troops during the civil war.[46]

Like thousands of Fascists, he was saved by an amnesty and returned to Italy, after which he dedicated himself to writing his memoirs, *Eight Million Bayonets*. In the preface, he promised the reader that he would have the 'greatest objectivity' in his reconstruction of the facts, but he was too vacillating and manipulative to keep to his word. This, for example, is how he describes and justifies the Slovenian deportations:

> The inhabitants of entire areas were put under the protection of our troops as the Red Army began to close in. This is why tens of thousands of people and their livestock and goods were transferred to other locations and to 'protective', voluntary internment camps. (These provisions were transformed by the enemy propaganda into mass 'deportations', exaggerating the

45 'High Commission for Purging': the *Alta commissione per l'epurazione*. [Trans.]
46 For Roatta's role in Spain, see Gabriele Ranzato, *L'eclissi della democrazia. La guerra civile spagnola e le sue origini, 1931–1939* (Turin: Bollati Boringhieri, 2004).

numbers out of all proportion. In reality, the 2nd army interned just over 30,000 people in well-equipped camps, *of which only a few thousand non-voluntarily).*[47]

It is difficult to make so many shameful lies in so few words, but the former head of the intelligence services—a talented agent of international destabilization—was capable of much more besides. Nevertheless, there was one project that he did not manage to complete: the ethnic cleansing of Ljubljana province. But only because he lacked enough time.

Despite the damage and hatred that Fascism caused—from the burning of the cultural centres (the *Narodni dom*) in Trieste to the annexation of southern Slovenia, and the harsh treatment of the Yugoslavians, that caused the death of thousands of Italians and the forced exodus of at least 250,000 people from the regions of Giulia and Dalmatia[48]— fortunately the divide between two populations that confronted each other on the Eastern front did not represent an insuperable abyss. Even though the history of Venezia-Giulia had been distorted and instru- mentalized for decades, in autumn 1993 a mixed Italian-Slovenian com- mission was established to shed some light on the focal points of the controversy (i.e. the violations carried out by the Fascists in the 1920s and 1930s, the deportations, the *foibe* killings, the exodus), which has

---

47 Mario Roatta, *Otto milioni di baionette. L'esercito italiano in guerra dal 1940 al 1944* (Milan: Mondadori, 1946), p. 174.

48 On the *foibe* and the forced exodus of 250,000 people from Dalmatian Giulia, see Giampaolo Valdevit (ed.), *Foibe, il peso del passato. Venezia Giulia 1943–1945* (Venice: Marsilio, 1997); Gianni Oliva, *Foibe. Le stragi negate degli italiani della Venezia Giulia e dell'Istria* (Milan: Mondadori, 2002); Giacomo Scotti, *Goli Otok. Italiani nel gulag di Tito* (Trieste: Lint, 2002); Raoul Pupo and Roberto Spazzali, *Foibe* (Milan: Bruno Mondadori, 2003); Raoul Pupo, *Il lungo esodo. Istria: le perse- cuzioni, le foibe, l'esilio* (Milan: Rizzoli, 2005); Guido Crainz, *Il dolore e l'esilio. L'Istria e le memorie diverse d'Europa* (Rome: Donzelli, 2005).

provided extremely encouraging results, both in political and historical terms.

Fourteen Slovenian and Italian historians spent seven years trying to reconstruct the history of relations between Italy and the Slovenian people, focusing on the years 1880–1956. In revisiting the Fascist period, for example, the group of scholars wrote in agreement with each other that:[49]

> Fascism's denationalizing drive went beyond political perse-
> cution and aimed at an 'ethnic cleansing' of Venezia-Giulia
> [. . .]. While it is true that in the same epoch most European
> countries demonstrated little respect for the rights of ethnic
> minorities present within their borders—when they were not,
> indeed, actively trying to trample those rights—but this does
> not remove the fact that the Fascist policy of 'ethnic cleansing'
> was particularly extreme. This was in part because a nationalist
> intolerance—sometimes with veritable strands of racism—
> was combined with the regime's totalitarian methods. [. . .]
> What Fascism tried to effect in Venezia-Giulia was a program
> for the full destruction of Slovenian and Croatian national
> identity.[50]

Writing about the following period, from 1941 to 1945, the study touches on two painful moments: the Italian annexation of southern

---

49 The Italian side of the commission included Sergio Bartole, Fulvio Tomizza, Lucio Toth, Fulvio Salimbeni, Elio Apih, Paola Pagnini and Angelo Ara. In a second phase, Battole, Tomizza and Apih resigned their seats, and were replaced by Giorgio Conetti, Marina Cattaruzza and Raoul Pupo. The Sloveninan side was represented by Milica Kacin Wohinz, France Dolinar, Boris Gombax, Branko Marusic, Boris Mlakar, Novenka Troha and Andrey Vovko. The co-presidents were Conetti and Wohinz.

50 *I rapporti italo-sloveni 1880–1956. Relazione della Commissione storico culturale italo-slovena* (Capodistria: Koper, 25 July 2000), pp. 85–88.

Slovenia, and the massacre of Italians in autumn 1943 and spring–summer 1945. Here is the version that the 14 scholars provide of the first episode: 'From the start, the Fascist aggressor thought to subjugate the Slovenians thanks to the clear superiority of Italian civilization, meaning that the first period of occupation established by the Italian authorities was relatively moderate.' When the Slovenian Liberation Front launched a resistance to the occupying forces, however, 'Mussolini responded by handing over all civilian powers to the military, which adopted drastic repressive measures. [. . .] Between the soldiers killed in battle, people sentenced to death, the hostages shot and the civilians murdered, thousands of people died. Approximately 30,000 people were deported, for the most part civilians, women and children, and many died of hardship.'[51]

With the same sense of responsibility and objectivity, the members of the mixed commission also examined the equally controversial issue of the massacre of Italians in local sinkholes (*foibe*), a topic on which a guilty silence had been maintained for a long time, as well as a highly politicized instrumentalization. The murder of Italians in autumn 1943 was interpreted as 'killings perpetrated not only for ethnic and social reasons, but most of all to strike at the ruling class, driving most Italians in the region to fear for their own national survival and for their own safety.'[52]

As for the more widespread and bloody events of spring and summer 1945, here is the conclusion provided by the group of scholars:

> The people of Giulia who supported Italy considered the Yugoslavian occupation as the darkest moment of their history, among other reasons because this period also witnessed a wave of violence in the regions of Trieste, Gorizia and Capodistria; this sentiment was expressed through the arrest

---

51 *I rapporti italo-sloveni*, p. 93. and pp. 94–95, respectively.

52 *I rapporti italo-sloveni*, p. 98.

of thousands of people [. . .], hundreds of whom were executed on the spot—then were thrown into sinkholes—and through the deportation of a large number of soldiers and civilians, a portion of whom died from hardship or were killed during the journey, in prisons or in prison camps (among which we note the camp at Borovnica) erected across different parts of Yugoslavia [. . .]. The driving force of this repression came from a revolutionary movement that was transforming itself into a regime, and thus converting a national and ideological animosity present among the partisan cadres into state violence.[53]

The report was presented in July 2000 and received a positive reception. Corrado Belci, for example, highlighted the 'spirit of calm research' that motivated the Commission, the usefulness of the 'methodological cross-over' and above all the fact that the two groups of historians had 'undertaken a commendable effort without bending their own interpretations to the needs of propaganda'.[54] For his own part, Manlio Cecovini wrote that:

This is a serious report which, wherever possible, bases itself on certain fact, leaving little space for conjecture [. . .]. Errors on both sides can explain—if certainly not justify—the violations of elementary human rights; but I believe that instead of fomenting the reasons for division, we need to learn that on any border the first law must be that of peaceful cohabitation, which must mean personal contact, respect for all cultures, freedom from prejudice. Languages can be learnt; culture knows no borders.[55]

---

53 *I rapporti italo-sloveni*, pp. 101-02.

54 Manlio Cecovini, 'Una relazione seria per costruire il futuro con gli sloveni', *Il Piccolo*, 4 April 2001.

55 Cecovini, 'Una relazione seria per costruire il futuro con gli sloveni'.

The report of the Italo-Slovenian commission, in our view, represents the most detailed, clear and respectful response to General Roatta's heinous Note no. 3C. But what is more surprising still is that the report has been—and continues to be—almost entirely ignored.

TWLEVE

THE RECKONING

The radio had just announced, at 10.47 p.m. on 25 July 1943, that 'His Majesty the King and Emperor has accepted the resignation of the Head of Government, Prime Minister and Secretary of State, His Excellency, *Cavaliere* Benito Mussolini, and has named *Marasciallo* Badoglio as Head of Government'. Despite the late hour, people flowed into the streets in disbelief, to check that Fascism really had come to an end.

Even if there were important details missing—had Mussolini resigned or had he been toppled? Was he free or in prison?—the people's joy was uncontainable, in part because they interpreted the end of the regime as a declaration of Italy's imminent exit from the global conflict. For many, it seemed that the time had come for revenge, the long-awaited moment of reckoning. That same night, between 25 and 26 July, a dozen local headquarters of the National Fascist Party were ransacked. In Milan, the offices in Via Paolo da Cannobbio, the historic headquarters of Mussolini's newspaper and one of the symbols of Fascism's origins, was devastated. In Rome, the crowd invaded the deserted courtyard of Palazzo Venezia (which housed the Fascist council) and then marched towards the Quirinale (the Royal Palace) and the headquarters of the Fascist Party in Piazza Colonna. In Florence, a young lieutenant, Giorgio Spini, recovering from tuberculosis in a military hospital, reacted thus to the news of Mussolini's fall: 'A group of us on the ward escaped from our confinement and went to make some din in the streets, demanding immediate peace with the Allies and war on the Germans.'[1]

Not everyone, however, was in a state of mind to be able to participate in the explosion of joy that extraordinary night. Here is the recollection of Nuto Revelli, who would later become a partisan leader and historian of the doomed Russian campaign:

> Fascism fell on 25 July 1943. Around midnight, a short demonstration of anti-Fascists passed down Via Roma and under my window. I heard them shouting 'Down with Fascism', 'Long live the army!' But which army? I went over to the window, I wanted to go down and talk with them, to tell them that the war wasn't over, that our soldiers who fell in Russia died for nothing! My head was all over the place, I could feel this enormous conflict in me. Only my father's tears stopped me. If I had gone down to the street, they would have taken me for a Fascist.[2]

Let us travel from Cuneo down to Sorrento. After a particularly hard day's work, Benedetto Croce went to bed at 11 p.m. But he was immediately woken up by a phone call from the Elena di Serracapriola, who informed him of Mussolini's fall. A few minutes later, the philosopher's house was full of 'jubilant' friends. Croce recalled: 'I went back to bed and could not close my eyes until four in the morning, nor after that. The sensation that I felt was of the liberation from a sickness that weighed upon the core of my soul: other dangers and deriving illnesses remained, but that one would not return.' Two days later, he noted in his diary: 'Yet again last night I slept very little, from midnight till four. The future of

---

1 Giorgio Spini, *La strada della liberazione. Dalla riscoperta di Calvino al Fronte della VII Armata* (Turin: Claudiana, 2002), p. 90.

2 Nuto Revelli, *Le due guerre. Guerra fascista e guerra partigiana* (Turin: Einaudi, 2003), p. 129.

Italy is fixed in my mind: Fascism seems already in the past, a closed circuit, and I have no taste for revenge.'[3]

Revenge arrived, nevertheless, on 26 July when people learnt about the details of the stormy session at the Great Fascist Council, Mussolini's meeting with the King and the former's arrest. The confirmation that the regime truly had fallen let the crowd break loose. Thirteen Fascist clubs were ransacked in Rome, while a few soldiers shot at them from the barracks on Via Depretis, killing two demonstrators. The prison was besieged in Turin and 300 political prisoners freed; in the same city, the German embassy was destroyed and a swastika flag set light to. In Cuneo, the lawyer Tancredi 'Duccio' Galimberti turned to the crowd flowing into Piazza Vittorio and exhorted them to take up arms against the Nazis, because only armed struggle could reclaim Italy's honour. A journalist for *Corriere della Sera*, Andrea Damiano, jotted in his diary:

> The state of siege that has been proclaimed in order to maintain order has not lessened the fervour of the people. The troops are applauded, there is celebration everywhere. The curfew is harsh, at 9.30 no one is allowed to move around without papers. The night resounds with gunshots: soldiers taking aim at suspicious persons, Fascists barricaded in neighbourhood groups that are resisting; workers pushing back against the troops guarding the jails holding political prisoners. [...] Listening carefully to the nocturnal echoing of gunfire, a little voice warns me that the worst is yet to come, that 20 years of Fascism cannot be stamped out in 48 hours of chaos. It's meaningless. But no one is using

---

3 Benedetto Croce, *Taccuini di guerra, 1943–1945* (Milan: Adelphi, 2004), p. 13 and p. 14, respectively. [The Duchess Elena di Serracapriola's brother, Duke Giovanni Maresca, was a committed Fascist who fought in both Spain and Ethiopia, a detail that doubtless did not escape Del Boca.—Trans.]

their heads today. A delicious unconsciousness has ignited the crowd, and hope is being reborn.[4]

Not everyone, obviously, participated in the general enthusiasm. Vincenzo Costa, who was to be the last Federal Fascist Secretary in Milan, commented on these stormy hours following the announcement of the fall of the regime thus: 'The anti-Fascists are coming out from their holes, followed by a mob nurtured on theft and violence; thus began the siege on the Fascist neighbourhood centres, that destruction and burning of the offices in Via Paolo da Cannobbio. The manhunt for Fascists had begun.'[5]

Costa was exaggerating, however. While there were certainly punches thrown, the Fascists killed during the 45 days of chaos numbered less than 10. The balance sheet of repression towards the demonstrators, on the other hand, was extremely high: 93 dead, 536 wounded, 2,276 arrested. In truth, the Fascist Party, which could boast 4,700,000 members in 1943, had practically been eliminated with Mussolini's arrest. Even the armed guard that were meant to defend the Duce down to the last drop of blood had ingloriously dissolved itself without even attempting an opposition.

The rioting after the fall of the regime was not to last long. Even though at its very first meeting on 27 July, Badoglio's government had decided to dissolve the Fascist organs of state,[6] incorporate the volunteer guards into the army and free the political prisoners (except for communists and anarchists), the mere fact that a state of siege had been proclaimed

---

4 Andrea Damiano, *Rosso e grigio* (Bologna: Il Mulino, 2000), pp. 70–71.

5 Vincenzo Vosta, *L'ultimo federale. Memorie della guerra civile, 1943–1945* (Bologna: Il Mulino, 1997), p. 6.

6 The Gran Consiglio del fascismo, the Camera dei fasci, the Fascist 'corporations' and the special court for the defence of the state.

throughout the country stubbed out the enthusiasm and hope that the fall of Fascism meant the end of the war.

Describing the period of Badoglio's military dictatorship, Dino Grandi—whose parliamentary order had provoked Mussolini and Fascism's fall—wrote in his memoirs: 'It is the men of the 45-day regime who led Italy into the tragic chapter of 8 September, sidestepping the monarchy, the constitution, the army, national honour and the hopes of the Italian people. They put the seal on Mussolini's errors. They dragged the nation into ruin, they have been its grave diggers.'[7] A harsh judgement, but not unreasonable. It is certainly true that Badoglio's decisional incompetence—or better, his meagre tricks to try and buy some time—is clear enough. The man who had managed to transform the disastrous defeat at Caporetto into a springboard for his own career was now convinced that he knew how to take care of the Germans and, at the same time, make peace with the Anglo-Americans. But he was wrong. On 26 July, the German 44th Infantry Division and the 136th Dolha Mountain Brigade forced the Brenner Pass and occupied South Tyrol. Over the following days, nine further divisions, including the 24th Panzer division and the *SS Hitler* swarmed into Italy and took hold of important communication points. The Allies, for their part, trying to put pressure on Badoglio to request an armistice, carried out massive air strikes on Milan, Turin, Genoa and Rome between 7 and 16 August. There were 510 casualties (all of which can be attributed to Badoglio) and 240,000 houses destroyed in Milan alone. As Elena Aga Rossi has rightly observed:

> There was no exit from Italy's situation, caught as it was between an ally that was preparing to act as an enemy, pouring divisions into the country in order to occupy key strategic positions, and enemies that were readying their own landing on the peninsula, rejecting any pre-emptive pact. There was no space for negoti-

---

7 Dino Grandi, *25 luglio. Quarant'anni dopo* (Renzo De Felice ed.) (Bologna: Il Mulino, 1983), p. 310.

ations, neither with one nor the other, but Badoglio and the King failed to realize this, proving themselves to be entirely incapable of confronting the situation. Through their very inaction, they dragged Italy into the worst military disaster in history.[8]

Badoglio's announcement on the radio, at 7.45 p.m. on 8 September, that the armistice had been signed with the Anglo-American forces, without taking any of the necessary measures to face up to the Germans, could only lead to catastrophe. Left without any orders (the famous 'Memo 44 OP', drawn up by the chief of staff, provided only the vaguest of indications), the armed forces simply melted away, without providing any resistance, and the majority were captured by the Germans and deported to Germany. The most undignified spectacle, however, was performed by the King, Badoglio and the mass of ministers, generals and assorted courtiers, who fled Rome at dawn, heading to Pescara and then, by sea, to Brindisi.

The thwarting of the Italian army, the full German occupation of more than half of Italy, Mussolini's liberation from his imprisonment on Gran Sasso on 12 September, and the announcement (three days later, by the Italian news service Agenzia Stefani) that the Duce had reprised 'the supreme leadership of Fascism in Italy', were all facts that had a precise and deadly meaning: despite the collapse of 25 July, the regime had been resurrected; Italy was split in two, with two governments, two occupying powers, two different ideologies. Each side felt a strong desire to dirty their hands, to satisfy a wish for revenge, to settle all the scores once and for all. The Fascists—old and new alike—wanted to reclaim the honour of the fatherland that had been lost by Badoglio and the King, and promised to strike out at anyone who thought differently. The anti-

---

8 Elena Aga Rossi, *Una nazionale allo sbando. L'armistizio italiano del settembre 1943* (Bologna: Il Mulino, 1993), p. 69.

Fascists, on the other hand, thought of fighting for democracy in Italy, and seemed unconcerned by the idea that this would mean facing off both the Germans and the Fascists simultaneously. From the outset, the conflict promised to be long, merciless and totalizing, both a civil war and a war of liberation.

The conclusion to the 45 days would have been very different if Badoglio, instead of the ambiguous 'Memo 44 OP', had sent the divisions in both Italy and abroad a pre-emptive order to attack the German forces. 'We needed to turn the mortars on the Germans,' warned Alfredo Pizzoni, president of the Committee for the National Liberation of Upper Italy, 'and shoot, shoot immediately, shoot first, without calculating if everyone could have contributed to the shooting. This is what Badoglio and his accomplices, the King and his family—all of them scared and uncertain—did not want to understand.'[9] Despite having been one of the most eminent figures of Fascism, Dino Grandi shared Pizzoni's view. Asked to provide his opinion during an audience with the King on the morning of 28 July, he replied: 'If our army does not defend itself and does not counter-attack the invading German forces that are crossing the Brenner Pass, and if the government does not simultaneously make any serious contact with the Allies, then I predict terrible days for the nation.'[10]

Those 'terrible days' inevitably arrived and with them, the first rumblings of the civil war. From one day to the next, while draft dodgers were hunted down in the cities, one had to choose between the resurgent Fascism and the anti-Fascist rebellion, between the Republic of Salò and waging guerrilla war.[11] It was a difficult choice for everyone, and even

---

9 Alredo Pizzoni, 'I quarantacinque giorni del Governo Badoglio', in *Alla guida del CLNAI. Memorie per i figli* (Bologna: Il Mulino, 1995), p. 42.

10 Grandi, *25 luglio*, pp. 369–70.

11 The Republic of Salò: an alternative name for the Italian Social Republic, the puppet state that controlled the northern half of Italy between 1943 and 1945. [Trans.]

more so for the young people who had been educated every day of their lives to venerate Mussolini and the symbols of Fascism, and who until then had never made an individual decision.

This choice of which side to take did not only concern those Italians who lived between the Alps and the River Garigliano—i.e. under the grip of Nazism—but also the 600,000 Italian soldiers deported by the Germans to the concentration camps. It is worth recalling that of these 600,000, only 15,000 adhered to the Republic of Salò. As Alessandro Natta wrote, a future general secretary of the Italian Communist Party:

> Non-collaboration, resistance in the face of incentives and threats, the refusal of work, sabotage—these were the weapons that the circumstances allowed the interned Italians to use, and which they used in an increasingly decisive way so that, through a long and laborious process, the motivations driving the struggle became clearer and, for the most part, began to coincide with those directing the simultaneous generalized liberation movement in Italy.[12]

Especially for the younger generation, the choices made in that moment were the result of spontaneous decisions, sometimes based on enthusiasm, others through long and arduous reflection. Either way, every choice had its own story, stimulus and horizon. The historian Roberto Vivarelli, for example, had two very precise reasons for joining the

---

12 Alessandro Natta, *L'altra Resistenza. I militari italiani internati in Germania* (Turin: Einaudi, 1997), p. 6. Also see Nicola Labanca (ed.), *Fra sterminio e sfruttamento. Militari internati e prigionieri di guerra nella Germana nazista, 1939–1945* (Florence: Le Lettere, 1992); Gerhard Schreiber, *I militari italiani internati nei campi di concentramento del Terzo Reich, 1943–1945. Traditi, disprezzati, dimenticati* (Rome: Stato Maggiore dell'Esercito, Ufficio Storico, 1992); Giuseppe Caforio and Marina Nuciati, '*No!' I soldati italiani internati in Germania. Analisi di un rifiuto* (Milan: Angeli, 1994); Gabriele Hammermann, *Gli internati militari italiani in Germania, 1943–1845* (Bologna: Il Mulino, 2004).

Republic of Salò: the memory that his father had been killed by Yugoslavian partisans, and an adamant faith in Mussolini and the values his regime represented:

> For us, Fascism was a myth that had filled our lives, to which we had given our fervent commitment with a kind of discipline and consistency that you only find in adolescent enthusiasm. They had taught us to 'believe, obey and fight', and so we continued to believe with complete faith, we were ready to obey, and as for fighting—that was our upmost ambition.[13]

Unlike Vivarelli, however, the journalist Massimo Rendina—a practising Catholic, and son of a police chief who was himself a lay member of the Dominican order—did not have any accounts to settle with anyone, nor any aspiration to fight and kill. Indeed, when an interviewer asked him whether it was 'true that you Catholics hoped to die rather than kill anyone', he replied: 'Yes. And still today I would prefer to die than kill anyone.' Nevertheless, on 9 September, in a Turin occupied by Nazi forces, and faced with the morbid spectacle of death, he decided to participate in the Resistance:

> The ferocity of the invaders was made clear to us after what happened at the train station at Porta Susa, when a German opened machine gun fire on a group of women shouting 'get out of here!', killing two or three of them. That was when we took our decision to act. [. . .] In the days following 8 September, we decided to form squadrons with a few other people. And we

---

13 Roberto Vivarelli, *La fine di una stagione. memoria 1943–1945* (Bologna: Il Mulino, 2000), pp. 18–19. Vivarelli participated in the war when he was only 15, and later taught contemporary history at the Scuola Normale Superiore in Pisa. On the enrolment of such young men, see Antonio Gibelli, 'Ragazzi di Salò, piccoli partiagini' in *Il popolo bambino. Infanzia e nazione dalla Grande Guerra a Salò* (Turin: Einaudi, 2005), pp. 366–401; Angelo Del Boca, 'Un cuore semplice' in *La scelta* (Vicenza: Neri Pozza, 2006), pp. 147–53.

proposed disarming the Germans—without killing them—so as to arm ourselves.[14]

There were also half-choices, or choices that were not spontaneous at all, but determined by exceptional circumstances, for example: by the gangs that enforced the call to arms. After the first press-ganging of November 1943, and even more so after the second wave in 18 February 1944 (which punished 'with death by gunshot in the chest' all Italian citizens between 19 and 22 years of age who had presented themselves to the relevant military department), many young people decided to enter the ranks of the Resistance. Between the risk of being sent to a German education camp and jumping into the unknown of armed resistance, they preferred the latter option—even though their mass movement into the mountains ended up bringing more problems for the partisan command than any real support.

Finally, there were those who decided not to make a real choice, whether through fear, indecision, civic apathy, historical refusal, or simply waiting to see what would happen. As Enzo Forcella wrote:

On 8 September I was in Rome, with permission to take leave after three years in the army. For me the war was over, I had no intention to begin again, whether for one side or the other. I hated the Nazis and neo-Fascists, but not to the point of conspiring against them or taking up arms. The only war that I was ready to fight was one for survival. [. . .] I simply wanted to

---

14 Account provided by Massimo Rendina in Walter E. Crevellin (ed.), *Cattolici, Chiesa, Resistenza. I testimoni* (Bologna: Il Mulino, 2000), pp. 115–34. A partisan commander, Rendina participated in the liberation of Turin and was later the director of the first TV news channel, RAI; at the time of writing he is a member of the scientific research committee at the Luigi Sturzo Institute for historical research into the Resistance. [Rendina died in 2015 at the age of 95. —Trans.]

hole myself up in my study, with my books and translations, immersed in my paralysing fear.[15]

This 'grey zone', which gave refuge to those who could not manage or did not want to identify themselves with either camp, was also inhabited by the journalist Andrea Damiano, who was nevertheless able to recognize the true enemy of the Italians, and did so masterfully:

Some of the good folk strolling around Milan remind one of Goya's works. You see them at daybreak, veterans of their 'work', riding on the tram or passing between people with a Basque beret or a black fez hanging off the backs of their necks, clasping an automatic rifle ready to shoot, a pistol on their belts, a dagger over their bellies: the latest degenerate version of a criminality that has been romanticized for too long. You see expressions half way between an eagle and a dog, finger-high foreheads under crisp, bloated hairstyles, thick arched noses on dull and gloomy faces, with disturbingly asymmetrical eyes. These are the hooligans who are supposedly teaching Italians civic virtues.[16]

Recalling that even a great writer like Cesare Pavese and other intellectuals of his calibre were hesitant of making any political commitment, Raffaele Liucci wrote: 'For them, the war offered above all the opportunity to take to the hills—metaphorically or otherwise—in order to preserve their own microcosm of values from the impact of history, thus avoiding taking any precise decision or responsibility, temporarily or forever.'[17]

---

15 Enzo Forcella, *La resistenza in convento* (Turin: Einaudi, 1999), pp. 216–29. A journalist and writer, Forcella worked for *La Stampa*, *Il Giorno* and *La Repubblica*. Along with Alberto Monitonce, he co-authored *Plotone d'esecuzione. I processi della priima guerra mondiale* (Bari: Laterza, 1968).

16 Damiano, *Rosso e grigio*, p. 113.

17 Raffaelle Luicci, *La tentazione della 'casa in collina'. Il disimpegno degli intelletuali nella guerra civile italiana, 1943–1945* (Milan: Unicopli, 1999). p. 36.

Finally, within this 'grey zone' were those who took the road of total indifference. My friend Mamante Rabozzi took this road: he had his father wall him up in his cottage in Cavaglio d'Agogna. A hole in the wall was used to pass him food and sheets of paper, on which he wrote beautiful nature poetry.[18]

Once the choices had been made, conflict was inevitable. At the beginning of 1944, around 100,000 men had joined the Republic of Salò, while no more than 10,000 partisans had taken to the mountains. It should be noted, however, that the Republic's soldiers were ill-equipped and untrained, lacking everything from guns to cars, clothes and petrol, blankets and mess-tins. Officers, on the other hand, were not in short supply (including 300 generals) who had joined the Republic above all for the bloated salaries. When the army expanded after Graziani's press-ganging in 1944, its effectiveness still left much to be desired. 'The barracks are slowly filling up,' reported Giampaolo Pansa, 'even if the youth are driven by bayonets rather than any love for their country, or the Fascist creed. The Republican National Guard make this clear in nearly all of their reports.'[19]

---

18 Angelo Del Boca, *Il mio Novecento* (Vicenza: Neri Pozza, 2008), p. 58. [Rabozzi then became a historian and school teacher in Novara.—Trans.]

19 Giampaolo Pansa, *Il gladio e l'alloro. L'esercito di Salò* (Milan: Mondadori, 1991), p. 48. On the events around the army of the Republic of Salò, also see Roberto Battaglia, *Storia della Resistenza italiana* (Turin: Einaudi, 1953); Frederick William Deakin, *Storia della Repubblica di Salò* (Turin: Einaudi, 1963); Silvio Bertoldi, *Salò. Vita e morte della Repubblica sociale italiana* (Milan: Rizzoli, 1976); Giorgio Bocca, *La Repubblica di Mussolini* (Rome and Bari: Laterza, 1977); Renzo De Felice, *Mussolini l'alleato, Volume 2: La guerra civile, 1943–1945* (Turin: Einaudi, 1997); Giovanni De Luna, Adolfo Mignemi and Carlo Gentile (eds), *Storia fotografica della Repubblica sociale italiana* (Turin: Bollati Boringhieri, 1997); Luigi Ganapini, *La repubblica delle camicie nere* (Milan: Garzanti, 1999); Aurelio Lepre, *La storia della Repubblica di Mussolini. Salò: il tempo dell'odio e della violenza* (Milan: Mondadori, 1999); Santo Peli, *La Resistenza in Italia. Storia e critica* (Turin: Einaudi, 2004); Pasquale Chessa,

Another reason that explained the weakness of the army was its fragmentation and the lack of a unified command. Renato Ricci effectively led the National Guard, while Alessandro Pavolini established and led the Black Brigades from June 1944. Junio Valerio Borghese led the X^a Flottiglia MAS as if it were his family's private property.[20] In his role as Minister of War, Graziani was meant to command all the armed forces, but in reality he controlled only the four divisions that had been trained in Germany.[21] The 20,000 Italian SS troops reported directly to the German command. The autonomous 'Ettore Muti' legion was led by Sergeant Francesco Colombo, who promoted himself to the rank of colonel. Another dozen legions, battalions, divisions and gangs enjoyed either total or partial independence, not to mention the police departments which tortured and killed hundreds of anti-Fascists with complete autonomy.

The only things that the army of Salò did not lack—especially the independent sections and the police—was the most extreme, vile and dishonourable forms of violence. One recalls the horrors accomplished by the Muti Legion and the Koch and Carità gangs.[22] 'The activities of these groups will scar the name of the Republic beyond all its other crimes', wrote the partisan Giogio Bocca. 'They will cover everything and everyone with their fog, so that even the better part of the new

---

Guerra civile, 1943, 1945, 1948. Una storia fotografica (Milan: Mondadori, 2005).

20 X^a Flottiglia MAS: literally 'the tenth flotilla of the armed torpedo unit', which after September 1943 became effectively a separate army under Borghese's command, and notorious for the extremism of both its adherence to Fascism and its use of violence. [Trans.]

21 For the training of the Monterosa, Littorio, San Marco and Italia divisions in Germany, see Angelo Del Boca, 'Gesù mio, aiutami' in *La Scelta*, pp. 68–128.

22 There were at least 20 police departments that practised torture. We can name some of them: the gangs run by Bardi and Pollastrini, Chiurco, Finizio, Bernasconi, Fumai, Sorlini, Ruggiero, Pennachio, Collotti and Guelli, De Santis, De Larderel, Castellanzi, Alfieri and Fiorentini, Bossi.

Fascism will try in vain to dissociate itself; in vain because the warped logic of the civil war necessitates and creates such groups.'[23] All the same, Mussolini himself acted as godfather and supporter of the Muti legion. After visiting their barracks, this is what he wrote to Commander Colombo: 'Fascists of your temperament and men of the kind in your command demonstrate the certainty that the "Muti", by developing its activities, will be up to its tasks tomorrow even more than today.'[24]

The Koch gang enjoyed the protection and financial support of the Minister for the Interior himself, Guido Buffarini Guidi, who was well aware of the abject methods employed by Pietro Koch to extract information from the captives who ended up at the Jaccarino hostel in Rome, or at Villa Fossati in Milan. 'Comparing the conditions of those who were subject to arrest in Via Tasso, the terrible site of detention run by the German police,' Massimiliano Griner tells us, 'with the conditions of those held in the reconverted rooms of the Jaccarino hostel, one might arrive at the conclusion—and perhaps without error—that from every point of view it was worse to fall victim to Koch than to the Germans.'[25]

---

23 Bocca, *Le Repubblica di Mussolini*, p. 191. Some of those who took part in the Resistance look on the use of the term 'civil war' with disdain: 'It was a war of liberation, not a civil war,' wrote Paolo Emilio Taviani. 'So long as the French and Norwegians do not accept calling their Resistance a civil war, then I will continue to call our Resistance an armed war of liberation'—*Politica e memoria d'uomo* (Bologna: Il Mulino, 2002), pp. 59–60. The position is also shared by Guido Quazza, Sergio Cotta, Livio Bianco, Giorgio Agosti and Ermanno Gorrieri. The last of these has written that 'reducing the Resistance to a conflict between Italians does not take account of the fact that over those 20 months there was a *third actor* in play: the German army, which had occupied Italy with efficient brutality' (Ermanno Gorrieri and Giulia Bondi, *Ritorno a Montefiorino. Dalla Resistenza sull'Appenino alla violenza del dopoguerra* (Bologna: Il Mulino, 2005), p. 167.

24 Cited in Massimilliano Griner, *La pupilla del duce. La Legione autonoma mobile 'Ettore Muti'* (Turin: Bollati Boringhieri, 2004), p. 107.

25 Massimilliano Griner, *La 'banda Koch'. Il reparto speciale di polizia, 1943–1945* (Turin: Bollati Boringhieri, 2000), p. 211.

Aside from the Muti, there were other Fascist brigades who distinguished themselves for their ferocity, such as sections of the X^a Flottiglia MAS and above all the Italian SS which had taken an oath of loyalty to Hitler and answered directly to the SS General, Peter Hansen. Albeit in an auxiliary position, they participated in several of the massacres carried out by the Nazis, including at Marzabotto, Sant'Anna di Stazzema, Bardine di San Terenzio and Vallucciole. They boasted about not taking prisoners, and did not fail to demonstrate proof for this claim.[26]

The history of violence in the Republic of Salò is marked by a certain sadism, a pleasure in violating civilians' feelings, a terrifying warning signal. 'The public display of the bodies of the hanged and the shot,' writes Sergio Luzzatto, 'was practised by the soldiers of Salò as an extreme form of controlling the Italian streets, one that was both the most silent and the most expressive; the butcher's hooks served their purpose as a tool for denigrating men as beasts.'[27] Partisans were hanged with butchers' hooks and with iron wires, as at Fivizzano di Massa; or with barbed wire, as at Pioppeti di Camaiore. Mirco Dondi informs us:

> It became impossible to avoid the displays of the dead. They chose crucial points in the cities to leave the dead on display. [...] One of the most famous theatres of death was the nerve centre at Piazzale Loreto in Milan, where 15 anti-Fascists were piled up. [...] One of the most mournful episodes of spectacularity happened in Bassano del Grappa, when 31 partisans were hanged from the trees along the town's main street.[28]

Sometimes this spectacle of death would last days, and the relatives of those killed, or members of the clergy, would intervene to end the torture,

26 On the activities of the Italian SS, see Ricciotti Lazzero, *Le SS italiane* (Milan: Rizzoli, 1982); Primo De Lazzari, *Le SS italiane* (Milan: Teti, 2002).

27 Sergio Luzzatto, *Il corpo del duce* (Turin: Einaudi, 1998), p. 58.

28 Mirco Dondi, *La lunga liberazione. Giustizia e violenza nel dopoguerra italiano* (Rome: Editori Riuniti, 1999), pp. 18–19.

without results. This is what took place at Fondotoce, in Verbano; at San Maurizio Canavese; at Vignale, just outside Novara; at Bagnolo in Piano, in the province of Reggio Emilia; and in a dozen other places. The prolonging of the deathly display did not aim only to inflict hours or days of agony on the population, but also to make it clear that those bodies—strewn with lead or the noose—did not deserve any mercy, any consideration, as if they belonged to a subhuman category.

Nevertheless, it would be a mistake to see the Republic of Salò's violence as somehow new, as the poisonous product of the 'Caporetto' of 8 September.[29] It has much deeper origins. It harks back to the castor oil used for the horrifying humiliation of the abused victim. It latches onto the baton, the pistol, the dagger, the hand bomb—the tools employed before the March on Rome. It reconnects with the gallows erected in Libya and Ethiopia, with the firing squads used in the Balkans, with the use of fire as a totalizing punishment. Even the public exhibition of the hanged and shot corpses has an endless line of precedents in the dark colonial night. There can be little doubt of the continuity between the 20 years of Fascist rule and the 600 days of the Republic of Salò.

The most illustrious victim of this kind of violence—which always ends up turning on those who have practised it—was Mussolini. He found himself in its cross-hairs like no one else. He had preached hatred his entire life, in all his writings, inciting the abuse of power and praising every kind of brutality. He had scolded his people for being insufficiently bellicose, unworthy of the empire he was granting them. With his usual disrespect, on 6 March 1945, he declared to the officers of the national guard: 'One cannot aim to transform a people's moral structure on a deep level within 20 years. For that, you need generations.'[30] His bitterness

---

29 The Battle of Caporetto (see Chapter 20) was the moment of Italy's greatest defeat in the First World War and thus also the symbolic beginning of Fascism, inasmuch as it was a movement that emerged from the veterans' anger. [Trans.]

30 Cited in Damiano, *Rosso e grigio*, p. 143. Mussolini and some of his followers,

towards the Italian people, who had disappointed all his high hopes, knew no limits. And it was mutual, a fact evidenced by the rage with which the crowd reacted to his body, hanged from the pylons of a petrol station in Piazzale Loreto, or the five shots that a woman fired into his head, or the lashes inflicted by an old woman who held him responsible for the death of her two sons.

Suddenly emerging from his makeshift 'grey zone' of the last 20 months, Andrea Damiano made his way to Piazzale Loreto on 29 April and, observing the barbaric display of bodies, mercilessly reported that:

> Mussolini's meaty visage was the most horrendous of them all. A gaping red mouth vomited a trickle of blood that glinted in the sunlight, spoiling the rest of his face; the two enormous nostrils, large as goblets, took over and formed a kind of chasm in the centre of the deformed mask. The bald, fat head seemed swollen. He was in a black shirt, open at the chest, and you could see his robust torso all smeared with blood.[31]

To avoid the idea that all the bad guys chose the side of Salò and all the good ones the Resistance, it is necessary at this point to establish the dimensions and some details of the partisans' own violence. In his book *The End of a Season*, Roberto Vivarelli claimed that he had no regrets about having fought in the ranks of the Republic of Salò, and even that he was 'proud of having done so, even while aware that the cause was

---

such as Filipo Anfuso, were persuaded that the creation of the Republic of Salò had been necessary in order to save Italy from Hitler's revenge. Francesco Germinario writes: 'A theory thus emerged—which was to be reprised by all the neo-Fascist press—of Salò as a cushion state required to avoid that Italy fall foul to the same fate as other nations occupied by the Nazis: thanks above all to Mussolini's political abilities, the Republic of Salò—instead of being imposed by Hitler on a politically shredded Mussolini—thus became an obstacle to the Nazi's project of 'Polandification'—*L'altra memoria. L'estrema destra, Salò e la Resistenza* (Turin: Bollati Boringhieri, 1999), p. 44.

31 Damiano, *Rosso e grigio*, p. 157.

morally and historically unjust'.[32] He put the enemy violence in the following terms:

> The idea that the violence exercised by the Resistance was qualitatively different from that exercised by the Fascists does not seem to me to correspond to any historical or psychological truth. Let me be quite clear: I have no intention of underestimating the savage cases of systematically organized torture, which are well known and have received the judgement they deserved both morally and, frequently, juridically. Nevertheless, it seems unjust to equate these numerically scarce criminal gangs with the entirety of the Fascist fighters, who numbered several hundred thousand. As far as the behaviour of these combatants—who we might call the ordinary ones—is concerned, I do not believe any real distinction can effectively be made between Fascist violence and partisan violence.[33]

First of all, it ought to be noted that torture was not practised by a few 'criminal gangs' but by all of the Republic of Salò's units, even if in a disorganized way. When it came to extorting information, even the four divisions of the regular army drew on the worst kinds of violence. 'The Littorio is here'—Livio Bianco wrote to Giorgio Agosti on 6 December 1944—'whose soldiers (not just the officers, but the troops too) *are worse than the Germans*, and they don't hold anything back. It was they who carried out the killings of the peaceful townsfolk a few days' back in the area around Cuneo, where around 50 people were found dead.'[34] At the

---

32 Vivarelli, *La fine di una stagione*, p. 104.

33 Vivarelli, *La fine di una stagione*, pp. 120–21.

34 Giorgio Agosti and Livio Bianco, *Un'amicizia partigiana. Lettere 1943–1945* (Turin: Meynier, 1990), p. 356. Giorgio Agosti, now a magistrate, was the regional commissar during the Resistance for the divisions of Giustizia e Libertà. Livio Bianco, now a lawyer, was first commander of the 1st division of GL, operating in Cuneo, and then—following the assassination of Duccio Galimberti—the regional commander.

end of the summer in 1944, a section of the Monterosa division in Bobbio filled up the underground cells in the carabinieri barracks with men and women connected to the Resistance, and unleashed their rage upon them to understand what the partisan forces were really made of (forces which at that point were laying siege to the city).[35]

It does not appear, however, that the Resistance had its own 'houses of tragedy' or practised torture. As the historian Claudio Pavone has rightly noted, resistance violence was above all 'defensive' and dictated by necessity.[36] In order to establish its own legitimacy, the partisan movement needed above all to enjoy the support and trust of the population among which it was operating, and to be able to distinguish itself clearly from Nazi-Fascism. This is why it fiercely condemned any moments of hooliganism, whether within or without of the movement. Those partisans who spoilt their records with any kind of criminality were almost always punished with death. Having heard sufficient evidence regarding thefts and burglaries carried out by a partisan from the 1st Giustizia e Libertà division in Piacenza, its commander—Fausto Cossu—immediately gave the order for him to be shot, an act which was carried out in front of the cemetery gates at Agazzano.[37]

Other units, such as the 'Pinan-Cichero' unit operating in the Alps between Liguria and Alessandria, provide themselves with an extremely harsh code of behaviour. In *Rules for Partisan Discipline* sent by the command to the detachments, one reads: 'Armed robbery, sexual violence: immediate shooting by the brigades' court'.[38] Sentencing by the special

35 This is Del Boca's own experience, see *Da Mussolini a Gheddafi, Nella notte ci guidano le stelle* and pp. *xxvii–xxviii* above. [Trans.]

36 Claudio Pavone, *Una guerra civile. Saggio storico sulla moralità nella Resistenza* (Turin: Bollati Boringhieri, 1991), pp. 446–47.

37 See Romano Repetti and Gian Luigi Cavanna, *Comandanti partigiani giunti da lontano*, (Bobbio: Pontegobbo, 2018). [Trans.]

38 See Roberto Botta, 'Il senso del rigore, il codice morale della giustizia partigiana' in Massimo Legnani and Ferruccio Vendramini (eds), *Guerra, guerra di liberazione,*

military courts held by the communist divisions in Valsesia was also severe. Commander Ciro (nom de guerre of Eraldo Gastone) felt no regret for

> having seized, tried and sentenced to death true and false partisans who committed theft, robbery or utilized the units' name for their own advantage. To tell the truth, there were few such cases. The severity with which we punished the actors of such undertakings in the first few months dissuaded the majority of anyone else with bad intentions from imitating such acts in the territory of the Valsesian Command. Those that did follow through soon fell into the hands of the partisan police, were tried and sentenced with the only possible punishment: death by shooting.[39]

Capital punishment was also wreaked upon deserters, above all those who passed over to the enemy camp. In mid-June 1944, Livio Bianco wrote to Giorgio Agosti about 'the elimination of Prato, former commander of Val Susa' who had surrendered to the Fascists in January, 'thwarting the division'. There was also no mercy for spies and infiltrators. The problem had arisen since the moment the divisions had been formed. In November 1943, Giorgio Agosti, while laying out which actions needed to be given utmost priority, identified as 'essential the killing of as many spies as can be identified'. A little later, writing to Livio Bianco, he picked out a particular danger: 'It appears that the police want to send an agent to the division with a forged note signed "Fausto" in order to lure some of you in. The above has already been communicated: stay alert and double your attention to spies. If the agent is found, dispose of him immediately.'[40]

---

guerra civile (Milan: Angeli, 1990), p. 145.

39 Cesare Bermani, 'Giustizia partigiana e guerra di popolo in Valsesia' in Legnani and Vendramini, *Guerra, guerra di liberazione, guerra civile*, p. 167.

40 Agosti and Bianco, *Un'amicizia partigiana*, p. 152, p. 72 and p. 179, respectively.

The problem of spies was no small matter. 'The ambiguity of their presence transformed into a halo of uncertainty surrounding their world,' explained Pavone. 'On the one hand, this uncertainty relied on a frequent light-handedness in planning, and on the other produced a widespread, exaggerated air of suspicion and a certain severity of repression.'[41] Indeed, evidence of the guilt of those arrested was not always demonstrated, and there was a clear risk of eliminating innocent people. In the Antigorio valley (then in the province of Novara), Franco Marini was executed along with his young wife, as well as former-squadrista Giovanni Cardano, about whose espionage there were more doubts than certainties.[42]

Partisan violence was also expressed through the relations between divisions of different political allegiances. Paolo Emilio Taviani, leader of the war for liberation in Genovesato, did not cover over the problem, instead outlining its limitations: 'There certainly were moments of conflict between partisans during the Resistance, but there were less than 50 dead among us because of us. This is not a scandalous number if you compare it with what happened in other Resistance operations in Europe and Asia.'[43] The conflicts came about over questions of territorial command, rivalry between commanders and strategic decisions. Sometimes, however, such conflicts also related to the problem of violence itself. As Ermanno Gorrieri recalled:

> There were two deeply different conceptions of the struggle that came to head. There were two cardinal points for the communist view: providing the armed struggle with the broadest possible participation by the masses, and characterizing it with an

---

41 Pavone, *Una guerra civile*, p. 473.

42 Del Boca, *Il mio Novecento*, p. 85.

43 Taviani, *Politica e memoria d'uomo*, p. 62. For example, this can be compared with the Algerian War, in which conflicts between the different divisions led to no less than 7,000 deaths among the resistance fighters. See Gilbert Mynier, *Histoire intérieure du FLN, 1954–1962* (Paris: Fayard, 2002), pp. 406–45.

unwavering severity. From the view of the Christian Democrats, however, importance lay in a rigid selection of the most effective fighters: their behaviour in terms of discipline and organization was not only a military necessity, but also a question of the dignity and prestige of the divisions in the eyes of the people; at the same time, their aimed at 'humanizing' the struggle, avoiding any unnecessary spilling of blood.[44]

One victim of these differing conceptions of the armed struggle was 'Azor' (Mario Simonazzi), vice-commander of the 76th Squadre d'Azione Pattriotica Brigade. A leading figure in the organization Catholic Action, he had been one of the first to push forward the Resistance in the province of Reggio Emilia, soon becoming renowned for the strikes he was counting up. But, as Massimo Storchi has noted, Azor had his own particular vision of the war of liberation, 'outside of any sides or ideologies', tending to spare human life because 'a man is always a man, even inside a black uniform'.[45] His independence of thought, and of action, would cost him dearly in a province that was so strongly characterized ideologically. On 21 March 1945, just a month from the end of the war, the partisan leader was killed with a gunshot to the back of the head by communist partisans; even though they were put on trial after the war, they spent little time in prison. Azor, however, continued to be insulted even in death: in 2003, his name appeared in the *Album of the Fallen and Missing of the Italian Social Republic* (i.e. the Republic of Salò), indicated as a 'soldier of the Republic, killed in ambush at Cesina on 22 April 1945'.[46]

---

44 Massimo Storchi, *Sangue al bosco del Lupo. Partigiani che uccidono partigiani: la storia di 'Azor'* (Reggio Emilia: Aliberti, 2005), p. 17.

45 Storchi, *Sangue al bosco del Lupo*, p. 17.

46 Arturo Conti (ed.), *Albo caduti e dispersi della Repubblica sociale italiana* (Milan: Istituto storico della Repubblica sociale italiana, 2003).

It was not always communist partisans who killed exponents of other ideologies however; for example, in the province of Piacenza the opposite took place. Here it was an old communist, Giovanni Molinari, who was shot by the carabinieri connected to the Partito d'azione; known as 'Piccoli' (he was the son of the first socialist mayor of Fiorenzuola), he was persecuted by the Fascists in 1921 and imprisoned for five years in Ponza and Ustica. Piccoli had been among the first organizers of the armed struggle in the province in 1942, leading his division into the Tidone valley behind another division, the 'Company of Patriotic Carabinieri', led by Fausto Cossu, who was of a different political persuasion. On 5 June 1944, Piccoli and three of his comrades were disarmed and shot by Cossu's carabinieri; in court, Cossu justified his cruel action by claiming that Piccoli and his men had committed terrible crimes. While there is no doubt that some of Piccoli's partisans carried out aimless requisitioning for their own benefit, they clearly did not merit so serious a punishment. As historian Mirco Dondi has written, 'the event can easily be read as the consequence of an anti-communist feeling, a political trait that, with a few attenuating factors, would continue to characterize Cossu and some of his officers.'[47] Dondi continues: 'The trial documents not only confirm that the operation against Piccoli's division was premeditated by Cossu, but also demonstrate the involvement of members of the military section of the Committee for the National Liberation of Upper Italy in initiating the operation and then in guaranteeing the protection of those who effected it.'[48]

The elimination of Piccoli was not the only case of the elimination of a division leader. There were at least four other cases: that of Colonel Raffaele Menici, decommissioned by the 'Green Flames' Brigade; that of the Russian commander Nicola Pankov, killed by one of the Garibaldi

---

47 Mirco Dondi, *La Resistenza tra unità e conflitto. Vicende parallele tra dimensione nazionale e realtà piacentina* (Milan: Bruno Mondadori, 2004), p. 204.

48 Dondi, *La Resistenza tra unità e conflitto*, p. 224.

Brigades; that of Angelo Del Bello, tried and shot for 'insubordination and abandoning his position'; and finally of Angelo Prete, wiped out by one of his officers in a power struggle. As far as territorial control is concerned, we can note the killing of Saturno Gagliardelli, a Christian Democrat runner in the 'Italia' Brigade, charged with maintaining the connection between the divisions on the flatlands and in the mountains.[49]

The most bloody and infamous of the conflicts among partisans, however, was that which led to the killings at the chalet in Porzûs, one of the darkest pages in the history of the Resistance. On 7 February 1945, a hundred communist fighters in the Natisone division, led by Mario Toffanin of the GAP (Gruppi d'Azione Patriotica) reached the valley of Porzûs, in Eastern Fruili, capturing the command of the 1st East 'Osoppo' Brigade, killing 19 partisan men and one woman. The victims included the brigade commander Francesco De Gregori, the political commissioner Gastone Valente—and Guildo Pasolini, brother of the writer Pier Paolo Pasolini. The partisan fighters of the Osoppo Brigade, for the most part Catholics, were suspected of having cut a deal with the Fascists in order to block the annexation of a section of Italian territory by Tito's Yugoslav divisions—an annexation which was supported by the communist Natisone brigade.

On 29 November 1951, during the trial against Toffanin (*in absentia*) and a dozen communist partisans, held at the Court of Assizes in Lucca, a lengthy contribution was given by Alfredo Pizzoni, who had led the national liberation committee continuously throughout the war.[50] After outlining the historical context in which the events that led up to the massacre at Porzûs took place, Pizzoni stated:

---

49 For a detailed analysis of the conflicts between partisan divisions, see the chapter 'Il peso dei contrasti nel movimento di Resistenza. La sfera militare' in Dondi, *La Resistenza tra unità e conflitto*, pp. 87–142.

50 On Alfredo Pizzoni, see the article by Dino Messina, 'E l'Italia oscurò il capo della Resistenza', *Corriere della Sera*, 27 April 2005.

I do not know the accused, nor who they are; they were simply the executors, partisans who tarnished the nobility of their prior actions, who forgot they were Italians—that they were above all else Italians, sons of this earth; they were led astray, their minds confused by concepts that no doubt can be admired and even loved, but which ought never lead one to take up arms against comrades in struggle.[51]

Toffanin, in fact, was only the executor of orders 'that emanated from the highest authorities or, if not so high, authorities that were sure they were following clearly given orders in turn.'[52] We know for certain that the green light was given to him by the communist federation in Udine, in particular by its secretary, Ostelio Modesti. This fact was confirmed on 9 February 2003 by Giovanni Padoan, former commissar of the Natisone Brigade, in a cordial meeting in Attimis with the President of the Osoppo Brigade, Federico Tacoli. In his intervention, Padoan recognized that 'the villainous attack' was organized with the agreement of the Communist Party of Udine. He repeated the accusation, specifying that 'the leadership was complicit in the barbarous crime'. Furthermore, Padoan admitted that his words 'ought to have been included in the trial in Lucca, which sentenced the [direct] authors of the crime', but that 'the political situation of the Cold War meant that, back then, this was not possible'.[53] Dondi, however, notes quite rightly that not all the responsibility for the killings should lie with Ostelio Modesti, 'because he in turn was influenced by the orders handed down by the leadership of

---

51 Pietro Negli, 'La questione della frontiera orientale italiana tra CLN e Alleati. Deposizione al processo per l'eccidio di Porzus di Alfredo Pizzoni', *Nuova Storia contemporanea*, 1 (1997), pp. 104–42.

52 Negli, 'La questione della frontiera orientale italiana', p. 127.

53 See Dario Ferdilio, 'Chiediamo perdono per la strage di Porzûs', *Corriere della Sera*, 10 February 2003.

the Italian Communist Party on 19 October 1944' which equated to 'authorizing the use of force, especially in relation to the Osoppo brigades.'[54]

The Allied offensive began in April 1945. Within a few days, the United States Fifth Army and British Eighth Army broke through the Gothic Line, conquering Massa-Carrara, Bologna and Ferrara, and crossing the Po River. Between 22 and 25 April, the partisan forces also engaged in fighting, abandoning their bases in the mountains and attacking the locations at the foot of the mountains that were still in Nazi hands. On the agreed signal (*'Aldo says 26 x 1'*), the descent from the mountains became generalized and uncontainable.[55] Every means necessary was acceptable to speed up the descent: tanks and carts, cars and bicycles. And while the valleys flowed with armed fighters, an extraordinary but little-known occurrence took place: as the partisans passed through, people climbed onto their roofs and lay white sheets across them, so that the Allied air force would know the breadth of the liberated zones.

The descent onto the plains took place in an atmosphere of unspeakable joy, because the 20 months in the mountains had seen incomparable challenges. The war, however, was not over yet. There were still 135,000 soldiers in the Republic of Salò's army and 90,000 Germans—armed even if completely demotivated—as well as those who had withdrawn from the Gothic Line. The Fascists searched for

---

54 Dondi, *La Resistenza tra unità e conflitto*, p. 130. A particularly detailed study of those 20 months of civil war can be found, for the Pavese, in Giulio Guderzo, *L'altra guerra. Neofascisti, tedeschi, partigiani, popolo in una provincia padana. Pavia 1943–1945* (Bologna: Il Mulino, 2002) and for the Varesotto see Franco Giannantoni, *Fascismo, guerra e società nella Repubblica sociale italiana. Varese, 1943–1945* (Milan: Angeli, 1984); Franco Giannantoni, *La notte di Salò, 1943–1945. L'occupazione nazifascista di Varese dai documenti delle camicie nere*, 2 VOLS (Varese: Edizioni Arrerigere, 2001).

55 The telegram communicated that the troops were to descend from the mountains at 1 a.m. on 26 April. [Trans.]

salvation in the mythical 'redoubt of Valtellina'.[56] the Germans aimed for the Alpine crossings to return to Germany. They were desperate but determined to fight; and indeed, on 25 April and 1 May, 4,000 partisans fell in combat, i.e. 10 per cent of the losses throughout the war of liberation.

While the partisans spread out across the plains of the Po and closed in on the large urban centres, in Milan the Fascists decided to abandon the city and head for the mountains of Valtellina, according to a plan hastily drawn up by Alessandro Pavolini. At 4 a.m. on 26 April, in Piazza San Sepolcro (where Mussolini had founded the Fascist combat units in 1919), the last Fascist federal secretary of Milan, Vincenzo Costa, notified the end of a Fascism in a brief ceremony. Costa recalled:

> The bugle played the assembly call: the terrible moment to lower the flag had arrived. By my side were Franco Colombo, Giulio Rao Torres, Domenico Vianello, Pino Perrone; the Fascists took note and stood to attention, their arms raised in the Roman salute, and a solemn song rose from the historic piazza, the legionary's prayer. Slowly, weeping, the flag came down; everyone's eyes brimmed with tears, but from the back a lone voice cried out 'We will return!' I gave a small speech, cut short by the emotion of it all.[57]

Preceded by 10 tanks and 4 armed cars, the column of 228 vehicles and 6,694 men left Milan at 6.30 a.m. and reached Como at 10 a.m., where they learnt that Mussolini had rejected the plan of participating in a final, extreme battle in the redoubt, and was making his way to Menaggio

---

56 Redoubt (*ridotto*): the military term for a fortification system to which an army can return when necessary. [Trans.]

57 Costa, *L'ultimo federale*, p. 272. On the days following Liberation, see the following two excellent reconstructions: Raffaello Uboldi, *25 aprile 1945. I giorni dell'odio e della libertà* (Milan: Mondadori, 2004); Edgarda Ferri, *L'alba che aspettavamo. Vita quotidiania a Milano nei giorni di piazzale Loreto* (Milan: Mondadori, 2005).

with the intention of taking refuge in Switzerland. In the end, no one reached the redoubt for a heroic death. The majority of the fugitives disbanded within a few hours. A dozen leaders fell at Dongo under partisan gunfire. Mussolini ended his days at Giulino di Mezzegra, caught in a machine-gun round after having attempted to flee beneath a German mantle and helmet. Croce noted in his diary on 29 April: 'News of the end of Mussolini and his circle. It seems natural to me. The man was a nothing, and his end confirms this judgement. It will be necessary to forget him, but at the same time to remember that, both in Italy and abroad, many people—most, perhaps—believed that he was both intelligent and beneficial, providing him with years of support and applause.'[58] No epitaph has been so concise, so scornful, so annihilating.

The descent of the partisans onto the plains also meant the beginning of a long reckoning. The questions to be dealt with covered not only recent events but also matters as far back as the struggles of 1921–22. What was clear to everyone was that there would be no half measures. A calm, responsible man such as Giorgio Agosti, from the political organization Giustizia e Libertà, had no hesitation in giving the following orders to Livio Bianco on 4 September 1944: 'Two matters remain to us: (1) to carry out the largest possible number of acts (merciless liquidation of Fascists and collaborators, and the radical liquidation of figures of authority and rank); (2) to not disarm ourselves during the inevitable democratic, fraternal embrace of victory, but to keep our spirits, men and weapons ready.'[59] A 'merciless liquidation' it was to be then. This does not, however—at least for the period of insurrectionary violence—mean that the period can be defined as 'a savage purge' (Hans Woller)[60] or 'a

---

58 Croce, *Taccuini di guerra*, p. 289.

59 Agosti and Bianco, *Un' amicizia partigiana*, p. 235.

60 Hans Woller, *I conti con il fascismo. L'epurazione in Italia, 1943–1948* (Bologna: Il Mulino, 1997), p. 383.

mix of gratuitous ferocity and desire for frequently misplaced revenge'
(Giampaolo Pansa).[61]

In truth, the insurrectionary violence should be judged according
to certain factors. To begin with, it should be measured against the
intensity of the conflicts, ambushes, raids and massacres carried out by
the Republic of Salò over the 600 days. It was also determined by the
more or less criminal behaviour of the Nazi leadership. Finally, an important role was also played by what had happened in cities and countryside
alike under Fascism and before, during the years of the Fascist pseudo-
revolution, which concluded with the death or exile of thousands of
anti-Fascists. The example of Turin is a case in point—the city that
begins the list of reprisals after 25 April, with 1,138 killings. The numbers
of the anti-partisan repression in Turin over the 20 months of the civil
war were extremely high, higher than any other city in Italy: 11 hanged,
271 shot, 132 fallen in combat, 611 wounded, 12,000 arrests, 20,000
deported.[62] Over the course of the two decades of Fascism, Turin had
already paid for its weak adhesion to the regime, with hundreds of arrests
and hundreds of years of prison sentences. This is without mentioning
the scars the city bore from the thuggery of Brandimarte and De Vecchi,
which culminated in the burning down of the trade-union chamber and
the workers' clubs on 18 December 1922 (as well as the ransacking of
the headquarters of *Ordine Nuovo*, Gramsci's newspaper), leaving 22
dead. Finally, it should be noted that at the moment of the insurrection,
the head of the Fascist Party was Federal Secretary Giuseppe Solaro: a
fanatic who had led operations against the local partisans with the utmost
brutality, and who had organized—in view of the Republic's imminent

---

61 Gianpaolo Pansa, *Il sangue dei vinti. Quello che accadde in Italia dopo il 25 aprile*
(Milan: Sperling & Kupfer, 2003), p. 49.
62 Centro di Documentazione—Presidenza del Consiglio dei Ministri della
Repubblica Italiana, 'Dati sulla lotta partigiana', *Documenti di vita italiana*, n. 29
(1954), pp. 2271–74.

collapse—an extended network of snipers to inflict maximum damage on the Resistance forces.

There were, therefore, all the premises necessary for a rapid and harsh reckoning at Turin. Further fomenting the climate, General Hans Schlemmer was practically laying siege to the city with two divisions (one in armed cars) and threatening to bomb the city.[63] The fighting to liberate the city lasted four days, despite the full collaboration of the large partisan divisions from the mountains with the workers' units that had taken control of the factories. During the fighting—above all, due to the snipers—320 partisans were killed, which increased the general thirst for revenge and justice.

Save for a limited number of arbitrary executions, the repression in Turin—as in the rest of Northern Italy—followed the partisan norms that accepted capital punishment for ministers, undersecretaries, provincial governors and federal secretaries in office from 8 September 1943. The same punishment was established for members of the Fascist special courts and components of all of the party's military divisions, including the Black Brigades, the Italian SS, the X^a Flottiglia MAS and the Muti. Defending himself from accusations of excessive severity, Giovanni Colli—judge and head of the justice section of the Piedmont military command, stated:

> For those who were not there and therefore know nothing of that dark and bloody battle, which lasted twenty months, or for those who have forgotten it, one can only respond that this explosion of hatred cannot be condemned, because its roots lie in a sea of blood and tears. And one can also say that the people's revenge would have had much vaster and extensive proportions if the immediate severity of the military courts had not shown

---

63 At Grugliasco, in order to demonstrate his refusal to allow the CNL to cross the city, General Schlemmer enacted his final massacre, killing 66 people between Garibaldi resistance fighters and civilians.

that justice was on the move, displaying neither weakness nor hesitation. It was harsh justice, a soldier's justice—but it was justice.[64]

On 2 May 1945, nevertheless, the military command issued an order with a peremptory tone: 'Every outbreak of madness must cease. It will end up striking down anyone, partisan or otherwise, rendering people cruel, leading to torture in interrogations and burglaries under the pretext of justice. [. . .] The military courts refuse to protect anyone who does not honour the law.'[65] A few weeks later, a few Roman newspapers claimed that in Turin the partisans had summarily sentenced 8,000 Fascists to death—and that a part of the executions was to take place in the second half of May, despite the presence of the Allied forces. Giorgio Agosti, now chief-of-police in Turin, refuted the news (which was clearly of Fascist inspiration) with the following words:

> The investigations carried out by the police have allowed us to establish that the number of people summarily sentenced to death by firing squad by the military courts of the volunteer freedom corps over the period between 26 April and 5 May (the day that the state of emergency came to a halt) numbers less than 2,000; this figure includes the Fascist divisions killed in combat and the vast number of 'snipers' shot on site. Since the second half of May, order has been completely re-established and the cases of violent death due to political causes over the period have numbered 41, and over the whole month of June dropped to 13.[66]

---

64 Giancarlo Carcano, 'Note sull'ordine pubblico a Torino dopo la liberazione', *Studi piacentini*, 8 (1990), p. 81.

65 Carcano, 'Note sull'ordine pubblico a Torino', p. 79.

66 Carcano, 'Note sull'ordine pubblico a Torino', p. 73. According to calculations produced by Mirco Dondi (*La lunga liberazione*, p. 97), the 'suppression' of Fascists between 25 April 1945 and October 1946 numbered: Turin, 1138; Treviso, 735;

Over the first weeks of Liberation, there was a concerted attempt to slander the Resistance by attributing it with massacres of enormous dimensions. Supporters of Salò attempted to attribute absurd figures such as 300,000 deaths, later reduced to 70,000 and then to 40–50,000. In his *History of the Civil War in Italy*, Giorgio Pisanò further reduced the number of killings to 34,000. Richard Lamb, for his own part, estimated the real number at 30,000 executions.[67] More recently, Giampaolo Pansa has taken into consideration the research conducted by the Milanese institute for the history of the Republic of Salò, writing: 'In all, 20,000 people—between soldiers and civilians—were swallowed up by the reckoning of accounts and successive political murders. This is a provisional figure, because a range of studies are still underway. But I do not feel able to say what a real total might be.'[68] I am of the opinion that even the figure provided by Pansa could be halved; the figure of 9,519—provided by the General Directorship for Public Security in October 1946—seems credible. Utilizing further data drawn from analyses of the provinces of Modena and Reggio Emilia, Dondi sets the figure at 9,911.[69]

In the conclusion to his commendable volume *Return to Montefiorino*—in many ways, his spiritual testimony—Ermanno Gorrieri, a former commander of Catholic partisan forces, and later Minister of Labour, recalls the Fascist victimism of the time:

> A great deal of anger had accumulated in people's souls. It was impossible for it not to explode after 25 April. Violence begets violence. Even if in part they represented a form of summary

Bologna, 675; Milan, 632; Genoa, 569; Udine, 472; Savona, 470; Cuneo, 426; Reggio Emilia, 425; Moden, 338; Ferrara, 276; Imperia, 274; Piacenza, 250; Bergamo, 247; Vercelli, 245; Asti, 216; Parma, 209; Sondrio, 208; Alessandria, 178; Novara, 160.

67 Richard Lamb, *War in Italy, 1943–1945: A Brutal Story* (London: John Murray, 1993), p. 236.

68 Pansa, *Il sangue dei vinti*, p. 371.

69 Dondi, *La lunga liberazione*, p. 93.

justice, the crimes suffered by the Fascists after Liberation cannot be justified, but they can nevertheless be explained by that which took place beforehand, and by the explosive atmosphere of the epoch. The Fascists have no right to play victim.[70]

Once the difficult but radiant days of Liberation were behind them, the demobilized partisans began a period full of both disappointment and rage. I will allow myself a personal recollection. On 29 April, following four days of fighting, I returned the remains of Nino Botti to his family. His chest had been burst apart by a bullet from a 12.7 mm calibre shot from an armoured car at the gates of Piacenza. Nino's funeral, in which everyone from the Luretta valley took part, was the final, unforgettable episode of the civil war. The endless line of people spiralled round and round, filling up the whole of Piazza Agazzano. Each person's face bore an expression of heavy sadness, but also of the awareness that the worst was now behind us, and that—in the name of our dead—we now faced the duty of building a better future.[71] But what future? We had been discharged with nothing but a uniform made of sack-cloth as a parting gift, which was so badly made and 'self-sufficient' that it came apart at the seams. This was our only pay, with which we would have to begin a new life, find employment and build a family.

From one day to the next, General Crittenberhe—commander of the United States Fourth Army—had expected the disarmament of 240,000 partisans, who were nevertheless almost pathologically attached to their weapons, given that for a long time they had depended on them for their survival. The fact that the Allies' request was an ultimatum was held to be offensive, with the result that the partisans handed over only the worst of their guns, conserving the newer and more efficient weapons

---

70 Gorrieri and Bondi, *Ritorno a Montefiorino*, p. 183.

71 Angelo Del Boca, 'La Resistenza in val Luretta', in Valeria Poli (ed.), *Gazzola. Emergenze e territorio* (Piacenza: Comune di Gazzola, 2002), p. 243.

for themselves, which ended up in the party deposits, whether the Communist Party, the Christian Democrats, the Partito d'Azione or the Socialists—tonnes of weaponry. 'The Christian Democrat disarmament,' Paolo Emilio Taviani wrote, 'was decided upon during a session in summer 1948, which I presided over. [. . .] In brief, we decided to consign all our arms to the carabinieri save for the pistols, which were to be reported and retained.'[72]

There were other factors aside from the forced disarmament of the Resistance soldiers that fed disappointment and bitterness. The partisans looked on with concern at the failed purges and with anger at the wave of arrests of their own numbers. While 35,000 Fascists were released from the concentration camp at Coltano, including war criminals in every sense, 1,486 partisans were imprisoned in Piedmont alone. As Hans Woller noted: 'this sense of frustration and impotence deepened the belief that the Resistance's mission remained incomplete, and that the struggle had to continue until Fascism—and those forces that continued to support it—had been definitively wiped out.'[73] It should be noted, furthermore, that passions were also exacerbated by the provocative appearance of neo-Fascist groups such as the 'Mussolini Armed Squadrons', the 'Fasci of Revolutionary Action', the 'Italian Anti-Bolshevik Front' and 'Honour and Combat'.[74]

One reason behind the indignation was the superficial nature of the purge, which allowed criminals like Rodolfo Graziani, Mario Roatta, Junio Valerio Borghese, Piero Brandimarte, Tommaso Brachetti (who had assassinated the partisan Duccio Galimberti) and hundreds more to be released from prison after only a few years or even months of

---

72 Taviani, *Politica e memoria d'uomo*, p. 134.

73 Woller, *I conti con il fascismo*, p. 386.

74 See Silvio Lanaro, *Storia dell'Italia repubblicana. Dalla fine della guerra agli anni Novanta* (Venice: Marsilio, 1992), pp. 30–32.

detention. On 8 September 1947, the chief of police in Turin, Giorgio Agosti, wrote in his diary:

> Long meeting with Minister Scelba on the question of war criminals in Casale.[75] Clearly complete lack of understanding: talked about Beccaria and Sacco and Vanzetti, dredging up the 'massacres in the North' and other rubbish. I stressed my own point of view heavily: the sentences issued by the courts need to be carried out for the government to be maintained; if pardons are to be agreed on, then you need the courage to say so clearly, that way the whole country will know that the executors and mass-murderers of Fascism are alive and well, thanks to De Nicola's tender heart.[76]

If they had known what we do today, since the documents of the US Office of Strategic Services were declassified, the partisans' frustration and indignation would have been greater still. We learn from these papers that already in October 1945, 18 former officials and members of the Xª Flottiglia MAS had been utilized 'in an experimental Allied base in Venice, and are to be considered decriminalized and immune from any accusation of activity effected to date'.[77] On 6 November 1945, James Angleton of Special Counter Intelligence wrote to Colonel Earl B. Nichols at the Allied headquarters, suggesting the removal of Valerio Borghese from the Italian justice system:

---

75 Those responsible for the shooting of 13 partisans on 15 January 1945.

76 Giorgio Agosti, *Dopo il tempo del furore. Diario 1946–1988* (Turin: Einaudi, 2005), p. 12. [De Nicola was the first president of the Republic; Cesare Beccaria the founding father of Italian liberal jurisprudence; Ferdinando Sacco and Bartolomeo Vanzetti were two Italian anarchists unjustly sentenced to death in the US in 1927.— Trans.]

77 Nicola Tranfaglia, *Come nasce la Repubblica. La mafia, il Vatiano e il neofascismo nei documenti americani e italiani, 1943–1947* (Milan: Bompiani, 2004), p. 60.

It would be easy for us to request that the trial is pushed back, if the command sends a letter to the Italian minister *demanding that Borghese be handed back to the Allies immediately following interrogation*. We would thus be able to ask Washington about exploiting Borghese's superior knowledge in terms of secret naval weapons and techniques of submarine warfare [. . .]. I strongly believe that Borghese will be of great use to American naval intelligence.[78]

The inability (or unwillingness) of De Gasperi's governments to have justice carried out and to make a general purge into not only a tool of rightful punishment but also an opportune moment to renovate the organs of the state, as well as their tolerance for the resurgent neo-Fascist forces (when this tolerance did not spill over into active, anti-Communist collaboration), was an important factor in the prolonging of the civil war. And as time passed, relations between the National Committee for Liberation and the Allied forces were not particularly calm and constructive either. The former 'suspected the Allies of making deals with reactionary and monarchist forces, and suffocating the emergence of any reformist proposal; the military government, on the other hand, saw the Resistance as subversive movement that absolutely had to be kept under close watch to avoid the risk of another "Greek incident".'[79]

In this atmosphere of widespread mistrust and growing bitterness, word spread among the partisans that the Resistance had been betrayed, that 'the wind from the North' had ceased to blow and a 'restoration' was underway. In the summer of 1946, in the provinces of Turin, Cuneo, Asti, Verona, Pavia, Sondio, Mantova, Milan and Genoa, thousands of partisans returned to the mountain paths, digging up their weapons. Even if the revolt did not lead to episodes of violence, it was no easy task to keep it at bay, as the demands were both abundant and difficult to

---

78 Tranfaglia, *Come nasce la Repubblica*, pp. 64–65.

79 Woller, *I conti con il fascismo*, p. 386.

meet: the reneging on Palmiro Togliatti's amnesty (which had allowed too many Fascists back into circulation), the expulsion of people with Fascist backgrounds from public office; and that the police and armed forces hire former partisans, with an equivalence of rank.

The accent was laid most heavily on the amnesty, which was seen as a grave error and an unqualified act of injustice. Gian Enrico Rusconi wrote: 'Not only has Togliatti failed to reach his own goal of re-pacifying the nation, but indeed has obtained the opposite effect, leaving everyone unsatisfied, beginning with his own people.'[80] It was above all precisely the Communist partisans—even if they were later labelled as 'unhinged elements'—who had carried out that horrendous and entirely illegal series of crimes between the end of 1945 and the summer of 1946 (above all, in the province of Emilia-Romagna, the so-called triangle of death). Not only unpunished Fascists landed in their cross-hairs, but also members of the clergy (of the 31 priests killed, only five had been chaplains in the Republic of Salò) and a hundred landowners, who they viewed as provokers of famine, financers of Fascist thuggery and grave-diggers of the farm-labourers' movement.

These forms of proletarian and savage justice ceased over the course of 1946 when the Italian Communist Party and the 'Volunteers' Corps for Freedom' publicly condemned them. But the damage had already been done. The Resistance's critics would draw upon this animalistic episode to the utmost. They still do so today, 60 years later, sometimes justifying their work as the realization of a civic duty to shed light on pages from history that have been too-long ignored or deliberately covered over.

POSTILLA. We have examined a great number of newspapers, journals and documents from both sides for this chapter on the civil war. And

---

80 Gian Enrico Rusconi, *Resistenza e postfascismo* (Bologna: Il Mulino, 1995), p. 169.

yet, to our great surprise, as accustomed as we are to reading the most incredible acts of self-absolution, we never came across phrases that could be connected to the myth of *Italiani brava gente*. Why is this the case? Our thesis is perhaps not the only one possible, but we believe that it approaches the truth. The 20 months between 8 September 1943 and 25 April 1945 saw so much violence, blood and the public display of martyred corpses that no one could have thought to dust off a myth that was already so demonstrably incoherent, and which the brutal reality of daily life could only undermine. It should also be noted that the Fascists of the Republic of Salò never claimed to be merciful or generous. On the contrary, in the heat of struggle they tended to boast of their own ferocity as their principle virtue.

THIRTEEN

EVERYONE'S RICH, HAPPY AND ANTI-COMMUNIST

We have come to the end of our long journey through 150 years of Italian history. Over the course of this journey, we have frequently met episodes of particular ferocity, involving soldiers and civilians alike, and to a constantly increasing degree. War has certainly been the backdrop—but war cannot justify all such excesses. Some episodes of singular violence took place in colonies in periods of total calm and even while the results of a successful 'civilizing mission' were being celebrated.

As we have been able to see, the responsibility for these acts of brutality should be attributed above all to minorities who, often in imitation of contemporary projects by foreign powers, attempted to carry out programs of imperialist expansion and, within the country itself, the construction of a strong state able to compete with nearby nations, even exporting its own doctrines. We have seen what can happen when a leader like Mussolini inserts into his own project the transformation of a people like the Italians—then composed mainly of mild-mannered farmers—into a lineage of cruel warriors, making up for a lack of military traditions with demented imperatives such as reciting 'believe, obey, fight'. This was a risky operation; and in the end, instead of producing able soldiers, generated fanatics and crooks, as we have seen in the descriptions of the repression effected in both Ethiopia and the Balkans.

The episodes that we have recounted in this volume obviously represent a selection and not the total of the criminal undertakings effected by Italians over the last 150 years, even if they certainly do represent the worst such occurrences. For example, we examined the inferno of the prison at Nokra, but the concentration camp at Danane, with its 3,175 deaths by famine and sickness, was no less shocking. Similarly, in the chapter on the Libyan resistance, we focused too little on the desperate daily life of the 100,000 Libyan interned in the 15 camps of Syrte. Muammar Gaddafi did not exaggerate when, on 7 October 1975, he claimed during a speech celebrating the anniversary of the Italians been turfed out from his country: 'What Italy did in the zone of el-Agheila is a historic lesson for humanity and a tragic example of aggression, brutality and barbarity. It reflects the arrogance of the strong when they attack the poor and helpless.'[1]

When dealing with the events surrounding the reign of Rodolfo Graziani in Ethiopia, again we limited ourselves to illustrating the nefarious consequences of the assassination attempt of 19 February 1937, overlooking the daily destruction of the people, their goods and their culture. For a more detailed examination in cold prose, see the two volumes signed by General Ugo Cavallero, high commander of the armed forces of Italian East Africa, which describe the continued and ferocious raids in 1938 in Shewa, Gojiam, Begemder and Ankober, with an overall count of tens of thousands of dead, for the most part innocent peasants.[2] Among the various historical diaries kept by the irregular soldiers, we can turn to that of Major Piero Farello, who wielded the right to life and death over the population of entire Ethiopian regions for three years, suppressing the people with the very worst of raids and pillage.[3]

---

1 Cited in Eric Salerno, *Genocidio in Libia. Le atrocità nascoste dell'avventura coloniale italiana, 1911–1931* (Rome: manifestolibri, 2005), p. 17.

2 Ugo Cavallero, *Gli avvenimenti militari nell'impero. Dal 12 gennaio 1938 al 12 gennaio 1939*. 2 VOLS (Addis Ababa: Ufficio centrale topocartografico, 1939).

The behaviour of Ettore Formento was no different,[4] nor was that of hundreds of other officers to whom the extermination of an entire people was delegated, and who were guaranteed full impunity.

Having had to whittle down the number of violent encounters, we did not, furthermore, deal with the Italian expeditionary corps during the Spanish civil war. In this context, however, we ought to single out one particular figure: a real criminal, Arconovaldo Bonaccorsi, a Fascist thug from Bologna, who was sent on the express order of Mussolini to the island of Majorca to organize the struggle against the legitimate republican government. 'Clothed in Fascist black, with high black boots and a white cross at his neck, covered in pistols, hand grenades, daggers and cartridges, he exercised a striking charisma over the islanders and soon fifty young men formed the "dragons of death" under the orders of the "Count Rossi".[5] French writer Georges Bernanos, living in Majorca in the summer of 1936, wrote in his well-known *The Great Cemeteries Under the Moon* that, between September 1936 and March 1937, Bonaccorsi and his thugs put at least 3,000 republicans to death, the majority without trial.[6]

---

3 Documents on Ethiopia in the author's possession: *Bande irregolari dello Uollo, Diario storico,* MS of 153 pages, edited by Major P. Farello. On Farello's operations, see Angelo Del Boca, 'Le bande irregolari indigene a caccia di partigiani in Etiopia', *Studi piacentini,* 11 (1992): 137–62.

4 Ettore Formento, *Kai Bandera. Etiopia 1936–1941: una banda irregolare* (Milan: Mursia, 2000). General Formento's book is an unusual document, written with a frankness that borders on brutality. The author does nothing to hide the most violent and cruel aspects of his activities in Ethiopia. There are no euphemisms, no covering-over, no attempting to understand, no regrets, no requests to be pardoned. He spent five years as a perfect war machine, just as Mussolini had hoped. And this did not, in the postwar period, prevent him from becoming the head of Atlantic armed forces for Southern Europe.

5 John F. Coverdale, *Italian Intervention in the Spanish Civil War* (Princeton: Princeton University Press, 1976).

6 Georges Bernanos, *I grandi cimiteri sotto la luna (1938)* (Milan: il Saggiatore, 1963).

For the same reasons as above, during the chapter on the period Italian occupation of the Balkans, we limited ourselves to describing operations in the province of Ljubljana, overlooking the very serious events that took place in Dalmatia, Croatia, Montenegro, Albania, Greece and the Dodecanese. Finally, we also entirely ignored—for lack of accessible documentation—the behaviour of the 200,000 soldiers sent by Mussolini to the front with the USSR, who supported the German troops, albeit in secondary position. Historian Thomas Schlemmer, one of the few scholars attempting to fill this gap, while not comparing the crimes of the Fascist corp with those of the Nazis themselves, nevertheless describes how the Italians' anti-Communism

> was mixed with racism and anti-Semitism, producing a very aggressive amalgamation [...]. Episodes of brutality by Italian soldiers are known to have taken place not only in relation to the civilian population but above all in relation to prisoners of war. In December 1944, a member of a repair unit witnessed a horrifying act: a group of Soviet soldiers were soaked in patrol and set fire to by a group of Italian carabinieri.[7]

Even if incomplete, the overview that we have presented of the war crimes effected by Italians over the past 150 years seems sufficient to us to be able to formulate a severe judgement. This is not to say, however, that Italians top the list for criminal endeavours. While second to the Nazis, they are nevertheless equivalent to other peoples who, in the

---

7 From an article by Simonetta Fiori, 'Il volto feroce dei nostri soldati. Italiani, brava gente? I documenti lo negano', *la Repubblica*, 14 April 2005. Thomas Schlemmer's statements are taken from his intervention in Rome on 14 April 2005 during the conference *L'Asse in guerra* orgnized by the *Istituto storico germanico*. [The reader can now also consult Thomas Schlemmer, *Invasori, non vittime. La campagna italiana di Russia 1941–1943* (Bari: Laterza, 2009) and—in English—Bastian Matteo Scianna, *The Italian War on the Eastern Front, 1941–1943. Operations, Myths, Memories* (London: Palgrave Macmillan, 2019).—Trans.]

same period, drove forward colonial campaigns and took part in the last two world conflicts. Italians differ from other peoples through their continual appeal to a device of self-forgiveness, the myth of the *Italiani brava gente* which has covered up—and continues to conceal—a whole series of shameful acts. As David Bidussa has written: 'A certain commonplace saying returns each time the issue of anti-Semitism is discussed in Italy: the *natural* distance of Italians from this "virus". Italy, the happy little island of *brava gente*. It's a reassuring assertion, isn't it? Personally, I find it completely deprived of any meaning, a product of *false consciousness*.'[8] In truth, Italians have not been in any way extraneous to this 'virus' ever since the race laws of 1938, and above all during the 20 months of the Republic of Salò when the authorities handed over 2,210 Jews to the Nazis, knowing full well the end that they would meet.[9]

Fortunately, since 1945, Italy has not known the horrors and ruins of war, even if serious threats of involvement have arisen over the years. As Paolo Emilio Taviani has written: 'As the Defence Minister for five years, and eight as the Interior Minister, I can testify that the first Republic thrice ran the risk—perhaps even four times—of a third European war that would have involved Italy: in 1950 (Korea), 1956 (Suez and Hungary), 1961 (Cuba) and 1968 (Czechoslovakia).'[10] Italy has thus known the benefits of peace for 60 good years. This has allowed it, in the arc of a few years, to undergo a radical reconstruction of a country that was seriously damaged by the war, to increase its well-being and to enter into the small, privileged group of the most industrialized countries in the world.

---

8 David Bidussa, *Il mito del bravo italiano* (Milan: il Saggiatore, 1994), p. 12.

9 Bidussa, *Il mito del bravo italiano*, p. 65. For the complicity of the founders of Salò with the Nazi extermination of the Jews, see Antonio Carioti, 'Mussolini partecò all'orrore della Shoah. Lo storico Sarfatti: ci fu un accordo Berlino-Salò per la consegna degli ebrei italiani alle SS naziste', *Corriere della Sera*, 24 January 2005.

10 Taviani, *Politica e memoria d'uomo*, p. 413.

This does not mean, however, that these 60 years of peace with its neighbouring countries have been characterized by calm and reciprocal agreement. Indeed, we could say that between 1945 and 2005, Italy has seen it all: from attempts at coup d'etat to threats of secession, from barbarically repressed peasant revolts to alliances between Sicilian banditry and the Mafia; from the strategy of tension to terrorism on both right and left; from the colossal, unstoppable migration from the south to the 'industrial triangle' through to the revolt of Reggio Calabria; from the murder of Aldo Moro to the discovery of the P2 masonic lodge and its subversive conspiracy; from the liquidation of the men that symbolized the anti-Mafia (Carlo Alberto Della Chiesa, Giovanni Falcone and Paolo Borsellino) and the 'clean hands' operation, through to the crisis of the First Republic and the candidacy of Silvio Berlusconi.[11]

The years between 1960 and 1964 were especially unruly, when centrism saw its season close but any opening to the Socialists was still opposed by both the right-wing of the Christian Democrats, the Catholic hierarchy and the US. In entrusting Fernando Tambroni with the task of forming a government, President Gronchi was convinced that he had brought on the socialists. Tambroni, however, veered to the right, releasing the neo-Fascists of the 'Italian Social Movement' (MSI) and forming a government with their decisive votes. Tambroni's rightward shift not only surprised and concerned his own party but also alarmed the left-wing forces that saw the appeal to neo-Fascist votes as an intolerable provocation. When the MSI eventually decided to hold its sixth annual conference in Genoa, the golden city of the Resistance, the atmosphere was on fire; while the anti-Fascists organized demonstrations across the country, the police charged the protest marches, killing a protester in Licata, five in Reggio Emilia, two in Palermo and one in Catania. As

---

11 'Clean hands' operation: the juridical investigations that uncovered widespread corruption among the main political parties, especially the Socialists. [Trans.]

Francesco Biscione wrote, 'never had the country been so close to civil war since 1945'.[12]

Four years later, following the resignation of Aldo Moro as President of the Council, the commander of the carabinieri—General Giovanni De Lorenzo—believed the moment had become especially critical and required extraordinary measures to defend public order. He thus decided to activate the 'Solo' plan, which he had developed on request of President Segni. On 26 June, De Lorenzo called the heads of all three carabinieri divisions to Rome and handed them copies of the plan, which—aside from the occupation of strategic locations—included the arrest of hundreds of political figures and their internment in the military base at Capo Maragiu in Sardinia. On 22 July 1964, the governmental crisis was resolved and the Solo plan was put back in the drawer. Italy had avoided catastrophe by a hair's breadth.[13]

The plan that De Lorenzo had initiated—under Segni's watch—was not the only failed coup of the period. On the night between 7 and 8 December 1970, Junio Valerio Borghese triggered an operation that had the Ministries of the Interior and of Defence, the public television service and the phone lines as its objectives. Presumably with the complicity of government functionaries, activists from Avanguardia Nazionale occupied the Ministry of the Interior. Yet the operation was the interrupted, probably because some of the conspirators changed their minds. A group of Sicilian mafiosi were also involved in the attempted coup, with whom

---

12 Francesco M. Biscione, *Il sommerso della Repubblica. La democrazia italiana e la crisi dell'antifascismo* (Turin: Bollati Boringhieri, 2003), p. 84. Tamborni's intention to rehabilitate the neo-Fascists had already been demonstrated ten years earlier, as Enzo Santarelli recalls: 'It does not seem irrelevant that already by 1946, a man such as Tambroni could—during the course of the 2 June electoral campaign—propose the abandonment of any clearly anti-facist position.' Santarelli, *Fascismo e neofascismo. Studi e problemi di ricerca* (Rome: Editori Riuniti, 1974), p. 253.

13 For these events, see Anna Cento Bull, *Italian Neofascism* (New York: Berghahn Books, 2011). [Trans.]

Borghese had been in contact since the summer of 1944.[14] With an arrest warrant over his head, he fled to Spain.

But the darkest period in the country, which jeopardized all the conquests of the postwar period, beginning with the democratic institutions themselves, was that of the massacres at Piazza Fontana and at Via Fatebenefratelli in Milan, and at Piazza della Loggia in Brescia, the deaths on the Italicus train and the bombs in the train station in Bologna. Between 1 January 1969 and 31 December 1987, 14,591 acts of politically motivated violence were recorded in Italy, counting 491 casualties and 1,181 wounded. Giovanni Fasanella and Claudio Sestieri:

> These are war-like numbers that have no equivalent in another European country. Faced with such figures, for years we were forced to ask ourselves, searching for some kind of answer: how come there were so many killings in Italy? Why were those responsible for them so often protected and covered for? And why, once Fascist terrorism had been defeated, was Red terrorism left to grow until it ended up threatening the very heart of the state?[15]

These are questions to which, two decades after the 'years of lead', there is still no satisfactory response. Just yesterday, on 1 June 2005, the news arrived of five life sentences for the members of the last nucleus of the Red Brigades, those responsible for the assassination of Marco Biagi. Will this be the last such group? The last such sentence?

---

14 The discovery of connections between Borghese and the Giuliano gang going back to 1944 was made by the historian Giuseppe Casarrubea while working in the National Archives in College Park, Maryland. See Vincenzo Vasile, 'Salvatore Giuliano arruolato dalla X Mas', *l'Unità*, 30 April 2005.

15 Giovanni Fasanella, Claudio Sestieri and Giovanni Pellegrino, *Segreto di Stato. La verità da Gladio al caso Moro* (Turin: Einaudi, 2000). For the 'years of lead', see Giorgio Galli, *Piombo rosso. La storia completa della lotta armata in Italia dal 1970 a oggi* (Milano: Baldini, Castoli, Dalai, 2004).

On 17 February 1992, Mario Chiesa, a Craxian socialist and president of the 'Pio Alberto Trivulzio' care home in Milan, fell into the trap laid for him by public prosecutor Antonio Di Pietro, and was arrested for corruption. Thus began the 'clean hands' operation, led by a pool of judges in Milan, who spent 10 years investigating over 5,000 people and sending 3,200 to trial. After the years of massacres and terrorism by right and left, the chastising campaign of 'clean hands' was welcomed by public opinion with an unprecedented enthusiasm. The Italian justice system, due to its extended, exasperating slowness, had never enjoyed great popularity, but this new operation from Milan changed matters swiftly. You could finally see the effects of an efficient and capable justice system, one that hit both the corrupted and the corrupters, thieves and fraudsters, and above all politicians of every colour who had distinguished themselves through their greed to money and power. As Gianni Barbacetto, Peter Gomez and Marco Travaglio have written:

> As the network of political corruption slowly came to light, the inquiry begun by the investigating magistrates in Milan gathered a mass support that transformed into a rally cry. The distrust of political parties was expressed electorally on 5 April, translating into a widespread, transversal and deep adhesion to the judiciary's activities, and above all to Antonio De Pietro. The mass media exulted him, describing him as the man who was cleaning up and renewing Italian politics. The public prosecutors gained an unimaginable level of popularity.[16]

Nevertheless, even if the drive against corruption was given clear support through backing from the President of the Republic, Scalfato, the popular consensus could not last for long. Too many interests were being hit by the inquiry, which had begun by clearing out important politicians from

---

16 For an exhaustive history of the *tangentopoli* scandal, see Gianni Barbacetto, Peter Gomez and Marco Travaglio, *Mani pulite. La vera storia* (Rome: Editori Riuniti, 2002); quote at p. 33.

the Christian Democrat and Socialist party traditions. It overturned all the mechanisms of handouts and kickbacks, forcing some of those investigated to take to suicide, and a leader of Bettino Craxi's stature to flee to Tunisia. The same newspapers that had lauded Di Pietro and his colleagues so highly now demanded that the devastating inquiry come to an end because, they claimed, the judiciary could not substitute politics.

One of the businessmen who had a great interest in interrupting the onward march of the judicial group in Milan, and began to delegitimize it, was Silvio Berlusconi. An important figure in the building sector since the 1960s, he had subsequently made a qualitative leap into the world of insurance, banking, industrial distribution, publicity, publishing and television. In January 1994, he made a final move by entering into politics, driven above all by the necessity to protect his own companies that had now landed in the cross-hairs of the judiciary. Even though he possessed no political experience whatsoever (but certainly did possess the qualities of a salesman and a great communicator), he managed to put together a heterogeneous coalition of political parties, including the neo-Fascists, the Lombard secessionists and the frayed surviving edges of the old parties of the First Republic. In a very short arc of time, he thus managed to form a new party, Forza Italia, 'invented, promoted and organized directly by Pubitalia, the publicity agency of Fininvest—with a marketing campaign that worked with extraordinary effectiveness'.[17]

Using this political tool, which included some very new and innovative aspects, profiting from the Italian people's disaffection from the old parties, he swept up a clear victory in the elections of 1994. Even though he was soon disrupted by the 'betrayal' of the Northern League, he did not lose hope, nor did he renege on his campaign. Over seven

---

17 Stuart Woolf, 'Crisi di un sistema e origini di una destra', in Gianpasquale Santomassimo (ed.), *La notte della democrazia italiana. Dal regime fascista al governo Berlusconi* (Milan: il Saggiatore, 2003), p. 63.

years of opposition, Berlusconi transformed Forza Italia into an effective electoral machine which, as the historian Paul Ginsborg has recognized, is 'capable of mobilizing consensus through a capillary presence across the entire peninsula'.[18] Displaying his talents at a communicator and public figure, on the eve of the 2001 elections, he presented 15 million families with a captivating small work, *An Italian Story*, which included a firm invitation to vote for a loyal, charismatic man surrounded by a beautiful, happy family, the funder of an important football club and, above all, an enormously successful businessman, to the extent that he had entered into the lists of the richest men on Earth. To this he added a constant, reassuring smile, one that invited optimism and seemed to promise a radiant and secure future. What could be more encouraging than a man who loves flowers, who cultivates them, who has himself photographed in the gardens of paradise?

These operations bore fruit. The 'House of Freedoms' obtained the majority of seats in the election on 13 May 2001, both in parliament and in the senate, with margins broad enough to govern without any problems. Crowning his extraordinary victory with a truly spectacular moment, Berlusconi appeared before the television cameras to sign a 'contract with the Italians', in which he solemnly promised to not stand for election in 2006 if he had not realized the cardinal points of his program over the following five years. At the time of writing, the last year of his legislature is quickly sliding away, and it is clear that he has not managed to maintain the excessive number of promises that he had made, and that the act of disproportionate pride that he performed for the cameras is about to come back and bite him.

This explanation for this failure is given by Giorgio Bocca, a scholar who has never taken his eyes off Berlusconi since he 'entered the ring', and has written hundreds of articles and a series of books on him:

---

18 Paul Ginsborg, *Berlusconi. Ambizioni patrimoniali in una democrazia mediatica* (Turin: Einaudi, 2003), p. 11.

A vast majority is not enough for him. He wants an absolute majority; three television channels are not enough, he wants all of them, and wants to put his own people there. The country is in urgent need of a decent politics, yet he provides simply a horrible spectacle, horrible rhetoric; he steps away for a month just to have a facelift. He knows very well—and he says this—that half of Italians 'viscerally hate him' but he continues to provoke them, to humiliate them. He tolerates neither brakes nor advice. If the authorities block his laws as subversive, he touches them up and then gets the majority in the house to re-propose them.[19]

Berlusconi's great strength—but also his weakness—is denying the evidence of the facts in moments of great difficulty for himself. After a defeat such as the one he sustained in the regional elections of 2005, any other political leader would have rushed to put together a program for relaunching their government. Not Berlusconi. He took the blow, avoided commenting on it and reacted by proposing to his allies to create a single, monolithic party and use it as a weapon against his enemies who were advancing in a sporadic manner. It was his last card and he played it fearlessly, in the moment in which—perhaps in too much haste—many had already begun to proclaim the end of 'Berlusconismo'. Instead, Italy has seen the latest undignified spectacle of 'transformismo'.[20]

Another example of his denying the evidence was provided in 2005 when, nearly every day, the European Commissioner for Economic Affairs, Joaquìn Almunia, noted that the Italian accounts were in trouble, that the deficit was overblown, that a corrective manoeuvre was unavoid-

---

19 Giorgio Bocca, *L'Italia l'è malada* (Milan: Feltrinelli, 2005), p. 17.

20 As Roberto Petrini writes: '*transformismo*, i.e. passing from one parliamentary group to another, has reached an unprecedented frequency. In the period between 1996 and 1999, 261 MPs and 129 Senators changed grouping.' In *Il declino dell'Italia* (Rome and Bari: Laterza, 2003), p. 130.

able. An outraged Berlusconi simply denied everything. When Tony Blair came to Italy on an official visit, Berlusconi told him that Italy was in perfectly good economic health, and that Italians had never been as rich or happy.

This un-novel statement should not be overlooked. It reveals a certain project that Berlusconi has kept on the back burners for a long time, perhaps his most ambitious project of all, and with which he enters straight into our inquiry into the destiny of the Italian people. As Giovanni De Luna has so sharply observed:

> with the right-wing in power, the project of 'making Italians' had found new life, following the construction of a national identity completely rooted in a very clean coincidence between values and material interests. Aside from any ethnic or geographical coordinates, Berlusconi invites Italians from north and south alike to recognize themselves in a common sense of belonging defined around the categories of the market, production and economic development. On a collision course with all the tools of political artifice that characterized the twentieth-century projects of 'making Italians', he seems to want to latch onto an unlimited faith in material progress and the expansion of goods and commodities, holding them to be able to reabsorb or at least smooth over any differences, constituting a 'nation' in which everyone feels they are 'children of the same well-being' [...]. After the good family father of the Catholic-rural tradition and the industrial worker from Borgo San Paolo of the communist tradition, now comes another model of the Italian—defined entirely through the couplet 'warehouse unit'—on which to imprint the project for building our national identity.[21]

---

21 Giovanni De Luna, 'Introduzione' to Santomassimo, *La notte della democrazia italiana*, pp. 31–32. [Trans: the 'warehouse unit' is a '*casa-cappanone*', literally a

Unless the centre-left wakes up and unites, another couple of mandates under the 'House of Freedoms' will be enough to prepare a new model of Italian. This twenty-first-century citizen represents not only an impressive worker and producer, but also an untiring consumer of goods that demonstrates he has earned an enviable status. He follows the cult of the boss, one that Berlusconi represents above all, and demonstrates an absolute loyalty to him. Among the various political programs, his most constant are those of reducing taxes, blocking immigration from non-European countries and a decisive reform of the judiciary—especially its power to open inquests. Because he is not encouraged to take any interest in the integrity, transparency or honesty of political leaders, he also has no interest in the country's moral renewal or a law that might block conflicts of interests. He is quite capable of completely repressing the Fascist, racist and colonial past, but is careful not to minimize the threat of communism—even if it vanished with the fall of the Berlin Wall. He says that the Mafia does not present a serious threat, that it is concentrated in Sicily and Calabria—and that anyway, you can live with it. Finally, continuously bombarded by images on a mass level, he is not able to distinguish between television as education and television as mere waste material. He reads neither often nor refined material, and often has difficulty in locating a country on a world map. He is computerized, even if he does not always know how to use such tools: the importance lies in possessing them.

While the most recent model, this Italian—a clear product of consumerism, ignorance and egoism—is certainly not the one imagined by

---

'house-warehouse'. In the Italian context, however, this is not so much a warehouse conversion but rather a large, prefabricated home spanning an area of terrain, 'a type that, in the current imagination, is still connected to the idea of multiple generations living in a building for the extended family, according to a logic of mutual support, and when necessary taking advantage of the flexibility of the prefab structure in order to adapt it to the habitational or productive requirements of the family enterprise.' Antonio De Rossi, *Riabitare l'Italia* (Rome: Donzelli, 2019).]

Massimo d'Azeglio and the other founding fathers. Fortunately, this is still a model in gestation (even while examples are already in circulation), and can yet be blocked. For despite its woes and defects, both old and new, that we have listed in these pages, Italy is nevertheless far better than it might seem. It is still capable of great refusals, of vast mobilizations, of courageous choices. We hold onto the belief that one day, perhaps not so far in the future, when all of the repressions and false revisionism has ceased, when there are no longer documents hidden away in a 'filing cabinet of shame' and when the legend of a 'good Fascism' has finally seen its last day (along with that of Mussolini's detention facilities being passed off as holiday camps)[22]—then finally we will also be able to bury the false myth of the *Italiani brava gente* which has covered over and absolved so many atrocities.

An important fact, which indicates a favourable reversal of the normal tendency, is the exquisitely professional behaviour maintained by the Italian troops sent on peacekeeping missions over the last 20 years in Lebanon, Bosnia, Albania, Kosovo, East Timor, Mozambique, Afghanistan and Iraq. If comparisons were to be made, one could even claim that the Italian soldiers have behaved better than many of their colleagues in other national contingents. Considering the past account, this is not without significance.[23]

This is not, however, the only element of reassurance available. There is also another army in Italy, which neither wears uniform nor bears arms, nor does it reside in barracks. It is an army of millions of young people—and those who are not so young—which grows in number every

---

22 See Silviero Corvizieri, *La villeggiatura di Mussolini. Il confino da Bocchini a Berlusconi* (Milano: Baldini, Castoli, Dalai: 2004).

23 There is a blot on the record however. During the operation 'Restore Hope' in Somalia, which included an Italian contingent, allegations were made of violence committed against Somali prisoners; the case related to events in Jowhar on the eve of 1994. [See Piero Ignazi, Giampiero Giacomello and Fabrizio Coticcha, *Italian Military Operations Abroad* (New York: Palgrave Macmillan, 2012), p. 106.—Trans.]

year and which is bound together by a love for one's neighbour, and by a vast, limitless passion for alleviating the suffering and fears of others. It is the army of the 4 million volunteers who, in silence and almost in secret, take to the streets every day, in Italy and the world over, to combat the thousand faces of suffering. It is an army composed of 38,000 organizations, who work in the fields of healthcare, emergency support, ambulances, house-calls to the sick and disabled, in school clubs for children and in support of immigrants. It is an army without generals, insignia, medals or fanfares, in which no one has a salary and in which the only recompense begins and ends in a gesture of love. If there are Italians who merit the definition of *brava gente*, in the true meaning of these words—not in terms of mythologization or self-absolution—then it is deserved by these humble and splendid labouring volunteers.

BIBLIOGRAPHY

ABBATTISTA, Guido (ed.). *Global Perspectives on Modern Italian Culture: Knowledge and Representation of the World in Italy from the Sixteenth to the Early Nineteenth Century*. London and New York: Routledge, 2021.

ABDI SHEIK-'ABDI. *Divine Madness: Mohammed Abdulle Hassan*. London: Zed Books, 1993.

ADDISON, Joseph. *Remarks on Several Parts of Italy*. London, 1705.

ADORNO, Theodor W. *Critical Models: Interventions and Catchwords* (Henry Pickford trans.). New York: Columbia University Press, 2005.

AGA ROSSI, Elena. *Una nazionale allo sbando. L'armistizio italiano del settembre 1943*. Bologna: Il Mulino, 1993.

AGOSTI, Giorgio. *Dopo il tempo del furore. Diario 1946–1988*. Turin: Einaudi, 2005.

——, and Livio Bianco. *Un'amicizia partigiana. Lettere 1943–1945*. Turin: Meynier, 1990.

AGRELLI, Enrico. 'C'è uno scheletro nel deserto'. *Panorama*, 18 September 1988.

AL-DAQÂLÎ, Muhammad 'Abd al-Nabî. 'Gli esiliati libici nell'arcipelago delle Termiti. Una pagina drammatica' in Francesco Sulpizi and Salaheddin Hasan Sury (eds), *Gli esiliati libici nel periodo coloniale*. Rome: IsIAO Centro Libico per gli Studi Storici, 2003.

ALBERTINI, Luigi. *Epistolario, 1911–1926, Volume 1: Dalla guerra di Libia alla Grande Guerra*. Milan: Mondadori, 1968.

ALFANI, Augusto. *Il carattere degli italiani*. Florence: Barbèra, 1878.

ALIANELLO, Carlo. *La conquista del Sud. Il Risorgimento nell'Italia meridionale*. Milan: Rusconi, 1994.

ALLARD, Paul, and Frédéric Drach. *Images Secrètes de la guerre*. Paris: Les Illustrés Francais, 1933.

ALTIERI, Guido [Emilio Salgari]. *Lo schiavo di Somalia*. Palermo: Salvatore Biondo, 1903.

ANDERSON, Perry. *Passages from Antiquity to Feudalism*. London: New Left Books, 1974.

ANGRISANI, Alberto. *Immagini della guerra di Libia* (Nicola Labanca and Luigi Tomassini eds). Manduria: Lacaita, 1997.

ANONIMO, Tenente [Anonymous Lieutenant]. *Campagna d'Africa. 1885–1896*. Milan: Ed. Agom, 1935.

ARCHENHOLZ, Johann Wilhelm von. *England und Italien*, VOL. 2 (Michael Maurer ed.). Heidelberg: Winter, 1993.

ARTIERI, Giovanni. *Cronaca del Regno d'Italia. Da Porta Pia all'Intervento*. Milan: Mondadori, 1977.

Associazione Italiana per il Controllo Democratico. *Il governo fascista nelle colonie. Somalia, Eritrea, Libia*. Milan: Corbaccio, 1925.

BALBO, Cesare. *Pensieri sulla storia d'Italia*. Florence: Felice Le Monnier, 1858.

BALCONI, Lorenzo M. *Trentatré anni in Cina*. Milan: Pontificio Istituto delle Missioni Estere, 1943.

BALLINGER, Pamela. *The World Refugees Made: Decolonization and the Foundation of Postwar Italy*. Ithaca and London: Cornell University Press, 2020.

BARBACETTO, Gianni, Peter Gomez, and Marco Travaglio. *Mani pulite. La vera storia*. Rome: Editori Riuniti, 2002.

BARBERO, Alessandro. *I prigionieri dei Savoia*. Bari and Rome: Laterza, 2012.

BARETTI, Giuseppe. 'Degli ordini monastici e dei frati in Italia a mezzo il secolo XVIII' in Giosuè Carducci (ed.), *Letture del Risorgimento. 1749–1870*. Bologna: Zanichelli, 1920.

BARZILAI, Salvatore. *Vita internazionale*. Florence: Quattrini, 1911.

BARZINI, Luigi. *Avventure in Oriente*. Milan: Mondadori, 1959.

BASTIDE, Marianne, Marie-Claire Bergère, and Jean Chesneaux. *China from the Opium Wars to the 1911 Revolution* (Anne Destenay trans.). New York: Pantheon Books, 1976.

BATTAGLIA, Roberto. *Storia della Resistenza italiana*. Turin: Einaudi, 1953.

BATTINI, Michele. *Peccati di memorie. La mancata Norimberga italiana*. Rome and Bari: Laterza, 2003.

BATTISTELLI, Fabrizio. *Gli italiani e la guerra. Tra senso di insicurezza e terrorismo internazionale*. Rome: Carocci, 2004.

BAUR, Giovanni. *Il servo di Dio P. Giuseppe Freinademez.* Vienna: Tipografia missionaria San Gabriele, 1942.

BAZIN, René. *Les Italiens d'aujourd'hui.* Paris: Calmann-Lévy, 1894.

BECCARIA, Cesare. *Dei delitti e delle pene.* Turin: Einaudi, 1994.

——. *On Crimes and Punishments* (David Young trans.). Indianapolis: Hackett, 1986.

BEN-GHIAT, Ruth, and Mia Fuller (eds). *Italian Colonialism.* New York: Springer Link, 2005.

BERHANE SELASSIE, Tsehai. 'An Ethiopian Medical Text-Book'. *Journal of Ethiopian Studies* 9(1) (1971): 95–180.

BERMANI, Cesare. 'Giustizia partigiana e guerra di popolo in Valsesia' in Massimo Legnani and Ferruccio Vendramini (eds), *Guerra, guerra di liberazione, guerra civile.* Milan: Angeli, 1990.

BERNANOS, Georges. *I grandi cimiteri sotto la luna.* Milan: il Saggiatore, 1963[1938].

BERNINI, Simone. 'Documenti sulla repressione italiana in Libia agli inizi della colonizzazione, 1911–1918' in Nicola Labanca (ed.), *Un nodo. Immagini e documenti sulla repressione coloniale italiana in Libia.* Manduria: Lacaita, 2002.

BERRA, Pierina. *I redentori d'Italia, ossia la storia patria contemporanea narrata per bravi cenni ai giovinetti.* Turin: Tip. Unione dei Maestri, 1888.

BERTOLDI, Silvio. *Salò. Vita e morte della Repubblica sociale italiana.* Milan: Rizzoli, 1976.

BEVIONE, Giuseppe. *Come siamo andati a Tripoli.* Turin: Bocca, 1912.

BIAMONTE, Carlo Angelo. *Il brigantaggio alla frontiera pontifica dal 1800 al 1863.* Milan: Daelli and C., 1864.

BIANCHINI, Paolo. 'I testi di lingua italiani prima e dopo l'unità' in Giorgio Chiosso (ed.), *Teseo. Tipografia e editori scolastico-educativi dell'Ottocento.* Milan: Editrice bibliografica, 2003.

BIASUTTI, Giambattista. *La politica indigena italiana in Libia. Dall'occupazione al termine del governatorato di Italo Balbo, 1911–1940.* Pavia: Università degli Studi di Pavia, 2004.

BICK, Tenley. 'Ghosts for the Present: Countercultural Aesthetics and Postcoloniality for Contemporary Italy: The Work of Wu Ming 2 and Fare Ala' in Martin Munro et al. (eds), *Global Revolutionary Aesthetics and Politics After Paris '68.* London: Lexington, 2020, pp. 45–78.

BIDUSSA, David. *Il mito del bravo italiano.* Milan: il Saggiatore, 1994.

BISSOLATI, Leonida. *La politica estera dell'Italia dal 1897 al 1920*. Milan: Treves, 1923.

BIZZONI, Achille. *Eritrea nel passato e nel presente. Ricerche, impressioni, delusioni di un giornalista*. Milan: Zonzogno, 1897.

BLAND, John Ottway Percy, and Edmund Trelawny Backhouse. *China Under the Empress Dowager*. London: Heinemann, 1910.

BOCCA, Giorgio. *L'Italia l'è malada*. Milan: Feltrinelli, 2005.

———. *La Repubblica di Mussolini*. Rome and Bari: Laterza, 1977.

BOLLA, Pietro. *Dell'amor patrio. Dialoghi per fanciulli ad uso delle scuole e delle famiglie*. Cremona: Tipo. Ronzi e Signori, 1864.

BOLLATI, Giulio. *L'Italiano*. Turin: Einaudi, 1983.

BONAVIA, Loria, and Luca Bonavia. *Cantar storie. Un viaggio nel canto popolare tra i monti dell'Ossola*. Domodossola: Grossi, 1999.

BONAZZA, Giulia. *Abolitionism and the Persistence of Slavery in the Italian States, 1750–1850*. London: Palgrave Macmillan, 2019.

BOTTAI, Giuseppe. *Quaderno affricano*. Florence: Sansoni, 1938.

BRAMBILLA, Gerardo. *La Chiesa di Cina e i suoi fasti*. Milan: Istituto delle Missioni Estere, 1917.

BRODER, David. *Mussolini's Grandchildren: Fascism in Contemporary Italy*. London: Pluto Press, 2023.

BRUNER, Stephen C. *Late Nineteenth-Century Italy in Africa: The Livraghi Affair and the Waning of Civilizing Aspirations*. Newcastle-Upon-Tyne: Cambridge Scholars Publishing, 2017.

BURNET, Gilbert. *Some Letters Containing an Account of What Seemed Most Remarkable in Travelling Through Switzerland, Italy, Some Parts of Germany, etc., in the Years 1685 and 1686*. Rotterdam: Abraham Acher, 1686.

CADORNA, Luigi. *Altre pagine sulla Grande Guerra*. Milan: Mondadori, 1925.

———. *La guerra alla fronte italiana*. Milan: Treves, 1934.

CAFORIO, Giuseppe, and Marina Nuciati. *No! I soldati italiani internati in Germania. Analisi di un rifiuto*. Milan: Angeli, 1994.

CALVINO, Italo. *Letters: 1941–1985* (Martin McLaughlin trans.). Princeton, NJ: Princeton University Press, 2014.

CAMPBELL, Ian L. 'La repressione fascista in Etiopia: il massacro segreto di Engecha'. *Studi piacentini* 24–25 (1999): 23–46.

——, and Degife Gabre-Tsadik. 'La repressione fascista in Etiopia. La ricostruzione del massacro di Debrà Libanòs'. *Studi piacentini* 21 (1997): 100.

CANALI, Mauro. *Le spie del regime*. Bologna: Il Mulino, 2004.

CANDELORO, Giorgio. *Storia dell'Italia moderna, Volume 5: 1860–1871, La costruzione dello Stato unitario*. Milan: Feltrinelli, 1968.

CANEVARI, Emilio, and Giovanni Comisso. *Il generale Tommaso Salsa e le sue campagne coloniali. Lettere e documenti*. Milan: Mondadori, 1935.

CANOSA, Romano. *Graziani. Il Maresciallo d'Italia, dalla guerra d'Etiopia alla repubblica di Salò*. Milan: Mondadori, 2004.

CANTATORE, Lorenzo. 'La letteratura italiana sui banchi di scuola. Valori, modelli e antimodelli nelle antologie dell'età iberale' in Giorgio Chiosso (ed.), *Teseo. Tipografia e editori scolastico-educativi dell'Ottocento*. Milan: Editrice bibliografica, 2003.

CANTÙ, Cesare. *Storia d'Italia ne' suoi patimenti e nelle sue glorie raccontata ad uso del popolo e delle scuole*. Milan: Pagnoni, 1861.

CAPOBIANCO, Giuseppe Leonida. *Impressioni e ricordi della prigionia di guerra in Austria*. Naples: Federico & Ardia, 1928.

CARBONE, Carlo. *Italiani in Congo*. Milan: FrancoAngeli, 2019.

CARCANO, Giancarlo. 'Note sull'ordine pubblico a Torino dopo la liberazione'. *Studi piacentini* 8 (1990).

CARDINALI, Emidio. *I briganti e la Corte Pontificia ossia La cospirazione borbonico-clericale svelata*, 2 VOLS. Livorno: Davilli e C., 1862.

CARDUCCI, Giosue. *Contro l'eterno barbaro. Poesie e prose*. Florence: Società Dante Alighieri, 1915.

——. *Opere*, VOL. 25. Bologna: Zanichelli, 1938.

CARPI, Leone. *L'Italia vivente. Aristocrazia di nascitia e del denaro, borghesia, clero, aristocrazie*. Milan: Vallardi, 1878.

CARRIERI, Raffaele. 'La più bella notte d'Italia'. *Illustrazione italiana*, 17 May 1936.

CAVALLERO, Ugo. *Comando Supremo. Diario 1940–43 del capo di stato maggior generale*. Bologna: Cappelli, 1948.

——. *Gli avvenimenti militari nell'impero. Dal 12 gennaio 1938 al 12 gennaio 1939*, 2 VOLS. Addis Ababa: Ufficio centrale topocartografico, 1939.

CECOVINI, Manlio. 'Una relazione seria per costruire il futuro con gli sloveni'. *Il Piccolo*, 4 April 2001.

Centro di Documentazione (Presidenza del Consiglio dei Ministri della Repubblica Italiana). 'Dati sulla lotta partigiana.' *Documenti di vita italiana* 29 (1954): 2271–74.

CESARI, Cesare. *Il brigantaggio e l'opera dell'Esercito italiano dal 1860 al 1870*. Rome: Ausonia, 1920.

CH'EN, Jerome. *Yuan Shih-k'ai, 1859–1916. Brutus Assumes the Purple*. London: George Allen and Unwin, 1961.

CHATEAUBRIAND, Francois de. *Oeuvre complètes*, VOL. 7. Paris: Honoré Champion, 2008.

——. *Voyage en Italie* (A. S. Kline trans.). London: Poetry in Translation, 2010.

CHESSA, Pasquale. *Guerra civile, 1943, 1945, 1948. Una storia fotografica*. Milan: Mondadori, 2005.

CHIMINELLI, Eugenio. *Nel Paese dei Draghi e delle Chimere*. Perugia: Lapi, 1903.

CHOATE, Mark. *Emigrant Nation*. Cambridge, MA: Harvard University Press, 2008.

——. 'Tunisia, Contested: Italian Nationalism, French Imperial Rule, and Migration in the Mediterranean Basin.' *California Italian Studies* 1(1) (2010).

CIANO, Galeazzo. *Diario 1937–1943* (Renzo De Felice ed.). Milan: Rizzoli, 1980.

CIASCA, Raffaele. *Storia coloniale dell'Italia contemporanea*. Milan: Hoepli, 1940.

CINGARI, Gaetano. *Brigantaggio, proprietari e contadini nel Sud, 1799–1900*. Reggio Calabria: Editori Meridionali Riuniti, 1976.

CLARK, Christopher. *The Sleepwalkers: How Europe Went to War in 1914*. London: Penguin, 2012.

CLARK, Martin. *Modern Italy: 1871 to the Present*. London and New York: Routledge, 2014.

COLLOTTI, Enzo. *Il fascismo e gli ebrei. Le leggi razziali in Italia*. Rome and Bari: Laterza, 2003.

CONELLI, Carmine. *Il rovescio della Nazione. La costruzione coloniale dell'idea di Mezzogiorno*. Naples: Tamu, 2022.

CONRAD, Joseph. *Heart of Darkness*. New York: Barnes and Noble, 1994.

CONTI, Arturo (ed.). *Albo caduti e dispersi della Repubblica sociale italiana*. Milan: Istituto storico della Repubblica sociale italiana, 2003.

CORRADINI, Enrico. *L'ora di Tripoli*. Milan: Treves, 1911.

CORVIZIERI, Silviero. *La villeggiatura di Mussolini. Il confino da Bocchini a Berlusconi*. Milano: Baldini, Castoldi, Dalai, 2004.

COSTA, Vincenzo. *L'ultimo federale*. Milan: Rizzoli, 1982.

COVA, Alessandro. *Graziani. Un generale per il regime*. Rome: Newton Compton, 1987.

COVERDALE, John F. *Italian Intervention in the Spanish Civil War*. Princeton: Princeton University Press, 1976.

CRAINZ, Guido. *Il dolore e l'esilio. L'Istria e le memorie diverse d'Europa*. Rome: Donzelli, 2005.

CRESCITELLI, Luigi. *Noè Tacconi, 1879–1942. Il priimo Vescovo di Kaifeng (Cina)*. Bologna: EMI, 1999.

———. *Vita del servo di Dio Padre Alberico Crescitelli, missionario apostolico nello Scen-si meridionale in China*. Avellino: Tipografia Gennaro Ferraro, 1914.

CREVELLIN, Walter E. (ed.). *Cattolici, Chiesa, Resistenza. I testimoni*. Bologna: Il Mulino, 2000.

CROCE, Benedetto. *Taccuini di guerra, 1943–1945*. Milan: Adelphi, 2004.

———. *Teoria e storia della storiografia*. Bari: Laterza, 1966.

CURLI, Barbara (ed.). *Italy and the Suez Canal from the Mid-Nineteenth Century to the Cold War*. London: Palgrave Macmillan, 2022.

D'AGOSTINI, Paolo. 'Noi colonialist diventati censori'. *Repubblica*, 20 September 1988.

D'AZEGLIO, Massimo. *I miei ricordi*, 2 VOLS. Florence: Barbera Editore, 1867.

DALL'ORA, Fidenzio. *Intendenza in A.O.*. Rome: Istituto Nazionale Fascista di Cultura, 1937.

DAMIANO, Andrea. *Rosso e grigio*. Bologna: Il Mulino, 2000.

DE AMICIS, Edmondo. *La vita militare*. Milan: Treves, 1868.

DE BONO, Emilio. *La guerra alla fronte italiana*. Milan: Treves, 1934.

DE FELICE, Renato. *Mussolini il duce. Lo Stato totalitario 1936–1940*. Turin: Einaudi, 1996.

———. *Mussolini l'alleato, Volume 2: La guerra civile, 1943–1945*. Turin: Einaudi, 1997.

DE JACO, Aldo (ed.). *Brigantaggio meridionale. Cronaca inedita dell'Unità d'Italia*. Rome: Editori Riuniti, 1969.

DE LAZZARI, Primo. *Le SS italiane*. Milan: Teti, 2002.

DE LUIGI, Giuseppe. *La Cina contemporanea. Viaggio e note*. Milan: Treves, 1912.

DE LUNA, Giovanni, Adolfo Mignemi, and Carlo Gentile (eds). *Storia fotografica della Repubblica sociale italiana*. Turin: Bollati Boringhieri, 1997.

———. 'Introduzione' in Gianpasquale Santomassimo (ed.), *La notte della democrazia italiana. Dal regime fascista al governo Berlusconi.* Milan: il Saggiatore, 2003.

DE MAURO, Tullio. *Storia linguistica dell'Italia unita.* Bari: Laterza, 1963.

DE MICHELI, Mario. *Scalarini. Vita e disegni del grande caricaturista politico.* Milan: Feltrinelli, 1978.

DE NAPOLI, Olindo. 'Colonialism through Penal Deportation in the Italian Political and Legal Debate: From the Unification to the Beginning of the Colonial Enterprise'. *Quaderni fiorentini per la storia del pensiero giuridico moderno* 49 (2020): 185–220.

DE PÉLACOT, Edouard. *Expédition de Chine de 1900.* Paris: Charles-Lavanzelle, 1901.

DE SANCTIS, Francesco. *Saggi critici.* Bari: Laterza, 1957.

DE VECCHI, Cesare Maria. *Il quadrumviro scomodo. Il vero Mussolini nelle memorie del più monarchico dei fascisti.* Milan: Mursia, 1983.

———. *Orizzonti d'impero. Cinque anni in Somalia.* Milan: Mondadori, 1935.

DEAKIN, Frederick William. *Storia della Repubblica di Salò.* Turin: Einaudi, 1963.

DEL BOCA, Angelo. 'Chi ha paura di Omar?'. *Il Messaggero,* 14 March 1983.

———. 'La Resistenza in val Luretta' in Valeria Poli (ed.), *Gazzola. Emergenze e territorio.* Piacenza: Comune di Gazzola, 2002.

———. 'Rodolfo Graziani' in *Dizionario biografico degli italiani,* VOL. 58. Rome: Istituto della Enciclopedia Italiana, 2002, pp. 829–35.

———. 'Un cuore semplice' in *La scelta.* Vicenza: Neri Pozza, 2006, pp. 147–53.

———. *Apartheid. Affanno e dolore.* Milan: Bompriani, 1962.

———. *Da Mussolini a Gheddafi: Quaranta incontri.* Vicenza: Neri Pozza, 2012.

———. *The Ethiopian War 1935–1941* (Phyllis Deborah Cummins trans.). Chicago, IL: University of Chicago Press, 1965.

———. *Giornali in crisi: Indagine sulla stampa quotidiani in Italia e nel mondo.* Turin: Aeda, 1968.

———. *Gli italiani in Africa Orientale,* 4 VOLS. Bari: Laterza, 1976–84.

———. *Gli italiani in Libia,* 2 VOLS. Bari: Laterza, 1986.

———. *I gas di Mussolini. Il fascismo e la guerra d'Etiopia.* Rome: Editori Riuniti, 1996.

———. *Il mio Novecento.* Vicenza: Neri Pozza, 2008.

———. *L'altra Spagna.* Milan: Bompriani, 1961.

——. *La disfatta di Gars bu Hàdi. 1915: Il colonnello Miani e il più grande disastro dell'Italia coloniale.* Milan: Mondadori, 2004.

——. *La guerra d'Abissinia 1935–1941.* Milan: Feltrinelli, 1965.

——. *La scelta.* Vicenza: Neri Pozza, 2006.

——. *Manicomi come lager.* Turin: Edizioni dell'Albero, 1966.

——. *The Negus: The Life and Death of the Last King of Kings* (Anthony Shugaar trans.). Addis Ababa: Arada Books, 2012[1995].

——. *Nella notta ci guidano le stelle: La mia storia partigiana.* Milan: Mondadori, 2015.

——. *Occhio giapponese.* Novara: De Agostino, 1963.

——. *Rapporto dalla Jugoslavia.* Genoa: Valnoci, 1968.

——. *Un testimone scomodo.* Domodossola: Grossi, 2000.

——. *Vietnam* in *Lotte di liberazione e rivoluzioni.* Turin: Giappichelli, 1968.

——, and Mario Giovana. *Fascism Today: A World Survey* (R. H. Boothroyd trans.). London: William Heinemann, 1970.

——, and RAINERO, Paolo Valera. *Gli Italiani in Libia, Volume 1: Tripoli bel suol d'amore, 1860–1922.* Rome and Bari: Laterza, 1986.

DEL BOCA, Lorenzo. *Maledetti Savoia.* Casale Monferrato: Piemme, 1998.

DEL FRA, Lino. *Sciara Sciat. Genocidio nell'oasi: l'esercito italiano a Tripoli.* Rome: Datanews, 1995.

DELLAVALLE, Claudio. 'Il politico e l'organizzatore di cultura' in Luciano Boccalatte (ed.), *Guido Quazzi. L'archivio e la biblioteca come autobiografia.* Milan: FrancoAngeli, 2008, pp. 33–60.

Département de la Presse et de L'Information du gouvernement impérial D'Ethiopie. *La Civilisation de l'Italie fascite en Ethiope,* VOL. 1. Addis Ababa: Berhanena Selam, 1945.

DEPLANO, Valeria. 'Within and Outside the Nation: Former Colonial Subjects in Post-War Italy'. *Modern Italy* 23(4) (2018): 395–410.

DER LING, Princess. *Two Years in the Forbidden City.* New York: Moffat, Yard and Company, 1911.

DI FIORE, Gigi. *1861: Pontelandolfo e Casalduni. Un massacro dimenticato.* Naples: Grimaldi, 1998.

——. *I vinti del Risorgimento. Storia e storie di chi combatté per i Borbone di Napoli.* Turin: Utet, 2004.

DI FRANCESCO, Tommaso. Interview with Angelo Del Boca. *il manifesto*, 1 November 2019.

DI MAIO, Alessandra. 'Il mediterraneo nero. Rotte dei migranti nel millennio globale' in Giulia de Spuches (ed.), *La Città Cosmopolita*. Palermo: Palumbo Editore, 2012, pp. 143–63.

——. 'Italian Explorations in Southeast Asia' in Edoardo Tortarolo (ed.), *Cosmopolitan Italy in the Age of Nations*. London and New York: Routledge, 2023, pp. 161–74.

DI PASQUALE, Francesca. 'The "Other" at Home: Deportation and Transportation of Libyans to Italy During the Colonial Era (1911–1943)'. *International Review of Social History* 63 (2018): 211–31.

DI SANTE, Costantino (ed.). *Italiani senza onore. I crimini in Yugoslavia e i processi negati, 1941–1951*. Verona: Ombre Corte, 2005.

DOMENICO, Roy Palmer. *Processo ai fascisti, 1943–1948. Storia di un'epurazione che non c'è stata*. Milan: Rizzoli, 1996.

DOMINIONI, Matteo. 'Le fotografie di Danane nel contesto dell'immagine coloniale'. *Studi piacentini* 35 (2004): 213–26.

——. *Lo sfascio dell'impero*. Rome and Bari: Laterza, 2008.

DONDI, Mirco. *La lunga liberazione. Giustizia e violenza nel dopoguerra italiano*. Rome: Editori Riuniti, 1999.

——. *La Resistenza tra unità e conflitto. Vicende parallele tra dimensione nazionale e realtà piacentina*. Milan: Bruno Mondadori, 2004.

DRAGONI, Carlo. *La meravigliosa vita di Tzu Hsi, imperarice*. Milan: Mondadori, 1943.

DRUMMOND, David Thomas Kent. *Scenes and Impressions in Switzerland and the North of Italy*. Edinburgh: W. P. Kennedy, 1854.

ECO, Umberto. *Il costume de casa. Evidenze e misteri dell'ideologia italiana*. Milan: Bomponiani, 1973.

EDEEK, Mahmud. 'Les Dimensions politiques, économiques et sociales de la conquête italienne en Libya' in Anna Baldinetti (ed.), *Modern and Contemporary Libya: Sources and Historiographies*. Rome: IsIAO, 2003.

EVANS-PRITCHARD, Edward Evan. 'The Sanusi of Cyrenaica'. *Journal of the International Africa Institute* 15(2) (1945): 61–79.

FALDELLA, Emilio. *La Grande Guerra*. Chiari: Nordpress, 2004.

FARJENEL, Fernand. *La Morale chinoise, fondement des sociétés d'Extrême-Orient*. Paris: Giard & Brière, 1906.

FASANELLA, Giovanni, Claudio Sestieri, and Giovanni Pellegrino. *Segreto di Stato. La verità da Gladio al caso Moro*. Turin: Einaudi, 2000.

FERENC, Tone. *Si ammazza troppo poco: Condannati a morte—ostaggi—passati per le armi nella provincia di Lubiana, 1941–1943: documenti*. Ljubljana: Inštitut za novejšo zgodovino, 1999.

———. *Ubija se premalo: Obsojeni na smrt—Talci—Ustreljeni v Ljubljanski pokrajini 1941–1943: Dokumenti*. Ljubljana: Inštitut za novejšo zgodovino, 1999.

FERGUSON, Niall. *The Pity of War*. London: Allen Lane, 1998.

FERRI, Edgarda. *L'alba che aspettavamo. Vita quotidiana a Milano nei giorni di piazzale Loreto*. Milan: Mondadori, 2005.

FILANGIERI, Gaetano. 'Molti gran proprietarii, pocchi proprietarii piccoli, ostacolo alla popolazione' in Giosuè Carducci (ed.), *Letture del Risorgimento. 1749–1870*. Bologna: Zanichelli, 1920.

FILETI, Vincenzo. *La conessione italiana di Tien-Tsin*. Genoa: Barabino e Gravese, 1921.

FIORI, Simonetta. 'Il volto feroce dei nostri soldati. Italiani, brava gente? I documenti lo negano'. *La Repubblica*, 14 April 2005.

FLEMING, Peter. *The Siege at Peking*. Hong Kong, Oxford, and New York: Oxford University Press, 1986.

FONTANA, Ferdinando. *In viaggio per la Cina*. Milan: Tipografia Nazionale di V. Ramperti, 1900.

FORCELLA, Enzo. 'Grandezza e miseria del movimento dei giornalisti democratici' in *Il potere delle parole: come si diventa giornalista*. Rome: La Città del Sole, 1983.

———. *La resistenza in convento*. Turin: Einaudi, 1999.

———, and Alberto Monticone. *Plotone d'esecuzione. I processi della prima guerra mondiale*. Bari: Laterza, 1968.

FORGACS, David. *Italy's Margins: Social Exclusion and Nation Formation Since 1861*. Cambridge: Cambridge University Press, 2014.

FORMENTO, Ettore. *Kai Bandera. Etiopia 1936–1941: Una banda irregolare*. Milan: Mursia, 2000.

FOSCOLO, Ugo. *Ultime Lettere di Jacopo Ortis: A Translation* (Douglas Radcliff-Umstead trans.). Chapel Hill: University of North Carolina Press, 1970.

——. *Ultime lettere di Jacopo Ortis*. Cles: I libri dell'Unità, 1993.

FRANZINELLI, Mimmo. *Delatori. Spie e confidenti anonimi: l'arma segreta del regime fascista*. Milan: Mondadori, 2001.

——. *Le stragi nascoste. L'armadio della vergogna: impunità e rimozione dei crimini di guerra nazifascista, 1943–2001*. Milan: Mondadori, 2002.

FULLER, Mia. 'Italy: Beyond the Clichés that Obscure Unacceptable Histories'. *Journal of Genocide Research* 24(2) (2021): 298–307.

GALLI DELLA LOGGIA, Ernesto. 'Il brigantaggio' in Giovanni Belardelli (ed.), *Miti e storia dell'Italia unita*. Bologna: Il Mulino, 1999.

GALLI, Giorgio. *Piombo rosso. La storia completa della lotta armata in Italia dal 1970 a oggi*. Milan: Baldini, Castoldi, Dalai, 2004.

GALLO, Max. *Vita di Mussolini*. Bari: Laterza, 1967.

GAMBINO, Antonio. *Inventario italiano. Costumi e mentalità di un Paese materno*. Turin: Einaudi, 1998.

GANAPINI, Luigi. *La repubblica delle camicie nere*. Milan: Garzanti, 1999.

GENTILE, Anna Vertua. *Come devo comportarmi?*. Milan: Hoepli, 1921.

GENTILE, Carlo, and Francesco Corniani. 'Zur Geschichte der italienisch-faschistischen Division Monterosa im deutsch besetzten Italien 1944–1945'. *Quellen und Forschungen aus italienischen Archiven und Bibliotheken* 102(1) (2022).

GENTILE, Emilio. *Il culto del Littorio. La sacralizzazione della politica nell'Italia fascista*. Rome and Bari: Laterza, 1993.

GÉRARD, Auguste. *Ma mission en Chine, 1893–1887*. Paris: Plon, 1918.

GHISLERI, Arcangelo. *Tripolitania e Cirenaica dal Mediterrano al Sahara*. Milan and Bergamo: Società Editoriale Italiana–Istituto Italiano d'Arti Grafiche, 1912.

GIANNATONI, Franco, and Fabio Minazzi. *Il coraggio della memoria e la guerra civile spagnola*. Varese: Edizioni Arterigere, 2000.

GIBELLI, Antonio. 'Ragazzi di Salò, piccoli partigiani' in *Il popolo bambino. Infanzia e nazione dalla Grande Guerra a Salò*. Turin: Einaudi, 2005, pp. 366–401.

——. *L'officina della guerra. La Grande Guerra e le trasformazioni del mondo mentale*. Turin: Bollati Boringhieri, 1991.

GIGLI MARCHETTI, Ada (ed.). *'Il Giorno'. Cinquant'anni di un quotidiano anticonformista*. Milan: FrancoAngeli, 2007.

GILBERT, Martin. *The First World War: A Complete History*. New York: Henry Holt, 1994.

GINGERAS, Ryan. *The Fall of the Sultanate*. Oxford: Oxford University Press, 2016.

GINSBORG, Paul. *Berlusconi. Ambizioni patrimoniali in una democrazia mediatica*. Turin: Einaudi, 2003.

GIOIA, Melchiorre. 'Dissertazione sul problema "Quale dei governi liberi meglio convenga alla felicità d'Italia" ' in Giosuè Carducci (ed.), *Letture del Risorgimento. 1749–1870*. Bologna: Zanichelli, 1920.

GIOLITTI, Giovanni. *Quarant'anni di politica italiana. Dalle carte di Giovanni Giolitti, Volume 3: Dai prodromi della Grande guerra al fascismo, 1910–1928* (Claudio Pavone ed.). Milan: Feltrinelli, 1962.

GIOVANA, Mario. *L'avventura fascista in Etiopia*. Milan: Teti, 1976.

GIRETTI, Edoardo. 'A proposito della Tripolitania. Ottimismo o pessimismo coloniale?'. *La Riforma sociale*, December 1911.

GIUDICI, Marco. *Fascismo, guerra e società nella Repubblica sociale italiana. Varese, 1943–1945*. Milan: Angeli, 1984.

——. *La notte di Salò, 1943–1945. L'occupazione nazifascista di Varese dai documenti delle camicie nere*, 2 VOLS. Varese: Edizioni Arterigere, 2001.

GIUSTOLISI, Franco. *L'armadio della vergogna*. Rome: Nutrimenti, 2004.

GOBERTI, Vincenzo. *Del primato morale e civile degli italiani*, VOL. 1. Capolago: Tipografia Elvetica, 1846.

GOETHE, Johann Wolfgang von. *Italian Journey* (W. H. Auden and Elizabeth Mayer trans). New York: Schocken Books, 1968.

——. *Werkausgabe*, VOL. 7: Italienische Reise (Bettina Hessa ed.). Cologne: Könemann, 1998.

GOPAL, Priyamvada. *Insurgent Empire: Anticolonial Resistance and British Dissent*. London and New York: Verso, 2019.

GORRIERI, Ermanno, and Luigi Bondi. *Ritorno a Montefiorino*. Modena: Artioli Editore, 1987.

GRAMSCI, Antonio. 'Some Aspects of the Southern Question' in *Selections from Political Writings (1921–1926)* (Quentin Hoare trans. and ed.). London: Lawrence and Wishart, 1978.

GRANDI, Dino. *25 luglio. Quarant'anni dopo* (Renzo De Felice ed.). Bologna: Il Mulino, 1983.

GRAY, Ezio Maria. *La bella guerra*. Florence: Bemporad, 1912.

GRAZIANI, Rodolfo. *Cirenaica pacificata*. Milan: Mondadori, 1932.

———. *Pace romana in Libia*. Milan: Mondadori, 1937.

GRINER, Massimiliano. *La 'banda Koch'. Il reparto speciale di polizia, 1943–1945*. Turin: Bollati Boringhieri, 2000.

———. *La pupilla del duce. La Legione autonoma mobile 'Ettore Muti'*. Turin: Bollati Boringhieri, 2004.

HAMMERMANN, Gabriele. *Gli internati militari italiani in Germania, 1943–1845*. Bologna: Il Mulino, 2004.

HAWTHORNE, Camilla. 'Black Mediterranean Geographies: Translation and the Mattering of Black Life in Italy'. *Gender, Place and Culture: A Journal of Feminist Geography* 30(3) (2023): 484–507.

HEINE, Heinrich. *Gesammelte Werke, Volume 3: Reisebilder*. Berlin: Grote'sche Verlag, 1887.

———. *Pictures of Travel* (Charles Godfrey Leland trans.). Philadelphia: Schaefer and Koradi, 1879.

HIPPLER, Thomas. *Prologue to Governing from the Skies: A Global History of Aerial Bombing* (David Fernbach trans.). London and New York: Verso, 2017.

HOBSBAWM, Eric. *Bandits*. London: Weidenfeld and Nicolson, 1969.

HOM, Stefania Malia. *Empire's Moebius Strip: Historical Echoes in Italy's Crisis of Migration and Detention*. Ithaca, NY: Cornell University Press, 2019.

IGNAZI, Piero, Giampiero Giacomello, and Fabrizio Coticchia. *Italian Military Operations Abroad*. New York: Palgrave Macmillan, 2012.

ISNENGHI, Mario. *L'Italia in piazza*. Milan: Mondadori, 1994.

———, and Giorgio Rochat. *La grande guerra, 1914–1918*. Florence: La Nuova Italia, 2000.

IYOB, Ruth. *The Eritrean Struggle for Independence*. Cambridge: Cambridge University Press, 1995.

JESI, Furio. *Secret Germany* (Richard Braude trans.). London: Seagull Books, 2021.

JIAN, Bozan, Shao Xunzheng, and Hu Hua. *Concise History of China*. Beijing: Foreign Language Press, 1981.

KALI-NYAH, Imani. *Italy's War Crimes in Ethiopia, 1935–1941*. Chicago: The Ethiopian Holocaust Remembrance Committee, 2001.

KLINKHAMMER, Lutz. *L'occupazione tedesca in Italia, 1943–1945*. Turin: Bollati Boringhieri, 1993.

———. *Le stragi naziste in Italia. La guerra contro i civili, 1943–1944*. Rome: Donzelli, 1997.

LABANCA, Nicola (ed.). *Fra sterminio e sfruttamento. Militari internati e prigionieri di guerra nella Germana nazista, 1939–1945*. Florence: Le Lettere, 1992.

——— (ed.). *Un nodo. Immagini e documenti sulla repressione coloniale italiana in Libia*. Manduria: Lacaita, 2002.

———. 'Colonial rule, colonial repression and war crimes in the Italian colonies'. *Journal of Modern Italian Studies* 9(3) (2004): 300–313.

———. *In marcia verso Adua*. Turin: Einaudi, 1993.

———, and Carlo Spagnolo (eds). *Guerra ai briganti, guerra dei briganti (1860–1870). Storiografia e narrazioni*. Bari: Unicopli, 2021.

LAMB, Richard. *War in Italy, 1943–1945: A Brutal Story*. London: John Murray, 1993.

LANARO, Silvio. *Storia dell'Italia repubblicana. Dalla fine della guerra agli anni Novanta*. Venice: Marsilio, 1992.

LAREBO, Haile. 'Empire Building and Its Limitations: Ethiopia (1935–1941)' in Ruth Ben-Ghiat and Mia Fuller (eds), *Italian Colonialism*. New York: Springer Link, 2005.

LAZZERO, Ricciotti. *Le SS italiane*. Milan: Rizzoli, 1982.

LENCI, Marco. *All'inferno e ritorno. Storie di deportati tra Italia ed Eritrea in epoca coloniale*. Pisa: Biblioteca Franco Serantini, 2004.

LEOPARDI, Giacomo. *Discorso sopra lo stato presente dei costumi degli italiani*. Milan: Rissoli, 1998.

LEPRE, Aurelio. *La storia della Repubblica di Mussolini. Salò: il tempo dell'odio e della violenza*. Milan: Mondadori, 1999.

LESSONA, Alessandro. *Un ministro di Mussolini racconta*. Milan: Edizioni Nazionali, 1973.

LESSONA, Michele. *Volere è potere*. Florence: Barbèra, 1870.

LEVI, Carlo. *Christ Stopped at Eboli* (Frances Frenaye trans.). New York: Farrar, Straus and Company, 1947.

LEWIS, Ioan Myrddin. *A Modern History of Somalia*. London and Boulder: Westview Press, 1965.

LICATA, Glauco. *Notabili della terza Italia*. Rome: Cinque Luna, 1968.

LIDDELL HART, Basil Henry. *The Real War (1914–1918)*. London: Faber & Faber, 1930.

LIUCCI, Raffaele. *La tentazione della 'casa in collina'. Il disimpegno degli intellettuali nella guerra civile italiana, 1943–1945*. Milan: Unicopli, 1999.

LIVRAGHI, Dario. 'Gli assassini in Africa. 800 morti?'. *Il Secolo*, 5–6 March 1891.

LO BIANCO, Giuseppe. *Profondo Nero: Mattei, De Mauro, Pasolini*. Milan: Garzanti, 2009.

LOMBARDI SATRIANI, Luigi. *Menzogna e verità nella cultura contadina del Sud*. Naples: Guida, 1974.

LOMBARDI-DIOP, Cristina. 'Gifts, Sex, and Guns: Nineteenth-Century Italian Explorers in Africa' in Patrizia Palumbo (ed.), *A Place in the Sun*. Berkeley, CA: University of California Press, 2003, pp. 119–36.

LOTI, Pierre. *Les Deniérs jours de Pékin*. Paris: Calmann-Levy, 1901.

LUCARELLI, Antonio. *Il brigantaggio politico del Mezzogiorno d'Italia dopo la seconda restaurazione borbonica (1815–1818) e il brigantaggio politico delle Puglie dopo il 1860*. Milan: Longanesi, 1982.

LUDWIG, Emil. *Colloqui con Mussolini*. Milan: Mondadori, 1932.

LUZZATTO, Sergio. *Il corpo del duce*. Turin: Einaudi, 1998.

MABILLON, Jean. *Correspondance inèdite de Mobillon et de Monfaucon avec l'Italie* (Antoine-Claude Pasquin Valery ed.). Paris: J. Labitte, 1847.

MACCHIA, Giovanni. 'Introduzione' in Montesquieu, *Viaggio in Italia*. Rome and Bari: Laterza, 1995.

MAGRI, Enzo. 'Garibaldi della Libia'. *Oggi*, 10 August 1979.

MAIORINO, Taquino. *Storia e leggenda di briganti e brigantesse*. Casale Monferrato: Piemme, 1997.

MAKONNEN, T. Ras. *Pan-Africanism from Within: As Recorded and Edited by Kenneth King*. Nairobi and London: Oxford University Press, 1973.

MARCUS, Harold G. *Haile Selassie I, My Life and Ethiopia's Progress* (Edward Ullendorff trans.). New York: Frontline Books, 1999.

MARTONE, Luciano. *Giustizia coloniale. Modelli e prassi penale per i sudditi d'Africa dall'età giolittiana al fascismo*. Naples: Jovene, 2002.

MAVRAPOULOS, Nikolaus. 'The Latecomers' Early Colonial Experiment—The Uniqueness of the German Case'. *Athens Journal of History* 6(2) (April 2020): 157–74.

MAYDA, Giuseppe. *Graziani l'Africano. Da Neghelli a Salò*. Florence: La Nuova Italia, 1992.

MAZZINI, Giuseppe. 'Della giovine Italia' (1832) in *Opere*, VOL. 1. Milan: Daelli, 1861.

MELEGARI, Carlo. *Cenni sul brigantaggio. Ricordi di un antico bersagliere*. Turin: Roux Frassati & C., 1897.

MERCURI, Lamberto, and Carlo Tuzzi. *Canti politici italiani, 1793–1945*. Rome: Editori Riuniti, 1973.

MERETA, Francesco. 'Quando Italo Calvino ammirava Angelo Del Boca'. *Studi piemontesi* 35(1) (2006): 83–87.

MESSEROTTI BENVENUTI, Giuseppe. *Un italiano nella Cina dei Boxer. Lettere e fotografie, 1900–1901* (Nicola Labanca ed.). Modena: Associazione Giuseppe Panini Archivi Modenesi, 2000.

MILKIAS, Paulos, and Getachew Metaferia (eds). *The Battle of Adwa: Reflections on Ethiopia's Historic Victory Against European Colonialism*. New York: Algora, 2005.

Ministero per la Guerra. *Relazione sull'attività svolta per l'esigenza A.O.*. Rome: Istituto Poligrafico dello Stato, 1936.

MOFFA, Claudio. 'I deportati libici della guerra del 1911–1912 alle Tremiti' in Francesco Sulpizi and Salaheddin Hasan Sury (eds), *Gli esiliati libici*. Rome: IsIAO Centro Libico per gli Studi Storici, 2003.

MOLFESE, Franco. *Storia del brigantaggio dopo l'Unità*. Milan: Feltrinelli, 1964.

MONNIER, Marco. *Notizie storiche documentate sul brigantaggio nelle provincie napoletane*. Naples: Berisio, 1965.

MONTAGNARI, Ernesto. *I più grandi siamo noi. Per rivendicazione dell'italica superiorità*. Rome and Milan: Mondadori, 1924.

MONTANELLI, Indro. *XX Battaglione eritreo*. Milan: Panoramma, 1936.

MONTESQUIEU, Charles Louis de Secondat, Baron de. 'Voyage d'Italie' in *Oeuvres complètes de Montesquieu, Volume 10: Mes voyages*. Paris: Classiques Garnier, 2012.

MORONE, Antonio Maria. 'How Italy Returned to Africa' in Paolo Bertella Farnetti and Cecilia Dau Novelli (eds), *Colonialism and National Identity*. Newcastle: Cambridge Scholars Publishing, 2015, pp. 130–36.

MUSSOLINI, Benito. *Corrispondenza inedita*. Milan: Edizioni del Borghese, 1972.

——. *Scritti e discorsi*, 12 VOLS. Milan: Hoepli, 1935–39.

MUSSOLINI, Vittorio. *Voli sulle ambe*. Florence: Sansoni, 1937.

MYNIER, Gilbert. *Histoire intérieure du FLN, 1954–1962*. Paris: Fayard, 2002.

NASIBÙ, Martha. *Memorie di una principessa etiope*. Vicenza: Neri Pozza, 2005.

NATTA, Alessandro. *L'altra Resistenza. I militari italiani internati in Germania*. Turin: Einaudi, 1997.

NEGASH, Tekeste. *No Medicine for the Bite of a White Snake: Notes on Nationalism and Resistance in Eritrea, 1890–1940*. Uppsala: Nordiska Afrikainstituet, 1986.

OCCHINI, Pier Ludovico. *Corradini*. Florence: Rinascimeno del Libro, 1933.

OLIVA, Gianni. *Foibe. Le stragi negate degli italiani della Venezia Giulia e dell'Istria*. Milan: Mondadori, 2002.

ORANO, Paolo. *Rodolfo Graziani, generale scipionico*. Rome: Pinciana, 1936.

OUSBY, Ian. *The Road to Verdun*. New York: Anchor Books, 2002.

PANKHURST, Richard. 'Nuove rivelazioni sull'attentato alla vita di Graziani del 19 febbraio 1937'. *Studi piacentini* 36 (2004): 141–44.

PANSA, Giampaolo. *Comprati e venduti. I giornali e il potere negli anni '70*. Milan: Bompiani, 1977.

——. *Il gladio e l'alloro. L'esercito di Salò*. Milan: Mondadori, 1991.

——. *Il sangue dei vinti. Quello che accadde in Italia dopo il 25 aprile*. Milan: Sperling & Kupfer, 2003.

PARATO, Giovanni. *I doveri morali e civili. Insegnati ai giovinetti per via di precetti ed esempi*. Turin: Paravia, 1865.

PARINI, Giuseppe. 'Cagioni del presente decadimento delle belle lettere e delle belle arti in Italia' in Giosuè Carducci (ed.), *Letture del Risorgimento. 1749–1870*. Bologna: Zanichelli, 1920.

PASCOLI, Giovanni. *Fior da fiore. Prose e poesie scelte per la scuola italiana*. Palermo: Sandron, 1929.

PAVOLINI, Alessandro. *Disperata*. Florence: Vallecchi, 1937.

PAVONE, Claudio. *Una guerra civile. Saggio storico sulla moralità nella Resistenza*. Turin: Bollati Boringhieri, 1991.

PELI, Santo. *La Resistenza in Italia. Storia e critica*. Turin: Einaudi, 2004.

PETRINI, Roberto. *Il declino dell'Italia*. Rome and Bari: Laterza, 2003.

PICCININI, Giuseppe. *Guerra d'Africa*. Rome: Perino, 1887.

PICCIOLI, Felice. *Diario di un bersagliere*. Milan: Il Formichere, 1974.

PISACANE, Carlo. *La rivoluzione*. Turin: Einaudi, 1970.

——. *Revolution* (Richard Roberts trans.). Leicester: Troubador, 2010.

PISANÒ, Giorgio. *Storia della guerra civile in Italia*. Milan: Il Borghese, 1965.

PIZZONI, Alfredo. 'I quarantacinque giorni del Governo Badoglio' in *Alla guida del CLNAI. Memorie per i figli*. Bologna: Il Mulino, 1995.

——. 'La questione della frontiera orientale italiana tra CLN e Alleati. Deposizione al processo per l'eccidio di Porzus di Alfredo Pizzoni'. *Nuova Storia contemporanea* 1 (1997): 104–42.

POGGIALI, Ciro. *Diario AOI. 15 giugno 1936–4 ottobre 1937*. Milan: Longanesi, 1971.

POLITI, Giancarlo. *Martiri in Cina*. Bologna: EMI, 1998.

PRENZLER, Johannes (ed.). *Die Reden Kaiser Wilhelms II*. Leipzig: Reclan, 1904.

PROCACCI, Giovanna. *Soldati e prigionieri italiani nella Grande Guerra*. Turin: Bollati Boringhieri, 2000.

PUPO, Raoul. *Il lungo esodo. Istria: le persecuzioni, le foibe, l'esilio*. Milan: Rizzoli, 2005.

——, and Roberto Spazzali. *Foibe*. Milan: Bruno Mondadori, 2003.

PURCELL, Victor. *The Boxer Uprising*. Cambridge: Cambridge University Press, 1963.

QUADRONE, Ernesto. *Pionieri, donne e belve. Uebi Scelebi, Giuba*. Milan: Agnelli, 1934.

QUAZZA, Guido. *Resistenza e storia d'Italia*. Turin: Einaudi, 1965.

R. L. 'La Guerre de Tripoli et l'esprit public en Italie'. *Chronique sociale de France*, March 1912.

RAGIONIERI, Ernesto. 'La storia politica e sociale' in Ruggiero Romano and Corrado Vivanti (eds), *Storia d'Italian Einaudi, Volume 4: Dall'Unità d'Italia a oggi*. Turin: Einaudi, 1975.

RAINERO, Romain. *Paolo Vaera e l'opposizione democratica all'impresa di Tripoli*. Rome: L'Erma di Bretschneider, 1983.

RASTELLI, Vito. 'La civiltà del lavoro verso l'impero'. *Il Solco fascista*, 11 August 1935.

RE, Lucia. *Calvino and the Age of Neorealism: Fables of Estrangement*. Stanford, CA: Stanford University Press, 1990.

REPETTI, Romano, and Gian Luigi Cavanna. *Comandanti partigiani giunti da lontano*. Bobbio: Pontegobbo, 2018.

REVELLI, Nuto. *Le due guerre. Guerra fascista e guerra partigiana*. Turin: Einaudi, 2003.

RIALL, Lucy. 'Hidden Spaces of Empire. Italian Colonists in Nineteenth-Century Peru'. *Past and Present* 245 (February 2022): 209.

———. *The Italian Risorgimento: State, Society and National Unification*. London and New York: Routledge, 1994.

RICCI, Aldo, and Roland Giglio. 'Sconfitto, ma nella leggenda'. *Il Messaggero*, 6 February 1981.

RICCI, Giovanni, and Ercolano Porta. *Storia della missione francescana e del vicariato apostolico del Hunan meridionale dalle sue origini ai giorni nostri*. Bologna: Stabilimenti Poligrafici Riuniti, 1925.

ROATTA, Mario. *Otto milioni di baionette. L'esercito italiano in guerra dal 1940 al 1944*. Milan: Mondadori, 1946.

ROBECCHI BRICCHETTI, Luigi. *Dal Benadir. Lettere illustrate alla Società antischiavista d'Italia*. Milan: La Poligrafica, 1904.

ROCHAT, Giorgio, and Giulio Massobrio. *Breve storia dell'esercito italiano dal 1861 al 1914*. Turin: Einaudi, 1978.

ROGGERO, Caterina. 'The Italian Left and Ben Bella's Authoritarianism in Algeria, between Unconditional Support and Faint Criticism (1962–1965)'. *Journal of Asian and African Studies* 58(6) (2022): 16.

ROMANO, Sergio. *La quarta sponda. La guerra di Libia, 1911–1912*. Milan: Bompiani, 1977.

ROSA, Paolo. *Strategic Culture and Italy's Military Behavior*. London: Lexington Books, 2016.

RUINI, Meuccio. *L'Islam e le nostre colonie*. Città di Castello: Il Solco, 1922.

RUSCONI, Gian Enrico. *Resistenza e postfascismo*. Bologna: Il Mulino, 1995.

RUSSO, Giovanni. 'I briganti sono meglio di Cavour?'. *L'Indice* 6 (June 2004): 39.

SABATTINI, Mario, and Paolo Santangelo. *Storia della Cina. Dalle origini alla fondazione della Repubblica*. Rome and Bari: Laterza, 1986.

SALERNO, Eric. *Genocidio in Libia. Le atrocità nascoste dell'avventura coloniale italiana, 1911–1931*. Rome: manifestolibri, 2005.

SALERNO, Eric. *Genocidio in Libia*. Milan: Sugarco, 1979.

SALVEMINI, Gaetano. *La politica estera dell'Italia, 1871–1914*. Florence: Barbera, 1944.

SAMATAR, Abdi Ismail. *Africa's First Democrats*. Bloomington and Indianapolis: Indiana University Press, 2016.

SANTARELLI, Enzo, Giorgio Rochat, Romain Rainero, and Luigi Goglia. *Omar al-Mukhtar e la riconquista fascista della Libia*. Milan: Marzorati, 1981.

SAULNIER, Verdun-Louis. *La littérature francaise du siècle romantique*. Paris: Presse universitaires, 1961.

SCHINDLER, John R. *Isonzo: The Forgotten Sacrifice of the Great War*. London: Praeger, 2001.

SCHLEMMER, Thomas. *Invasori, non vittime. La campagna italiana di Russia 1941– 1943*. Bari: Laterza, 2009.

SCHMITT, Olivier. *Allies That Count*. Washington DC: Georgetown University Press, 2018.

SCHREIBER, Gerhard. *I militari italiani internati nei campi di concentramento del Terzo Reich, 1943–1945. Traditi, disprezzati, dimenticati*. Rome: Stato Maggiore dell'Esercito, Ufficio Storico, 1992.

SCIANNA, Bastian Matteo. *The Italian War on the Eastern Front, 1941–1943. Operations, Myths, Memories*. London: Palgrave Macmillan, 2019.

SCIROCCO, Alfonso. 'Introduzione' in Renato Dentoni-Letta (ed.), *Guida alle fonti per la storia del brigantaggio postunitario conservate negli Archivi di Stato*, VOL. 1. Rome: Ufficio Centrale per i Beni archivistici, 1999.

——. *Il Mezzogiorno nella crisi dell'unificazione, 1860–1865*. Naples: SEN, 1881.

——. *Garibaldi: A Citizen of the World* (Allan Cameron trans.). Princeton, NJ: Princeton University Press, 2007.

SCOTT, William R. *The Sons of Sheba: African-Americans and the Italo-Ethiopian War 1935–1941*. Bloomington: Indiana University Press, 2006.

SCOTTI, Giacomo. *Goli Otok. Italiani nel gulag di Tito*. Trieste: Lint, 2002.

SERRA, Fabrizio. *La conquista integrale dell'impero*. Rome: Unione Editoriale d'Italia, 1938.

SERRAZANETTI, Marcello. *Considerazioni sulla nostra attività coloniale in Somalia*. Bologna: Tipografia La Rapida, 1933.

——. *La politica indigena in Somalia*. Bologna: Tipografia La Rapida, 1934.

SETTEMBRINI, Domenico. *Storia dell'idea antiborghese in Italia, 1860–1989*. Bari and Rome: Laterza, 1991.

SHELLEY, Percy Bysshe. *The Prose Works*, VOL. 2. (Richard Herne Shepherd ed.). London: Chatto and Windus, 1888.

SILVESTRI, Roberto. 'Il "Leone del deserto" come la "Battaglia di Algeri" '. *Quaderni internazionali* 1 (1987): 113–18.

SISMONDI, Jean Charles Léonard Simonde de. *Histoire des républiques italiennes du moyenâge*, VOL. 8. Brussels: Société typographique belge, 1839.

SPAVENTA, Bertrando. *Opere*, VOL. 1. Florence: Sansoni, 1972.

SPINI, Giorgio. *La strada della liberazione. Dalla riscoperta di Calvino al Fronte della VII Armata*. Turin: Claudiana, 2002.

SRIVASTAVA, Neelam. *Italian Colonialism and Resistances to Empire: 1930–1970*. London: Palgrave Macmillan, 2019.

STENDHAL. *Rome, Naples et Florence*. Paris: Delaunry, 1826.

——. *Rome, Naples and Florence* (Richard N. Coe trans.). London: John Calder, 1959.

STEPHENSON, Charles. *A Box of Sand: The Italo-Ottoman War 1911–1912*. Ticehurst: Tattered Flag, 2014.

STORCHI, Massimo. *Sangue al bosco del Lupo. Partigiani che uccidono partigiani: la storia di 'Azor'*. Reggio Emilia: Aliberti, 2005.

STRANG, G. Bruce (ed.). *Collision of Empires: Italy's Invasion of Ethiopia and its International Impact*. New York and London: Routledge, 2016.

TADDEI, Irma. *Autobiografie Africane*. Milan: FrancoAngeli, 1996.

TAVIANI, Paolo Emilio. *Politica e memoria d'uomo*. Bologna: Il Mulino, 2002.

The Black Mediterranean Collective (ed.). *The Black Mediterranean: Bodies, Borders and Citizenship*. London: Palgrave Macmillan, 2021.

TOPA, Michele. *I briganti di sua Maestà*. Naples: Fratelli Fiorentino, 1993.

TORRES, Luigi. *Il brigantaggio nell'Abruzzo Peligno e nell'Alta Sangro, 1860–1870*. Alessandria: Majell, 2003.

TOSATTO, Claudio. 'Un film e la storia. Lion of the Desert, 1982'. *Studi piacentini* 36 (2004): 173–88.

TOSCANO, Alberto. *Late Fascism*. London: Verso Books, 2023.

TOSTI, Amedeo. *La spedizione italiana in Cina, 1900–1901*. Rome: Provveditorato Generale dello Stato, 1926.

TRANFAGLIA, Nicola. *Come nasce la Repubblica. La mafia, il Vaticano e il neofascismo nei documenti americani e italiani, 1943–1947*. Milan: Bompiani, 2004.

—— (ed.). *Ministri e giornalisti. La guerra e il Minculpop, 1939–1943*. Turin: Einaudi, 2005.

TRAPANI, Francamaria. *Le brigantesse*. Rome: Canesi, 1968.

TRAVERSO, Enzo. *The Origins of Nazi Violence*. New York: The New Press, 2003.

TRIULZI, Alessandro. 'Displacing the Colonial Event'. *Interventions* 8(3) (2006): 430–43.

UBOLDI, Raffaello. *25 aprile 1945. I giorni dell'odio e della libertà*. Milan: Mondadori, 2004.

Ufficio Storico della Regia Marina. *L'opera della R. Marina in Cina*. Florence: Vallecchi, 1935.

VALABREGA, Guido. 'Il servizio trasporti e tappe nella guerra libica'. *Africa* 3 (1984).

VALDEVIT, Giampaolo (ed.). *Foibe, il peso del passato. Venezia Giulia 1943–1945*. Venice: Marsilio, 1997.

VALERI, Nino. *Giolitti*. Turin: Utet, 1971.

VALLI, Mario. *Gli avvenimenti in Cina nel 1900 e l'azione della R. Marina italian*. Milan: Hoepli, 1905.

VARÈ, Daniele. *Yehonala. Storia dell'imperatrice Tzu Hsi e del trapasso dalla vecchia Cina alla nuova*. Florence: Bemporad, 1933.

VIGEZZI, Brunello. *L'Italia unita e le sfide della politica estera. Dal Risorgimento alla Repubblica*. Milan: Unicopli, 1997.

VIVARELLI, Roberto. *La fine di una stagione. Memoria 1943–1945*. Bologna: Il Mulino, 2000.

VOSTA, Vincenzo. *L'ultimo federale. Memorie della guerra civile, 1943–1945*. Bologna: Il Mulino, 1997.

WADA'AH EL-HASNAWI, Habîb. 'Effetti psico-sociali delle operazioni di deportazione dei libici nelle isole italiane sugli esiliati e i loro parenti in epoca coloniale, 1911–1943' in Francesco Sulpizi and Salaheddin Hasan Sury (eds), *Gli esiliati libici*. Rome: IsIAO Centro Libico per gli Studi Storici, 2003.

WANG, Yanwei. *Diplomatic Documents of the Qing Dynasty*. Taipei: Wen Hai Press, 1973.

WITT, Angelo de. *Storia politico-militare del brigantaggio nelle province meridionali d'Italia*. Florence: Coppini, 1884.

WOLLER, Hans. *I conti con il fascismo. L'epurazione in Italia, 1943–1948*. Bologna: Il Mulino, 1997.

WOOLF, Stuart. 'Crisi di un sistema e origini di una destra' in Gianpasquale Santomassimo (ed.), *La notte della democrazia italiana. Dal regime fascista al governo Berlusconi*. Milan: il Saggiatore, 2003.

XIANG, Lamxin. *The Origins of the Boxer War: A Multinational Study.* London and New York: Routledge, 2003.

ZECCHINI, S. P., and A. Vianti. *Esempi della virtù italiana narrati da nostri classici storici.* Turin: Stamperia sociale degli artisti tipografi, 1843.

ZIADEH, Nicola A. *Sanusiyah: A Study of a Revivalist Movement in Islam.* Leiden: Brill, 1958.